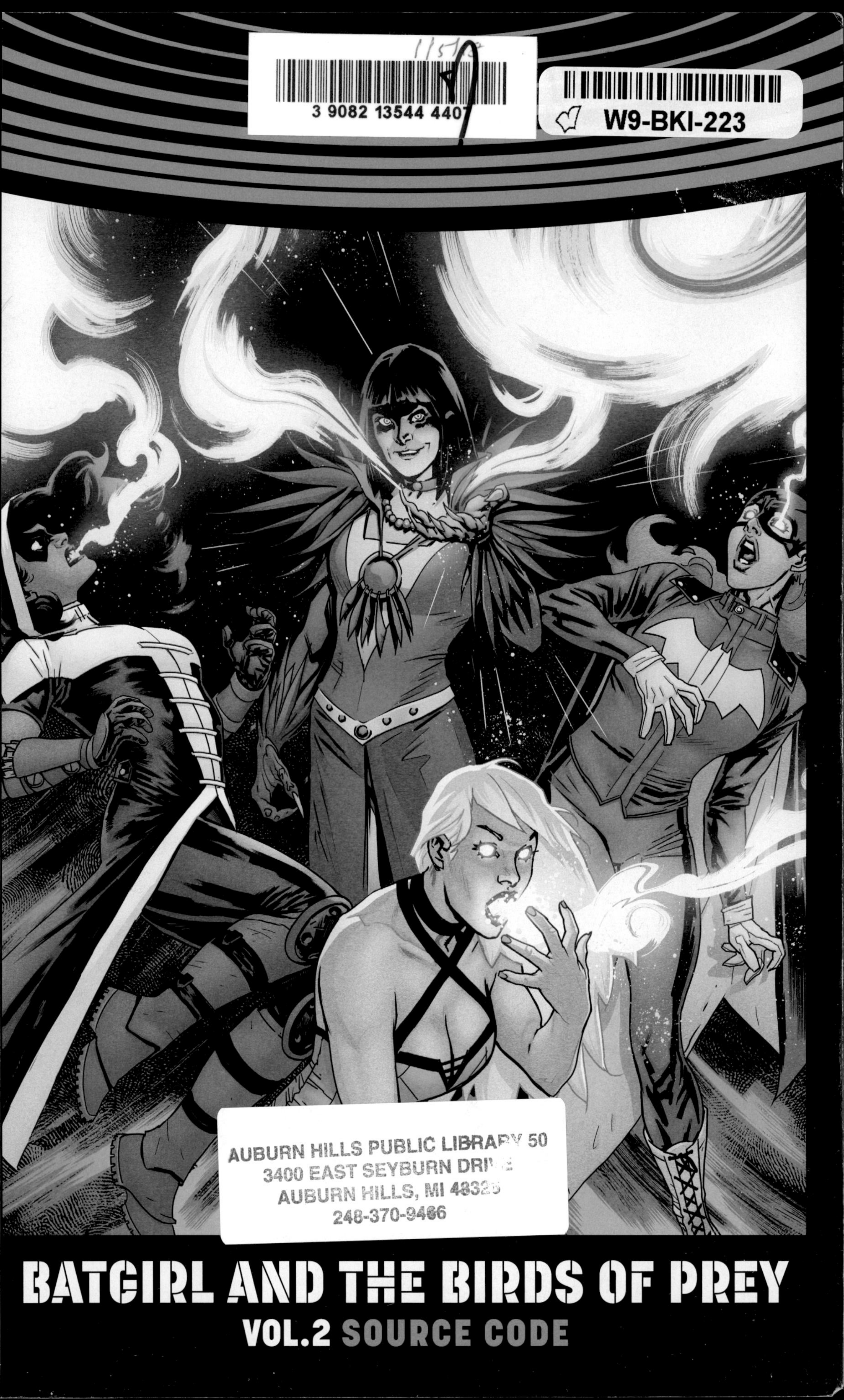

BATGIRL AND THE BIRDS OF PREY

VOL.2 SOURCE CODE

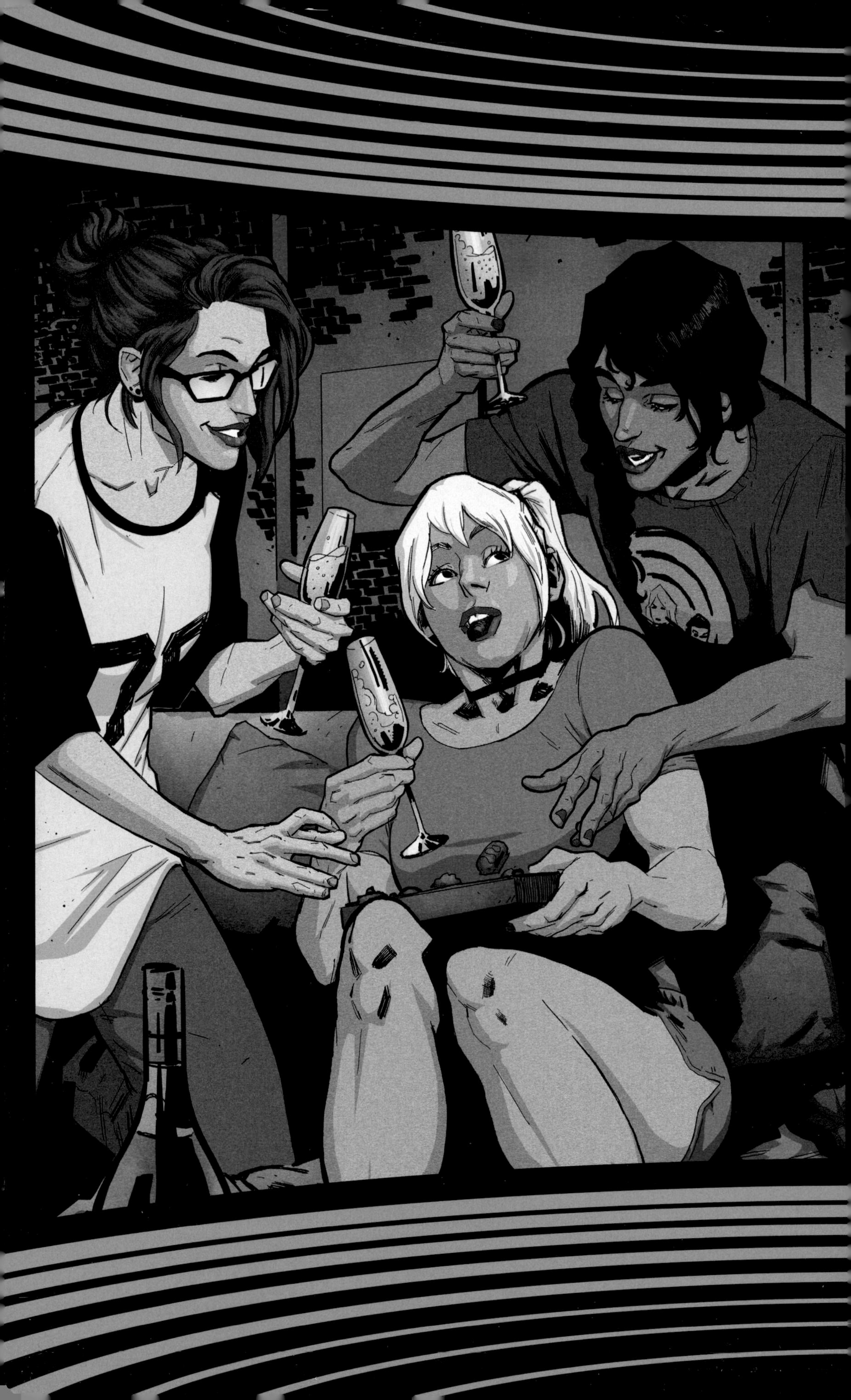

BATGIRL AND THE BIRDS OF PREY
VOL.2 SOURCE CODE

JULIE BENSON * **SHAWNA BENSON**
writers

ROGE ANTONIO * **CLAIRE ROE** * **BRENO TAMURA**
artists

ALLEN PASSALAQUA * **JOHN RAUCH** * **CHRIS SOTOMAYOR**
colorists

DERON BENNETT * **JOSH REED**
letterers

YANICK PAQUETTE and **NATHAN FAIRBAIRN**
series and collection cover artists

BATMAN created by **BOB KANE** with **BILL FINGER**
HUNTRESS created by **PAUL LEVITZ**, **BOB LAYTON** and **JOE STATON**

CHRIS CONROY Editor - Original Series ✳ **DAVE WIELGOSZ** Assistant Editor - Original Series
JEB WOODARD Group Editor - Collected Editions ✳ **LIZ ERICKSON** Editor - Collected Edition
STEVE COOK Design Director - Books ✳ **MONIQUE NARBONETA** Publication Design

BOB HARRAS Senior VP - Editor-in-Chief, DC Comics
PAT McCALLUM Executive Editor, DC Comics

DIANE NELSON President ✳ **DAN DiDIO** Publisher ✳ **JIM LEE** Publisher ✳ **GEOFF JOHNS** President & Chief Creative Officer
AMIT DESAI Executive VP - Business & Marketing Strategy, Direct to Consumer & Global Franchise Management
SAM ADES Senior VP & General Manager, Digital Services ✳ **BOBBIE CHASE** VP & Executive Editor, Young Reader & Talent Development
MARK CHIARELLO Senior VP - Art, Design & Collected Editions ✳ **JOHN CUNNINGHAM** Senior VP - Sales & Trade Marketing
ANNE DePIES Senior VP - Business Strategy, Finance & Administration ✳ **DON FALLETTI** VP - Manufacturing Operations
LAWRENCE GANEM VP - Editorial Administration & Talent Relations ✳ **ALISON GILL** Senior VP - Manufacturing & Operations
HANK KANALZ Senior VP - Editorial Strategy & Administration ✳ **JAY KOGAN** VP - Legal Affairs ✳ **JACK MAHAN** VP - Business Affairs
NICK J. NAPOLITANO VP - Manufacturing Administration ✳ **EDDIE SCANNELL** VP - Consumer Marketing
COURTNEY SIMMONS Senior VP - Publicity & Communications ✳ **JIM (SKI) SOKOLOWSKI** VP - Comic Book Specialty Sales & Trade Marketing
NANCY SPEARS VP - Mass, Book, Digital Sales & Trade Marketing ✳ **MICHELE R. WELLS** VP - Content Strategy

BATGIRL AND THE BIRDS OF PREY VOL. 2: SOURCE CODE

Published by DC Comics. Compilation and all new material Copyright © 2017 DC Comics. All Rights Reserved.
Originally published in single magazine form in BATGIRL AND THE BIRDS OF PREY 7-13 © 2017 DC Comics.
All Rights Reserved. All characters, their distinctive likenesses and related elements featured in this publication are trademarks of DC Comics.
The stories, characters and incidents featured in this publication are entirely fictional.
DC Comics does not read or accept unsolicited submissions of ideas, stories or artwork.

DC Comics, 2900 West Alameda Ave., Burbank, CA 91505.
Printed by LSC Communications, Kendallville, IN, USA. 11/3/17. First Printing.
ISBN: 978-1-4012-7380-4

Library of Congress Cataloging-in-Publication Data is available.

PEFC Certified

Printed on paper from
sustainably managed
forests, controlled
sources

PEFC/29-31-337   www.pefc.org

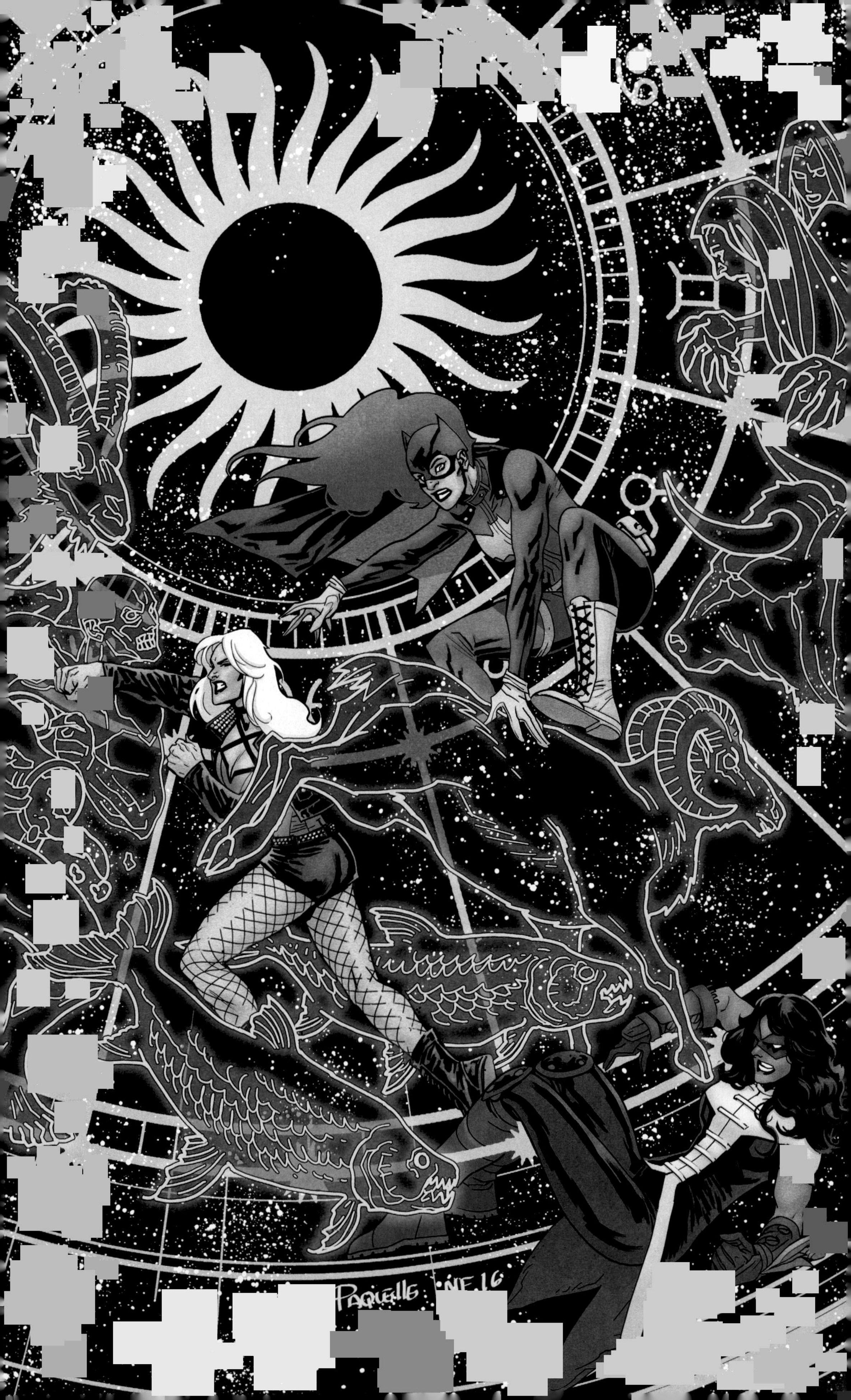
PAQUETTE NF 16

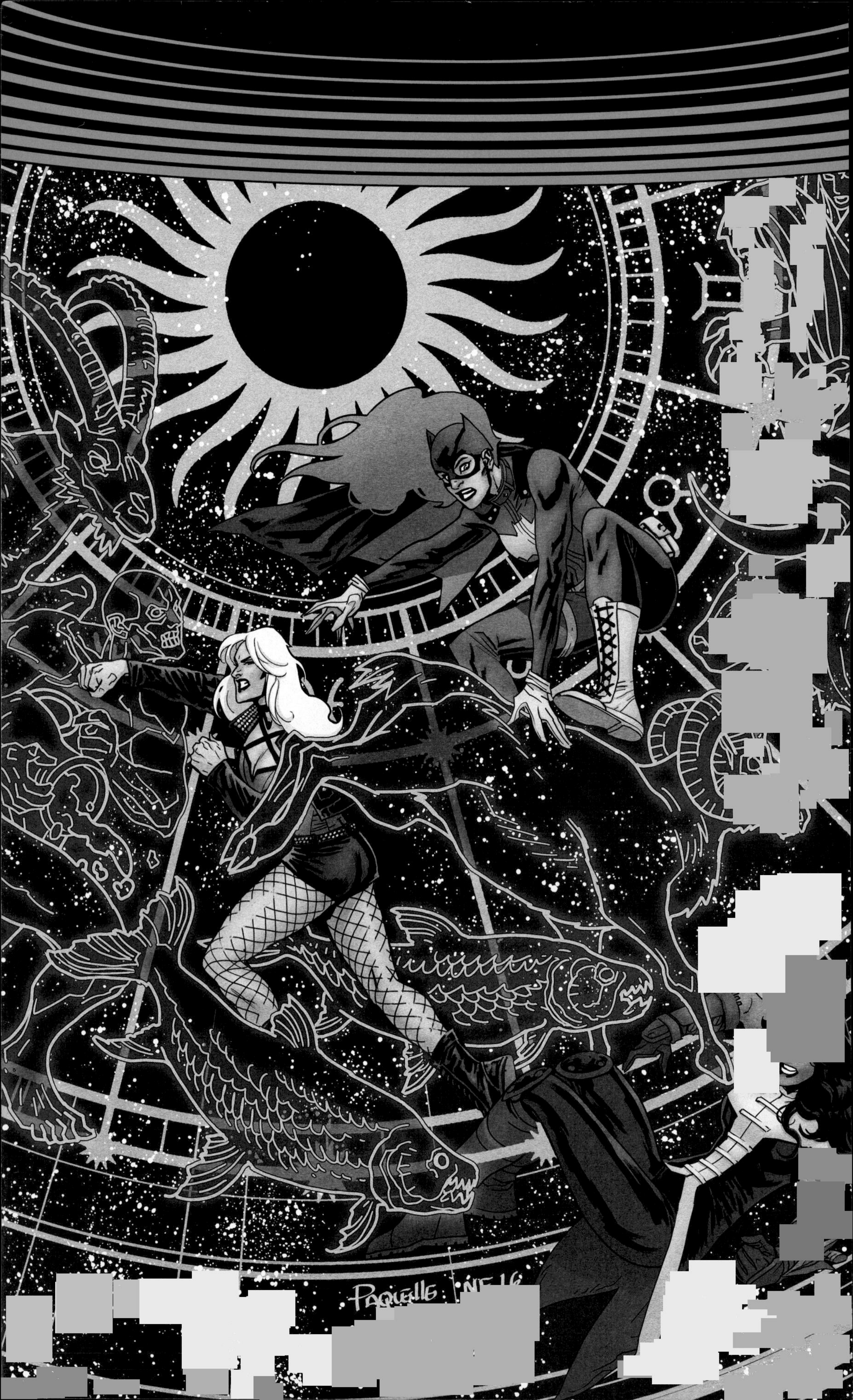

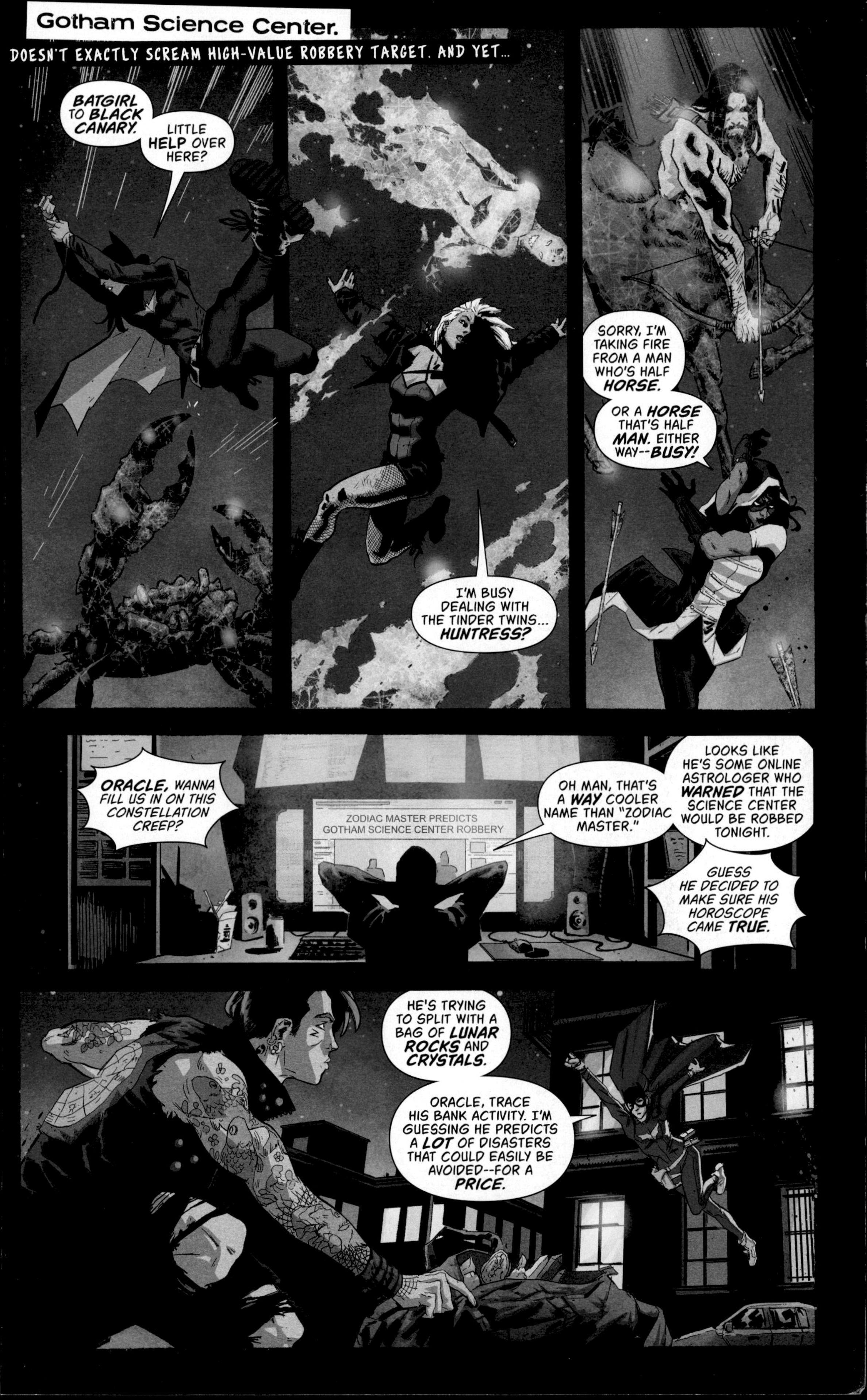
Gotham Science Center.
DOESN'T EXACTLY SCREAM HIGH-VALUE ROBBERY TARGET. AND YET...
BATGIRL TO BLACK CANARY.
LITTLE HELP OVER HERE?
I'M BUSY DEALING WITH THE TINDER TWINS... HUNTRESS?
SORRY, I'M TAKING FIRE FROM A MAN WHO'S HALF HORSE.
OR A HORSE THAT'S HALF MAN. EITHER WAY--BUSY!
ORACLE, WANNA FILL US IN ON THIS CONSTELLATION CREEP?
ZODIAC MASTER PREDICTS GOTHAM SCIENCE CENTER ROBBERY
OH MAN, THAT'S A WAY COOLER NAME THAN "ZODIAC MASTER."
LOOKS LIKE HE'S SOME ONLINE ASTROLOGER WHO WARNED THAT THE SCIENCE CENTER WOULD BE ROBBED TONIGHT.
GUESS HE DECIDED TO MAKE SURE HIS HOROSCOPE CAME TRUE.
HE'S TRYING TO SPLIT WITH A BAG OF LUNAR ROCKS AND CRYSTALS.
ORACLE, TRACE HIS BANK ACTIVITY. I'M GUESSING HE PREDICTS A LOT OF DISASTERS THAT COULD EASILY BE AVOIDED--FOR A PRICE.

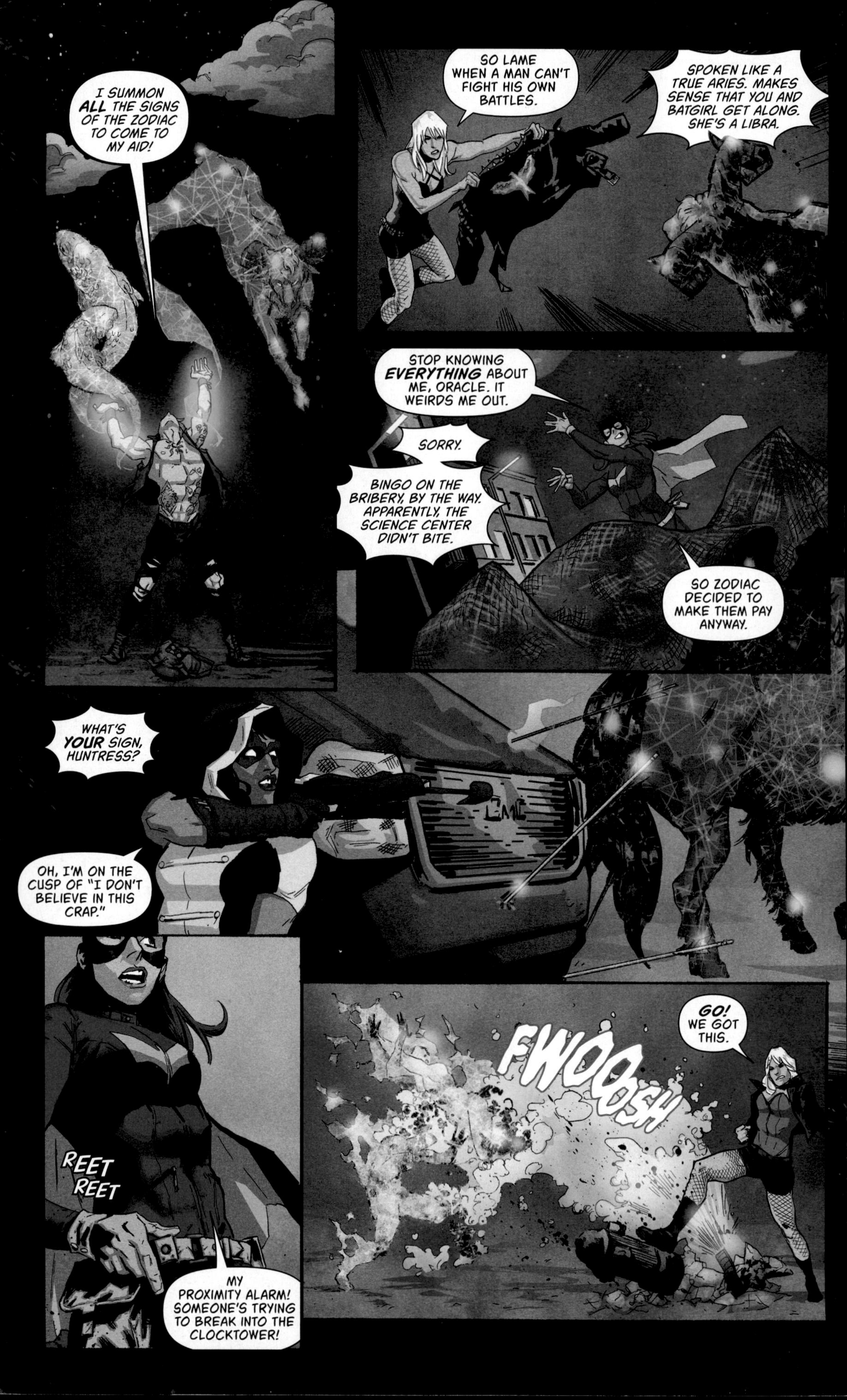
I SUMMON **ALL** THE SIGNS OF THE ZODIAC TO COME TO MY AID!
SO LAME WHEN A MAN CAN'T FIGHT HIS OWN BATTLES.
SPOKEN LIKE A TRUE ARIES. MAKES SENSE THAT YOU AND BATGIRL GET ALONG. SHE'S A LIBRA.
STOP KNOWING **EVERYTHING** ABOUT ME, ORACLE. IT WEIRDS ME OUT.
SORRY.
BINGO ON THE BRIBERY, BY THE WAY. APPARENTLY, THE SCIENCE CENTER DIDN'T BITE.
SO ZODIAC DECIDED TO MAKE THEM PAY ANYWAY.
WHAT'S **YOUR** SIGN, HUNTRESS?
OH, I'M ON THE CUSP OF "I DON'T BELIEVE IN THIS CRAP."
REET REET
MY PROXIMITY ALARM! SOMEONE'S TRYING TO BREAK INTO THE CLOCKTOWER!
FWOOOSH
GO! WE GOT THIS.

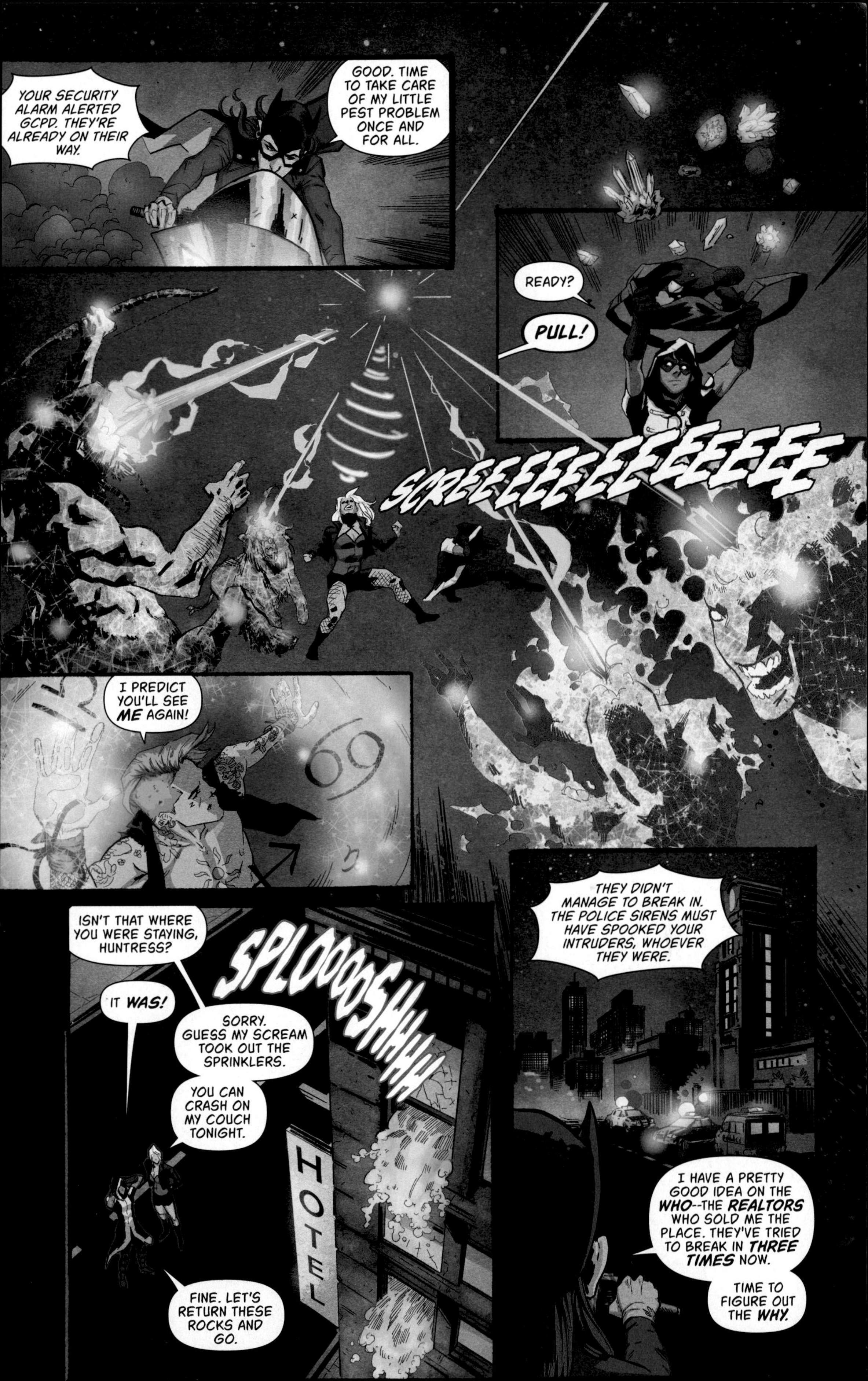
YOUR SECURITY ALARM ALERTED GCPD. THEY'RE ALREADY ON THEIR WAY.
GOOD. TIME TO TAKE CARE OF MY LITTLE PEST PROBLEM ONCE AND FOR ALL.
READY?
PULL!
SCREEEEEEEEEEEEEEEE
I PREDICT YOU'LL SEE ME AGAIN!
THEY DIDN'T MANAGE TO BREAK IN. THE POLICE SIRENS MUST HAVE SPOOKED YOUR INTRUDERS, WHOEVER THEY WERE.
I HAVE A PRETTY GOOD IDEA ON THE WHO--THE REALTORS WHO SOLD ME THE PLACE. THEY'VE TRIED TO BREAK IN THREE TIMES NOW.
TIME TO FIGURE OUT THE WHY.
ISN'T THAT WHERE YOU WERE STAYING, HUNTRESS?
SPLOOOOSHHHH
IT WAS!
SORRY. GUESS MY SCREAM TOOK OUT THE SPRINKLERS.
YOU CAN CRASH ON MY COUCH TONIGHT.
FINE. LET'S RETURN THESE ROCKS AND GO.
HOTEL

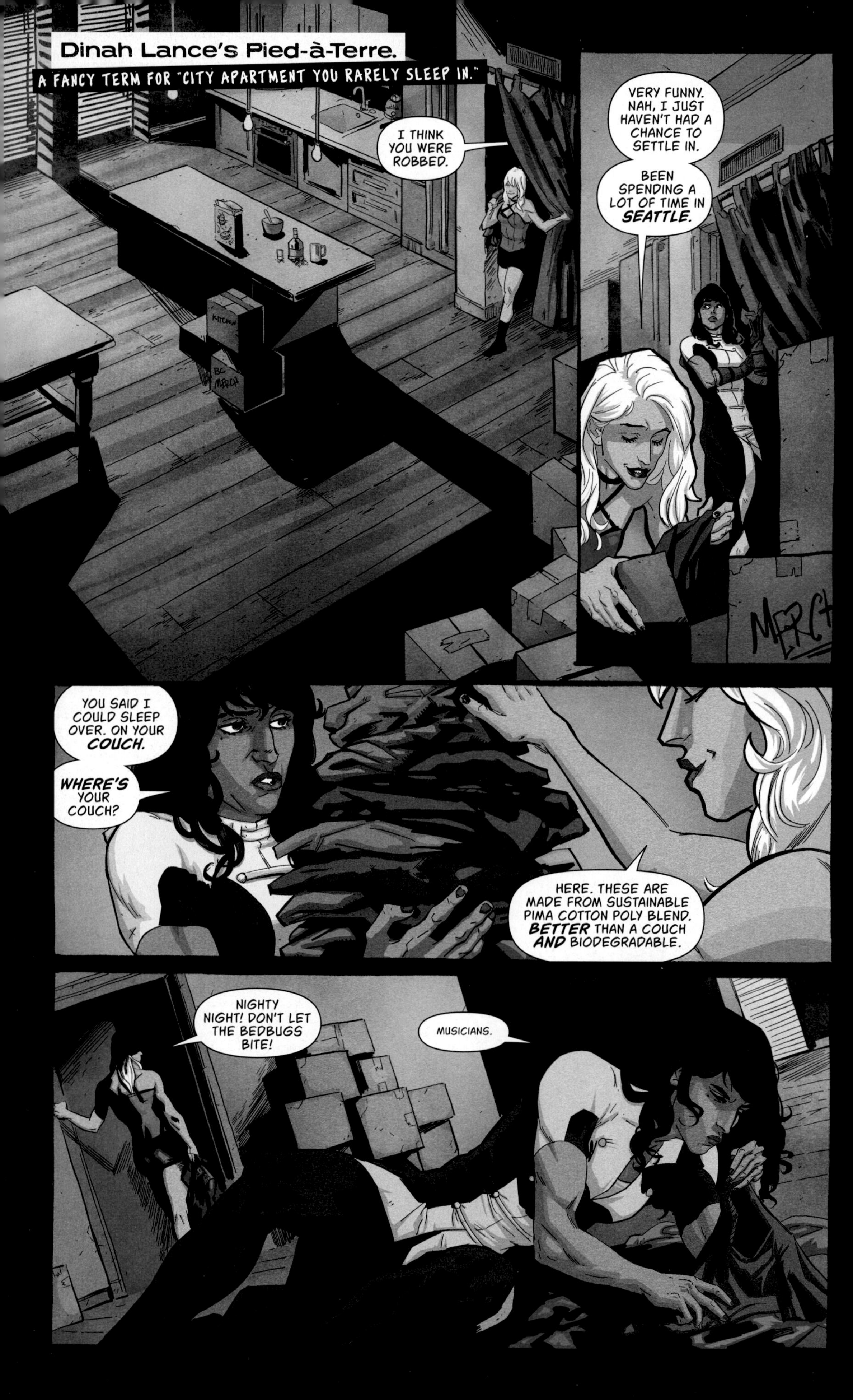
Dinah Lance's Pied-à-Terre.
A FANCY TERM FOR "CITY APARTMENT YOU RARELY SLEEP IN."
I THINK YOU WERE ROBBED.
VERY FUNNY. NAH, I JUST HAVEN'T HAD A CHANCE TO SETTLE IN.
BEEN SPENDING A LOT OF TIME IN SEATTLE.
MERCH
YOU SAID I COULD SLEEP OVER. ON YOUR COUCH.
WHERE'S YOUR COUCH?
HERE. THESE ARE MADE FROM SUSTAINABLE PIMA COTTON POLY BLEND. BETTER THAN A COUCH AND BIODEGRADABLE.
NIGHTY NIGHT! DON'T LET THE BEDBUGS BITE!
MUSICIANS.

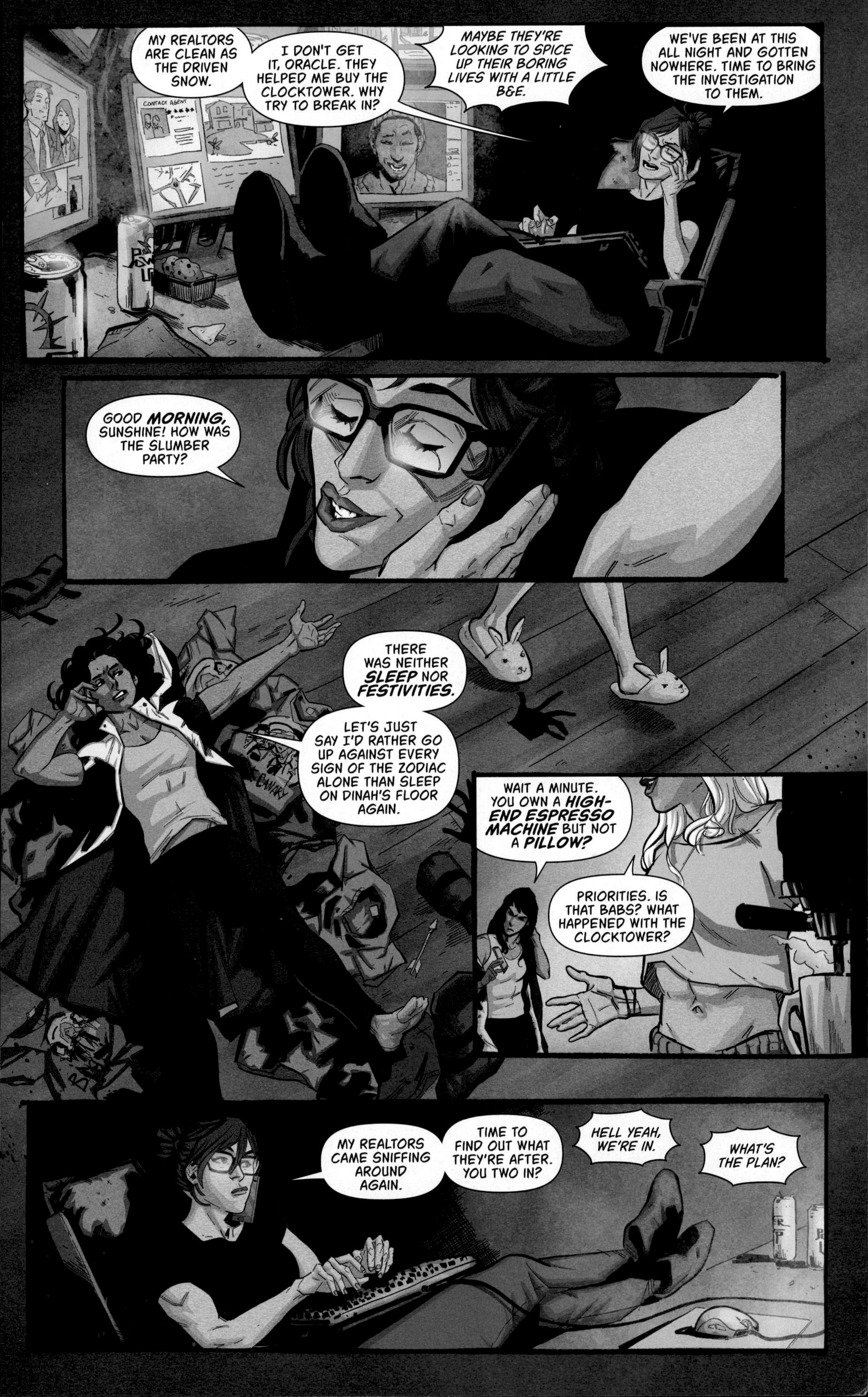
MY REALTORS ARE CLEAN AS THE DRIVEN SNOW.
I DON'T GET IT, ORACLE. THEY HELPED ME BUY THE CLOCKTOWER. WHY TRY TO BREAK IN?
MAYBE THEY'RE LOOKING TO SPICE UP THEIR BORING LIVES WITH A LITTLE B&E.
WE'VE BEEN AT THIS ALL NIGHT AND GOTTEN NOWHERE. TIME TO BRING THE INVESTIGATION TO THEM.
CONTACT AGENT
GOOD MORNING, SUNSHINE! HOW WAS THE SLUMBER PARTY?
THERE WAS NEITHER SLEEP NOR FESTIVITIES.
LET'S JUST SAY I'D RATHER GO UP AGAINST EVERY SIGN OF THE ZODIAC ALONE THAN SLEEP ON DINAH'S FLOOR AGAIN.
WAIT A MINUTE. YOU OWN A HIGH-END ESPRESSO MACHINE BUT NOT A PILLOW?
PRIORITIES. IS THAT BABS? WHAT HAPPENED WITH THE CLOCKTOWER?
MY REALTORS CAME SNIFFING AROUND AGAIN.
TIME TO FIND OUT WHAT THEY'RE AFTER. YOU TWO IN?
HELL YEAH, WE'RE IN.
WHAT'S THE PLAN?

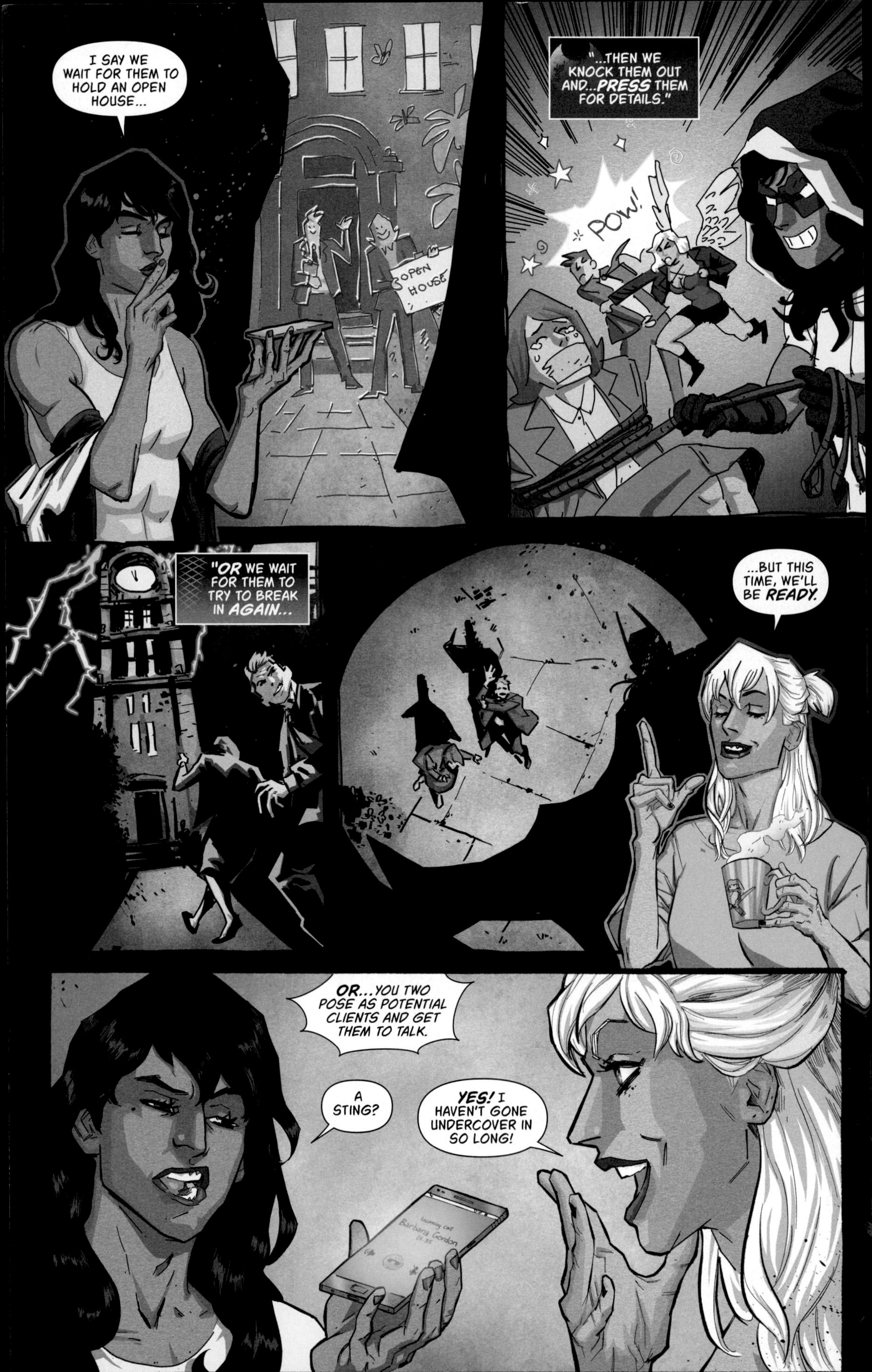

I SAY WE WAIT FOR THEM TO HOLD AN OPEN HOUSE...
OPEN HOUSE
"...THEN WE KNOCK THEM OUT AND...PRESS THEM FOR DETAILS."
POW!
"OR WE WAIT FOR THEM TO TRY TO BREAK IN AGAIN...
...BUT THIS TIME, WE'LL BE READY.
OR...YOU TWO POSE AS POTENTIAL CLIENTS AND GET THEM TO TALK.
A STING?
YES! I HAVEN'T GONE UNDERCOVER IN SO LONG!
Incoming call
Barbara Gordon

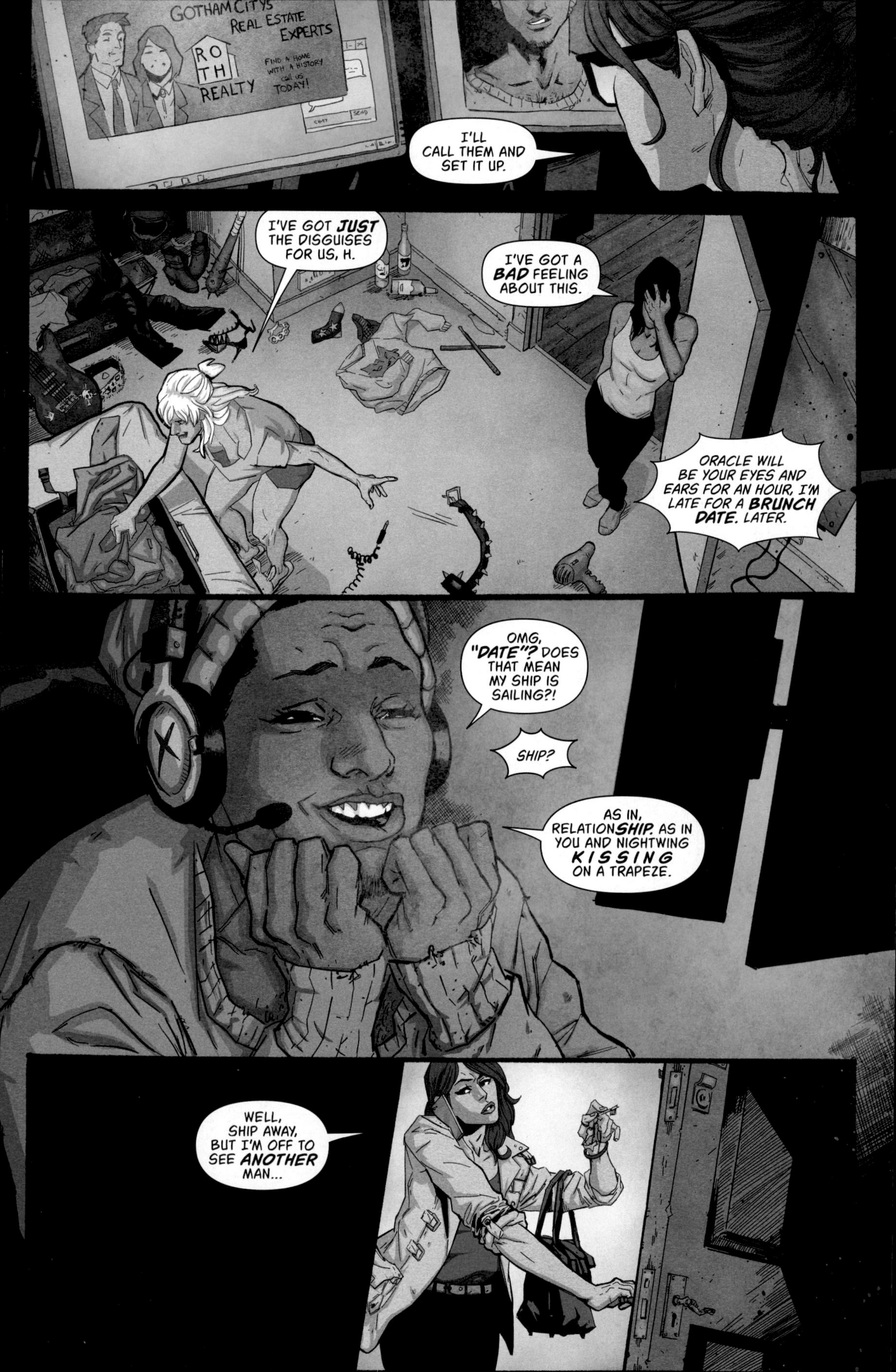
GOTHAM CITY'S REAL ESTATE EXPERTS
ROTH REALTY
FIND A HOME WITH A HISTORY
CALL US TODAY!
I'LL CALL THEM AND SET IT UP.
I'VE GOT JUST THE DISGUISES FOR US, H.
I'VE GOT A BAD FEELING ABOUT THIS.
ORACLE WILL BE YOUR EYES AND EARS FOR AN HOUR, I'M LATE FOR A BRUNCH DATE. LATER.
OMG, "DATE"? DOES THAT MEAN MY SHIP IS SAILING?!
SHIP?
AS IN, RELATIONSHIP. AS IN YOU AND NIGHTWING KISSING ON A TRAPEZE.
WELL, SHIP AWAY, BUT I'M OFF TO SEE ANOTHER MAN...

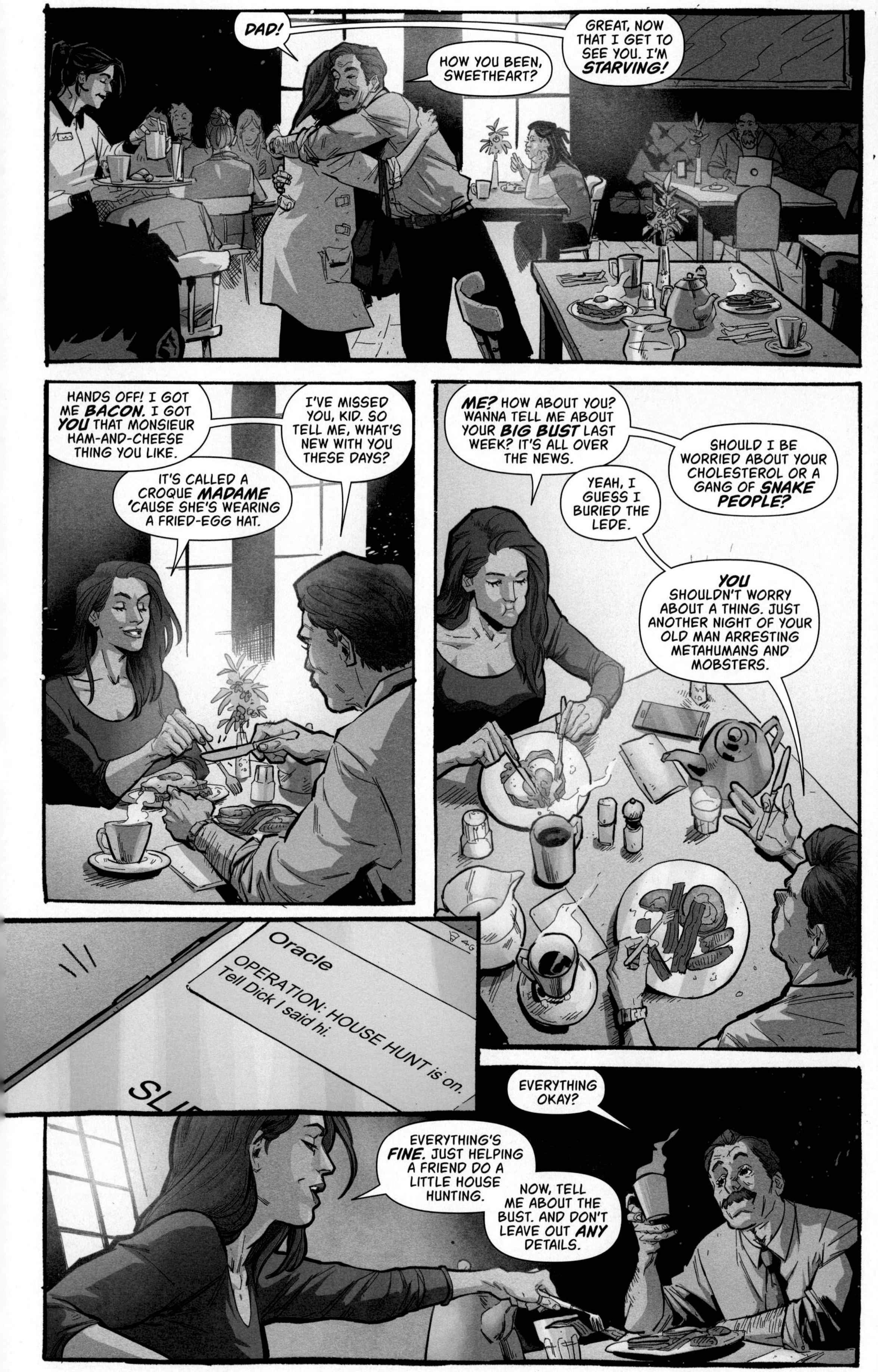
DAD!
HOW YOU BEEN, SWEETHEART?
GREAT, NOW THAT I GET TO SEE YOU. I'M STARVING!
HANDS OFF! I GOT ME BACON. I GOT YOU THAT MONSIEUR HAM-AND-CHEESE THING YOU LIKE.
IT'S CALLED A CROQUE MADAME 'CAUSE SHE'S WEARING A FRIED-EGG HAT.
I'VE MISSED YOU, KID. SO TELL ME, WHAT'S NEW WITH YOU THESE DAYS?
ME? HOW ABOUT YOU? WANNA TELL ME ABOUT YOUR BIG BUST LAST WEEK? IT'S ALL OVER THE NEWS.
YEAH, I GUESS I BURIED THE LEDE.
SHOULD I BE WORRIED ABOUT YOUR CHOLESTEROL OR A GANG OF SNAKE PEOPLE?
YOU SHOULDN'T WORRY ABOUT A THING. JUST ANOTHER NIGHT OF YOUR OLD MAN ARRESTING METAHUMANS AND MOBSTERS.
Oracle
OPERATION: HOUSE HUNT is on. Tell Dick I said hi.
EVERYTHING OKAY?
EVERYTHING'S FINE. JUST HELPING A FRIEND DO A LITTLE HOUSE HUNTING.
NOW, TELL ME ABOUT THE BUST. AND DON'T LEAVE OUT ANY DETAILS.

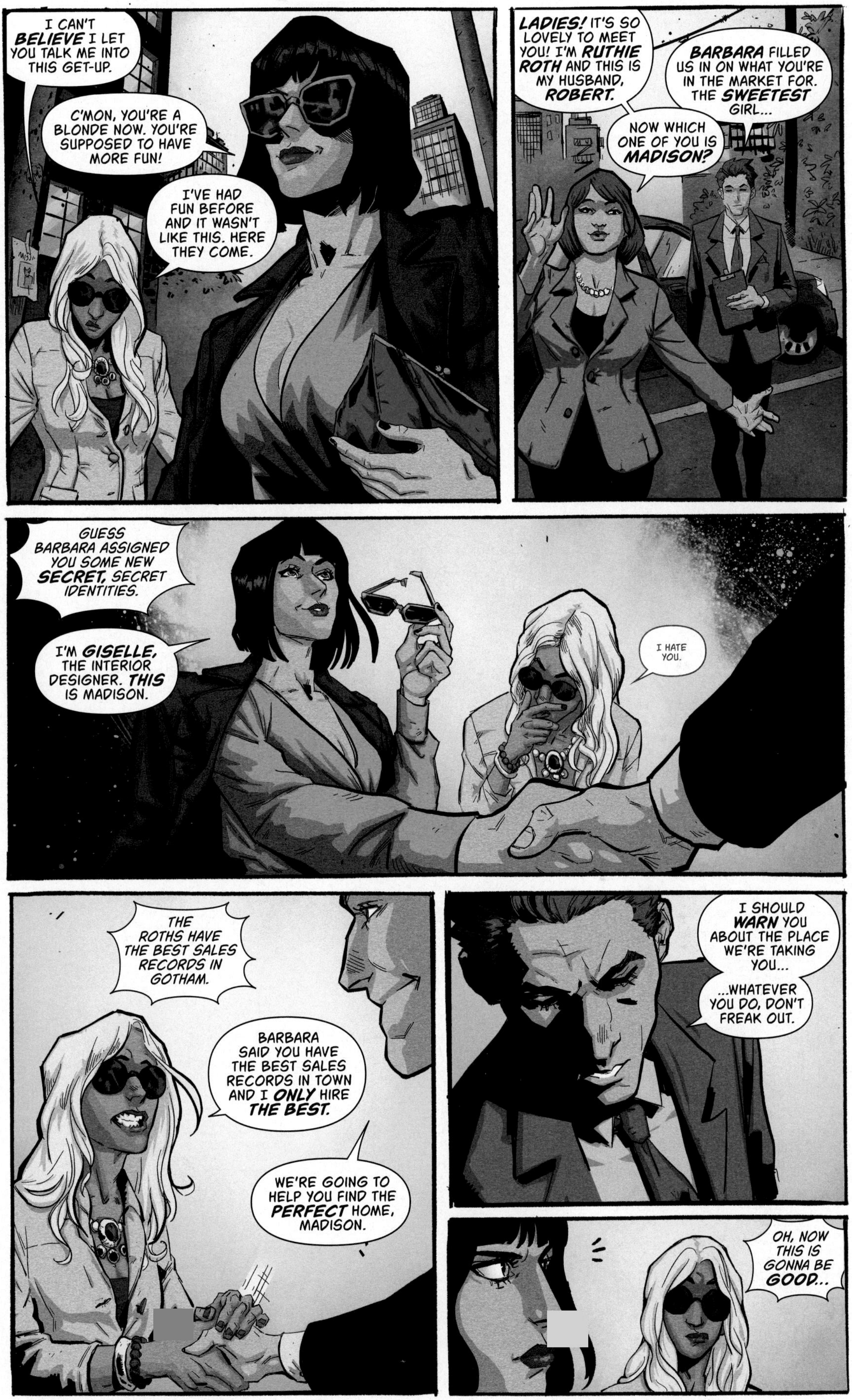

I CAN'T BELIEVE I LET YOU TALK ME INTO THIS GET-UP.
C'MON, YOU'RE A BLONDE NOW. YOU'RE SUPPOSED TO HAVE MORE FUN!
I'VE HAD FUN BEFORE AND IT WASN'T LIKE THIS. HERE THEY COME.
LADIES! IT'S SO LOVELY TO MEET YOU! I'M RUTHIE ROTH AND THIS IS MY HUSBAND, ROBERT.
BARBARA FILLED US IN ON WHAT YOU'RE IN THE MARKET FOR. THE SWEETEST GIRL...
NOW WHICH ONE OF YOU IS MADISON?
GUESS BARBARA ASSIGNED YOU SOME NEW SECRET, SECRET IDENTITIES.
I'M GISELLE, THE INTERIOR DESIGNER. THIS IS MADISON.
I HATE YOU.
THE ROTHS HAVE THE BEST SALES RECORDS IN GOTHAM.
BARBARA SAID YOU HAVE THE BEST SALES RECORDS IN TOWN AND I ONLY HIRE THE BEST.
WE'RE GOING TO HELP YOU FIND THE PERFECT HOME, MADISON.
I SHOULD WARN YOU ABOUT THE PLACE WE'RE TAKING YOU...
...WHATEVER YOU DO, DON'T FREAK OUT.
OH, NOW THIS IS GONNA BE GOOD...

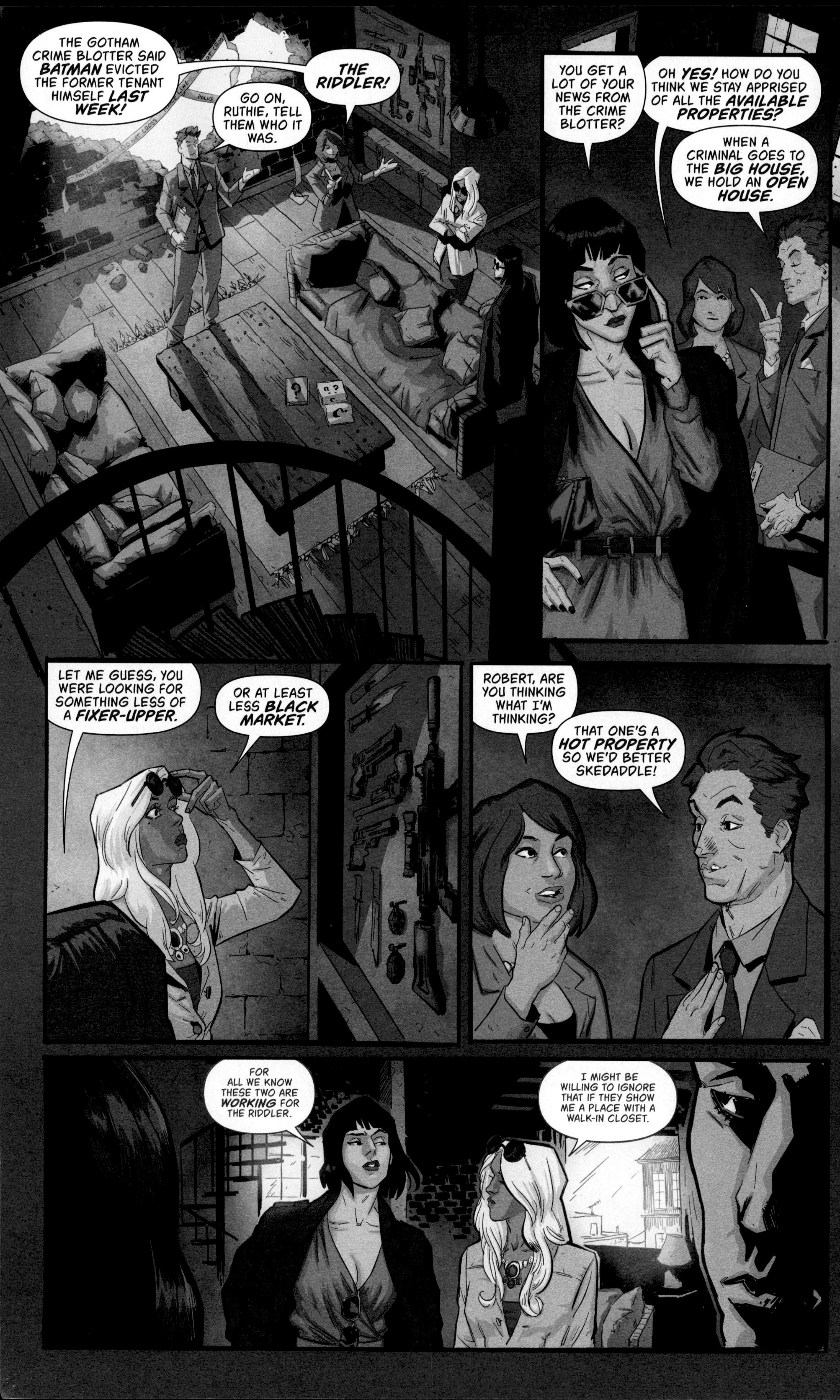

THE GOTHAM CRIME BLOTTER SAID BATMAN EVICTED THE FORMER TENANT HIMSELF LAST WEEK!
GO ON, RUTHIE, TELL THEM WHO IT WAS.
THE RIDDLER!
YOU GET A LOT OF YOUR NEWS FROM THE CRIME BLOTTER?
OH YES! HOW DO YOU THINK WE STAY APPRISED OF ALL THE AVAILABLE PROPERTIES?
WHEN A CRIMINAL GOES TO THE BIG HOUSE, WE HOLD AN OPEN HOUSE.
LET ME GUESS, YOU WERE LOOKING FOR SOMETHING LESS OF A FIXER-UPPER.
OR AT LEAST LESS BLACK MARKET.
ROBERT, ARE YOU THINKING WHAT I'M THINKING?
THAT ONE'S A HOT PROPERTY SO WE'D BETTER SKEDADDLE!
FOR ALL WE KNOW THESE TWO ARE WORKING FOR THE RIDDLER.
I MIGHT BE WILLING TO IGNORE THAT IF THEY SHOW ME A PLACE WITH A WALK-IN CLOSET.

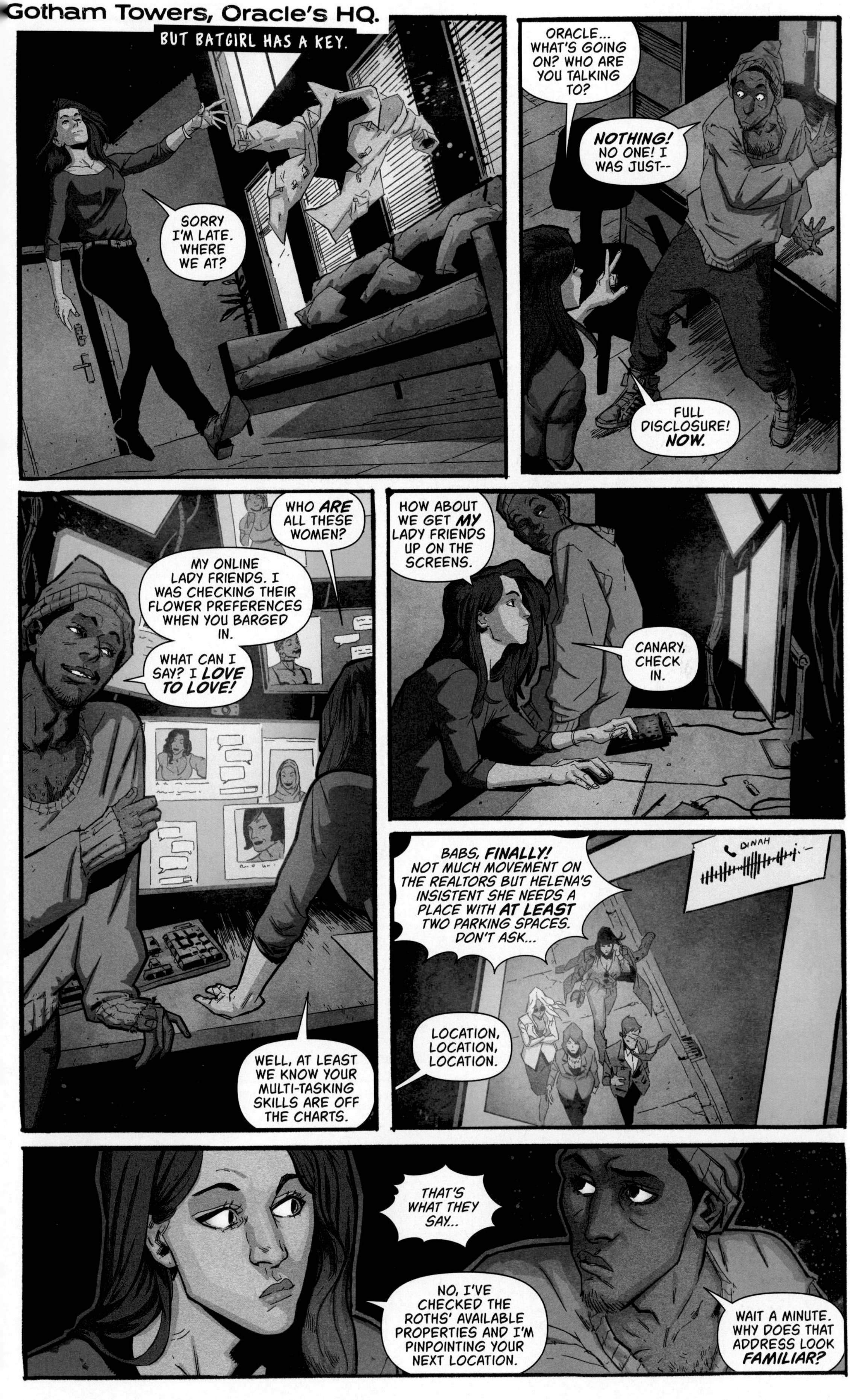
Gotham Towers, Oracle's HQ.
BUT BATGIRL HAS A KEY.
SORRY I'M LATE. WHERE WE AT?
ORACLE... WHAT'S GOING ON? WHO ARE YOU TALKING TO?
NOTHING! NO ONE! I WAS JUST--
FULL DISCLOSURE! NOW.
WHO ARE ALL THESE WOMEN?
MY ONLINE LADY FRIENDS. I WAS CHECKING THEIR FLOWER PREFERENCES WHEN YOU BARGED IN.
WHAT CAN I SAY? I LOVE TO LOVE!
WELL, AT LEAST WE KNOW YOUR MULTI-TASKING SKILLS ARE OFF THE CHARTS.
HOW ABOUT WE GET MY LADY FRIENDS UP ON THE SCREENS.
CANARY, CHECK IN.
DINAH
BABS, FINALLY! NOT MUCH MOVEMENT ON THE REALTORS BUT HELENA'S INSISTENT SHE NEEDS A PLACE WITH AT LEAST TWO PARKING SPACES. DON'T ASK...
LOCATION, LOCATION, LOCATION.
THAT'S WHAT THEY SAY...
NO, I'VE CHECKED THE ROTHS' AVAILABLE PROPERTIES AND I'M PINPOINTING YOUR NEXT LOCATION.
WAIT A MINUTE. WHY DOES THAT ADDRESS LOOK FAMILIAR?

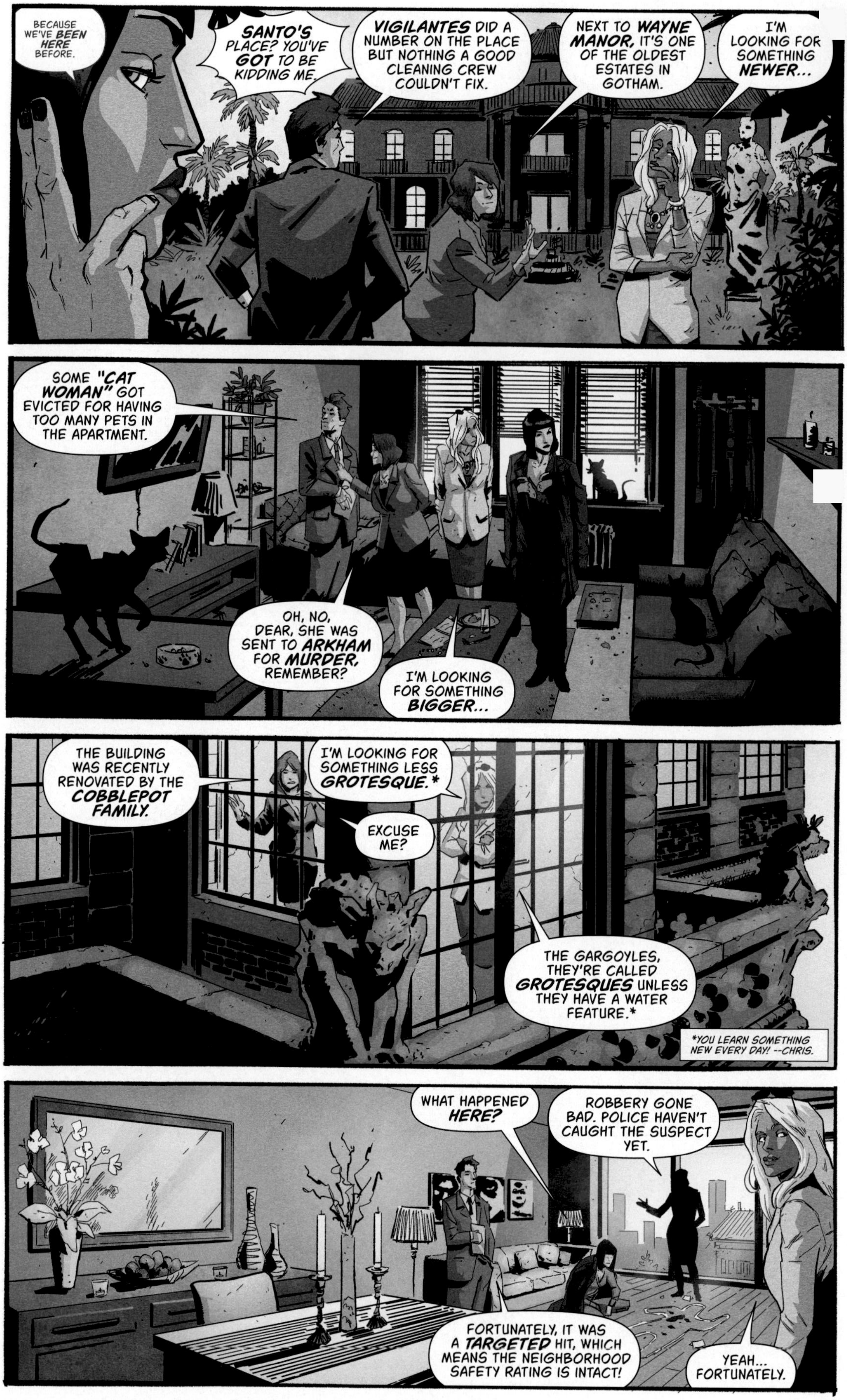
BECAUSE WE'VE BEEN HERE BEFORE.
SANTO'S PLACE? YOU'VE GOT TO BE KIDDING ME.
VIGILANTES DID A NUMBER ON THE PLACE BUT NOTHING A GOOD CLEANING CREW COULDN'T FIX.
NEXT TO WAYNE MANOR, IT'S ONE OF THE OLDEST ESTATES IN GOTHAM.
I'M LOOKING FOR SOMETHING NEWER...
SOME "CAT WOMAN" GOT EVICTED FOR HAVING TOO MANY PETS IN THE APARTMENT.
OH, NO, DEAR, SHE WAS SENT TO ARKHAM FOR MURDER, REMEMBER?
I'M LOOKING FOR SOMETHING BIGGER...
THE BUILDING WAS RECENTLY RENOVATED BY THE COBBLEPOT FAMILY.
I'M LOOKING FOR SOMETHING LESS GROTESQUE.*
EXCUSE ME?
THE GARGOYLES, THEY'RE CALLED GROTESQUES UNLESS THEY HAVE A WATER FEATURE.*
*YOU LEARN SOMETHING NEW EVERY DAY! --CHRIS.
WHAT HAPPENED HERE?
ROBBERY GONE BAD. POLICE HAVEN'T CAUGHT THE SUSPECT YET.
FORTUNATELY, IT WAS A TARGETED HIT, WHICH MEANS THE NEIGHBORHOOD SAFETY RATING IS INTACT!
YEAH... FORTUNATELY.

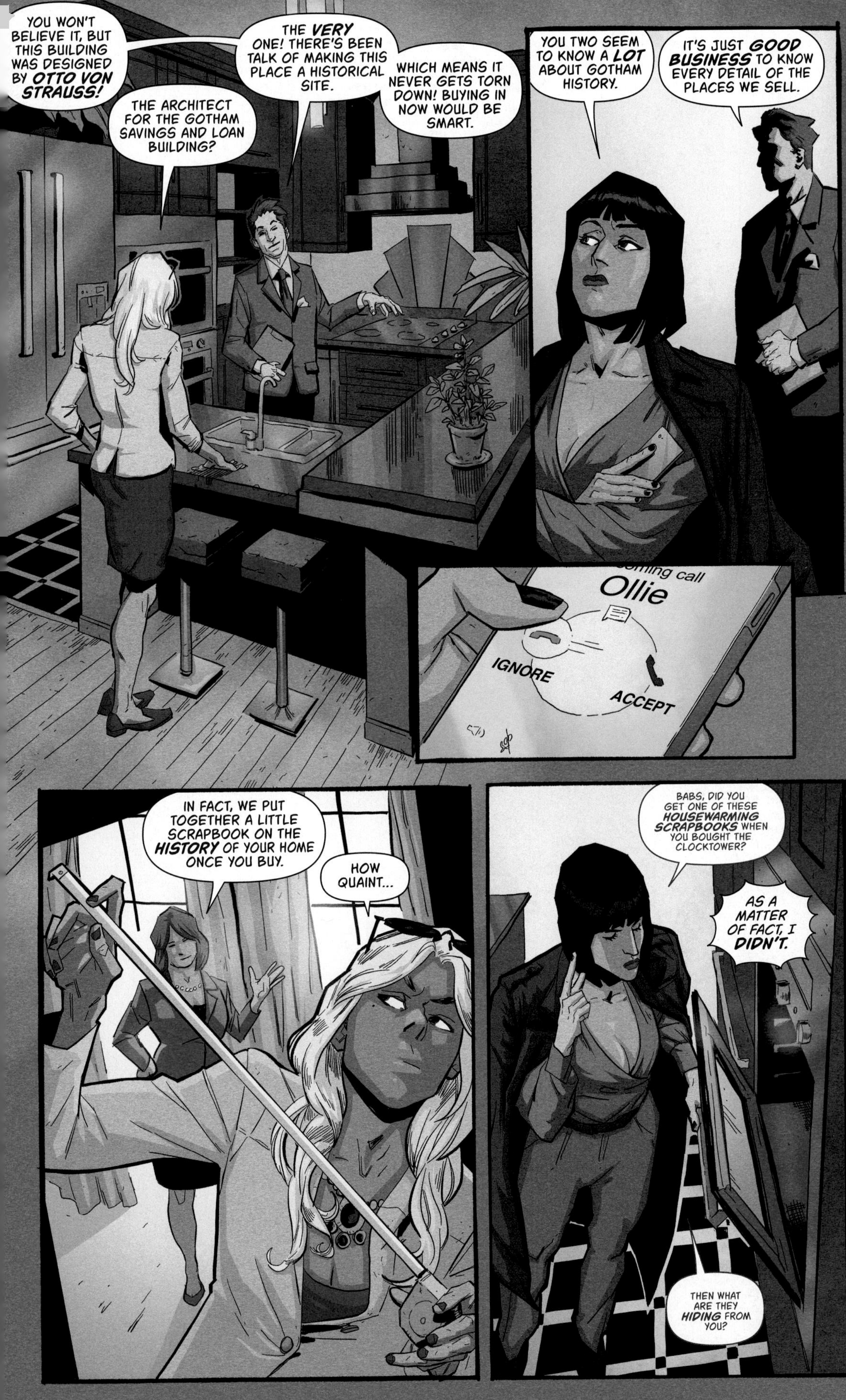

YOU WON'T BELIEVE IT, BUT THIS BUILDING WAS DESIGNED BY OTTO VON STRAUSS!
THE ARCHITECT FOR THE GOTHAM SAVINGS AND LOAN BUILDING?
THE VERY ONE! THERE'S BEEN TALK OF MAKING THIS PLACE A HISTORICAL SITE.
WHICH MEANS IT NEVER GETS TORN DOWN! BUYING IN NOW WOULD BE SMART.
YOU TWO SEEM TO KNOW A LOT ABOUT GOTHAM HISTORY.
IT'S JUST GOOD BUSINESS TO KNOW EVERY DETAIL OF THE PLACES WE SELL.
Ollie
IGNORE
ACCEPT
IN FACT, WE PUT TOGETHER A LITTLE SCRAPBOOK ON THE HISTORY OF YOUR HOME ONCE YOU BUY.
HOW QUAINT...
BABS, DID YOU GET ONE OF THESE HOUSEWARMING SCRAPBOOKS WHEN YOU BOUGHT THE CLOCKTOWER?
AS A MATTER OF FACT, I DIDN'T.
THEN WHAT ARE THEY HIDING FROM YOU?

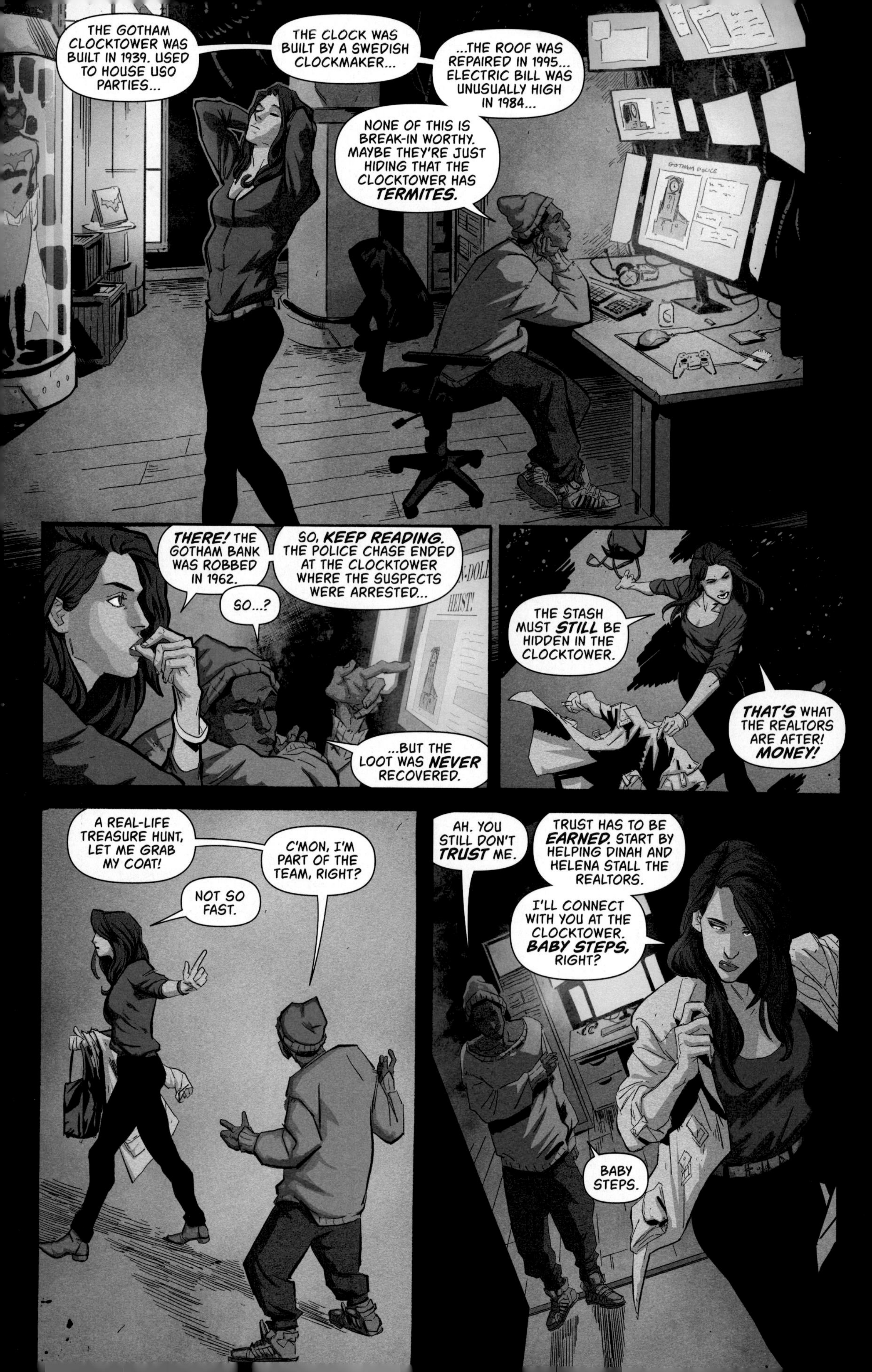

THE GOTHAM CLOCKTOWER WAS BUILT IN 1939. USED TO HOUSE USO PARTIES...
THE CLOCK WAS BUILT BY A SWEDISH CLOCKMAKER...
...THE ROOF WAS REPAIRED IN 1995... ELECTRIC BILL WAS UNUSUALLY HIGH IN 1984...
NONE OF THIS IS BREAK-IN WORTHY. MAYBE THEY'RE JUST HIDING THAT THE CLOCKTOWER HAS TERMITES.
GOTHAM POLICE
THERE! THE GOTHAM BANK WAS ROBBED IN 1962.
SO...?
SO, KEEP READING. THE POLICE CHASE ENDED AT THE CLOCKTOWER WHERE THE SUSPECTS WERE ARRESTED...
HEIST!
...BUT THE LOOT WAS NEVER RECOVERED.
THE STASH MUST STILL BE HIDDEN IN THE CLOCKTOWER.
THAT'S WHAT THE REALTORS ARE AFTER! MONEY!
A REAL-LIFE TREASURE HUNT, LET ME GRAB MY COAT!
NOT SO FAST.
C'MON, I'M PART OF THE TEAM, RIGHT?
AH. YOU STILL DON'T TRUST ME.
TRUST HAS TO BE EARNED. START BY HELPING DINAH AND HELENA STALL THE REALTORS.
I'LL CONNECT WITH YOU AT THE CLOCKTOWER. BABY STEPS, RIGHT?
BABY STEPS.

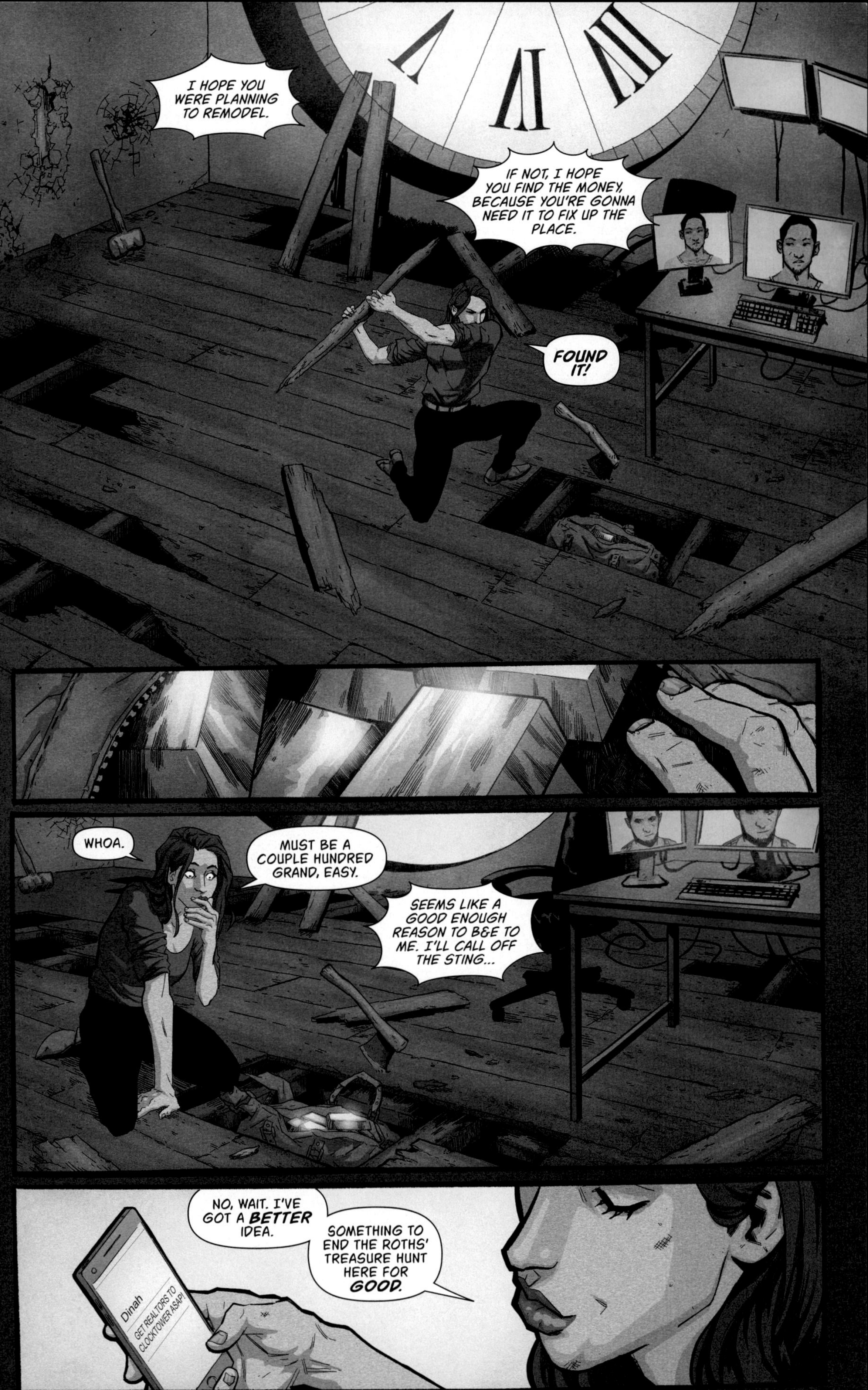
I HOPE YOU WERE PLANNING TO REMODEL.
IF NOT, I HOPE YOU FIND THE MONEY, BECAUSE YOU'RE GONNA NEED IT TO FIX UP THE PLACE.
FOUND IT!
WHOA.
MUST BE A COUPLE HUNDRED GRAND, EASY.
SEEMS LIKE A GOOD ENOUGH REASON TO B&E TO ME. I'LL CALL OFF THE STING...
NO, WAIT. I'VE GOT A BETTER IDEA.
SOMETHING TO END THE ROTHS' TREASURE HUNT HERE FOR GOOD.
Dinah
GET REALTORS TO CLOCKTOWER ASAP!

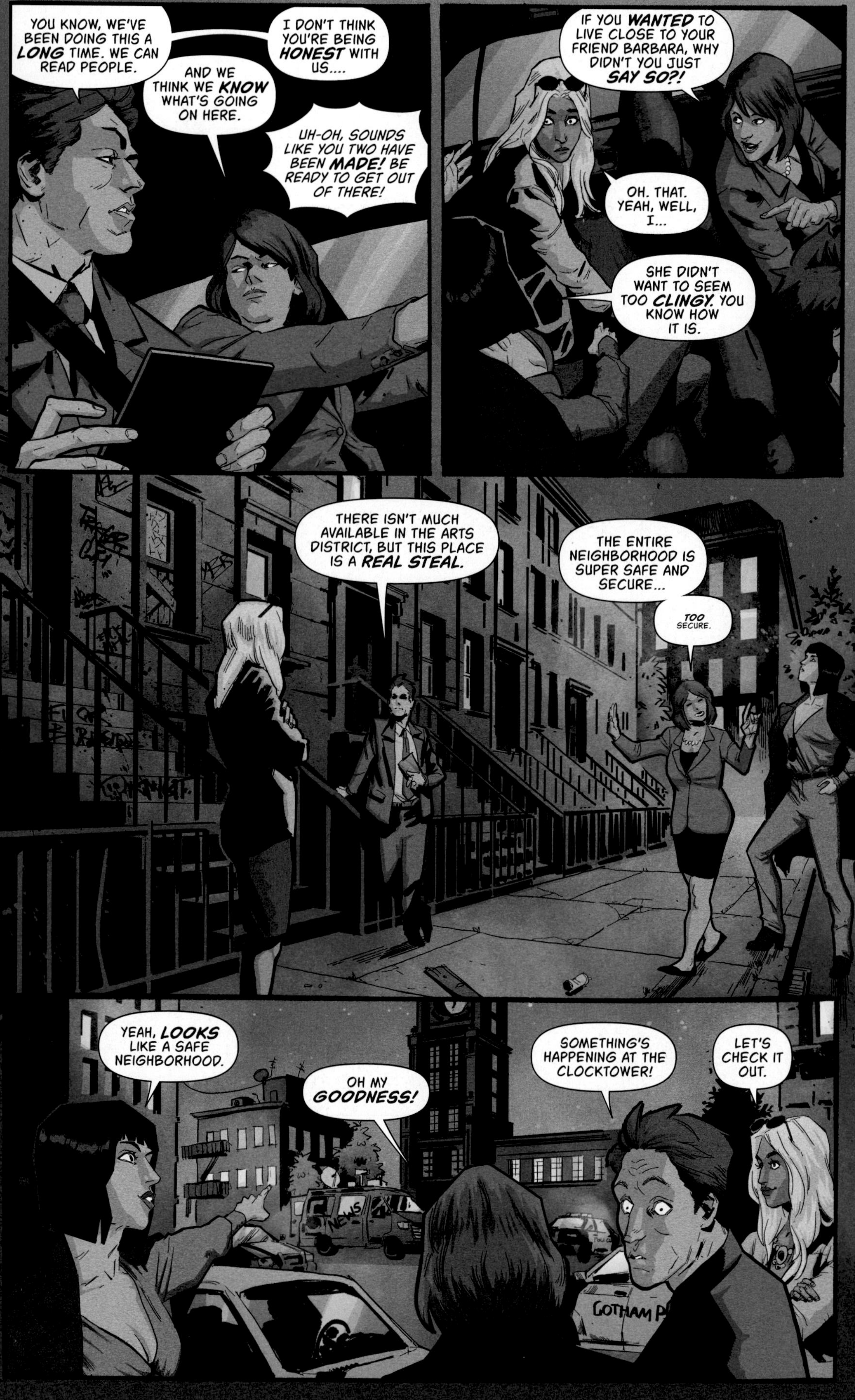

YOU KNOW, WE'VE BEEN DOING THIS A **LONG** TIME. WE CAN READ PEOPLE.
I DON'T THINK YOU'RE BEING **HONEST** WITH US....
AND WE THINK WE **KNOW** WHAT'S GOING ON HERE.
*UH-OH, SOUNDS LIKE YOU TWO HAVE BEEN **MADE!** BE READY TO GET OUT OF THERE!*
IF YOU **WANTED** TO LIVE CLOSE TO YOUR FRIEND BARBARA, WHY DIDN'T YOU JUST **SAY SO?!**
OH. THAT. YEAH, WELL, I...
SHE DIDN'T WANT TO SEEM TOO **CLINGY.** YOU KNOW HOW IT IS.
THERE ISN'T MUCH AVAILABLE IN THE ARTS DISTRICT, BUT THIS PLACE IS A **REAL STEAL.**
THE ENTIRE NEIGHBORHOOD IS SUPER SAFE AND SECURE...
TOO SECURE.
YEAH, **LOOKS** LIKE A SAFE NEIGHBORHOOD.
OH MY **GOODNESS!**
SOMETHING'S HAPPENING AT THE CLOCKTOWER!
LET'S CHECK IT OUT.

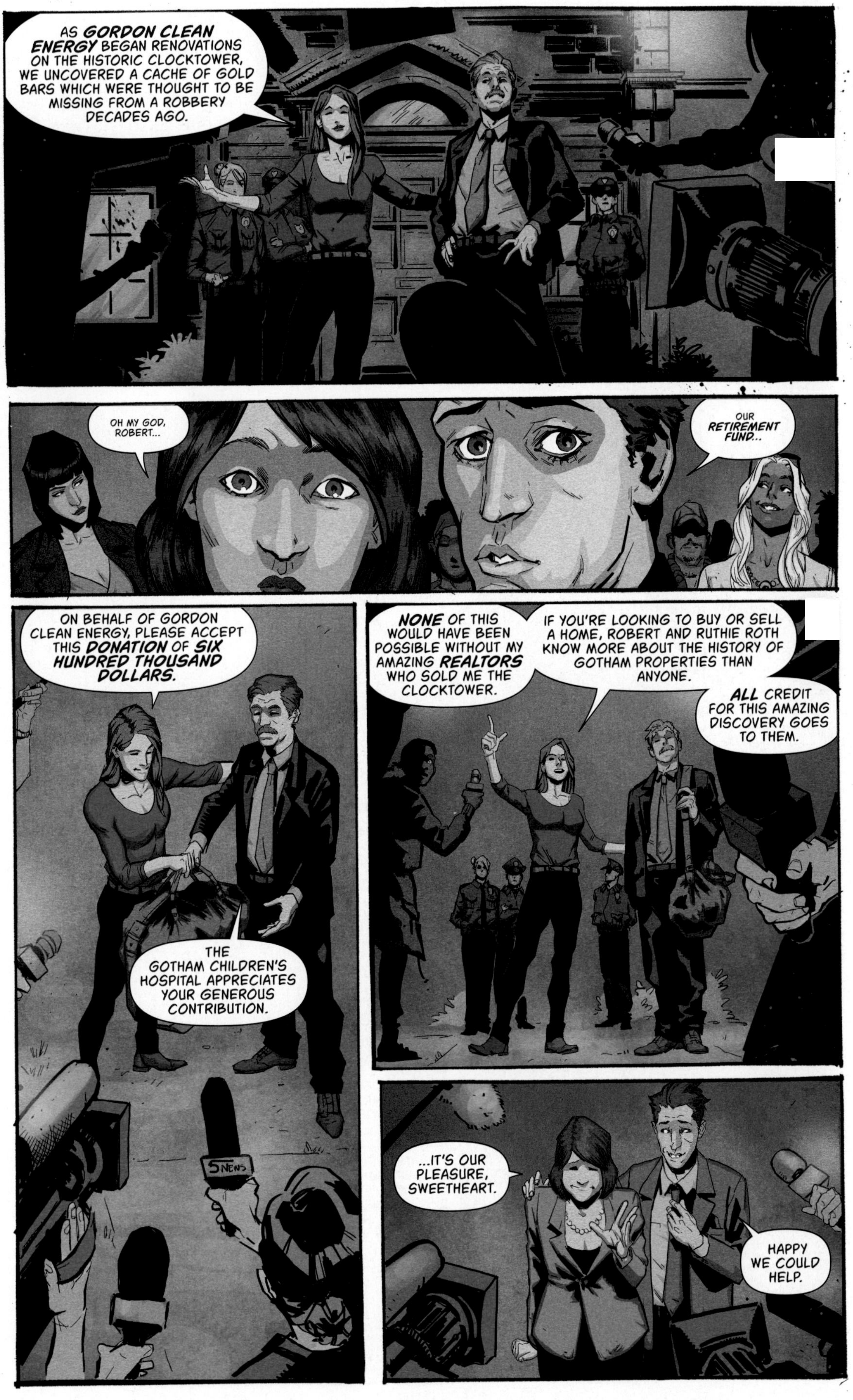
AS GORDON CLEAN ENERGY BEGAN RENOVATIONS ON THE HISTORIC CLOCKTOWER, WE UNCOVERED A CACHE OF GOLD BARS WHICH WERE THOUGHT TO BE MISSING FROM A ROBBERY DECADES AGO.
OH MY GOD, ROBERT...
OUR RETIREMENT FUND...
ON BEHALF OF GORDON CLEAN ENERGY, PLEASE ACCEPT THIS DONATION OF SIX HUNDRED THOUSAND DOLLARS.
THE GOTHAM CHILDREN'S HOSPITAL APPRECIATES YOUR GENEROUS CONTRIBUTION.
5 NEWS
NONE OF THIS WOULD HAVE BEEN POSSIBLE WITHOUT MY AMAZING REALTORS WHO SOLD ME THE CLOCKTOWER.
IF YOU'RE LOOKING TO BUY OR SELL A HOME, ROBERT AND RUTHIE ROTH KNOW MORE ABOUT THE HISTORY OF GOTHAM PROPERTIES THAN ANYONE.
ALL CREDIT FOR THIS AMAZING DISCOVERY GOES TO THEM.
...IT'S OUR PLEASURE, SWEETHEART.
HAPPY WE COULD HELP.

THE LOOKS ON THEIR FACES. *PRICELESS* MOVE, BABS.

I WASN'T SURE THEY WERE *CAPABLE* OF AN EXPRESSION OTHER THAN *TERRIFYING SMILES.*

I'M JUST GLAD THEY WON'T BE SNIFFING AROUND HERE ANYMORE.

WELL, *I* MAY NOT BE QUITE DONE WITH THEM YET. I THINK I SAW A PLACE I ACTUALLY LIKED.

YOU'RE GOING TO STAY? HELENA, *THAT'S AMAZING!*

FIGURED GOTHAM COULD USE A GOOD TEACHER. BESIDES, NOW THAT *MY MOM* IS BACK FROM THE DEAD AND IN JAIL, I NEED TO START LIVING MY LIFE FOR ME, AS HELENA BERTINELLI.

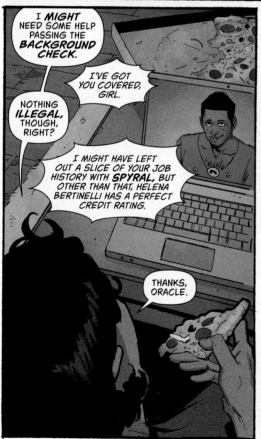

I *MIGHT* NEED SOME HELP PASSING THE *BACKGROUND CHECK.*

I'VE GOT YOU COVERED, GIRL.

NOTHING *ILLEGAL,* THOUGH, RIGHT?

I MIGHT HAVE LEFT OUT A SLICE OF YOUR JOB HISTORY WITH *SPYRAL,* BUT OTHER THAN THAT, HELENA BERTINELLI HAS A PERFECT CREDIT RATING.

THANKS, ORACLE.

THANKS FOR LETTING ME CRASH HERE TONIGHT.

HAPPY TO HELP! JUST DON'T FALL INTO MY ARCHAEOLOGICAL DIG HOLES.

COMPARED TO DINAH'S PLACE, THIS IS AN *UPGRADE.*

HEY! THOSE SHIRTS ARE REALLY SOFT!

THAT'S WEIRD, I MISSED SIXTEEN TEXTS FROM OLLIE.

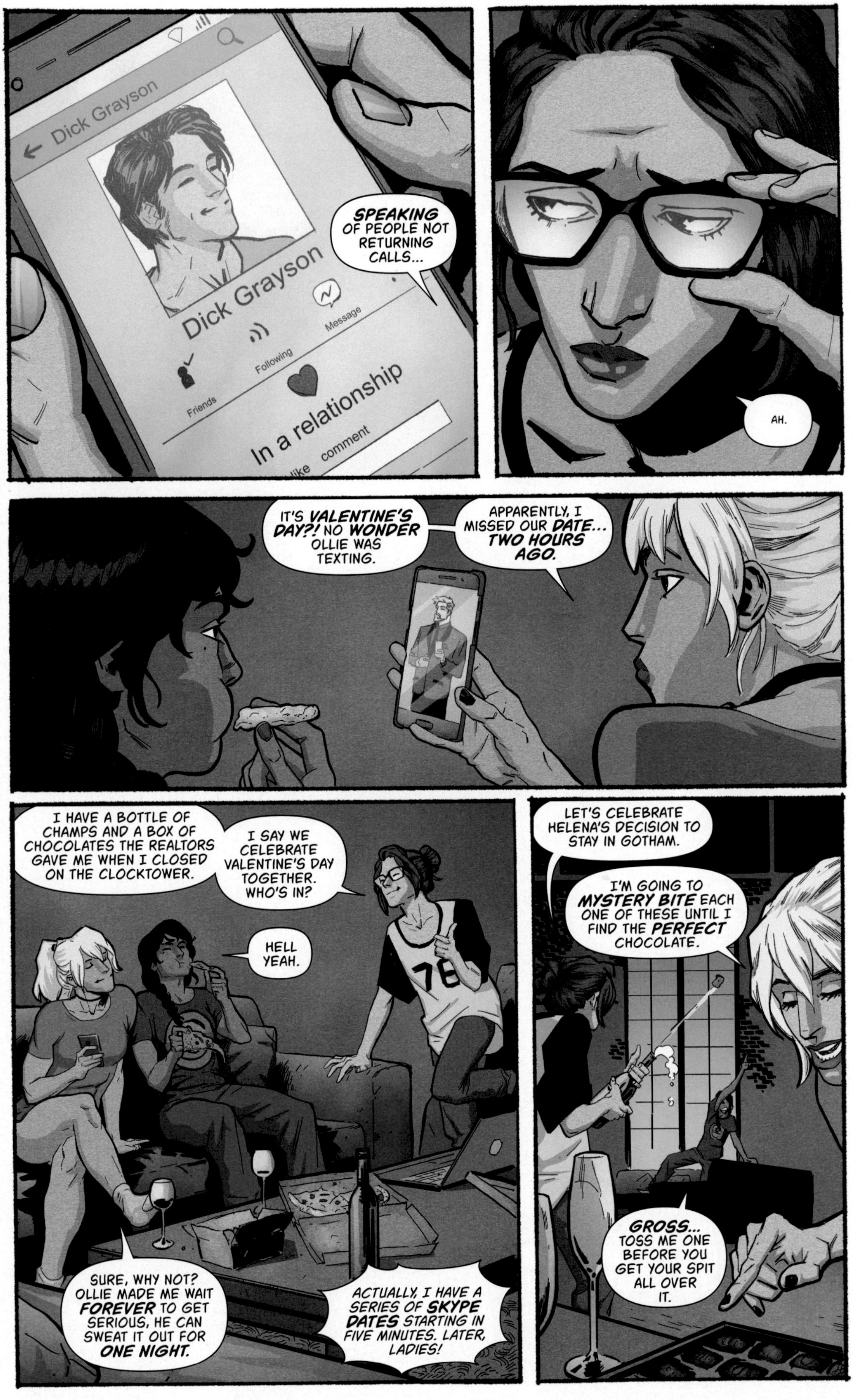
Dick Grayson
Dick Grayson
Friends
Following
Message
In a relationship
like comment
SPEAKING OF PEOPLE NOT RETURNING CALLS...
AH.
IT'S VALENTINE'S DAY?! NO WONDER OLLIE WAS TEXTING.
APPARENTLY, I MISSED OUR DATE... TWO HOURS AGO.
I HAVE A BOTTLE OF CHAMPS AND A BOX OF CHOCOLATES THE REALTORS GAVE ME WHEN I CLOSED ON THE CLOCKTOWER.
I SAY WE CELEBRATE VALENTINE'S DAY TOGETHER. WHO'S IN?
HELL YEAH.
SURE, WHY NOT? OLLIE MADE ME WAIT FOREVER TO GET SERIOUS, HE CAN SWEAT IT OUT FOR ONE NIGHT.
ACTUALLY, I HAVE A SERIES OF SKYPE DATES STARTING IN FIVE MINUTES. LATER, LADIES!
LET'S CELEBRATE HELENA'S DECISION TO STAY IN GOTHAM.
I'M GOING TO MYSTERY BITE EACH ONE OF THESE UNTIL I FIND THE PERFECT CHOCOLATE.
GROSS... TOSS ME ONE BEFORE YOU GET YOUR SPIT ALL OVER IT.

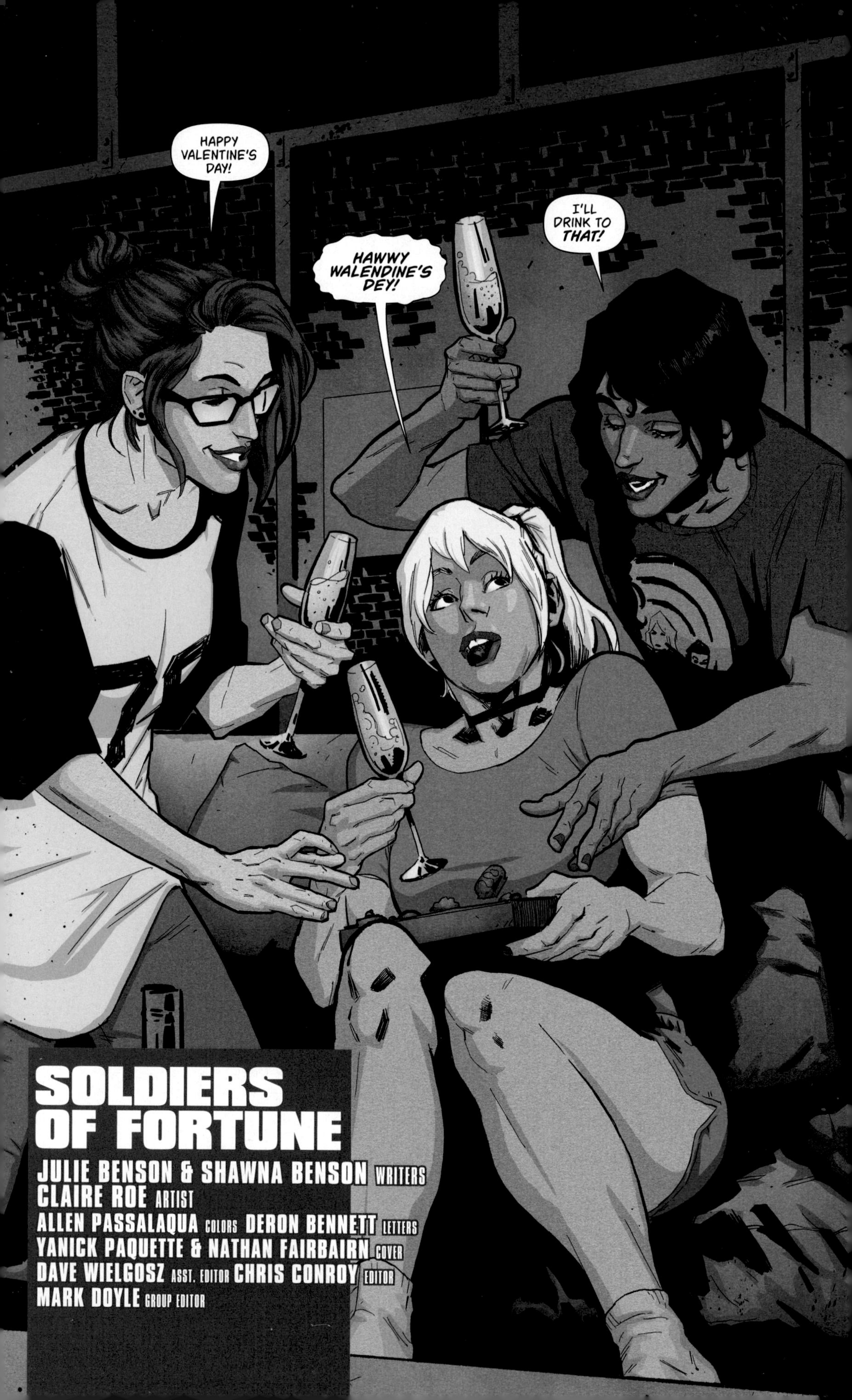
HAPPY VALENTINE'S DAY!
HAWWY WALENDINE'S DEY!
I'LL DRINK TO THAT!

SOLDIERS OF FORTUNE

JULIE BENSON & SHAWNA BENSON WRITERS
CLAIRE ROE ARTIST
ALLEN PASSALAQUA COLORS DERON BENNETT LETTERS
YANICK PAQUETTE & NATHAN FAIRBAIRN COVER
DAVE WIELGOSZ ASST. EDITOR CHRIS CONROY EDITOR
MARK DOYLE GROUP EDITOR

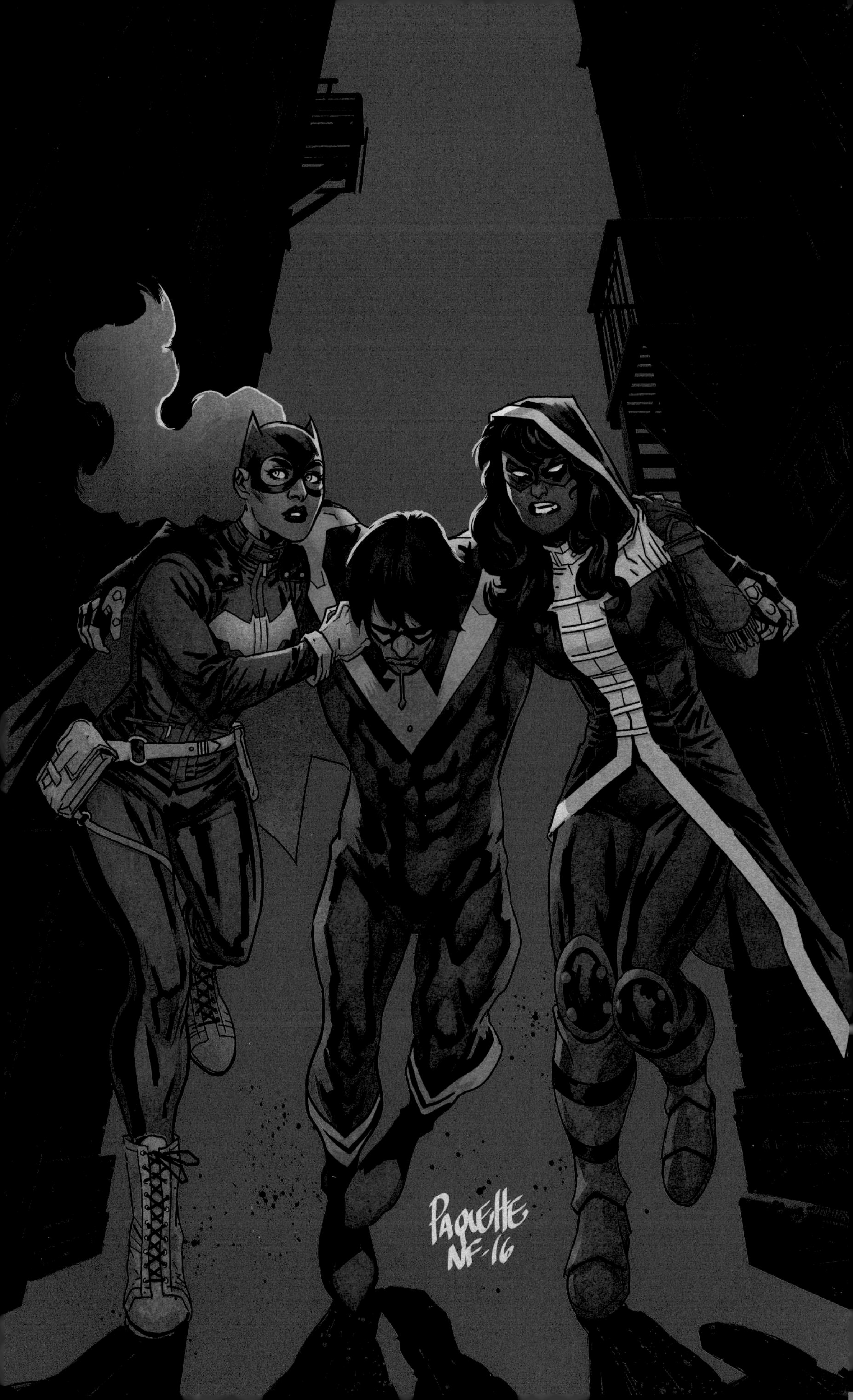
PAQUETTE
NF-16

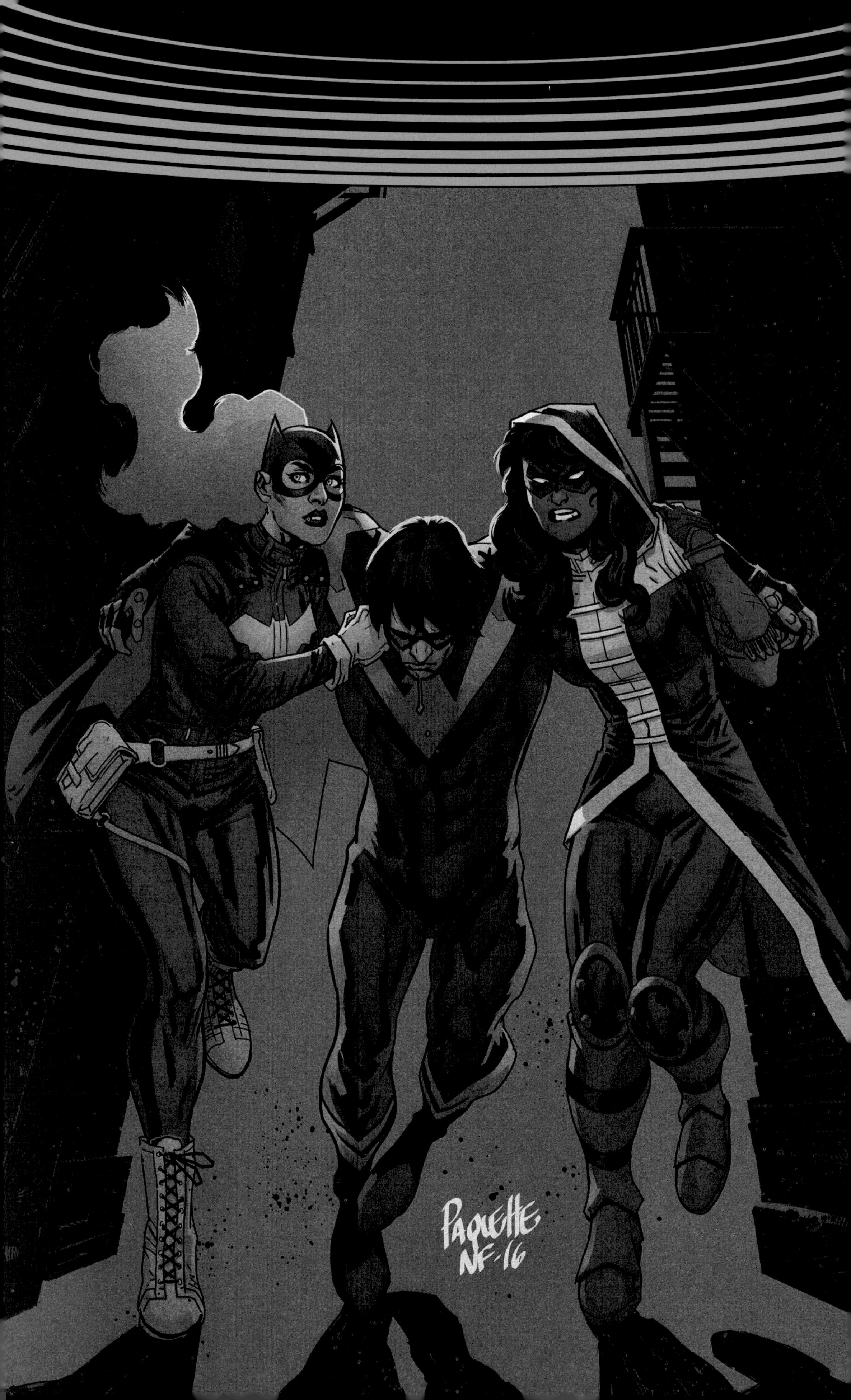
PAQUETTE
NF-16

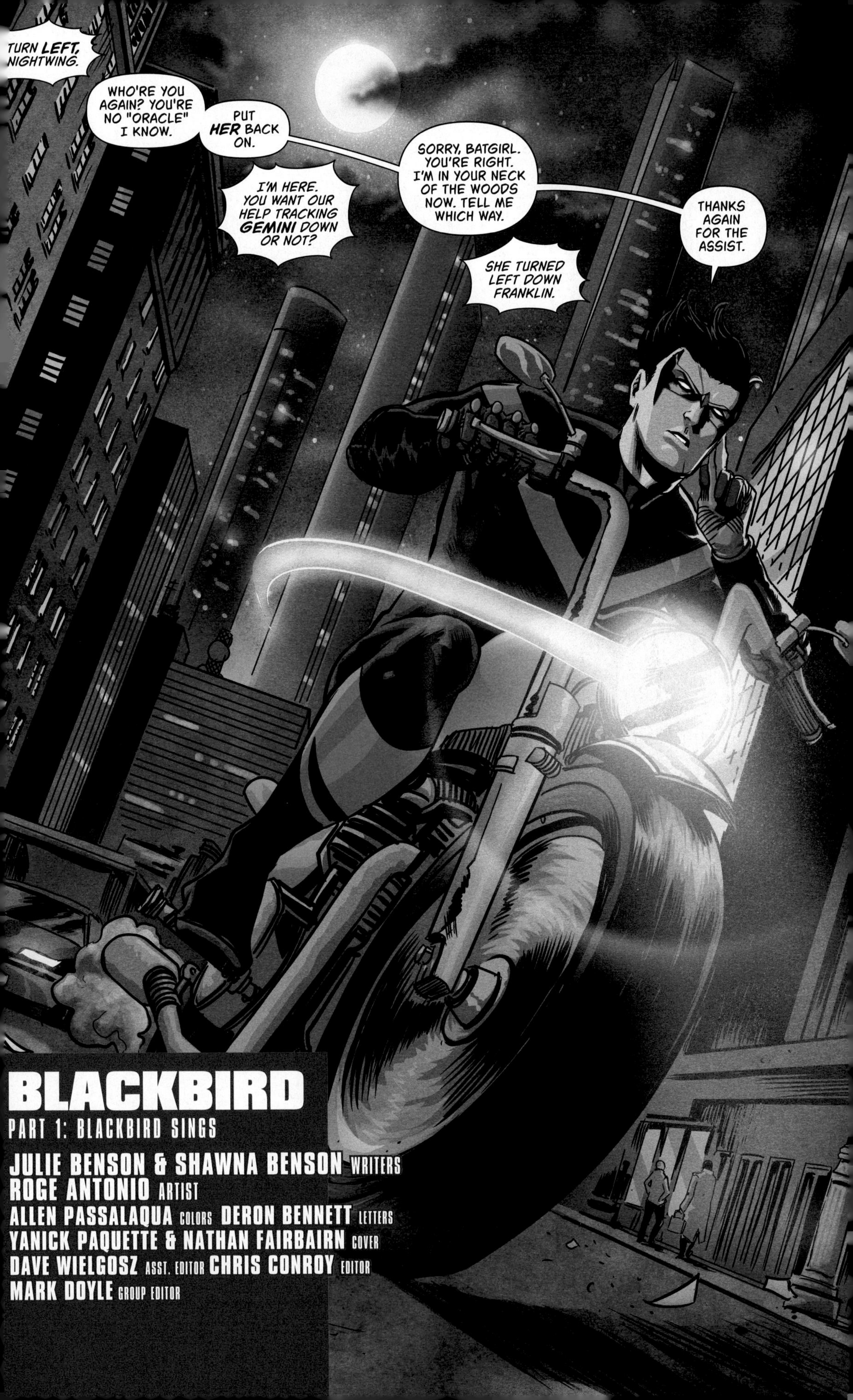
TURN LEFT, NIGHTWING.
WHO'RE YOU AGAIN? YOU'RE NO "ORACLE" I KNOW.
PUT HER BACK ON.
I'M HERE. YOU WANT OUR HELP TRACKING GEMINI DOWN OR NOT?
SORRY, BATGIRL. YOU'RE RIGHT. I'M IN YOUR NECK OF THE WOODS NOW. TELL ME WHICH WAY.
SHE TURNED LEFT DOWN FRANKLIN.
THANKS AGAIN FOR THE ASSIST.

BLACKBIRD

PART 1: BLACKBIRD SINGS

JULIE BENSON & SHAWNA BENSON WRITERS
ROGE ANTONIO ARTIST
ALLEN PASSALAQUA COLORS DERON BENNETT LETTERS
YANICK PAQUETTE & NATHAN FAIRBAIRN COVER
DAVE WIELGOSZ ASST. EDITOR CHRIS CONROY EDITOR
MARK DOYLE GROUP EDITOR

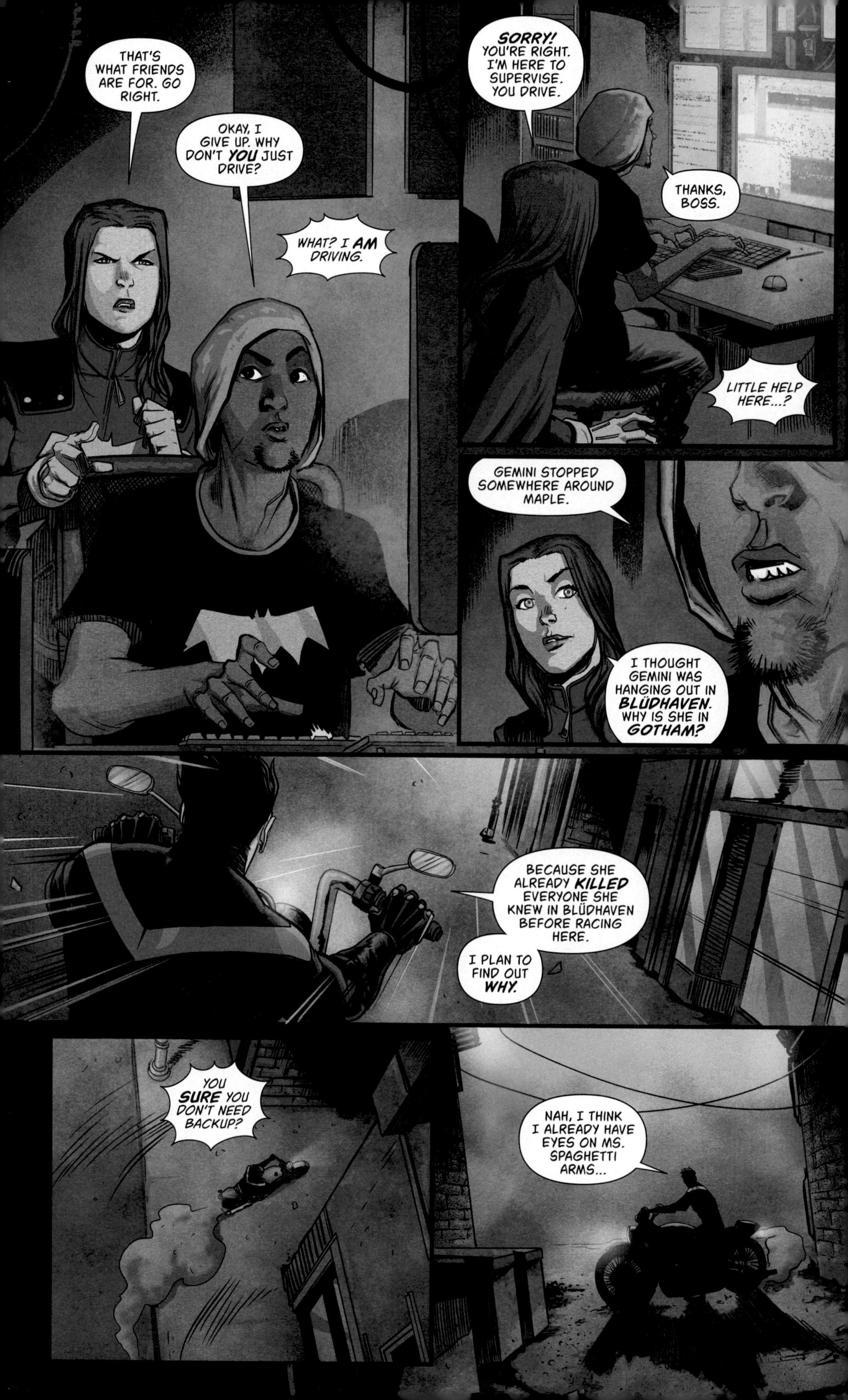
THAT'S WHAT FRIENDS ARE FOR. GO RIGHT.
OKAY, I GIVE UP. WHY DON'T **YOU** JUST DRIVE?
WHAT? I **AM** DRIVING.
SORRY! YOU'RE RIGHT. I'M HERE TO SUPERVISE. YOU DRIVE.
THANKS, BOSS.
LITTLE HELP HERE...?
GEMINI STOPPED SOMEWHERE AROUND MAPLE.
I THOUGHT GEMINI WAS HANGING OUT IN **BLÜDHAVEN**. WHY IS SHE IN **GOTHAM?**
BECAUSE SHE ALREADY **KILLED** EVERYONE SHE KNEW IN BLÜDHAVEN BEFORE RACING HERE.
I PLAN TO FIND OUT **WHY.**
YOU **SURE** YOU DON'T NEED BACKUP?
NAH, I THINK I ALREADY HAVE EYES ON MS. SPAGHETTI ARMS...

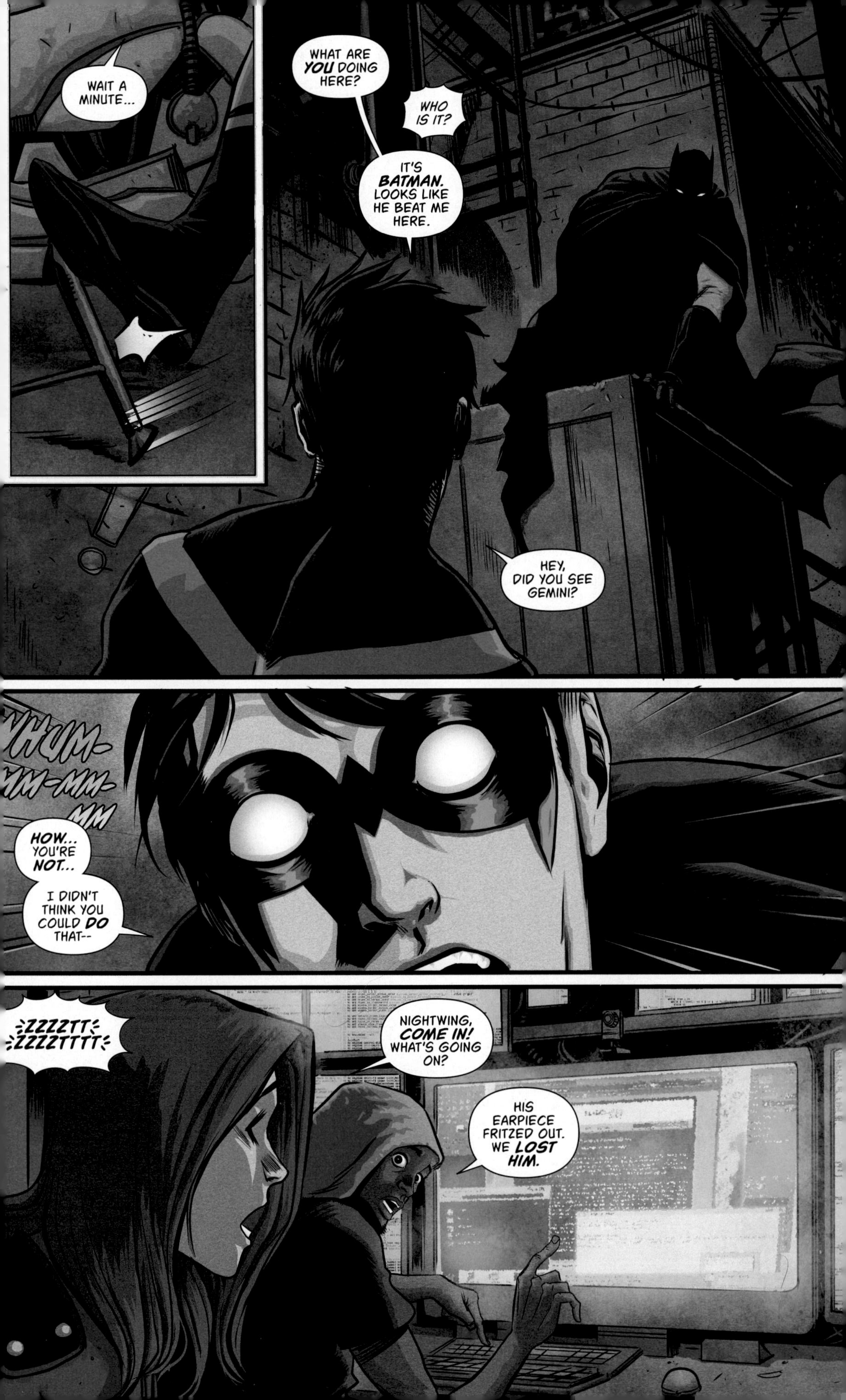
WAIT A MINUTE...
WHAT ARE YOU DOING HERE?
WHO IS IT?
IT'S BATMAN. LOOKS LIKE HE BEAT ME HERE.
HEY, DID YOU SEE GEMINI?
HUM-
MM-MM-
MM
HOW... YOU'RE NOT...
I DIDN'T THINK YOU COULD DO THAT--
ZZZZTT ZZZZTTTT
NIGHTWING, COME IN! WHAT'S GOING ON?
HIS EARPIECE FRITZED OUT. WE LOST HIM.

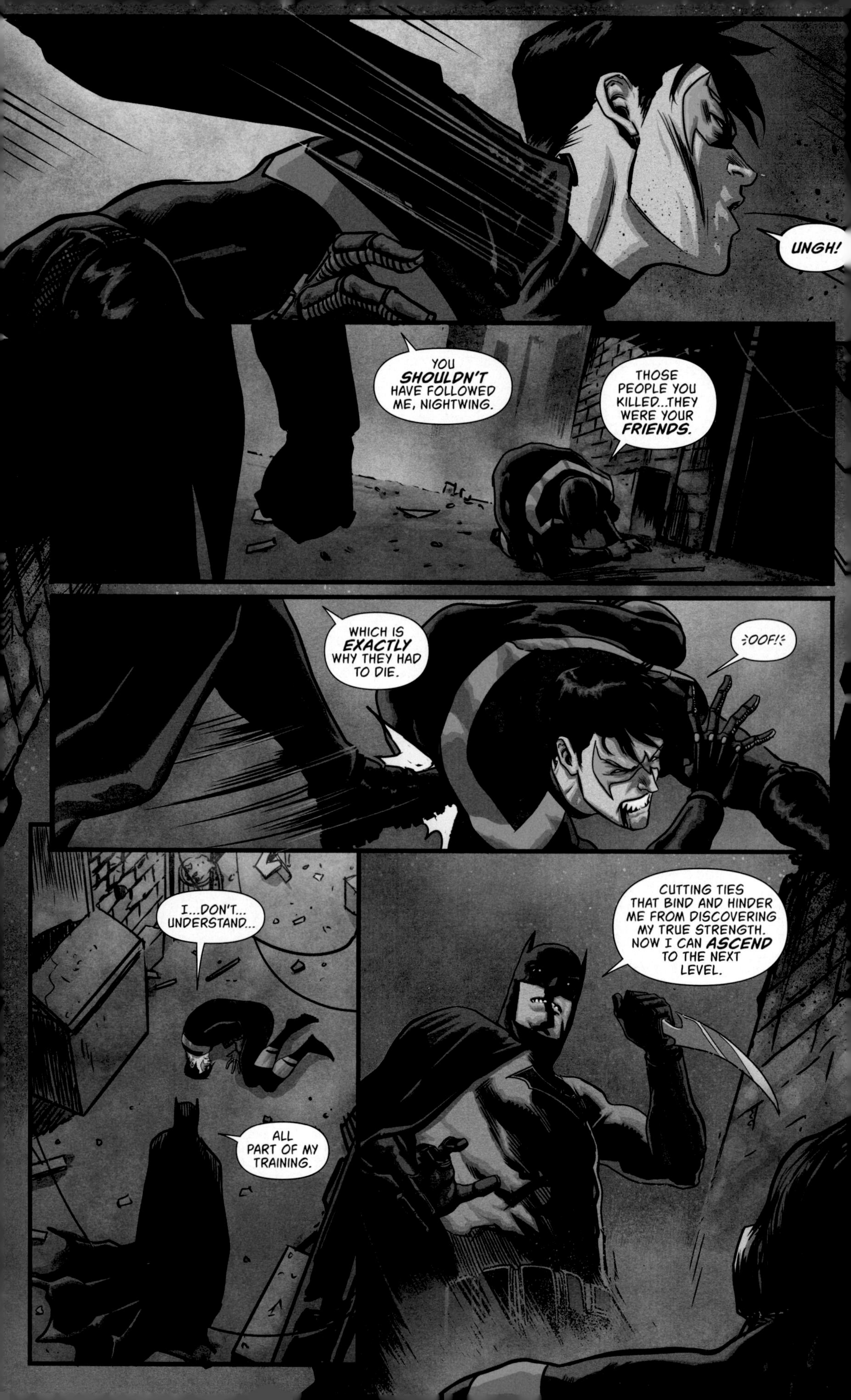
UNGH!
YOU SHOULDN'T HAVE FOLLOWED ME, NIGHTWING.
THOSE PEOPLE YOU KILLED...THEY WERE YOUR FRIENDS.
WHICH IS EXACTLY WHY THEY HAD TO DIE.
OOF!
I...DON'T... UNDERSTAND...
ALL PART OF MY TRAINING.
CUTTING TIES THAT BIND AND HINDER ME FROM DISCOVERING MY TRUE STRENGTH. NOW I CAN ASCEND TO THE NEXT LEVEL.

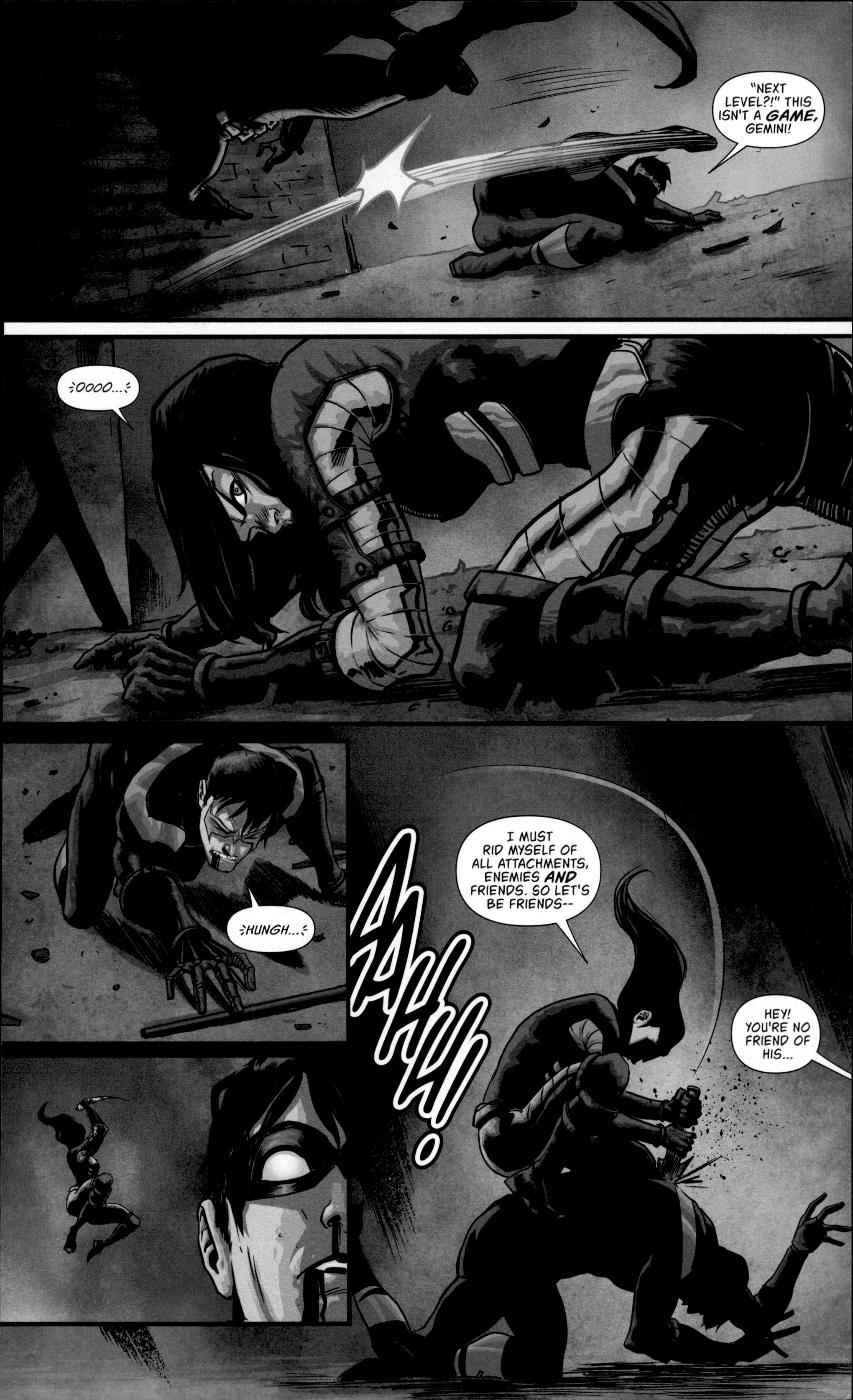
"NEXT LEVEL?!" THIS ISN'T A GAME, GEMINI!
OOOO...
HUNGH...
I MUST RID MYSELF OF ALL ATTACHMENTS, ENEMIES AND FRIENDS. SO LET'S BE FRIENDS--
AAHH!
HEY! YOU'RE NO FRIEND OF HIS...

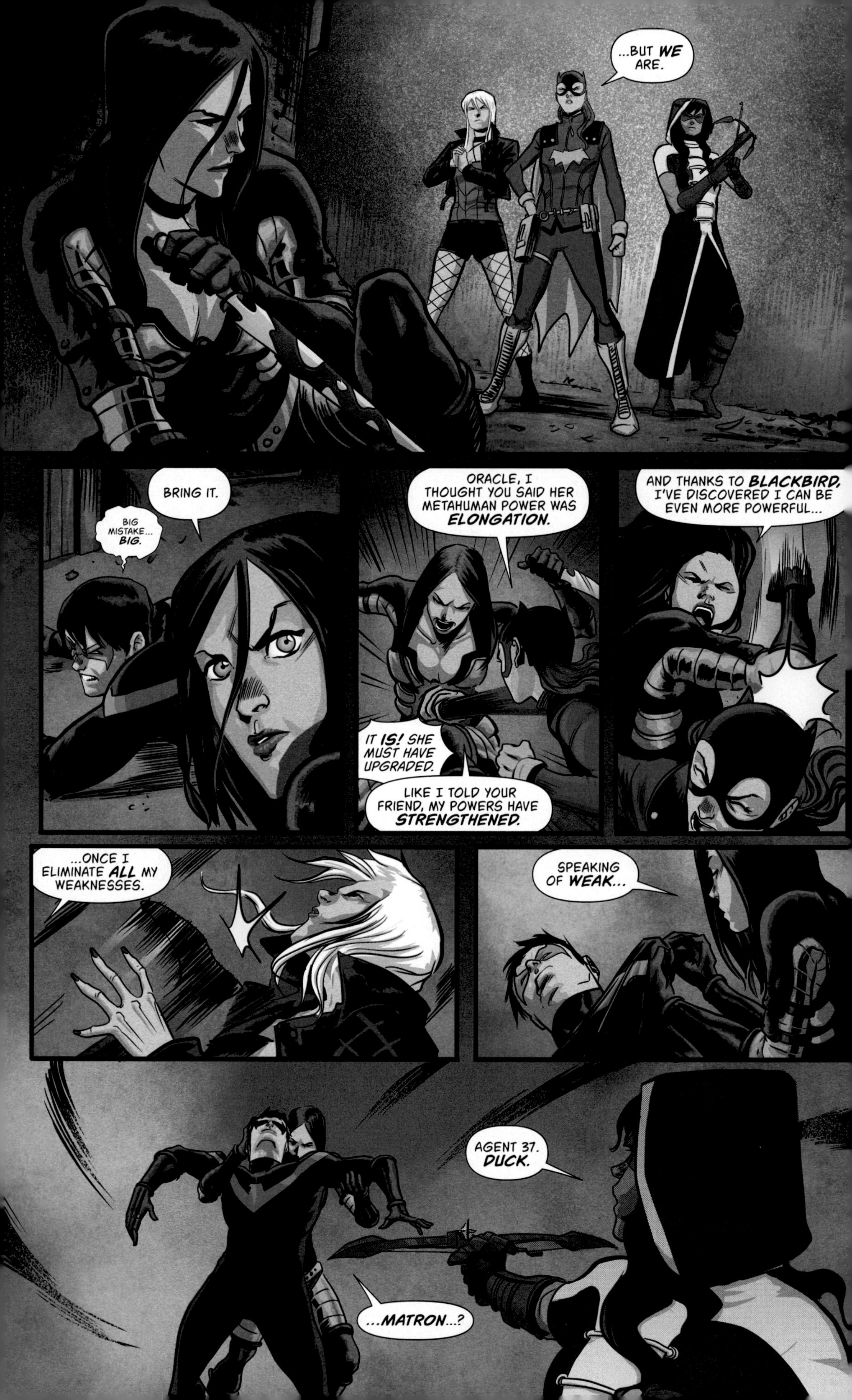
...BUT WE ARE.
BRING IT.
BIG MISTAKE... BIG.
ORACLE, I THOUGHT YOU SAID HER METAHUMAN POWER WAS ELONGATION.
IT IS! SHE MUST HAVE UPGRADED.
LIKE I TOLD YOUR FRIEND, MY POWERS HAVE STRENGTHENED.
AND THANKS TO BLACKBIRD, I'VE DISCOVERED I CAN BE EVEN MORE POWERFUL...
...ONCE I ELIMINATE ALL MY WEAKNESSES.
SPEAKING OF WEAK...
AGENT 37. DUCK.
...MATRON...?

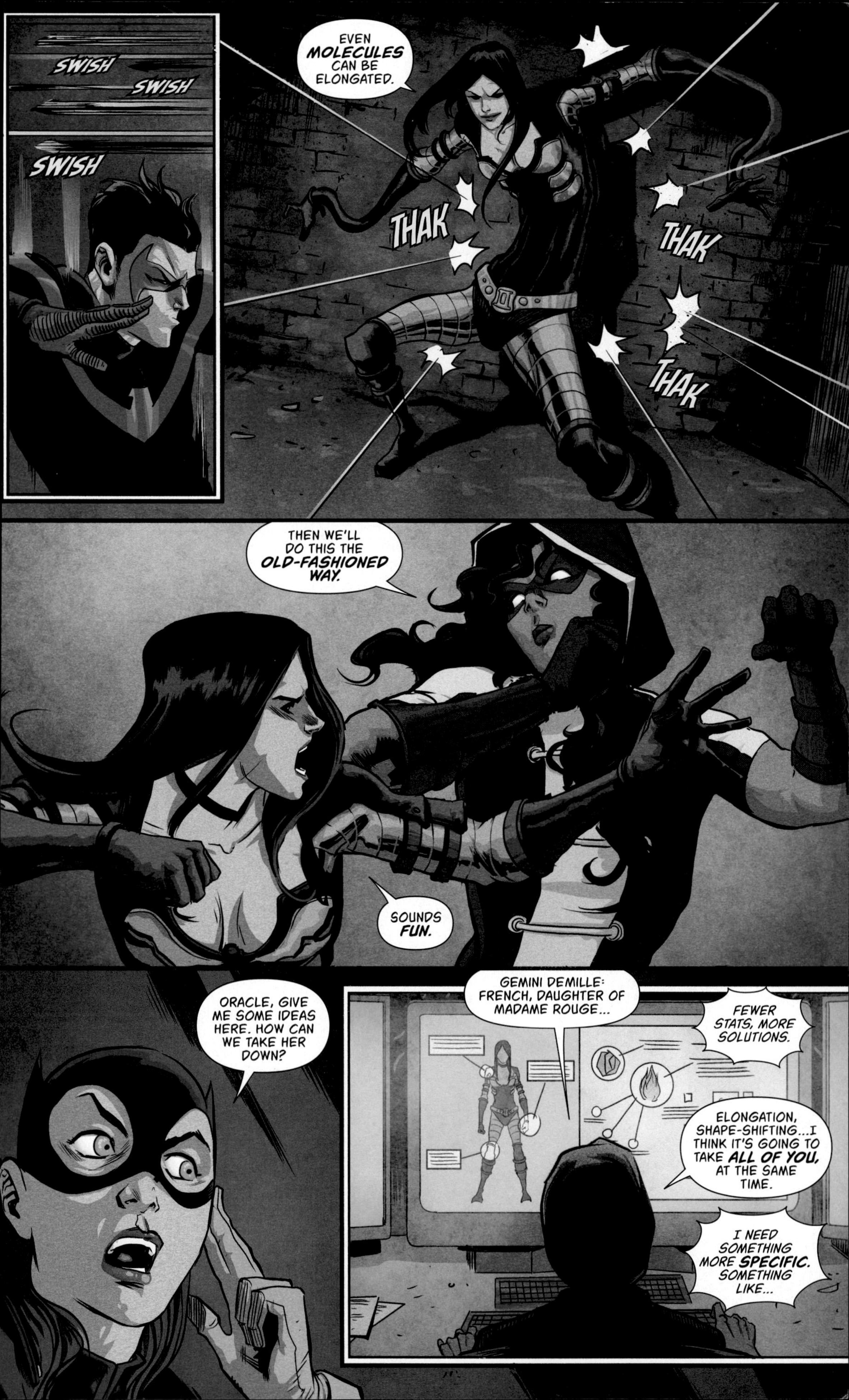
SWISH
SWISH
SWISH
EVEN MOLECULES CAN BE ELONGATED.
THAK
THAK
THAK
THEN WE'LL DO THIS THE OLD-FASHIONED WAY.
SOUNDS FUN.
ORACLE, GIVE ME SOME IDEAS HERE. HOW CAN WE TAKE HER DOWN?
GEMINI DEMILLE: FRENCH, DAUGHTER OF MADAME ROUGE...
FEWER STATS, MORE SOLUTIONS.
ELONGATION, SHAPE-SHIFTING...I THINK IT'S GOING TO TAKE ALL OF YOU, AT THE SAME TIME.
I NEED SOMETHING MORE SPECIFIC. SOMETHING LIKE...

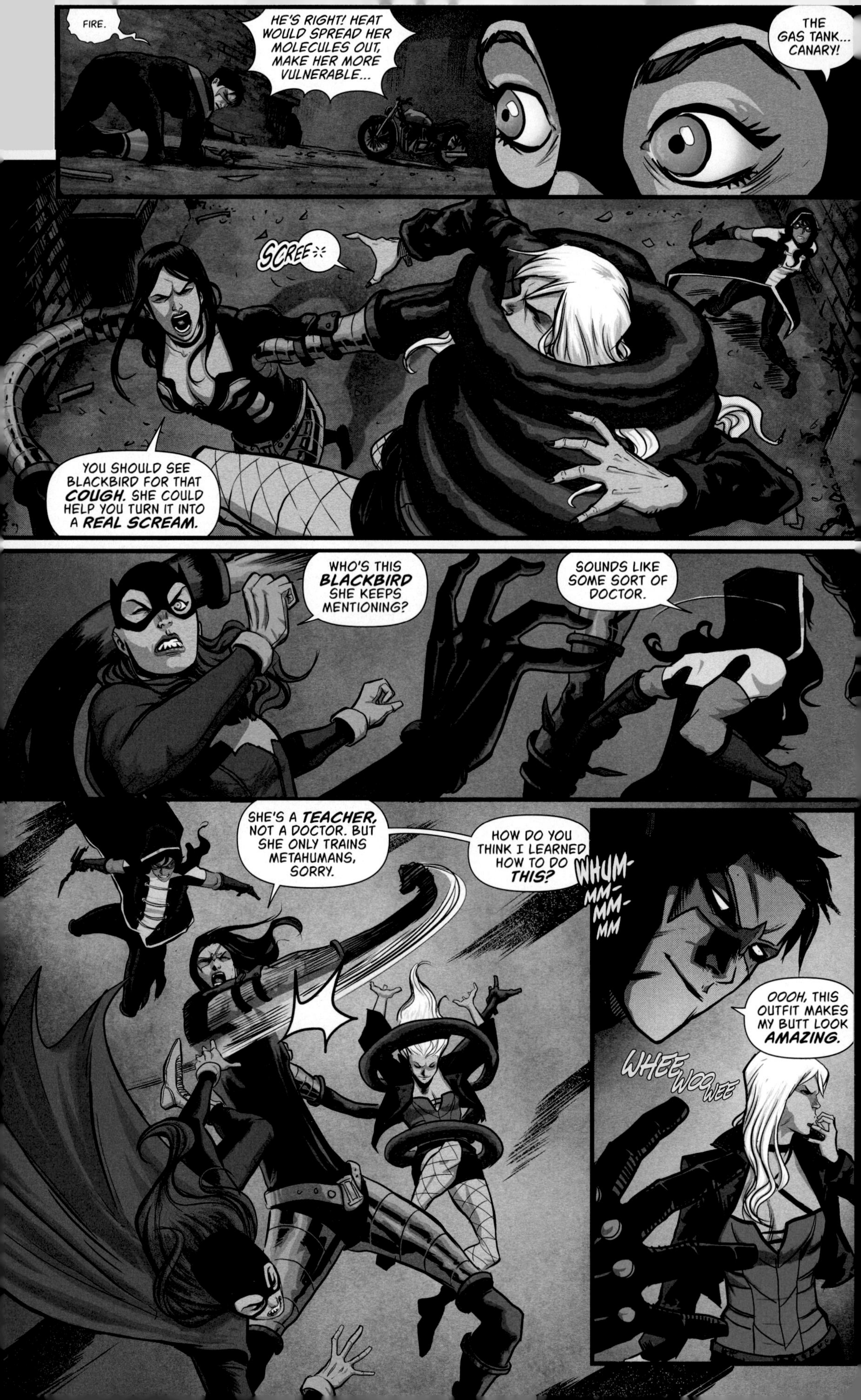
FIRE.
HE'S RIGHT! HEAT WOULD SPREAD HER MOLECULES OUT, MAKE HER MORE VULNERABLE...
THE GAS TANK... CANARY!
SCREE
YOU SHOULD SEE BLACKBIRD FOR THAT **COUGH.** SHE COULD HELP YOU TURN IT INTO A **REAL SCREAM.**
WHO'S THIS **BLACKBIRD** SHE KEEPS MENTIONING?
SOUNDS LIKE SOME SORT OF DOCTOR.
SHE'S A **TEACHER,** NOT A DOCTOR. BUT SHE ONLY TRAINS METAHUMANS, SORRY.
HOW DO YOU THINK I LEARNED HOW TO DO **THIS?**
WHUM-MM-MM-MM
OOOH, THIS OUTFIT MAKES MY BUTT LOOK **AMAZING.**
WHEE WOO WEE

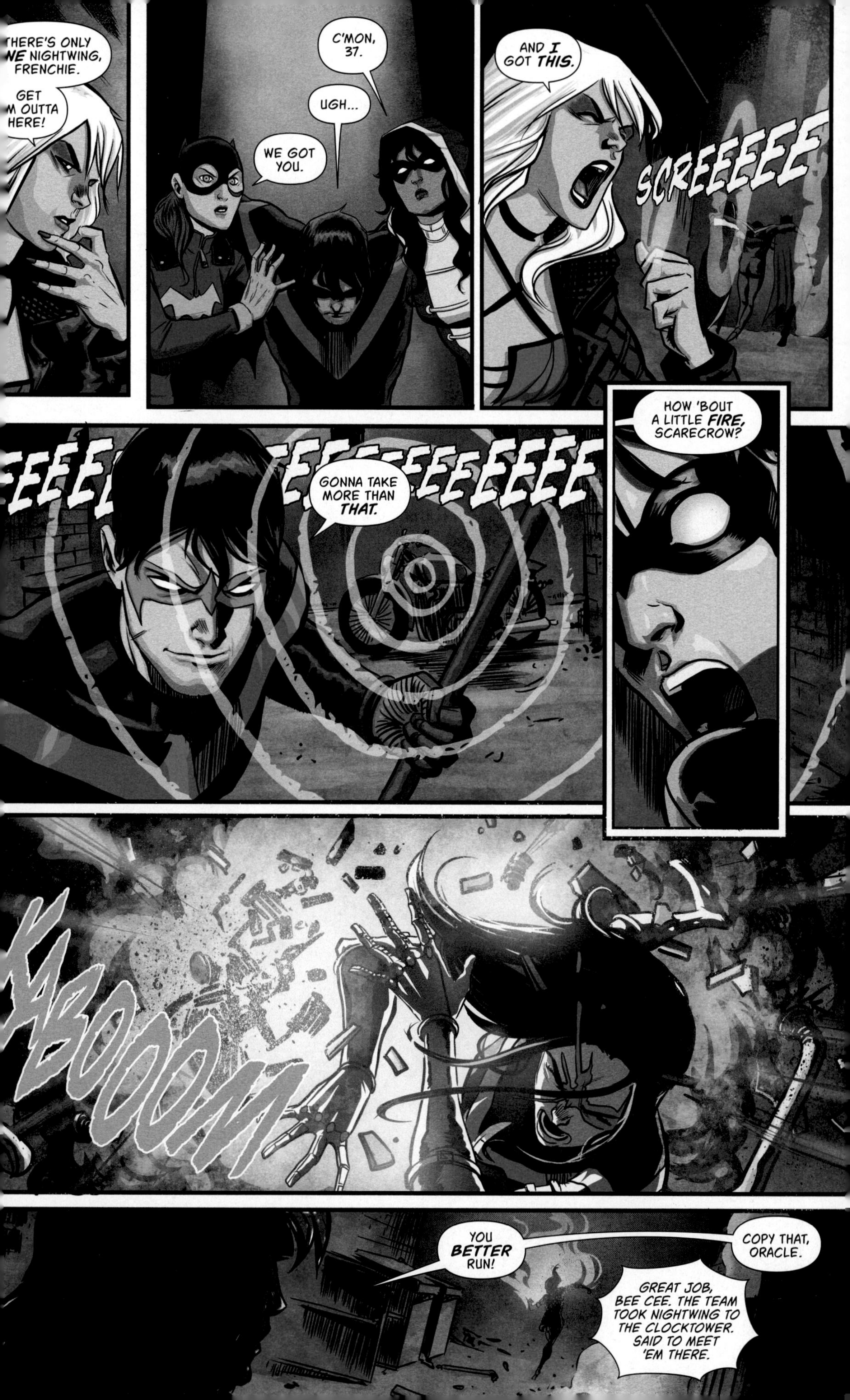
THERE'S ONLY NE NIGHTWING, FRENCHIE.
GET M OUTTA HERE!
C'MON, 37.
UGH...
WE GOT YOU.
AND I GOT THIS.
SCREEEEEE
EEEEEEEEEEEEEEE
GONNA TAKE MORE THAN THAT.
HOW 'BOUT A LITTLE FIRE, SCARECROW?
KABOOOM
YOU BETTER RUN!
GREAT JOB, BEE CEE. THE TEAM TOOK NIGHTWING TO THE CLOCKTOWER. SAID TO MEET 'EM THERE.
COPY THAT, ORACLE.

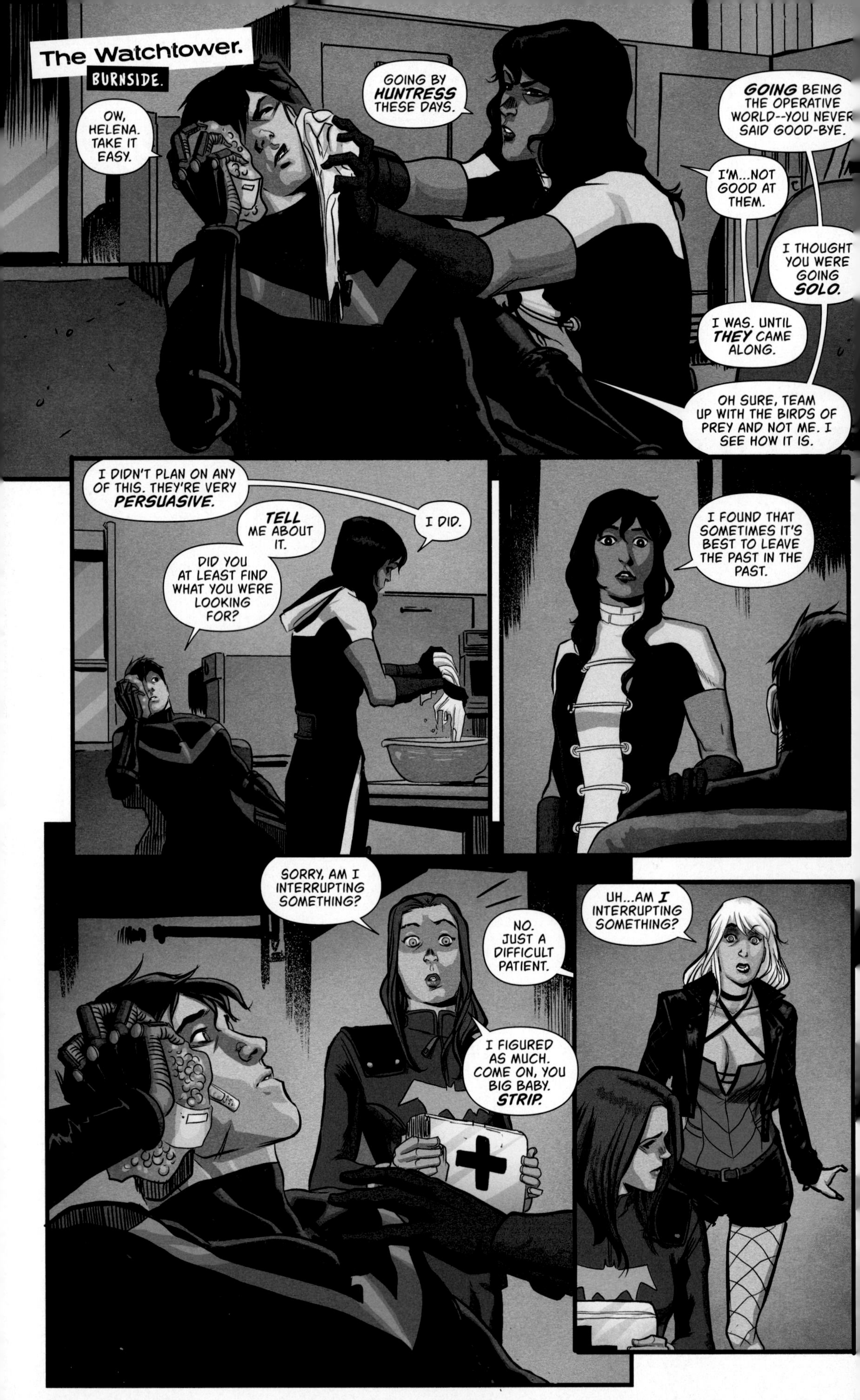
The Watchtower.
BURNSIDE.
OW, HELENA. TAKE IT EASY.
GOING BY HUNTRESS THESE DAYS.
GOING BEING THE OPERATIVE WORLD--YOU NEVER SAID GOOD-BYE.
I'M...NOT GOOD AT THEM.
I THOUGHT YOU WERE GOING SOLO.
I WAS. UNTIL THEY CAME ALONG.
OH SURE, TEAM UP WITH THE BIRDS OF PREY AND NOT ME. I SEE HOW IT IS.
I DIDN'T PLAN ON ANY OF THIS. THEY'RE VERY PERSUASIVE.
TELL ME ABOUT IT.
I DID.
DID YOU AT LEAST FIND WHAT YOU WERE LOOKING FOR?
I FOUND THAT SOMETIMES IT'S BEST TO LEAVE THE PAST IN THE PAST.
SORRY, AM I INTERRUPTING SOMETHING?
NO. JUST A DIFFICULT PATIENT.
I FIGURED AS MUCH. COME ON, YOU BIG BABY. STRIP.
UH...AM I INTERRUPTING SOMETHING?

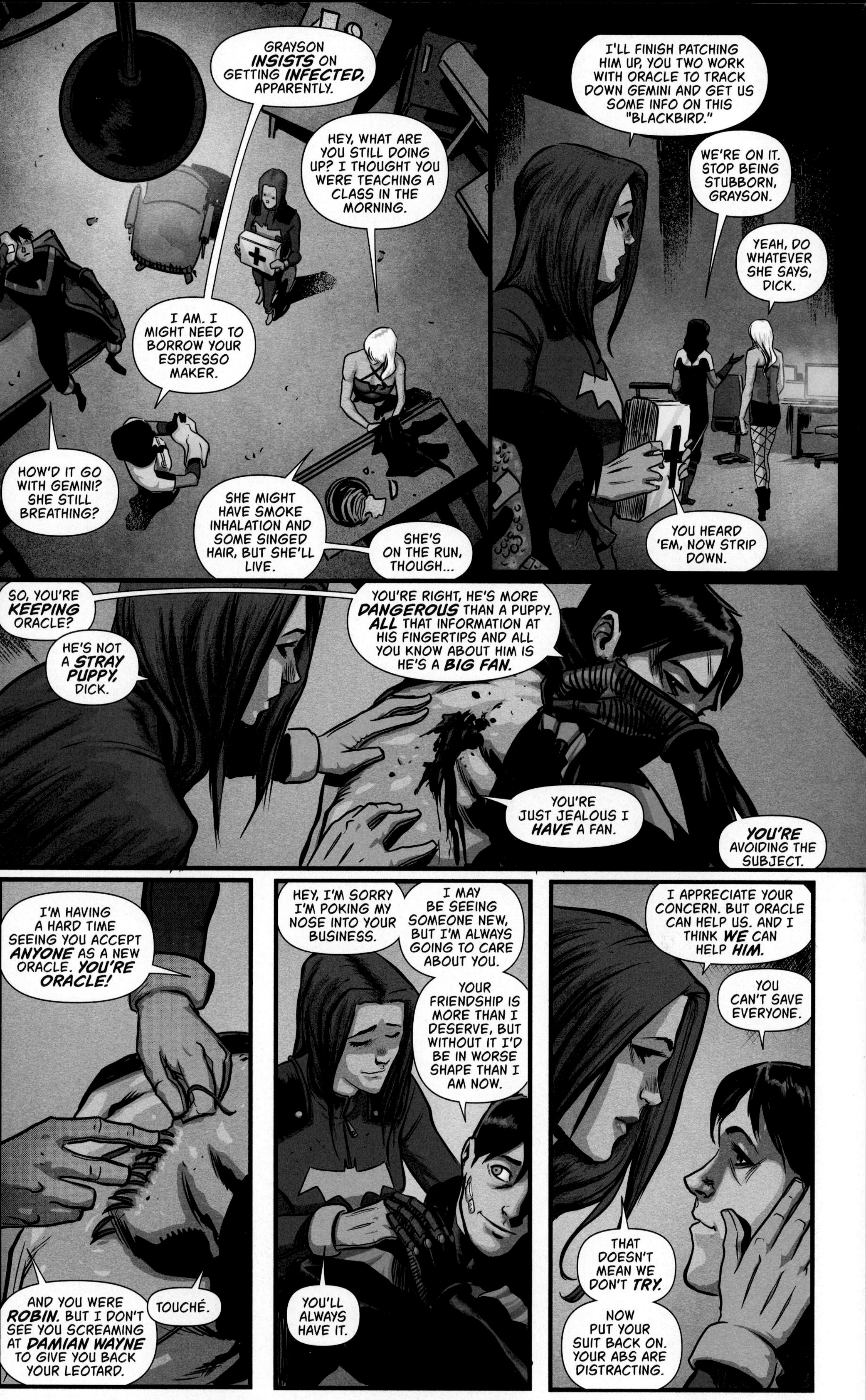
GRAYSON INSISTS ON GETTING INFECTED, APPARENTLY.
HEY, WHAT ARE YOU STILL DOING UP? I THOUGHT YOU WERE TEACHING A CLASS IN THE MORNING.
I AM. I MIGHT NEED TO BORROW YOUR ESPRESSO MAKER.
HOW'D IT GO WITH GEMINI? SHE STILL BREATHING?
SHE MIGHT HAVE SMOKE INHALATION AND SOME SINGED HAIR, BUT SHE'LL LIVE.
SHE'S ON THE RUN, THOUGH...
I'LL FINISH PATCHING HIM UP, YOU TWO WORK WITH ORACLE TO TRACK DOWN GEMINI AND GET US SOME INFO ON THIS "BLACKBIRD."
WE'RE ON IT. STOP BEING STUBBORN, GRAYSON.
YEAH, DO WHATEVER SHE SAYS, DICK.
YOU HEARD 'EM, NOW STRIP DOWN.
SO, YOU'RE KEEPING ORACLE?
HE'S NOT A STRAY PUPPY, DICK.
YOU'RE RIGHT, HE'S MORE DANGEROUS THAN A PUPPY. ALL THAT INFORMATION AT HIS FINGERTIPS AND ALL YOU KNOW ABOUT HIM IS HE'S A BIG FAN.
YOU'RE JUST JEALOUS I HAVE A FAN.
YOU'RE AVOIDING THE SUBJECT.
I'M HAVING A HARD TIME SEEING YOU ACCEPT ANYONE AS A NEW ORACLE. YOU'RE ORACLE!
AND YOU WERE ROBIN. BUT I DON'T SEE YOU SCREAMING AT DAMIAN WAYNE TO GIVE YOU BACK YOUR LEOTARD.
TOUCHÉ.
HEY, I'M SORRY I'M POKING MY NOSE INTO YOUR BUSINESS.
I MAY BE SEEING SOMEONE NEW, BUT I'M ALWAYS GOING TO CARE ABOUT YOU.
YOUR FRIENDSHIP IS MORE THAN I DESERVE, BUT WITHOUT IT I'D BE IN WORSE SHAPE THAN I AM NOW.
YOU'LL ALWAYS HAVE IT.
I APPRECIATE YOUR CONCERN. BUT ORACLE CAN HELP US. AND I THINK WE CAN HELP HIM.
YOU CAN'T SAVE EVERYONE.
THAT DOESN'T MEAN WE DON'T TRY.
NOW PUT YOUR SUIT BACK ON. YOUR ABS ARE DISTRACTING.

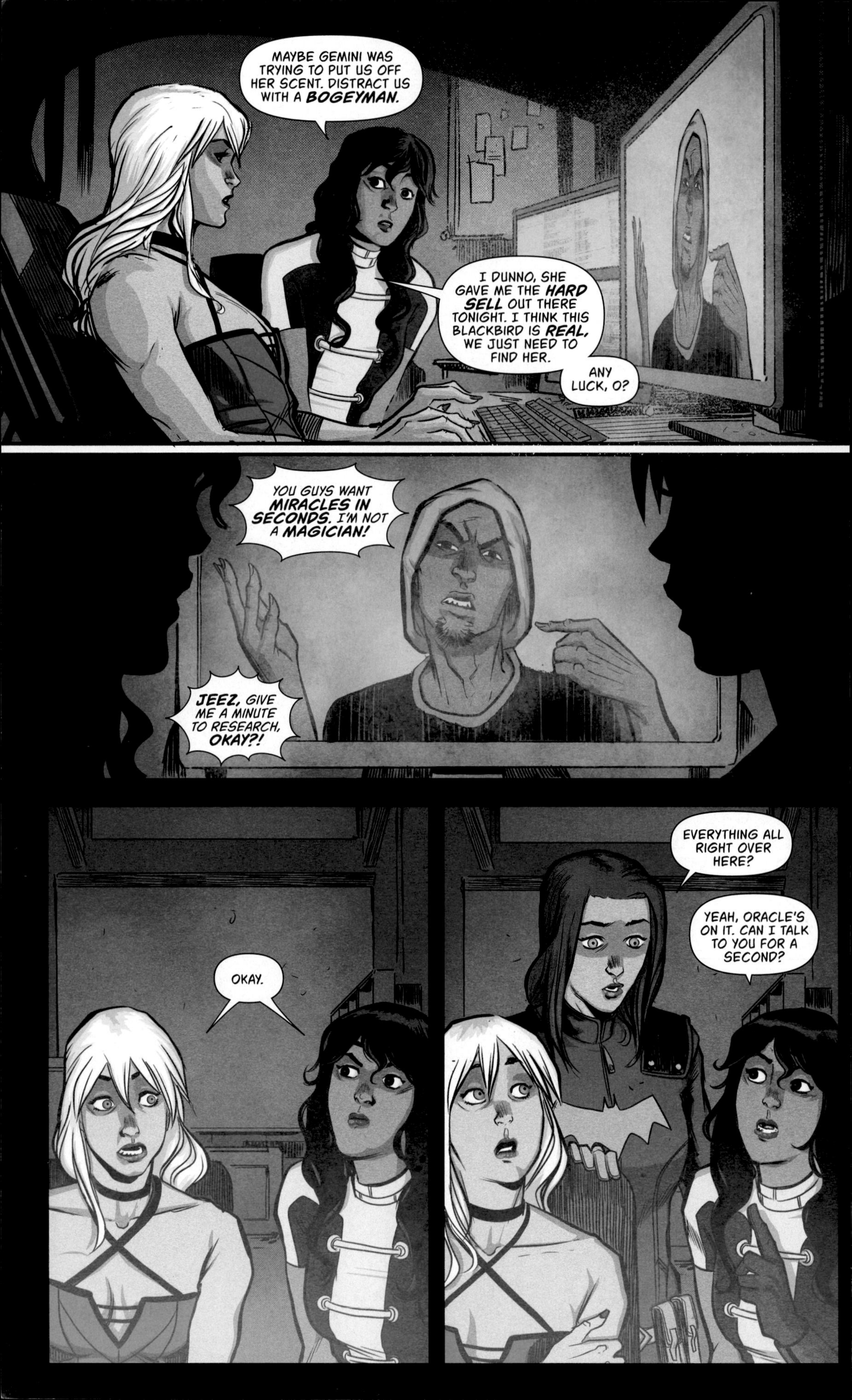
MAYBE GEMINI WAS TRYING TO PUT US OFF HER SCENT. DISTRACT US WITH A **BOGEYMAN.**
I DUNNO, SHE GAVE ME THE **HARD SELL** OUT THERE TONIGHT. I THINK THIS BLACKBIRD IS **REAL,** WE JUST NEED TO FIND HER.
ANY LUCK, O?
YOU GUYS WANT **MIRACLES IN SECONDS.** I'M NOT A **MAGICIAN!**
JEEZ, GIVE ME A MINUTE TO RESEARCH, **OKAY?!**
OKAY.
EVERYTHING ALL RIGHT OVER HERE?
YEAH, ORACLE'S ON IT. CAN I TALK TO YOU FOR A SECOND?

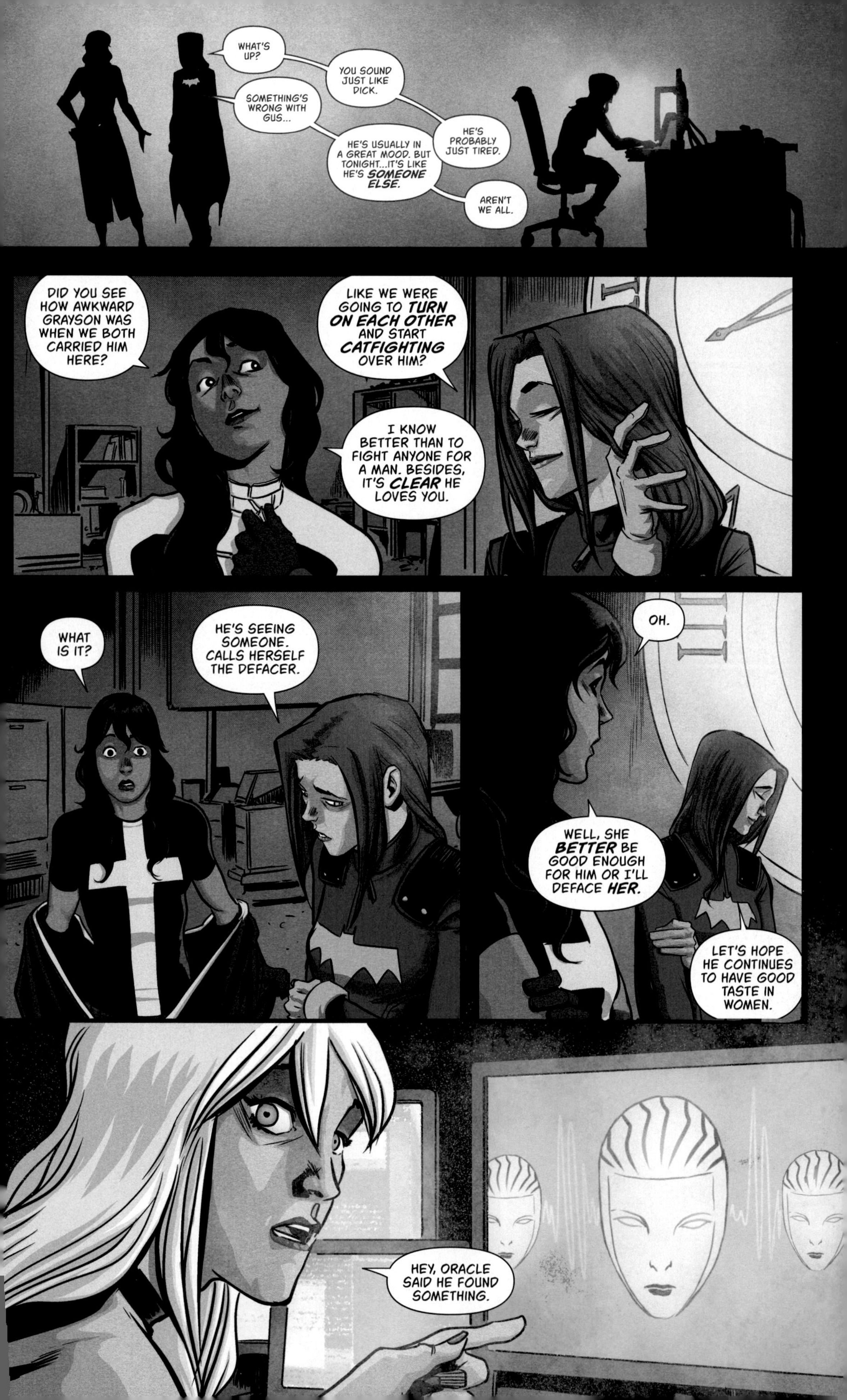
WHAT'S UP?
YOU SOUND JUST LIKE DICK.
SOMETHING'S WRONG WITH GUS...
HE'S PROBABLY JUST TIRED.
HE'S USUALLY IN A GREAT MOOD. BUT TONIGHT...IT'S LIKE HE'S SOMEONE ELSE.
AREN'T WE ALL.
DID YOU SEE HOW AWKWARD GRAYSON WAS WHEN WE BOTH CARRIED HIM HERE?
LIKE WE WERE GOING TO TURN ON EACH OTHER AND START CATFIGHTING OVER HIM?
I KNOW BETTER THAN TO FIGHT ANYONE FOR A MAN. BESIDES, IT'S CLEAR HE LOVES YOU.
WHAT IS IT?
HE'S SEEING SOMEONE. CALLS HERSELF THE DEFACER.
OH.
WELL, SHE BETTER BE GOOD ENOUGH FOR HIM OR I'LL DEFACE HER.
LET'S HOPE HE CONTINUES TO HAVE GOOD TASTE IN WOMEN.
HEY, ORACLE SAID HE FOUND SOMETHING.

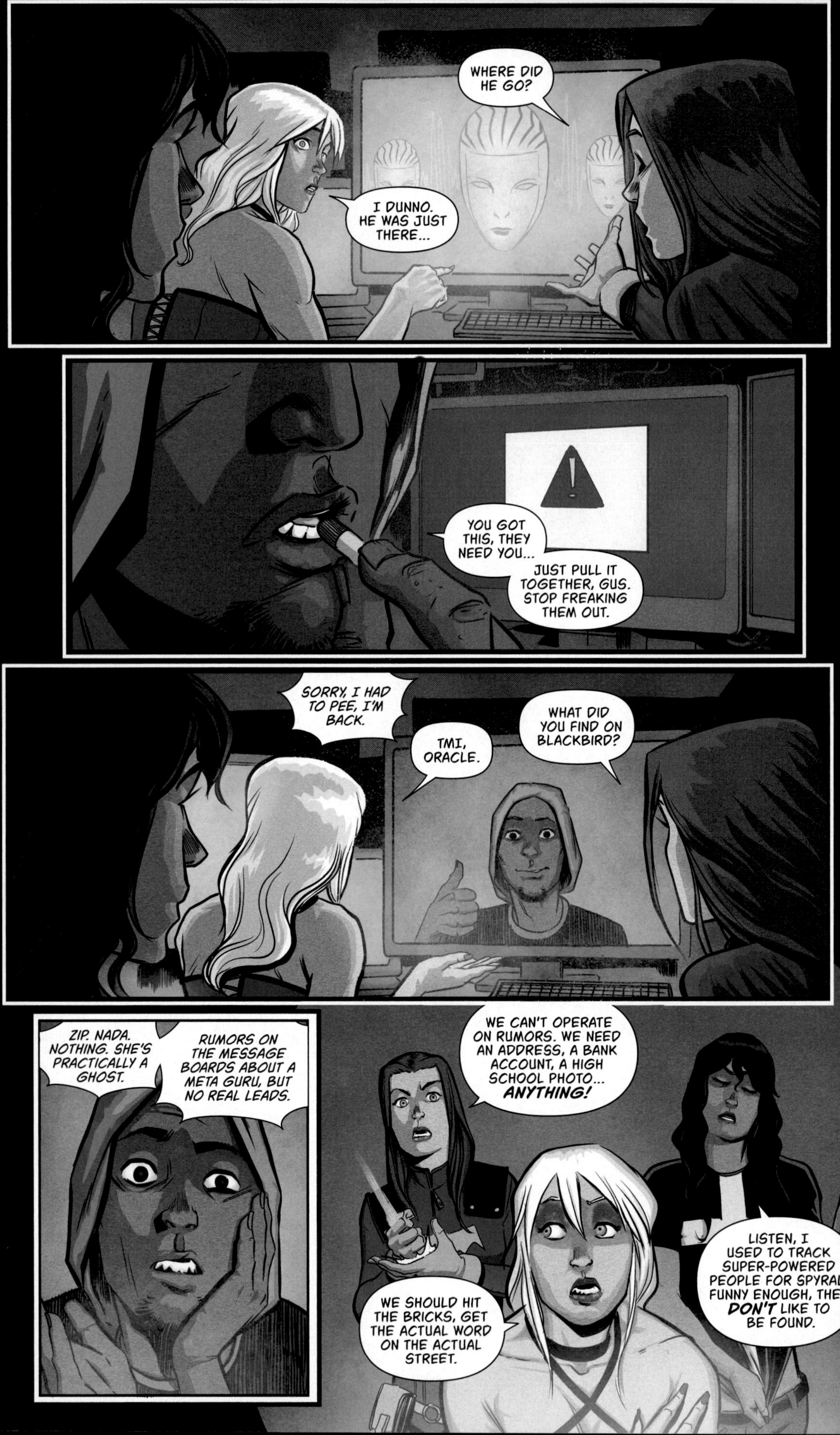
WHERE DID HE GO?
I DUNNO. HE WAS JUST THERE...
YOU GOT THIS, THEY NEED YOU...
JUST PULL IT TOGETHER, GUS. STOP FREAKING THEM OUT.
SORRY, I HAD TO PEE, I'M BACK.
TMI, ORACLE.
WHAT DID YOU FIND ON BLACKBIRD?
ZIP. NADA. NOTHING. SHE'S PRACTICALLY A GHOST.
RUMORS ON THE MESSAGE BOARDS ABOUT A META GURU, BUT NO REAL LEADS.
WE CAN'T OPERATE ON RUMORS. WE NEED AN ADDRESS, A BANK ACCOUNT, A HIGH SCHOOL PHOTO... ANYTHING!
WE SHOULD HIT THE BRICKS, GET THE ACTUAL WORD ON THE ACTUAL STREET.
LISTEN, I USED TO TRACK SUPER-POWERED PEOPLE FOR SPYRAL. FUNNY ENOUGH, THEY DON'T LIKE TO BE FOUND.

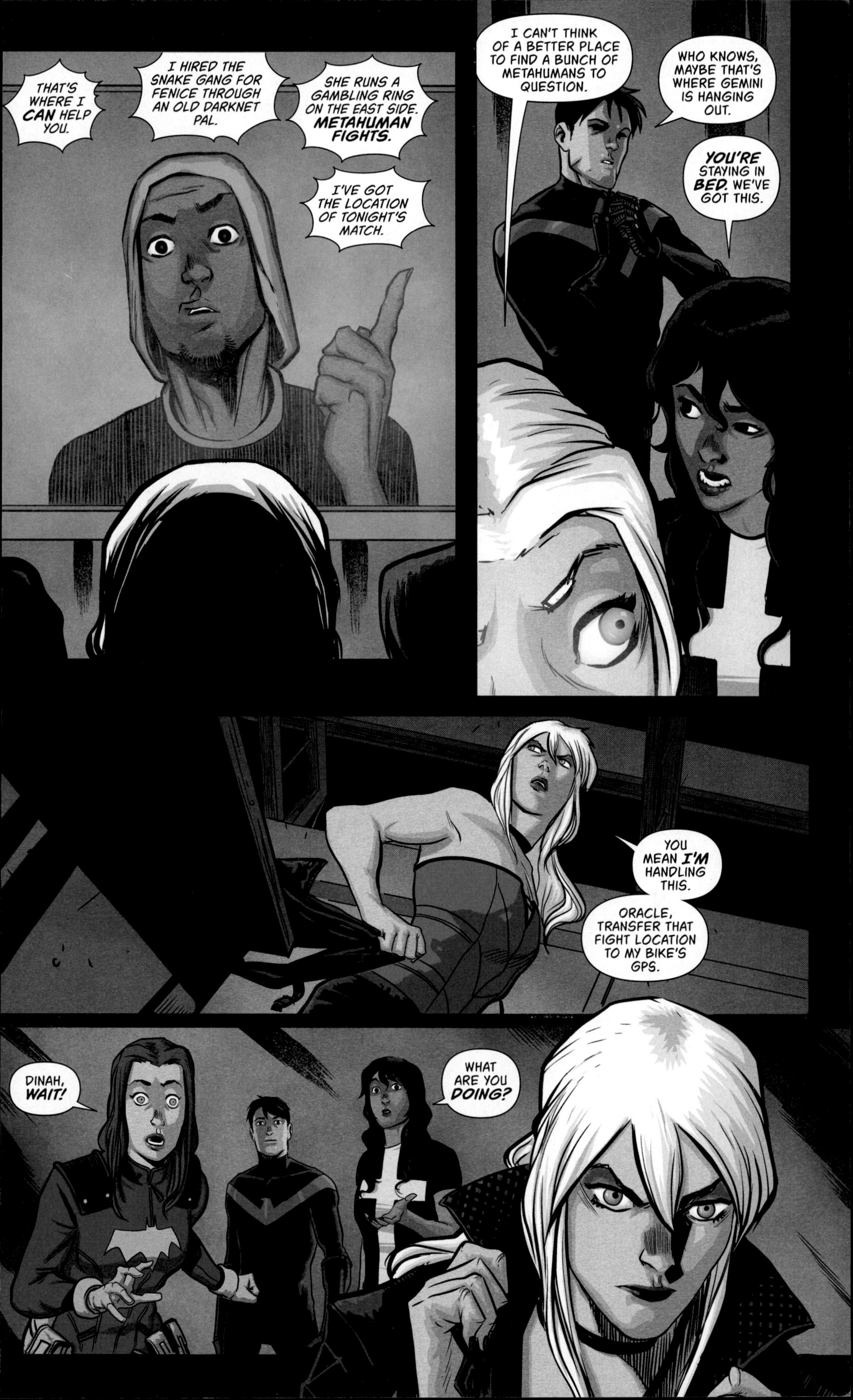

THAT'S WHERE I **CAN** HELP YOU.
I HIRED THE SNAKE GANG FOR FENICE THROUGH AN OLD DARKNET PAL.
SHE RUNS A GAMBLING RING ON THE EAST SIDE. **METAHUMAN FIGHTS.**
I'VE GOT THE LOCATION OF TONIGHT'S MATCH.
I CAN'T THINK OF A BETTER PLACE TO FIND A BUNCH OF METAHUMANS TO QUESTION.
WHO KNOWS, MAYBE THAT'S WHERE GEMINI IS HANGING OUT.
YOU'RE STAYING IN **BED.** WE'VE GOT THIS.
YOU MEAN **I'M** HANDLING THIS.
ORACLE, TRANSFER THAT FIGHT LOCATION TO MY BIKE'S GPS.
DINAH, **WAIT!**
WHAT ARE YOU **DOING?**

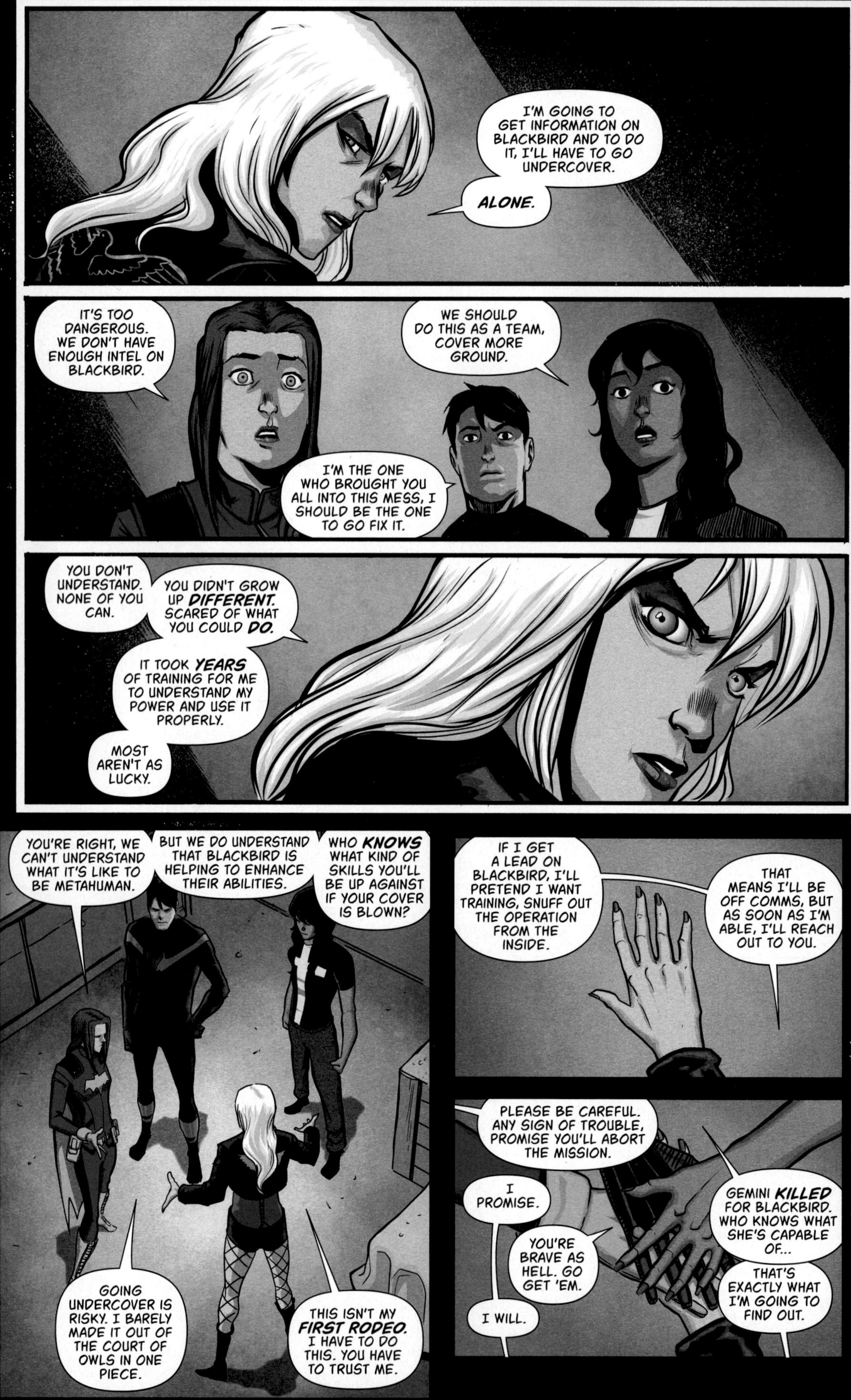

I'M GOING TO GET INFORMATION ON BLACKBIRD AND TO DO IT, I'LL HAVE TO GO UNDERCOVER.
ALONE.
IT'S TOO DANGEROUS. WE DON'T HAVE ENOUGH INTEL ON BLACKBIRD.
WE SHOULD DO THIS AS A TEAM, COVER MORE GROUND.
I'M THE ONE WHO BROUGHT YOU ALL INTO THIS MESS, I SHOULD BE THE ONE TO GO FIX IT.
YOU DON'T UNDERSTAND. NONE OF YOU CAN.
YOU DIDN'T GROW UP DIFFERENT. SCARED OF WHAT YOU COULD DO.
IT TOOK YEARS OF TRAINING FOR ME TO UNDERSTAND MY POWER AND USE IT PROPERLY.
MOST AREN'T AS LUCKY.
YOU'RE RIGHT, WE CAN'T UNDERSTAND WHAT IT'S LIKE TO BE METAHUMAN.
BUT WE DO UNDERSTAND THAT BLACKBIRD IS HELPING TO ENHANCE THEIR ABILITIES.
WHO KNOWS WHAT KIND OF SKILLS YOU'LL BE UP AGAINST IF YOUR COVER IS BLOWN?
GOING UNDERCOVER IS RISKY. I BARELY MADE IT OUT OF THE COURT OF OWLS IN ONE PIECE.
THIS ISN'T MY FIRST RODEO. I HAVE TO DO THIS. YOU HAVE TO TRUST ME.
IF I GET A LEAD ON BLACKBIRD, I'LL PRETEND I WANT TRAINING, SNUFF OUT THE OPERATION FROM THE INSIDE.
THAT MEANS I'LL BE OFF COMMS, BUT AS SOON AS I'M ABLE, I'LL REACH OUT TO YOU.
PLEASE BE CAREFUL. ANY SIGN OF TROUBLE, PROMISE YOU'LL ABORT THE MISSION.
I PROMISE.
YOU'RE BRAVE AS HELL. GO GET 'EM.
I WILL.
GEMINI KILLED FOR BLACKBIRD. WHO KNOWS WHAT SHE'S CAPABLE OF...
THAT'S EXACTLY WHAT I'M GOING TO FIND OUT.

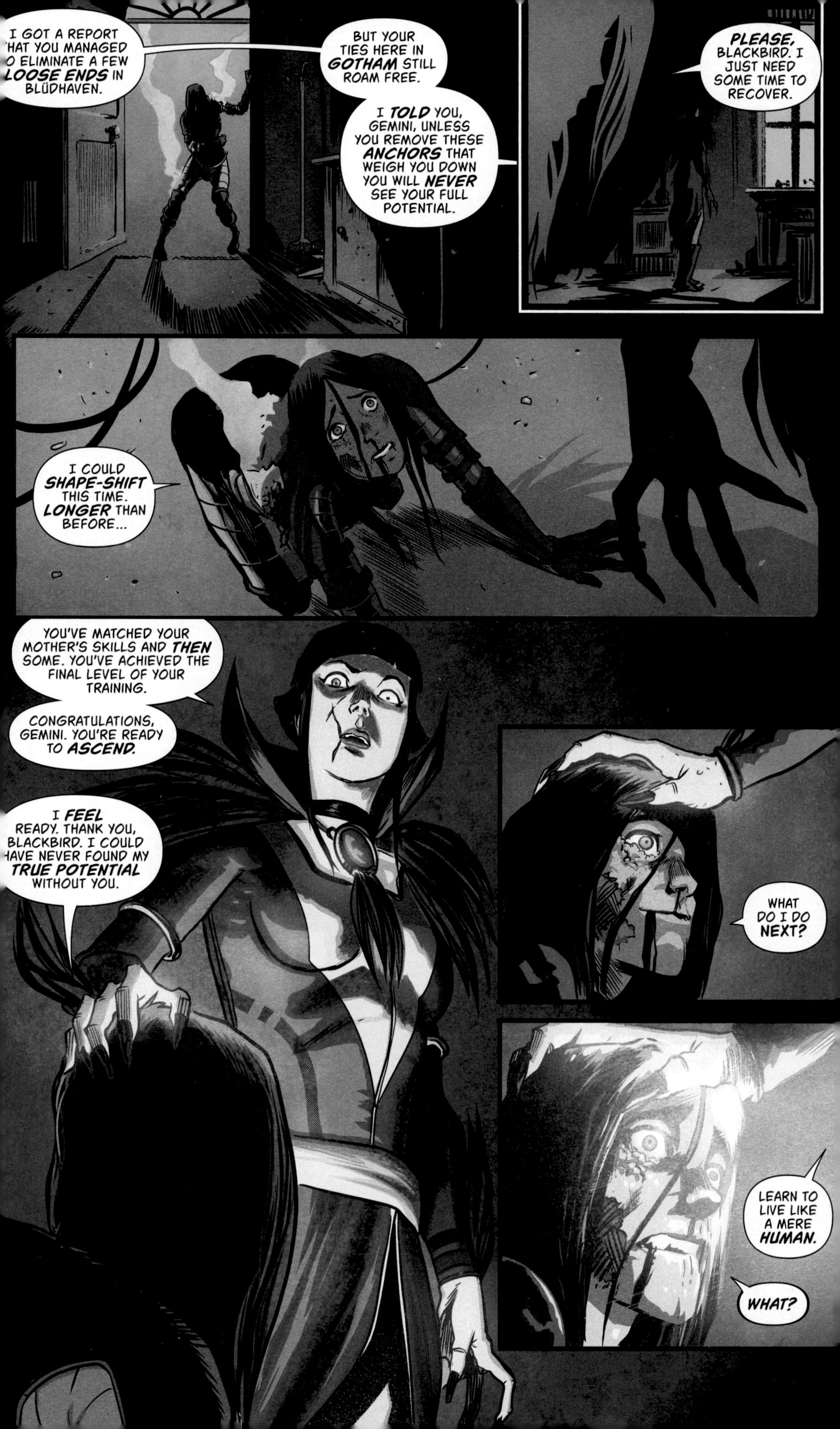

I GOT A REPORT THAT YOU MANAGED TO ELIMINATE A FEW LOOSE ENDS IN BLÜDHAVEN.
BUT YOUR TIES HERE IN GOTHAM STILL ROAM FREE.
I TOLD YOU, GEMINI, UNLESS YOU REMOVE THESE ANCHORS THAT WEIGH YOU DOWN YOU WILL NEVER SEE YOUR FULL POTENTIAL.
PLEASE, BLACKBIRD. I JUST NEED SOME TIME TO RECOVER.
I COULD SHAPE-SHIFT THIS TIME. LONGER THAN BEFORE...
YOU'VE MATCHED YOUR MOTHER'S SKILLS AND THEN SOME. YOU'VE ACHIEVED THE FINAL LEVEL OF YOUR TRAINING.
CONGRATULATIONS, GEMINI. YOU'RE READY TO ASCEND.
I FEEL READY. THANK YOU, BLACKBIRD. I COULD HAVE NEVER FOUND MY TRUE POTENTIAL WITHOUT YOU.
WHAT DO I DO NEXT?
LEARN TO LIVE LIKE A MERE HUMAN.
WHAT?

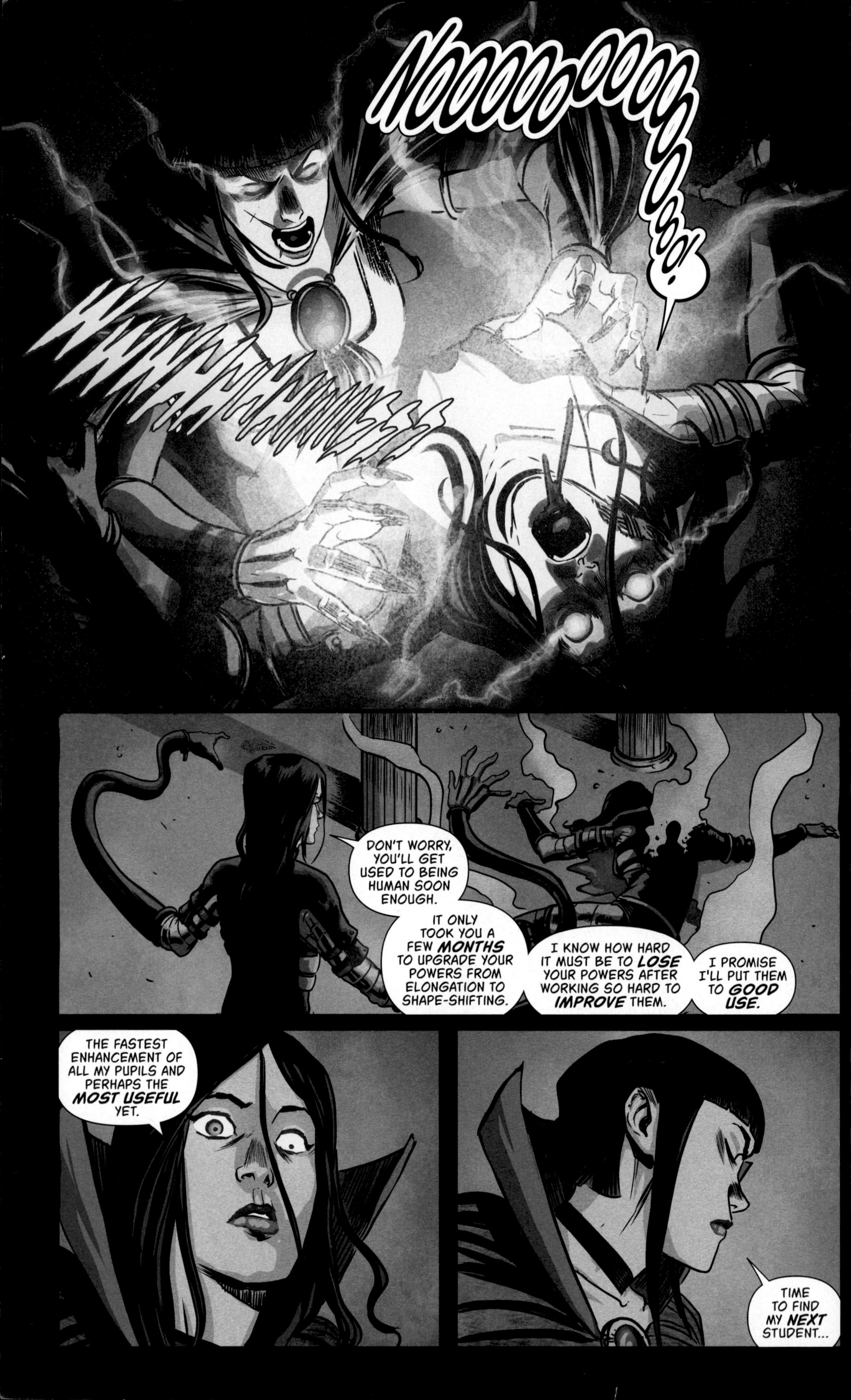

NOOOOOOOOOOOOOOOOOO!
DON'T WORRY, YOU'LL GET USED TO BEING HUMAN SOON ENOUGH.
IT ONLY TOOK YOU A FEW MONTHS TO UPGRADE YOUR POWERS FROM ELONGATION TO SHAPE-SHIFTING.
I KNOW HOW HARD IT MUST BE TO LOSE YOUR POWERS AFTER WORKING SO HARD TO IMPROVE THEM.
I PROMISE I'LL PUT THEM TO GOOD USE.
THE FASTEST ENHANCEMENT OF ALL MY PUPILS AND PERHAPS THE MOST USEFUL YET.
TIME TO FIND MY NEXT STUDENT...

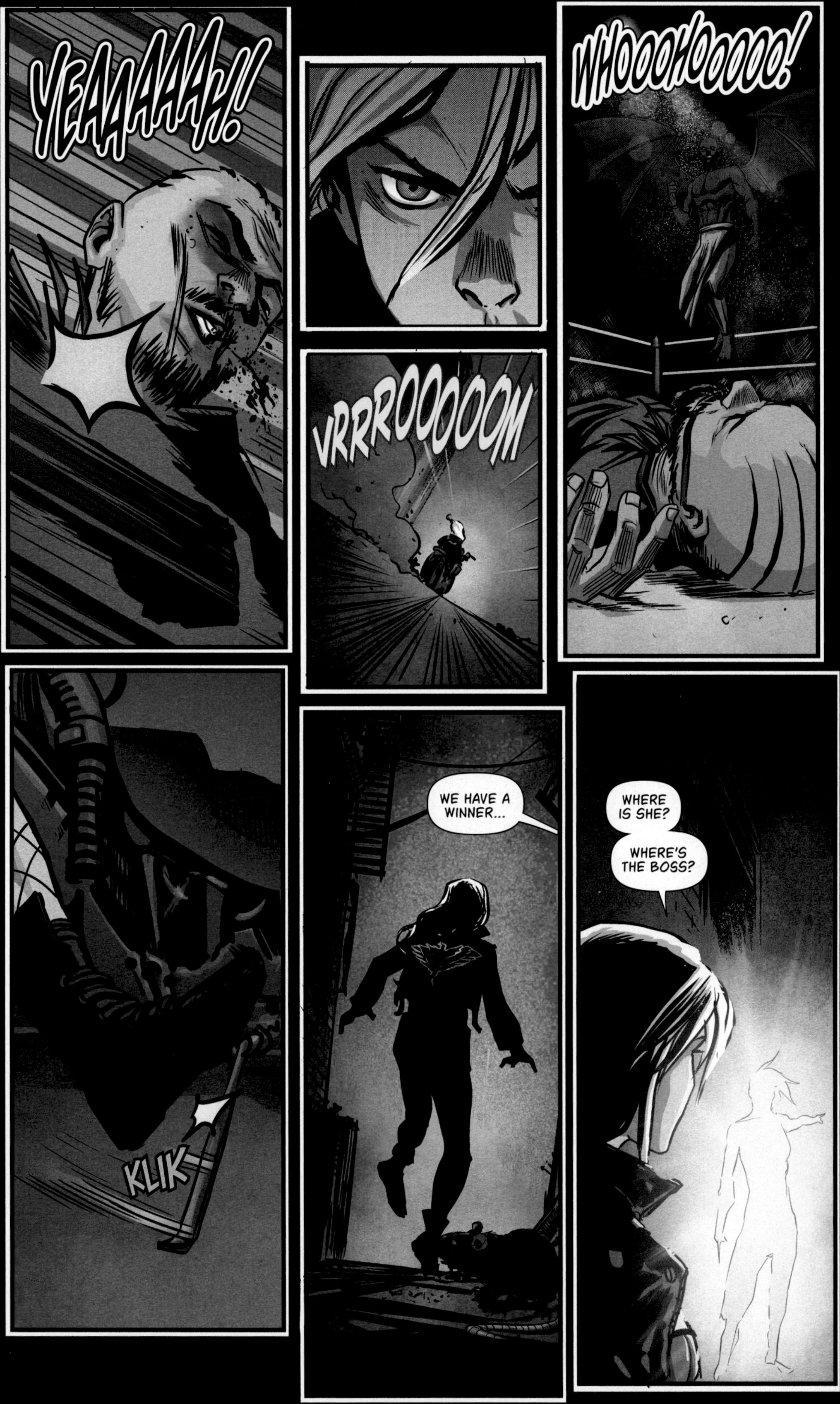
YEAAAAAH!
VRRROOOOOM
WHOOOHOOOOO!
KLIK
WE HAVE A WINNER...
WHERE IS SHE?
WHERE'S THE BOSS?

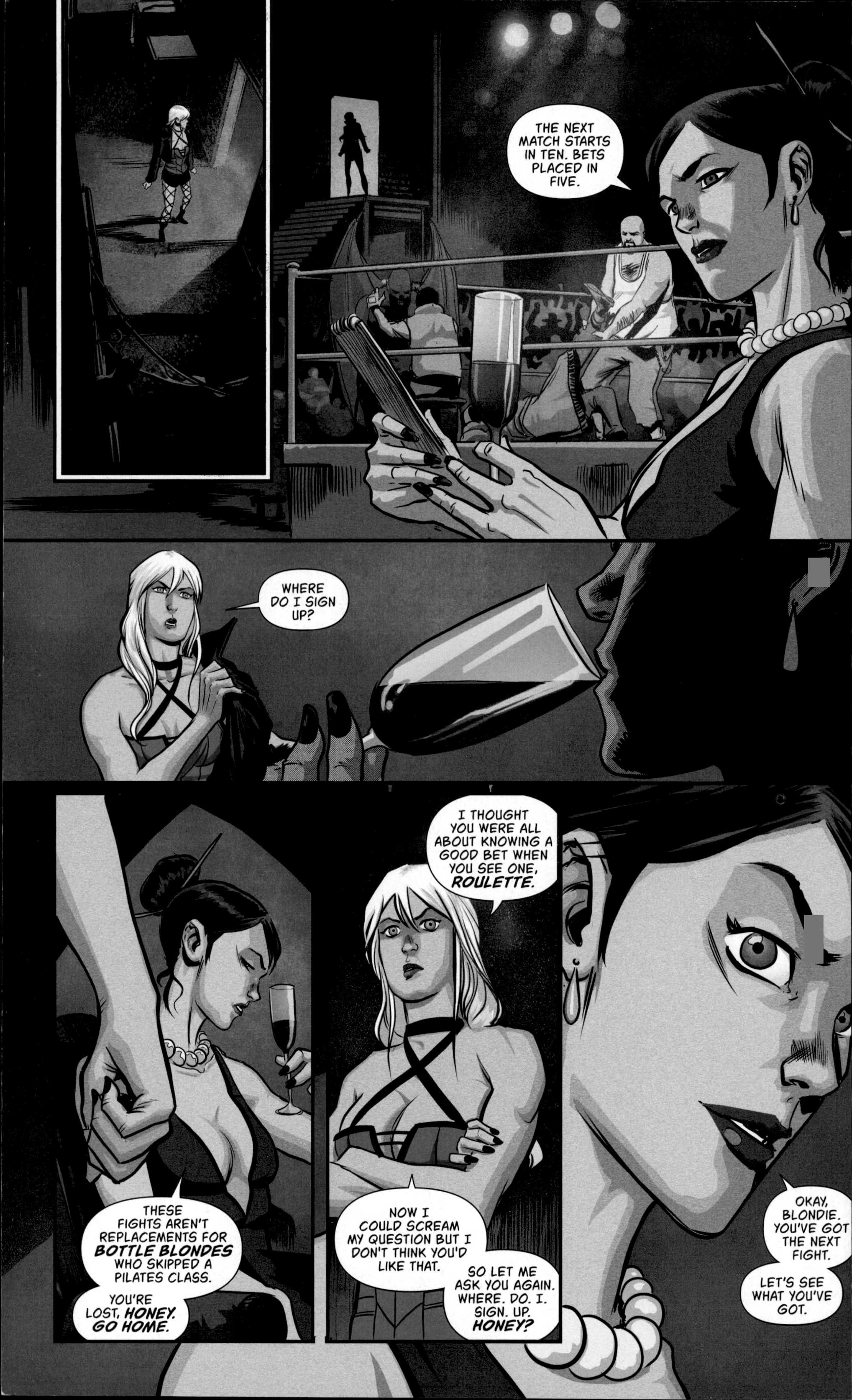
THE NEXT MATCH STARTS IN TEN. BETS PLACED IN FIVE.
WHERE DO I SIGN UP?
THESE FIGHTS AREN'T REPLACEMENTS FOR **BOTTLE BLONDES** WHO SKIPPED A PILATES CLASS.
YOU'RE LOST, **HONEY. GO HOME.**
I THOUGHT YOU WERE ALL ABOUT KNOWING A GOOD BET WHEN YOU SEE ONE, **ROULETTE.**
NOW I COULD SCREAM MY QUESTION BUT I DON'T THINK YOU'D LIKE THAT.
SO LET ME ASK YOU AGAIN. WHERE. DO. I. SIGN. UP. **HONEY?**
OKAY, BLONDIE. YOU'VE GOT THE NEXT FIGHT.
LET'S SEE WHAT YOU'VE GOT.

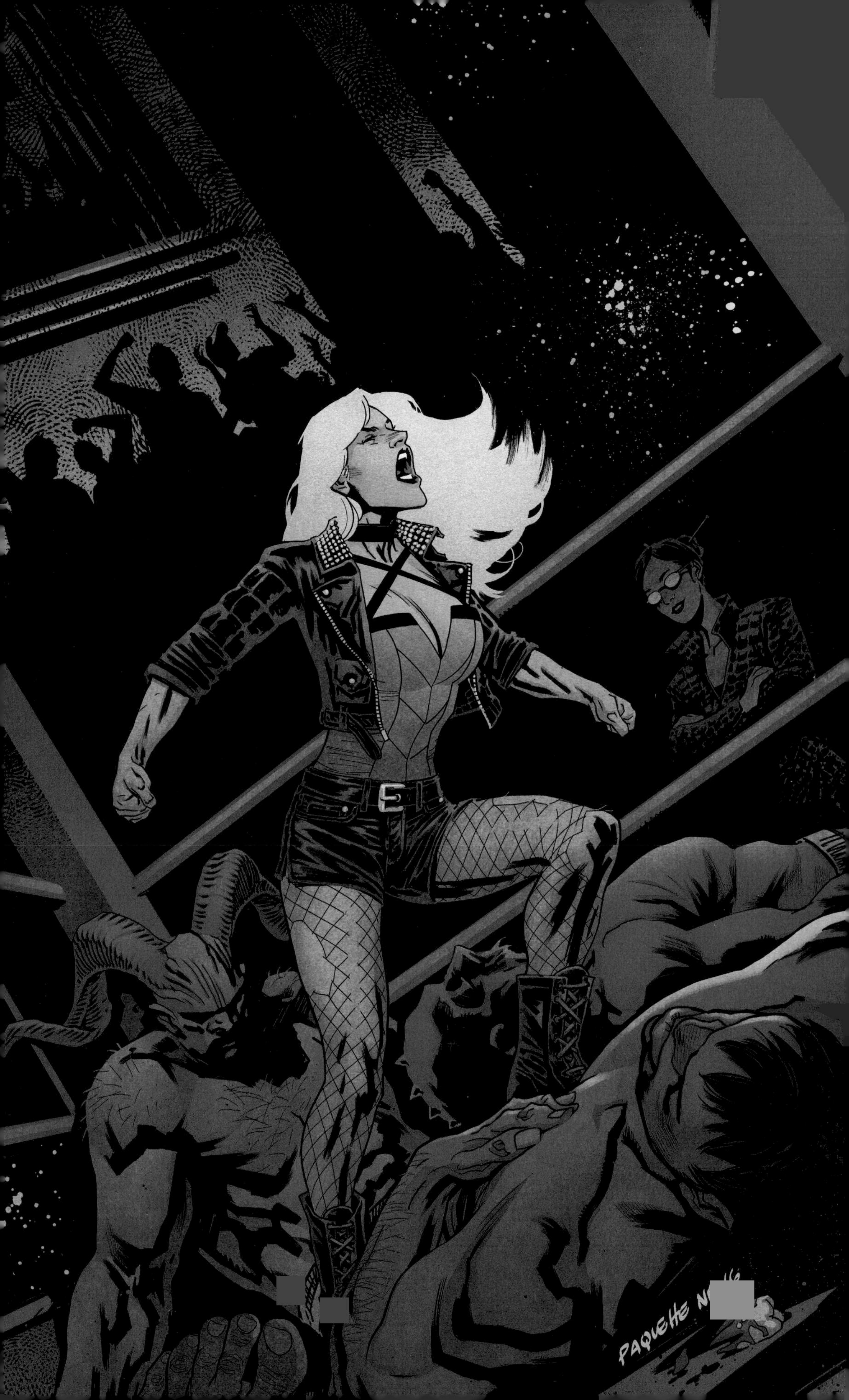

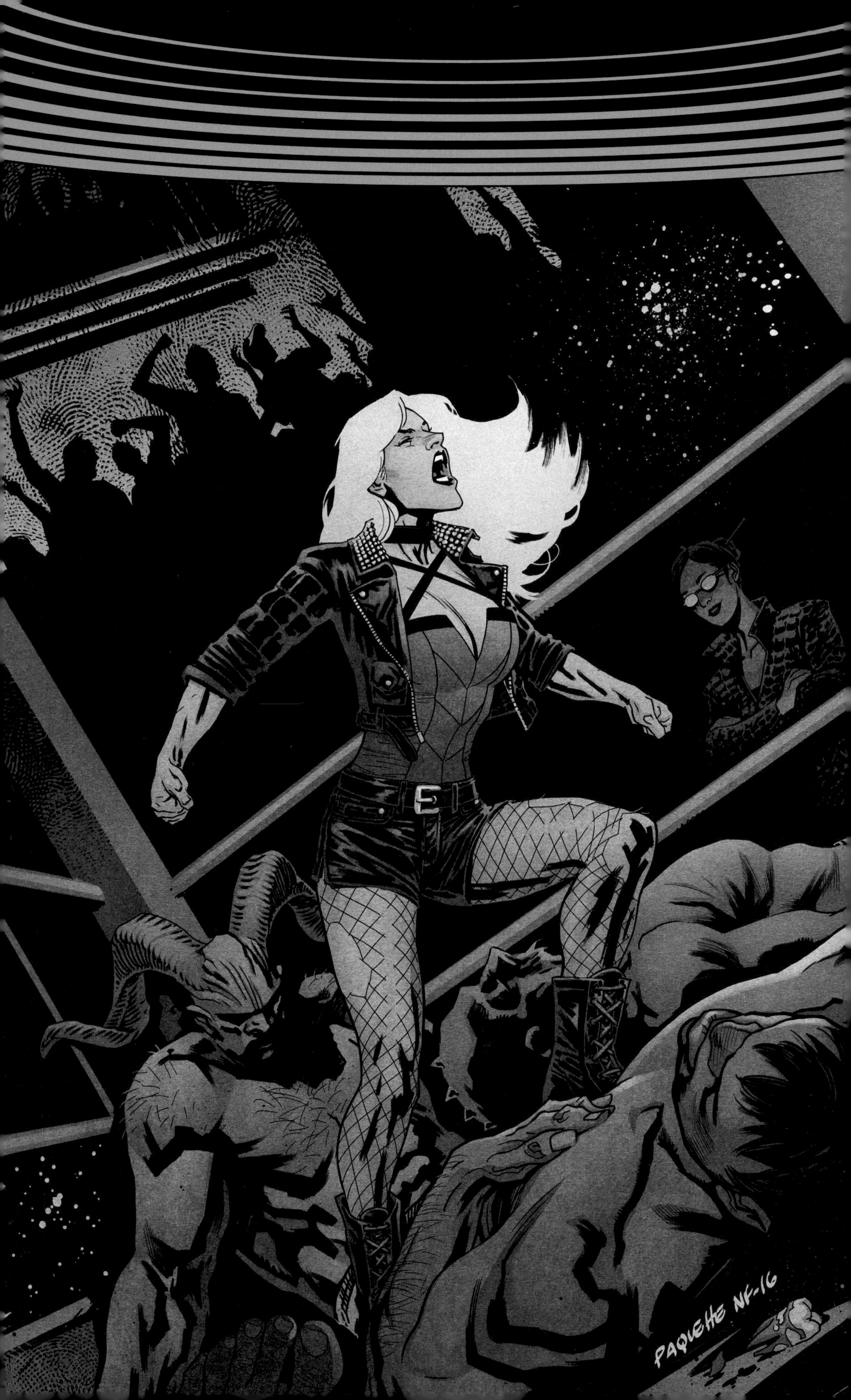
PAQUETTE NF-16

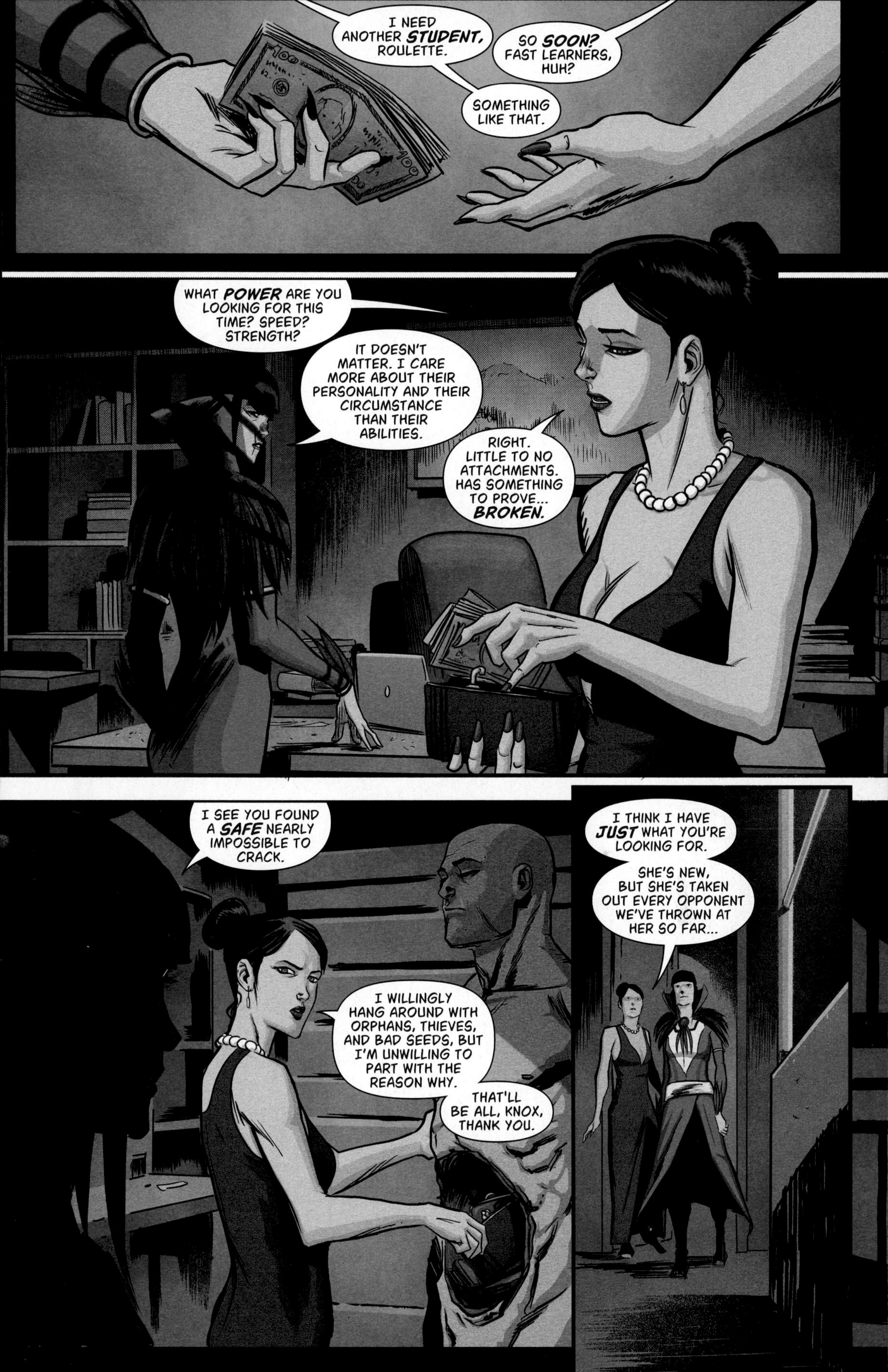
I NEED ANOTHER STUDENT, ROULETTE.
SO SOON? FAST LEARNERS, HUH?
SOMETHING LIKE THAT.
WHAT POWER ARE YOU LOOKING FOR THIS TIME? SPEED? STRENGTH?
IT DOESN'T MATTER. I CARE MORE ABOUT THEIR PERSONALITY AND THEIR CIRCUMSTANCE THAN THEIR ABILITIES.
RIGHT. LITTLE TO NO ATTACHMENTS. HAS SOMETHING TO PROVE... BROKEN.
I SEE YOU FOUND A SAFE NEARLY IMPOSSIBLE TO CRACK.
I WILLINGLY HANG AROUND WITH ORPHANS, THIEVES, AND BAD SEEDS, BUT I'M UNWILLING TO PART WITH THE REASON WHY.
THAT'LL BE ALL, KNOX, THANK YOU.
I THINK I HAVE JUST WHAT YOU'RE LOOKING FOR.
SHE'S NEW, BUT SHE'S TAKEN OUT EVERY OPPONENT WE'VE THROWN AT HER SO FAR...

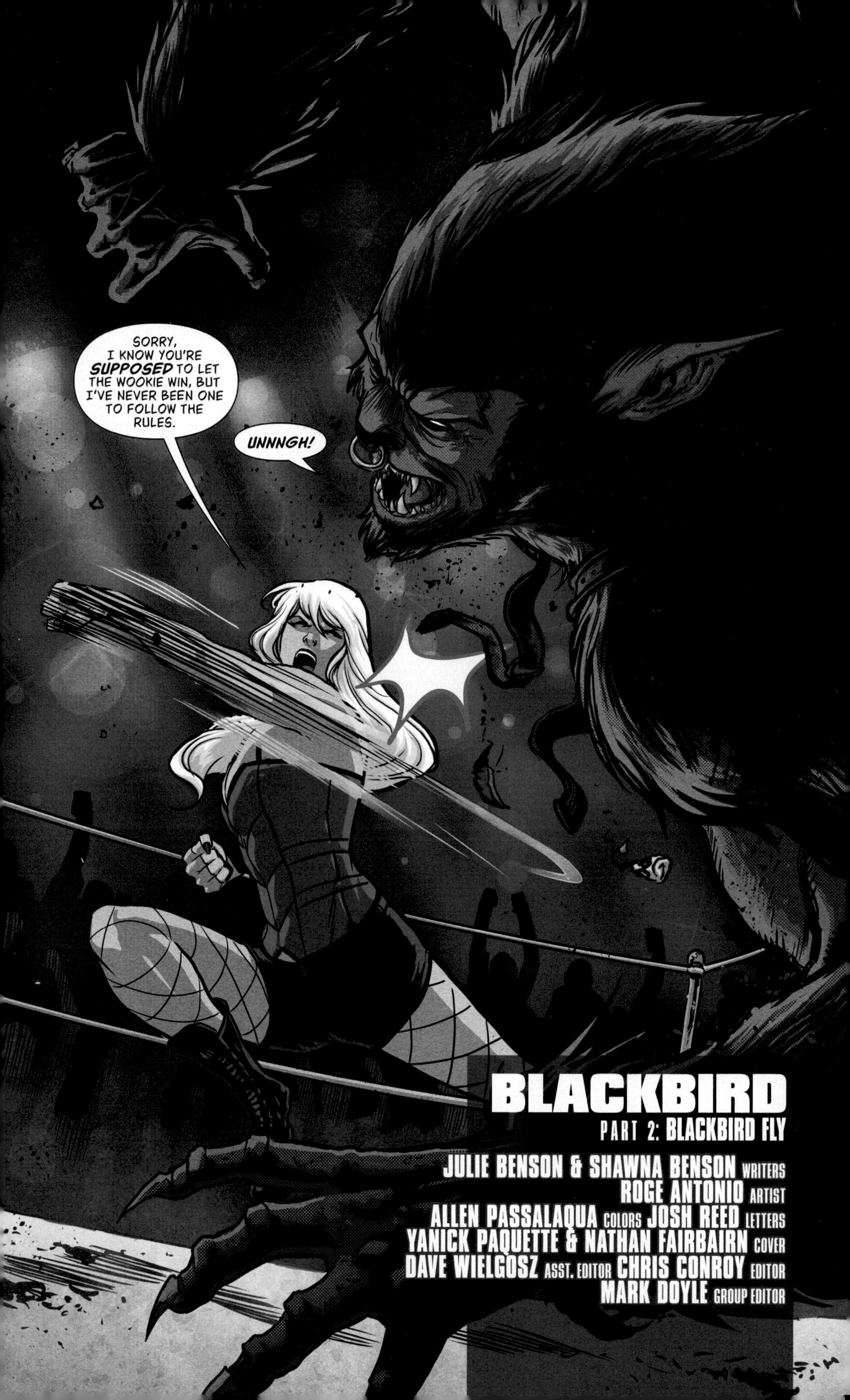
SORRY, I KNOW YOU'RE SUPPOSED TO LET THE WOOKIE WIN, BUT I'VE NEVER BEEN ONE TO FOLLOW THE RULES.
UNNNGH!
BLACKBIRD
PART 2: BLACKBIRD FLY
JULIE BENSON & SHAWNA BENSON WRITERS
ROGE ANTONIO ARTIST
ALLEN PASSALAQUA COLORS JOSH REED LETTERS
YANICK PAQUETTE & NATHAN FAIRBAIRN COVER
DAVE WIELGOSZ ASST. EDITOR CHRIS CONROY EDITOR
MARK DOYLE GROUP EDITOR

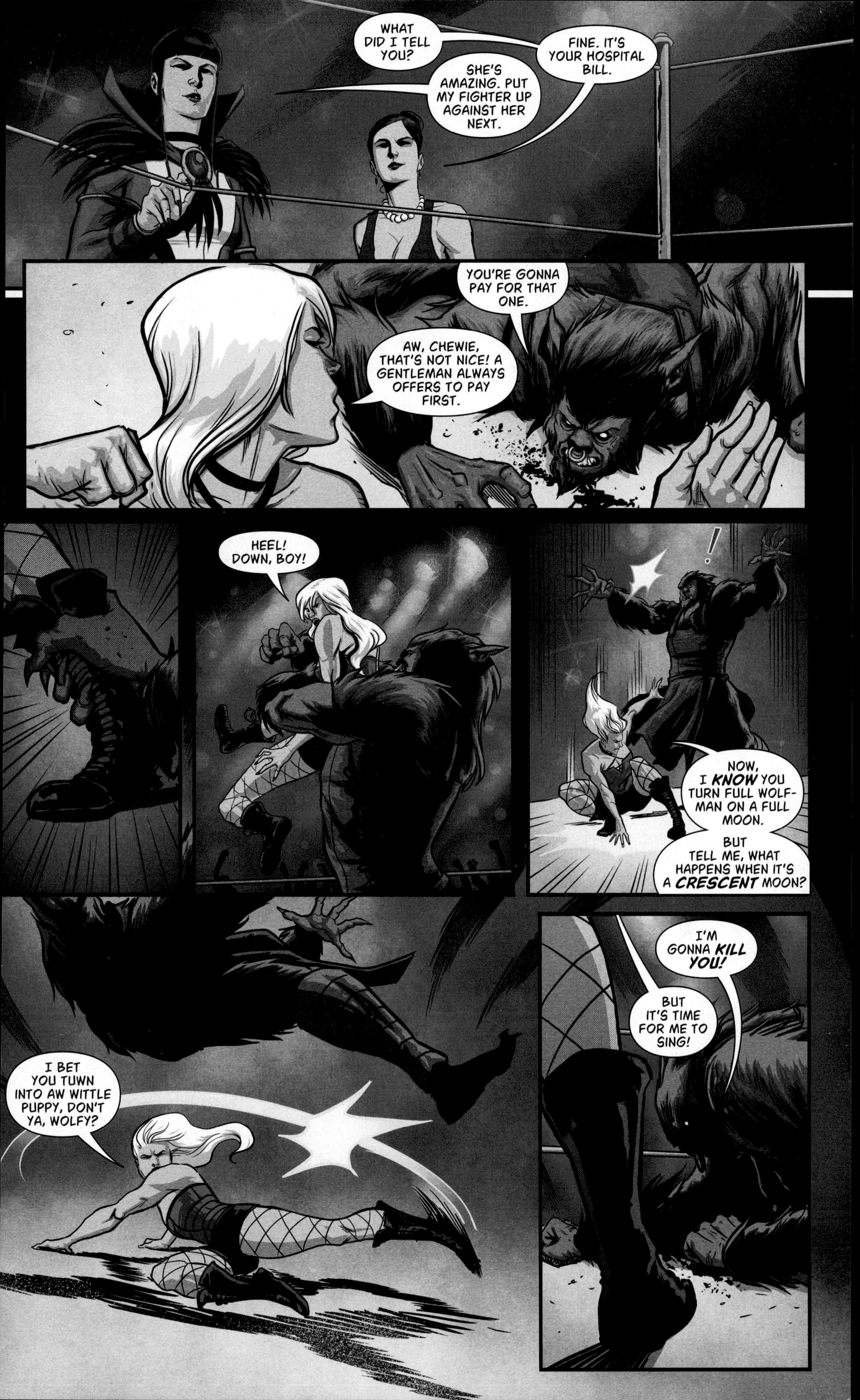
WHAT DID I TELL YOU?
SHE'S AMAZING. PUT MY FIGHTER UP AGAINST HER NEXT.
FINE. IT'S YOUR HOSPITAL BILL.
YOU'RE GONNA PAY FOR THAT ONE.
AW, CHEWIE, THAT'S NOT NICE! A GENTLEMAN ALWAYS OFFERS TO PAY FIRST.
HEEL! DOWN, BOY!
!
NOW, I KNOW YOU TURN FULL WOLF-MAN ON A FULL MOON.
BUT TELL ME, WHAT HAPPENS WHEN IT'S A CRESCENT MOON?
I BET YOU TUWN INTO AW WITTLE PUPPY, DON'T YA, WOLFY?
I'M GONNA KILL YOU!
BUT IT'S TIME FOR ME TO SING!

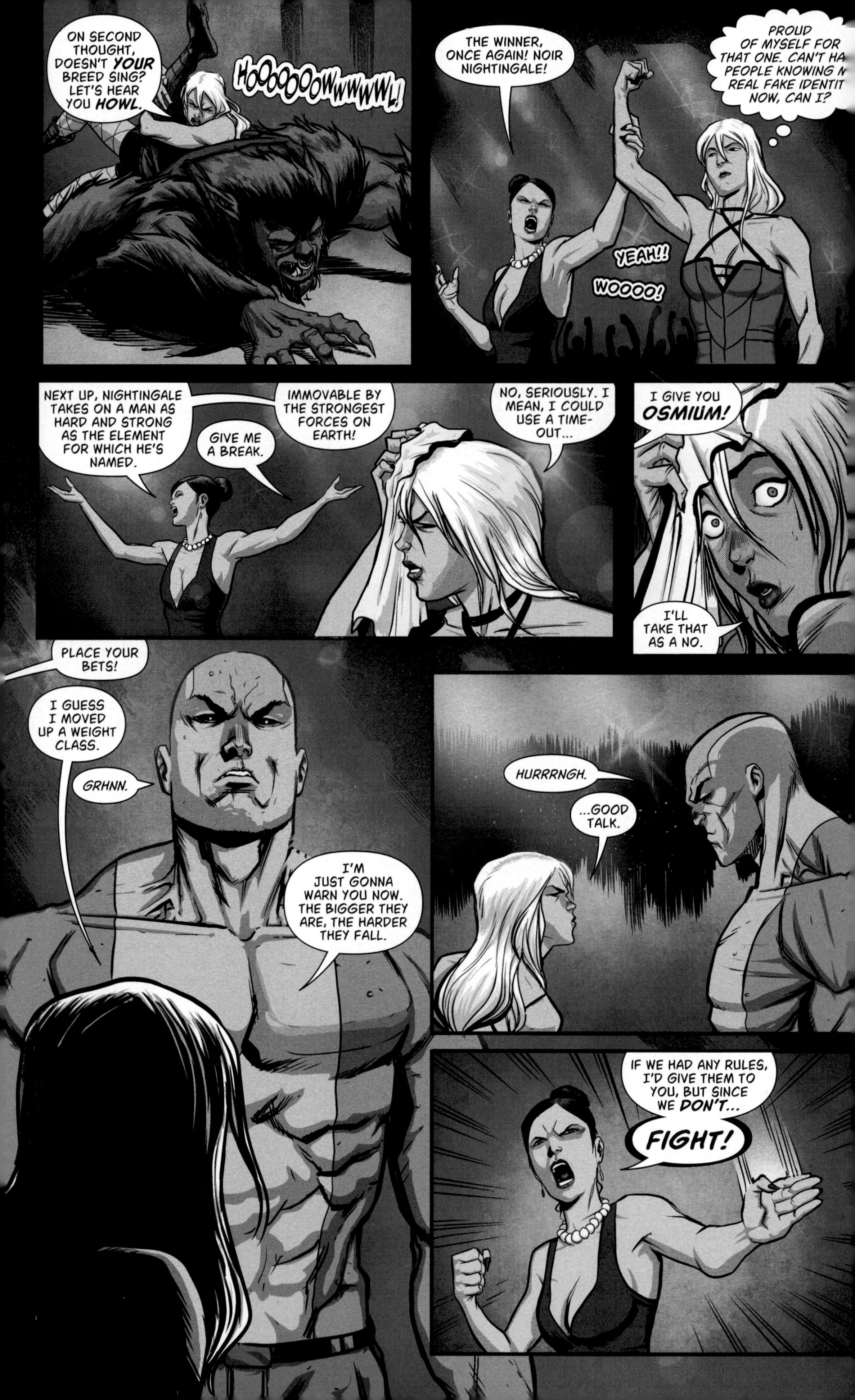
ON SECOND THOUGHT, DOESN'T YOUR BREED SING? LET'S HEAR YOU HOWL.
HOOOOOOOWWWWWL!
THE WINNER, ONCE AGAIN! NOIR NIGHTINGALE!
PROUD OF MYSELF FOR THAT ONE. CAN'T HA PEOPLE KNOWING M REAL FAKE IDENTIT NOW, CAN I?
YEAH!!
WOOOO!
NEXT UP, NIGHTINGALE TAKES ON A MAN AS HARD AND STRONG AS THE ELEMENT FOR WHICH HE'S NAMED.
IMMOVABLE BY THE STRONGEST FORCES ON EARTH!
GIVE ME A BREAK.
NO, SERIOUSLY. I MEAN, I COULD USE A TIME-OUT...
I GIVE YOU OSMIUM!
I'LL TAKE THAT AS A NO.
PLACE YOUR BETS!
I GUESS I MOVED UP A WEIGHT CLASS.
GRHNN.
I'M JUST GONNA WARN YOU NOW. THE BIGGER THEY ARE, THE HARDER THEY FALL.
HURRRNGH.
...GOOD TALK.
IF WE HAD ANY RULES, I'D GIVE THEM TO YOU, BUT SINCE WE DON'T...
FIGHT!

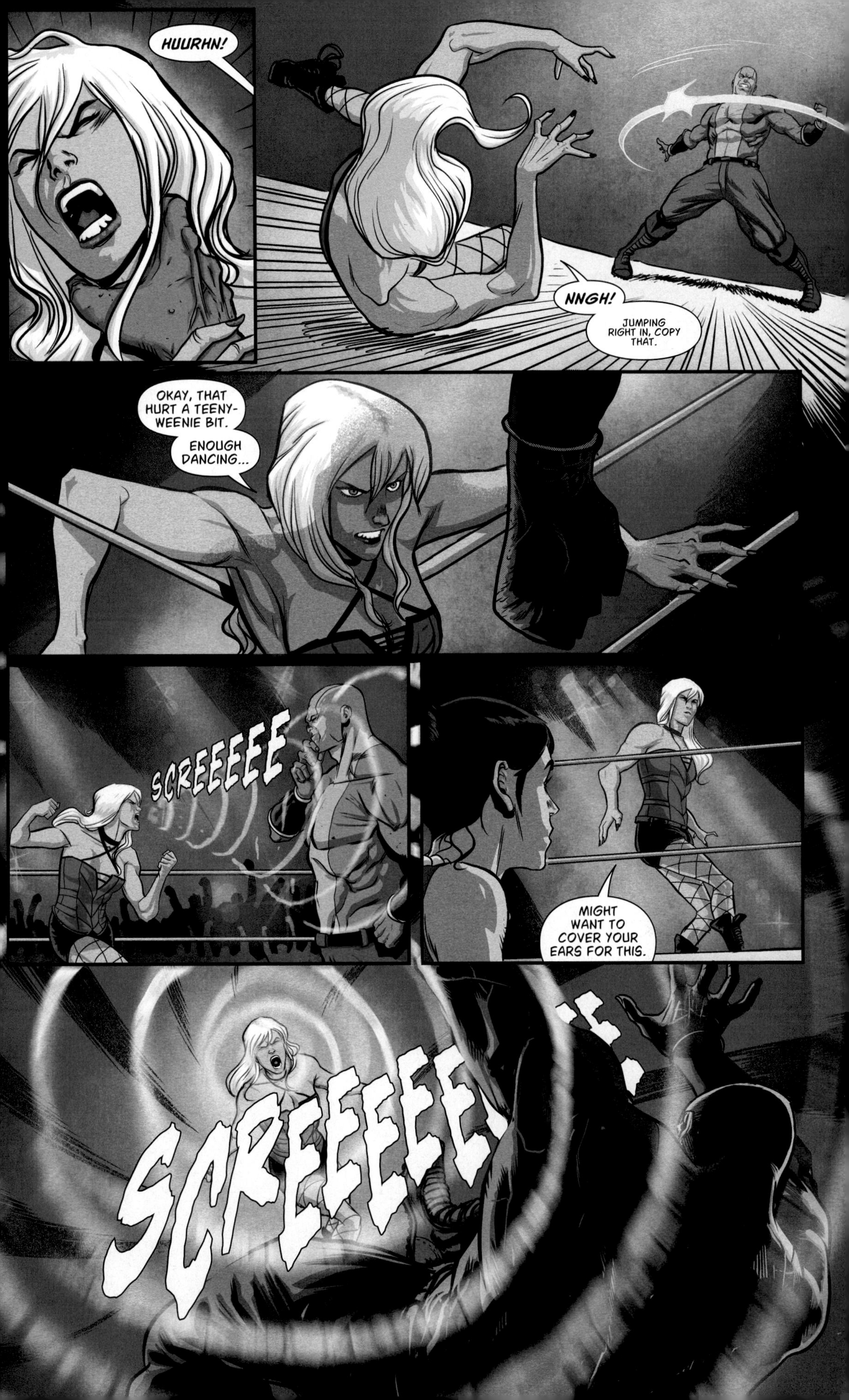
HUURHN!
NNGH!
JUMPING RIGHT IN, COPY THAT.
OKAY, THAT HURT A TEENY-WEENIE BIT.
ENOUGH DANCING...
SCREEEEEE
MIGHT WANT TO COVER YOUR EARS FOR THIS.
SCREEEEEE

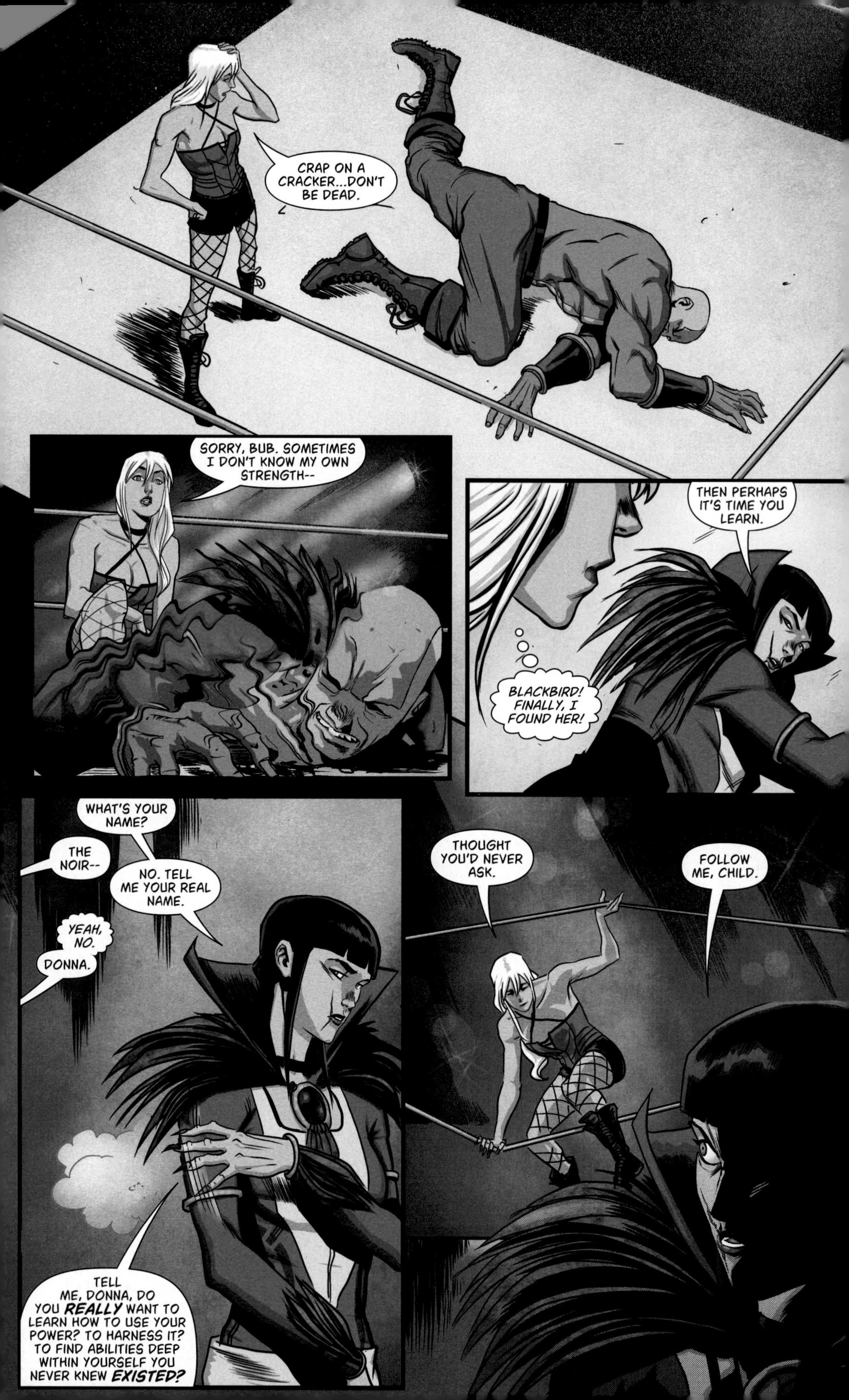
CRAP ON A CRACKER...DON'T BE DEAD.
SORRY, BUB. SOMETIMES I DON'T KNOW MY OWN STRENGTH--
THEN PERHAPS IT'S TIME YOU LEARN.
BLACKBIRD! FINALLY, I FOUND HER!
WHAT'S YOUR NAME?
THE NOIR--
NO. TELL ME YOUR REAL NAME.
YEAH, NO.
DONNA.
TELL ME, DONNA, DO YOU REALLY WANT TO LEARN HOW TO USE YOUR POWER? TO HARNESS IT? TO FIND ABILITIES DEEP WITHIN YOURSELF YOU NEVER KNEW EXISTED?
THOUGHT YOU'D NEVER ASK.
FOLLOW ME, CHILD.

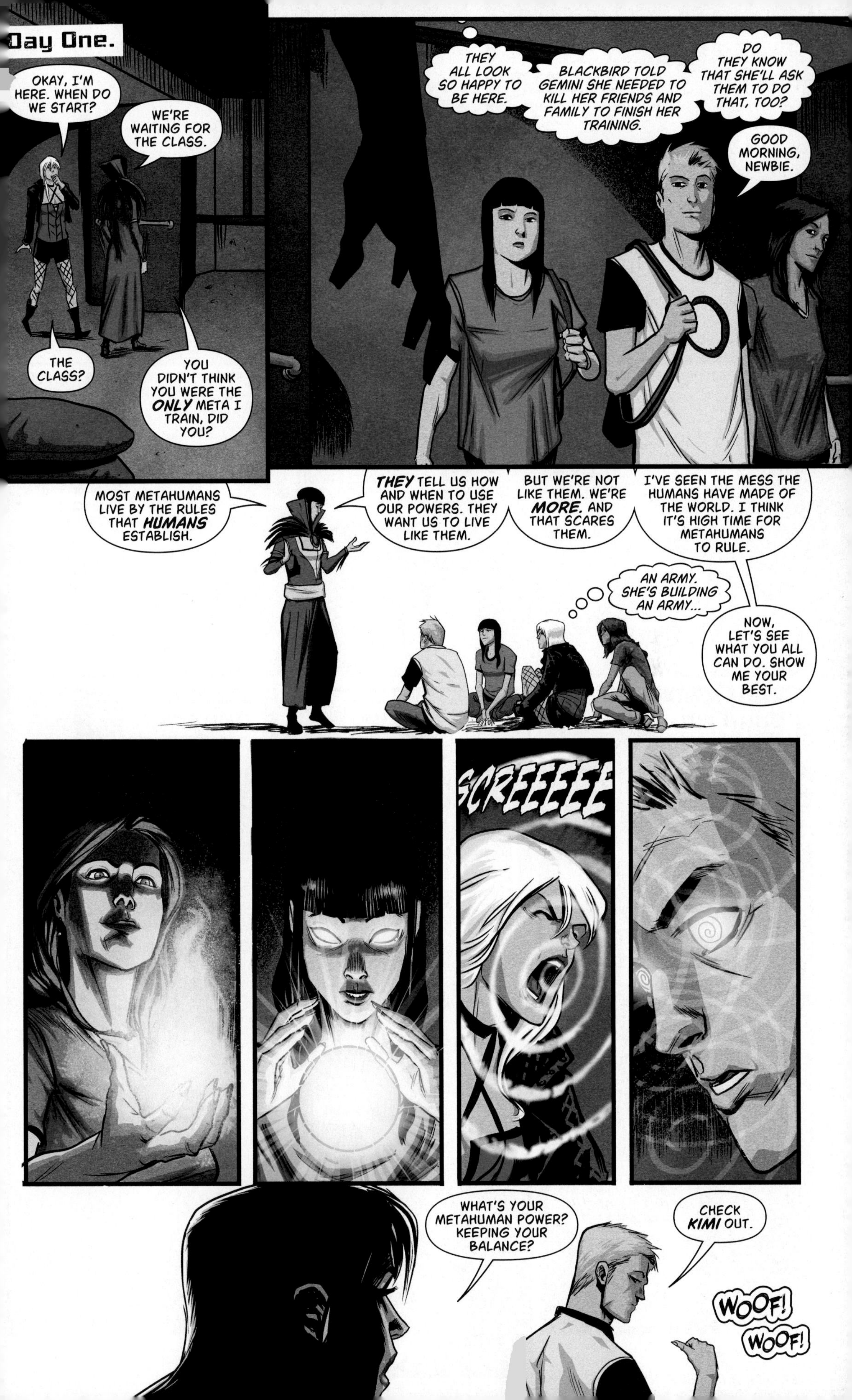

Day One.
OKAY, I'M HERE. WHEN DO WE START?
WE'RE WAITING FOR THE CLASS.
THE CLASS?
YOU DIDN'T THINK YOU WERE THE ONLY META I TRAIN, DID YOU?
THEY ALL LOOK SO HAPPY TO BE HERE.
BLACKBIRD TOLD GEMINI SHE NEEDED TO KILL HER FRIENDS AND FAMILY TO FINISH HER TRAINING.
DO THEY KNOW THAT SHE'LL ASK THEM TO DO THAT, TOO?
GOOD MORNING, NEWBIE.
MOST METAHUMANS LIVE BY THE RULES THAT HUMANS ESTABLISH.
THEY TELL US HOW AND WHEN TO USE OUR POWERS. THEY WANT US TO LIVE LIKE THEM.
BUT WE'RE NOT LIKE THEM. WE'RE MORE. AND THAT SCARES THEM.
I'VE SEEN THE MESS THE HUMANS HAVE MADE OF THE WORLD. I THINK IT'S HIGH TIME FOR METAHUMANS TO RULE.
AN ARMY. SHE'S BUILDING AN ARMY...
NOW, LET'S SEE WHAT YOU ALL CAN DO. SHOW ME YOUR BEST.
SCREEEEEE
WHAT'S YOUR METAHUMAN POWER? KEEPING YOUR BALANCE?
CHECK KIMI OUT.
WOOF!
WOOF!

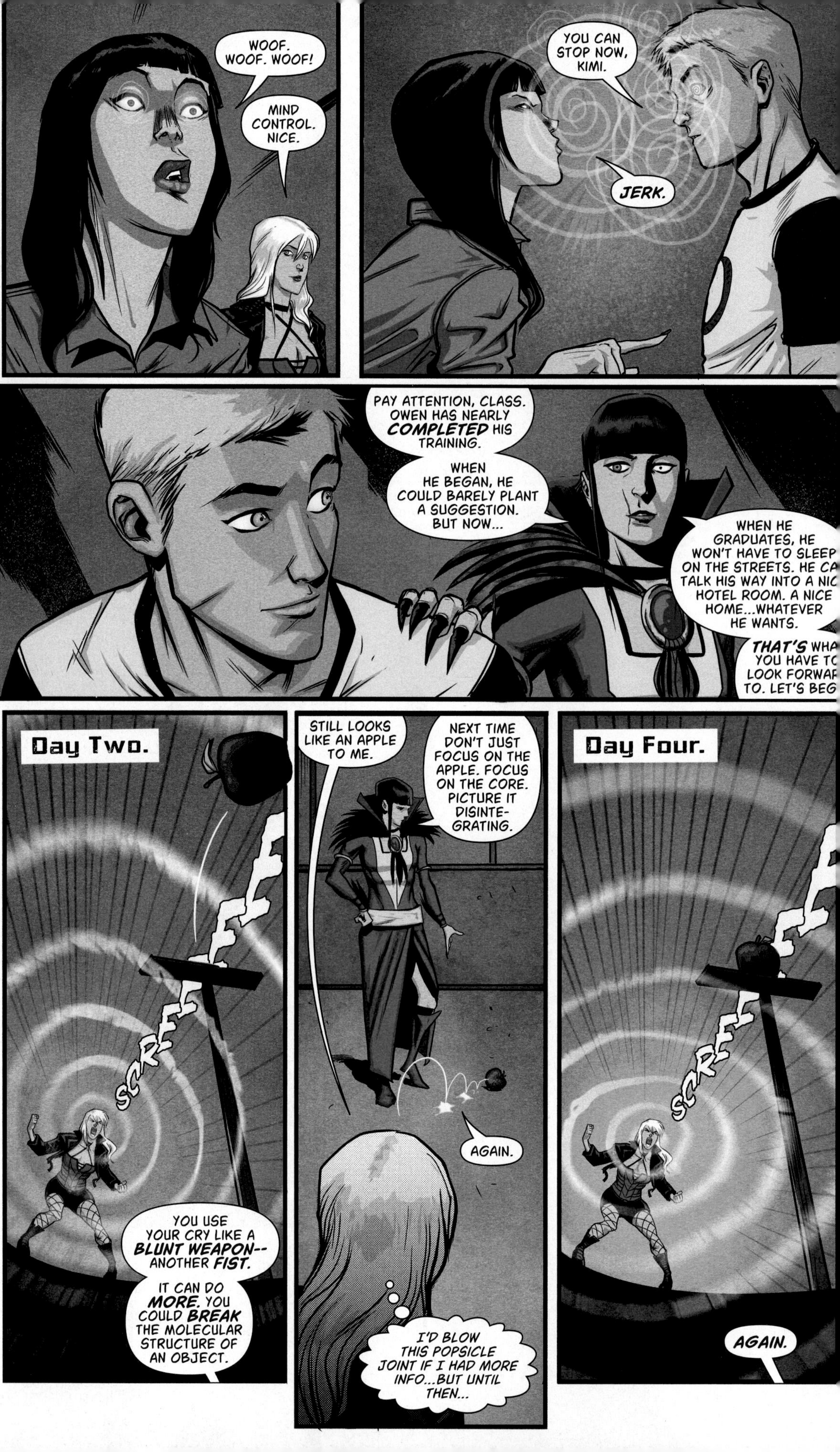
WOOF. WOOF. WOOF!
MIND CONTROL. NICE.
YOU CAN STOP NOW, KIMI.
JERK.
PAY ATTENTION, CLASS. OWEN HAS NEARLY COMPLETED HIS TRAINING.
WHEN HE BEGAN, HE COULD BARELY PLANT A SUGGESTION. BUT NOW...
WHEN HE GRADUATES, HE WON'T HAVE TO SLEEP ON THE STREETS. HE CA TALK HIS WAY INTO A NIC HOTEL ROOM. A NICE HOME...WHATEVER HE WANTS.
THAT'S WHA YOU HAVE TO LOOK FORWAR TO. LET'S BEG
Day Two.
SCREEEE
YOU USE YOUR CRY LIKE A BLUNT WEAPON--ANOTHER FIST.
IT CAN DO MORE. YOU COULD BREAK THE MOLECULAR STRUCTURE OF AN OBJECT.
STILL LOOKS LIKE AN APPLE TO ME.
NEXT TIME DON'T JUST FOCUS ON THE APPLE. FOCUS ON THE CORE. PICTURE IT DISINTE-GRATING.
AGAIN.
I'D BLOW THIS POPSICLE JOINT IF I HAD MORE INFO...BUT UNTIL THEN...
Day Four.
SCREEEE
AGAIN.

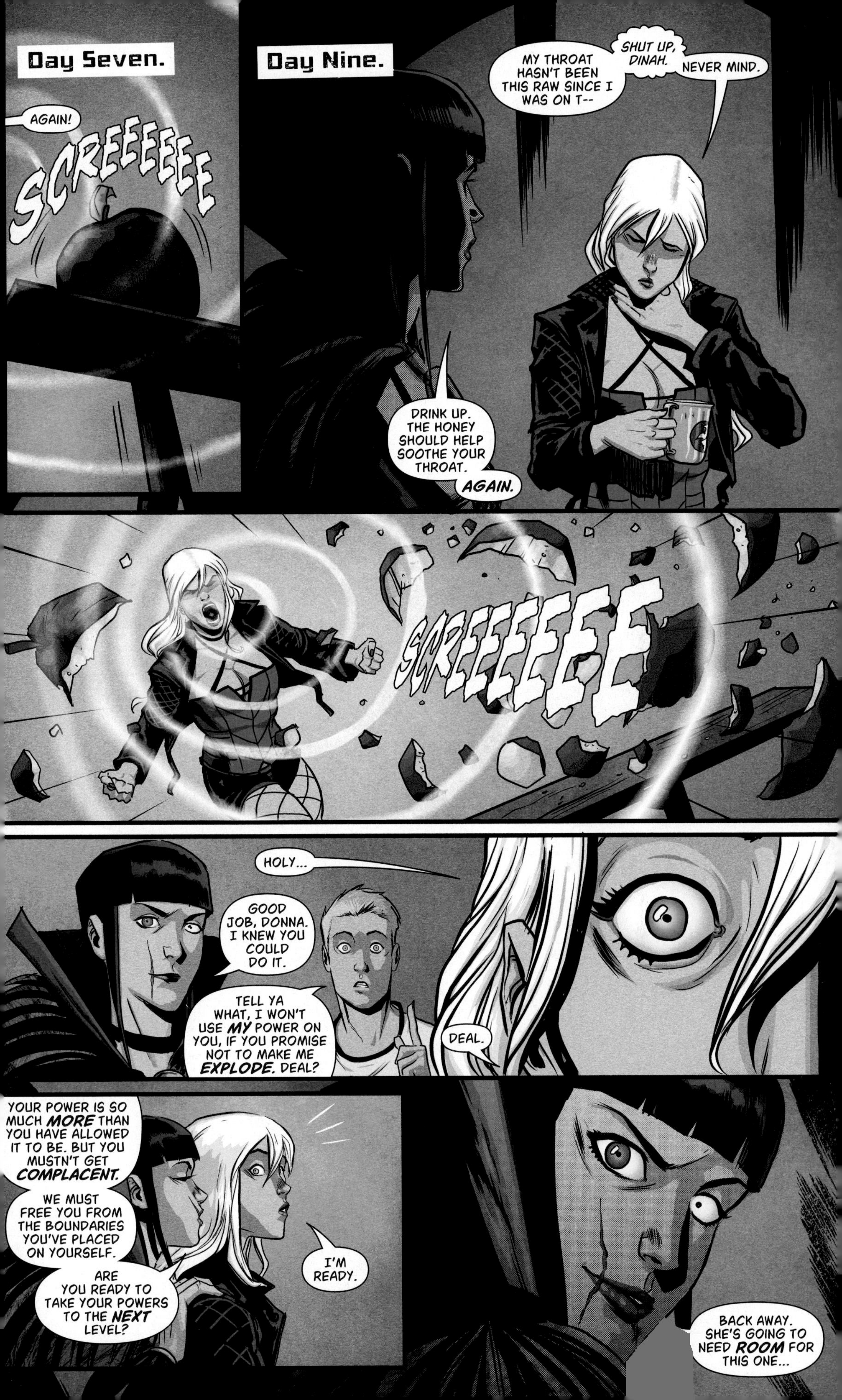
Day Seven.
AGAIN!
SCREEEEEEE
Day Nine.
MY THROAT HASN'T BEEN THIS RAW SINCE I WAS ON T--
SHUT UP, DINAH.
NEVER MIND.
DRINK UP. THE HONEY SHOULD HELP SOOTHE YOUR THROAT.
AGAIN.
SCREEEEEEEE
HOLY...
GOOD JOB, DONNA. I KNEW YOU COULD DO IT.
TELL YA WHAT, I WON'T USE MY POWER ON YOU, IF YOU PROMISE NOT TO MAKE ME EXPLODE. DEAL?
DEAL.
YOUR POWER IS SO MUCH MORE THAN YOU HAVE ALLOWED IT TO BE. BUT YOU MUSTN'T GET COMPLACENT.
WE MUST FREE YOU FROM THE BOUNDARIES YOU'VE PLACED ON YOURSELF.
ARE YOU READY TO TAKE YOUR POWERS TO THE NEXT LEVEL?
I'M READY.
BACK AWAY. SHE'S GOING TO NEED ROOM FOR THIS ONE...

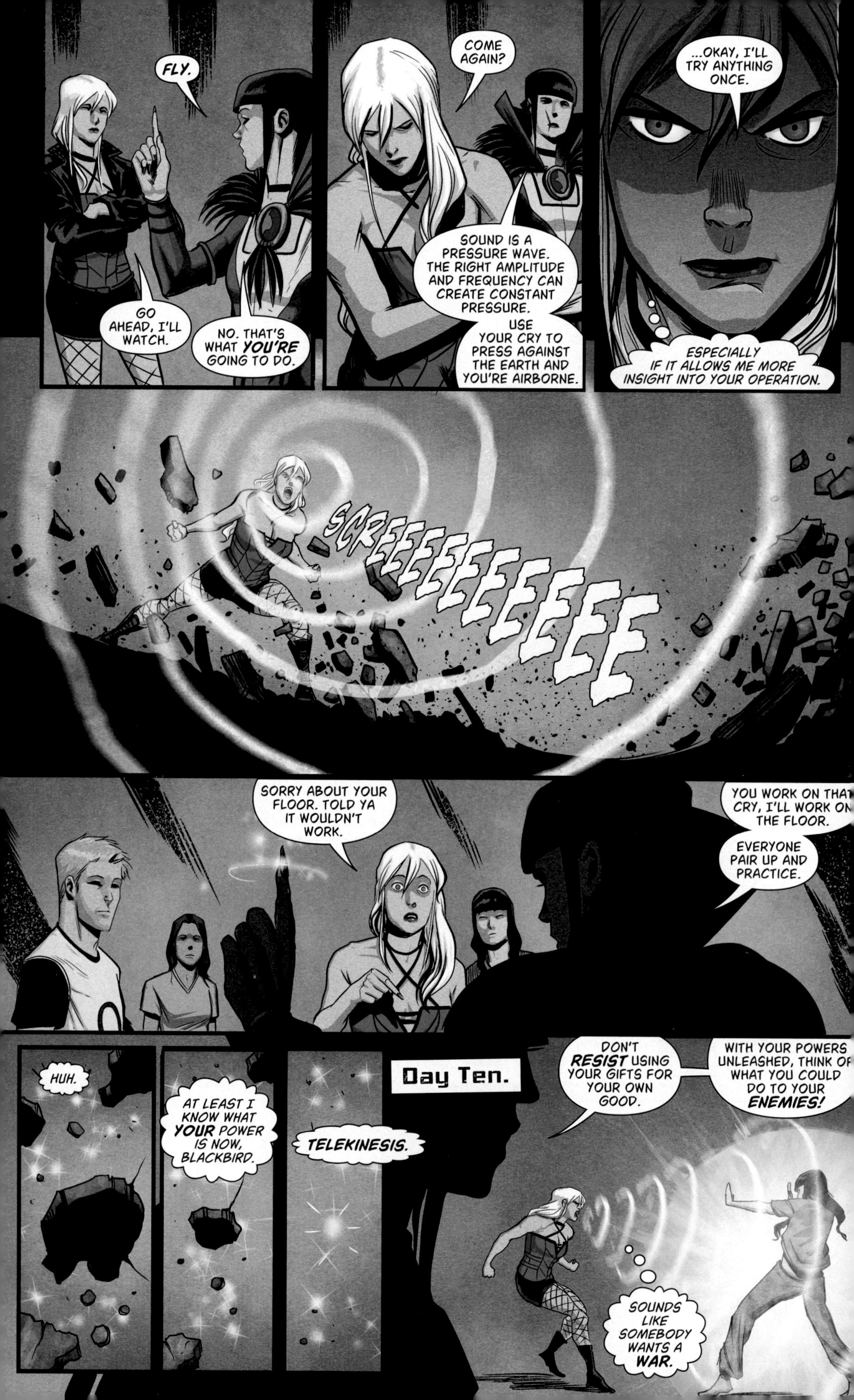
FLY.
GO AHEAD, I'LL WATCH.
NO. THAT'S WHAT YOU'RE GOING TO DO.
COME AGAIN?
SOUND IS A PRESSURE WAVE. THE RIGHT AMPLITUDE AND FREQUENCY CAN CREATE CONSTANT PRESSURE.
USE YOUR CRY TO PRESS AGAINST THE EARTH AND YOU'RE AIRBORNE.
...OKAY, I'LL TRY ANYTHING ONCE.
ESPECIALLY IF IT ALLOWS ME MORE INSIGHT INTO YOUR OPERATION.
SCREEEEEEEEEEEE
SORRY ABOUT YOUR FLOOR. TOLD YA IT WOULDN'T WORK.
YOU WORK ON THAT CRY, I'LL WORK ON THE FLOOR.
EVERYONE PAIR UP AND PRACTICE.
HUH.
AT LEAST I KNOW WHAT YOUR POWER IS NOW, BLACKBIRD.
TELEKINESIS.
Day Ten.
DON'T RESIST USING YOUR GIFTS FOR YOUR OWN GOOD.
WITH YOUR POWERS UNLEASHED, THINK OF WHAT YOU COULD DO TO YOUR ENEMIES!
SOUNDS LIKE SOMEBODY WANTS A WAR.

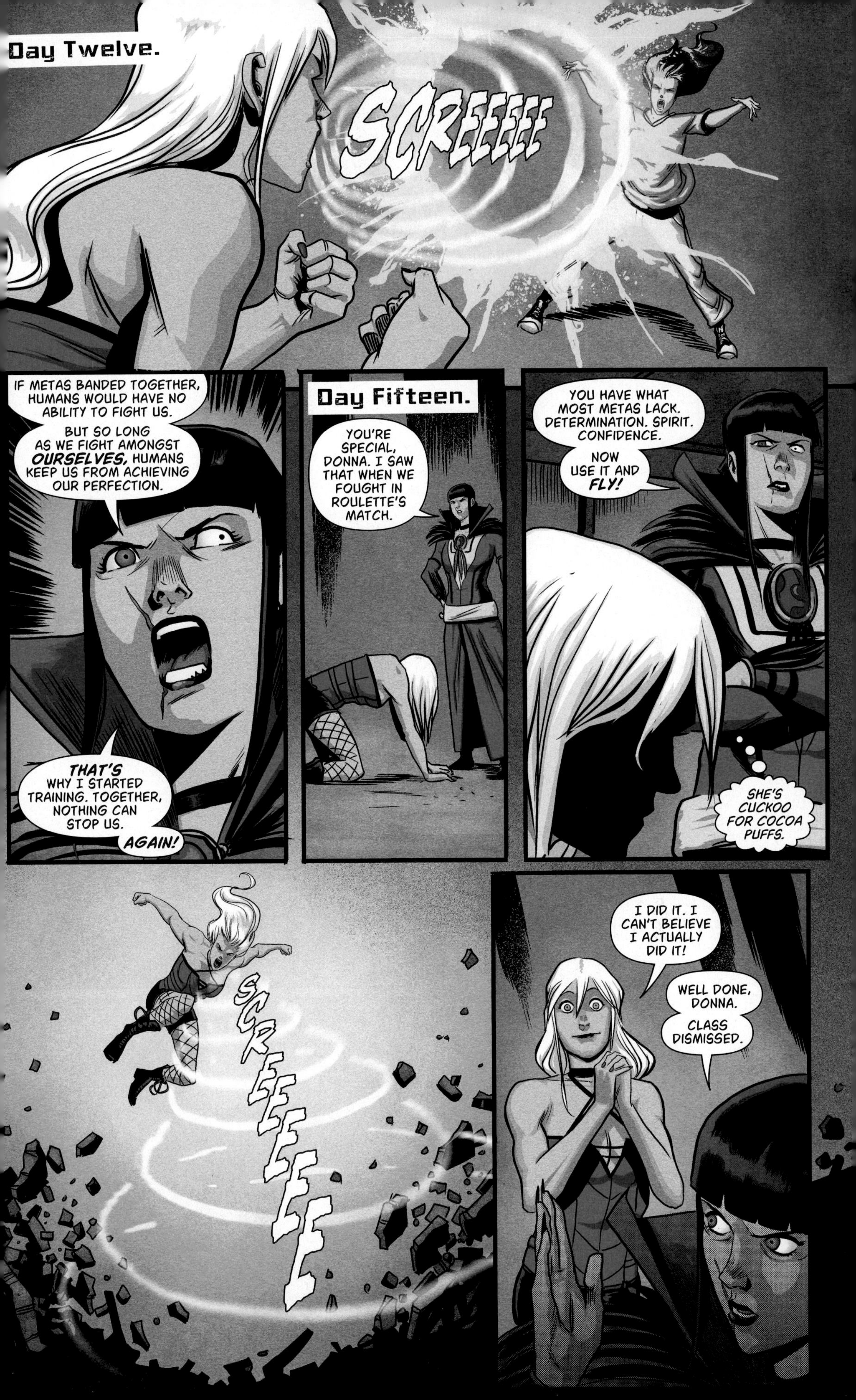
Day Twelve.
SCREEEEEE
IF METAS BANDED TOGETHER, HUMANS WOULD HAVE NO ABILITY TO FIGHT US.
BUT SO LONG AS WE FIGHT AMONGST OURSELVES, HUMANS KEEP US FROM ACHIEVING OUR PERFECTION.
THAT'S WHY I STARTED TRAINING. TOGETHER, NOTHING CAN STOP US.
AGAIN!
Day Fifteen.
YOU'RE SPECIAL, DONNA. I SAW THAT WHEN WE FOUGHT IN ROULETTE'S MATCH.
YOU HAVE WHAT MOST METAS LACK. DETERMINATION. SPIRIT. CONFIDENCE.
NOW USE IT AND FLY!
SHE'S CUCKOO FOR COCOA PUFFS.
SCREEEEEE
I DID IT. I CAN'T BELIEVE I ACTUALLY DID IT!
WELL DONE, DONNA.
CLASS DISMISSED.

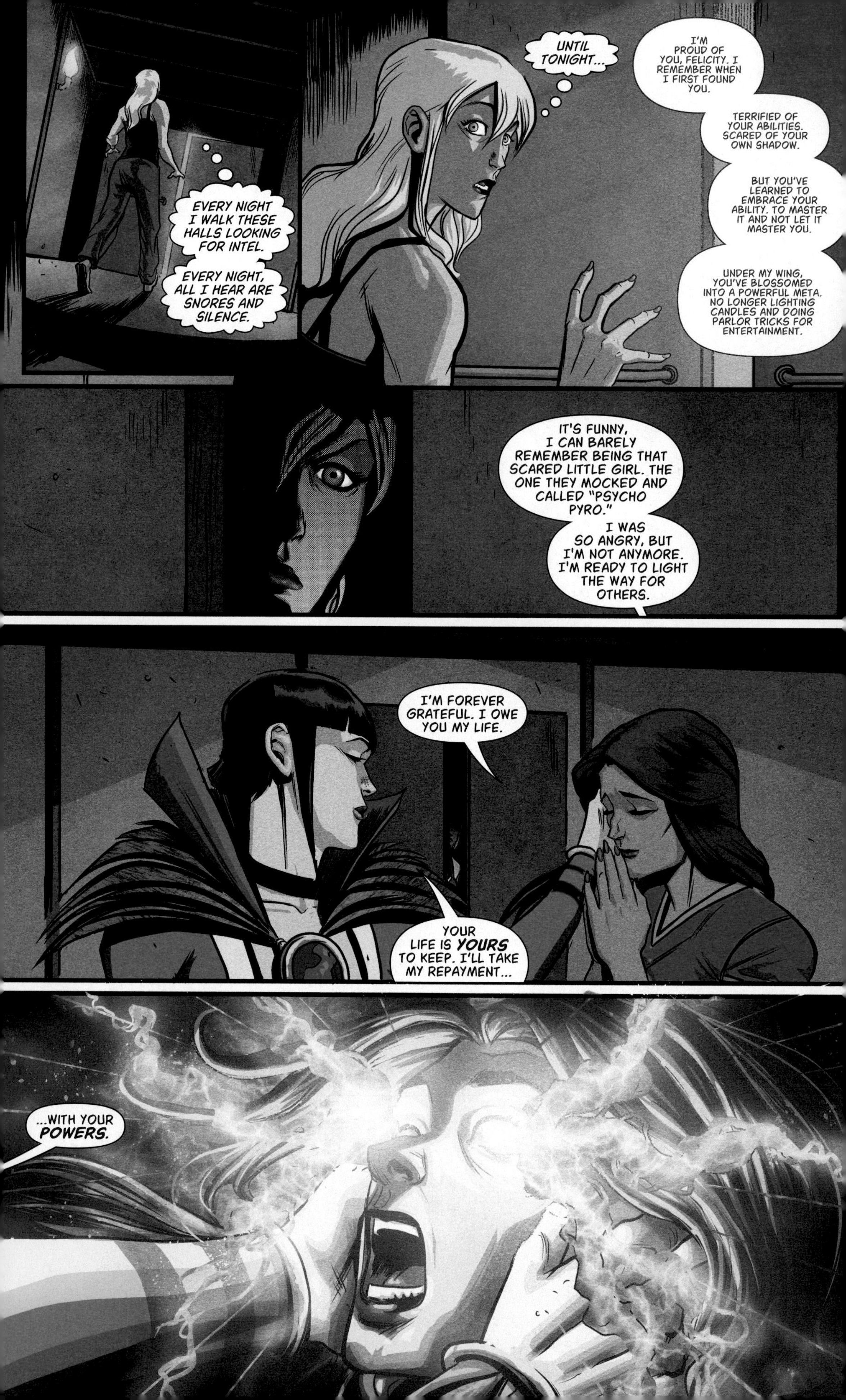
EVERY NIGHT I WALK THESE HALLS LOOKING FOR INTEL.
EVERY NIGHT, ALL I HEAR ARE SNORES AND SILENCE.
UNTIL TONIGHT...
I'M PROUD OF YOU, FELICITY. I REMEMBER WHEN I FIRST FOUND YOU.
TERRIFIED OF YOUR ABILITIES. SCARED OF YOUR OWN SHADOW.
BUT YOU'VE LEARNED TO EMBRACE YOUR ABILITY. TO MASTER IT AND NOT LET IT MASTER YOU.
UNDER MY WING, YOU'VE BLOSSOMED INTO A POWERFUL META. NO LONGER LIGHTING CANDLES AND DOING PARLOR TRICKS FOR ENTERTAINMENT.
IT'S FUNNY, I CAN BARELY REMEMBER BEING THAT SCARED LITTLE GIRL. THE ONE THEY MOCKED AND CALLED "PSYCHO PYRO."
I WAS SO ANGRY, BUT I'M NOT ANYMORE. I'M READY TO LIGHT THE WAY FOR OTHERS.
I'M FOREVER GRATEFUL. I OWE YOU MY LIFE.
YOUR LIFE IS **YOURS** TO KEEP. I'LL TAKE MY REPAYMENT...
...WITH YOUR **POWERS.**

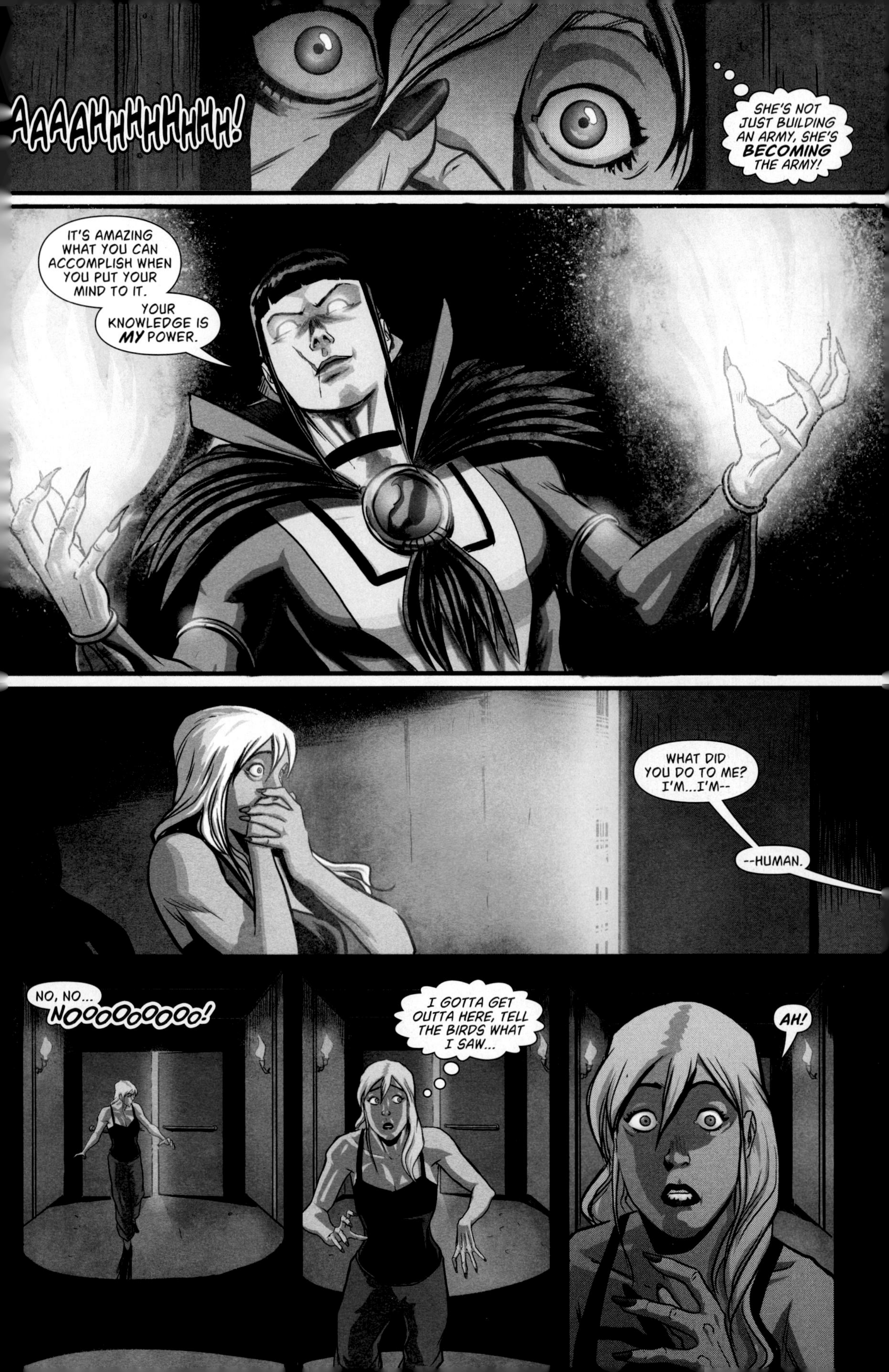
AAAAHHHHHHH!
SHE'S NOT JUST BUILDING AN ARMY, SHE'S BECOMING THE ARMY!
IT'S AMAZING WHAT YOU CAN ACCOMPLISH WHEN YOU PUT YOUR MIND TO IT.
YOUR KNOWLEDGE IS MY POWER.
WHAT DID YOU DO TO ME? I'M...I'M--
--HUMAN.
NO, NO... NOOOOOOOOO!
I GOTTA GET OUTTA HERE, TELL THE BIRDS WHAT I SAW...
AH!

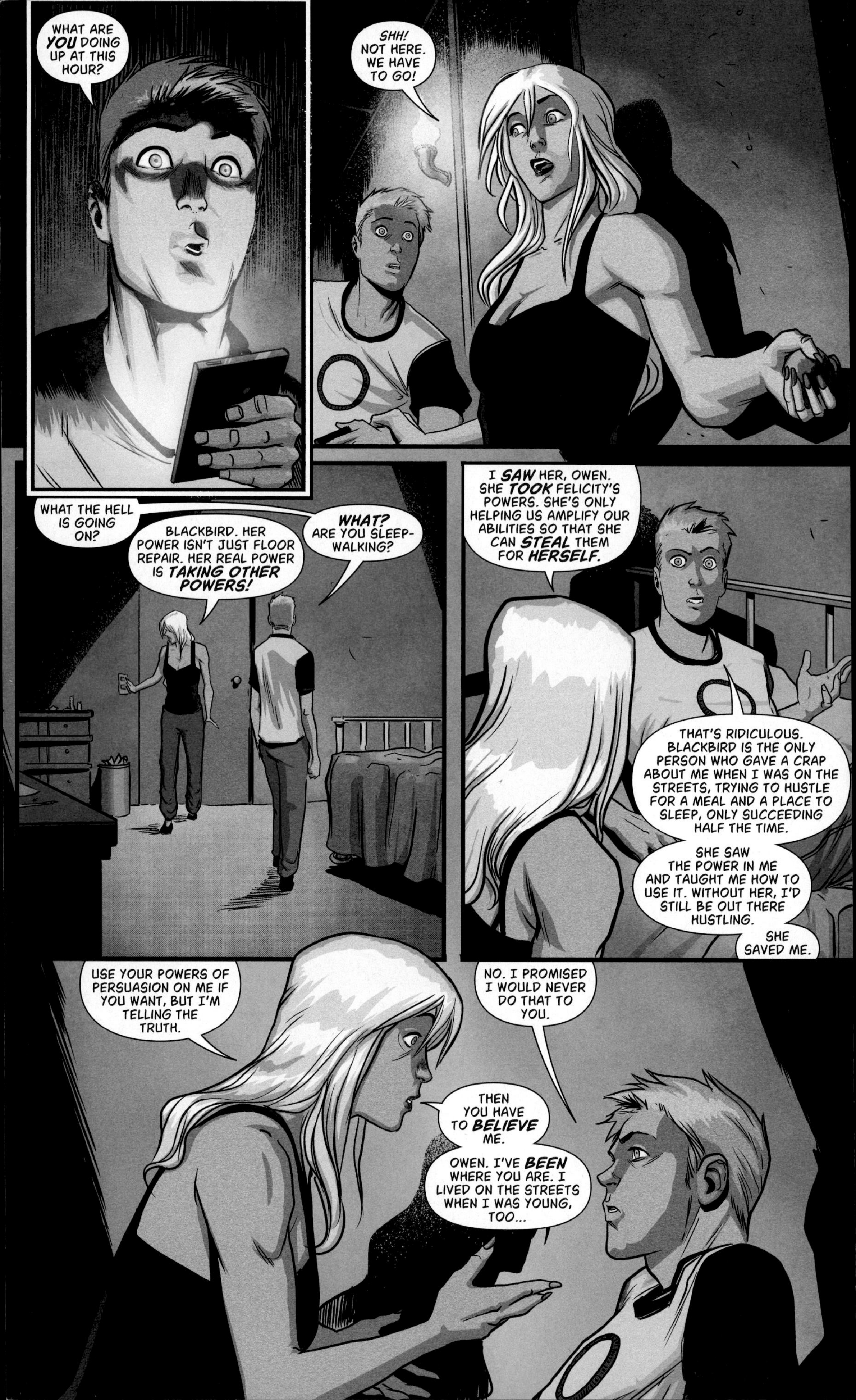
WHAT ARE YOU DOING UP AT THIS HOUR?
SHH! NOT HERE. WE HAVE TO GO!
WHAT THE HELL IS GOING ON?
BLACKBIRD. HER POWER ISN'T JUST FLOOR REPAIR. HER REAL POWER IS TAKING OTHER POWERS!
WHAT? ARE YOU SLEEP-WALKING?
I SAW HER, OWEN. SHE TOOK FELICITY'S POWERS. SHE'S ONLY HELPING US AMPLIFY OUR ABILITIES SO THAT SHE CAN STEAL THEM FOR HERSELF.
THAT'S RIDICULOUS. BLACKBIRD IS THE ONLY PERSON WHO GAVE A CRAP ABOUT ME WHEN I WAS ON THE STREETS, TRYING TO HUSTLE FOR A MEAL AND A PLACE TO SLEEP, ONLY SUCCEEDING HALF THE TIME.
SHE SAW THE POWER IN ME AND TAUGHT ME HOW TO USE IT. WITHOUT HER, I'D STILL BE OUT THERE HUSTLING.
SHE SAVED ME.
USE YOUR POWERS OF PERSUASION ON ME IF YOU WANT, BUT I'M TELLING THE TRUTH.
NO. I PROMISED I WOULD NEVER DO THAT TO YOU.
THEN YOU HAVE TO BELIEVE ME.
OWEN. I'VE BEEN WHERE YOU ARE. I LIVED ON THE STREETS WHEN I WAS YOUNG, TOO...

"I DECIDED THE FOSTER CARE SYSTEM NO LONGER HAD ANYTHING TO OFFER ME, SO I RAN AWAY."

"I HID FROM SKEEVY GUYS WHO WEREN'T LOOKING OUT FOR ME, EVEN IF THEY SAID THEY WOULD. I SAW WHAT HAPPENED TO OTHER GIRLS AND I KNEW TO STEER CLEAR."

"A COUPLE OF YEARS OF THAT AND I LEARNED NOT TO TRUST *ANYONE.*"

"DINING OPTIONS WEREN'T GREAT. SOMETIMES YOU'D FIND SOME LEFTOVER FRIES OR A PACKAGE OF STALE DONUTS."

"I GOT USED TO PEOPLE PASSING BY ME ON THE STREET LIKE I WAS INVISIBLE."

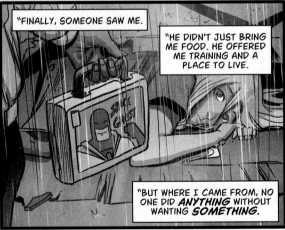

"FINALLY, SOMEONE SAW ME."

"HE DIDN'T JUST BRING ME FOOD. HE OFFERED ME TRAINING AND A PLACE TO LIVE."

"BUT WHERE I CAME FROM, NO ONE DID *ANYTHING* WITHOUT WANTING *SOMETHING.*"

"ALL HE WANTED IN RETURN WAS MY *TRUST,* JUST FOR ONE NIGHT. THEN ANOTHER NIGHT. AND ANOTHER."

"THE DAYS ADDED UP AND I REALIZED I WASN'T TERRIFIED ANYMORE."

"I'D FOUND SOMEONE WHO CARED ABOUT ME AND WASN'T LOOKING FOR ANYTHING IN RETURN."

THERE ARE GOOD PEOPLE OUT THERE WHO WILL HELP YOU, BUT BLACKBIRD ISN'T ONE OF THEM.

SHE'S BEEN USING YOU, BUILDING YOU UP TO TAKE YOUR POWER.

WE *NEED* TO GET OUT OF HERE. WE *NEED* TO STOP HER.

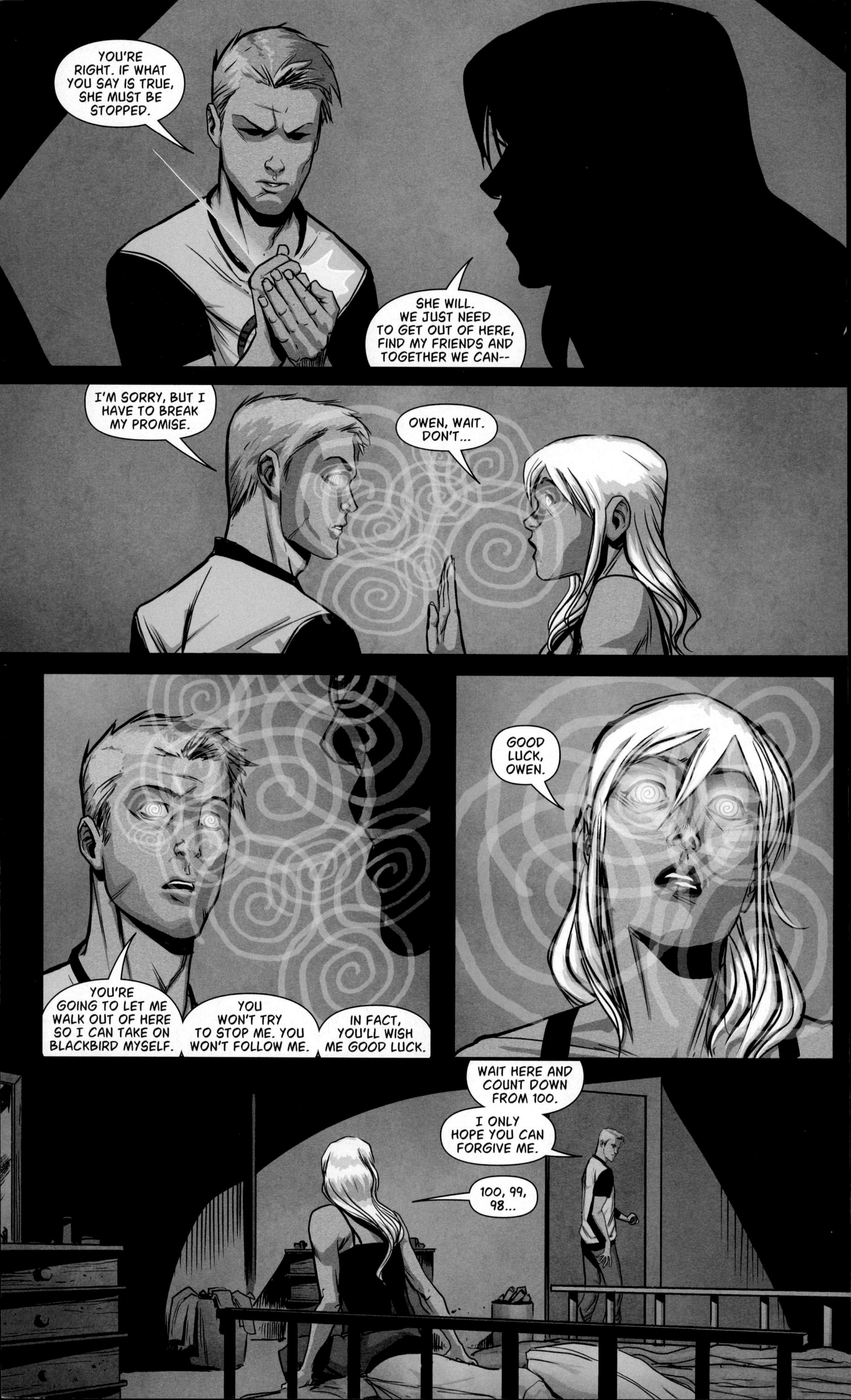
YOU'RE RIGHT. IF WHAT YOU SAY IS TRUE, SHE MUST BE STOPPED.
SHE WILL. WE JUST NEED TO GET OUT OF HERE, FIND MY FRIENDS AND TOGETHER WE CAN--
I'M SORRY, BUT I HAVE TO BREAK MY PROMISE.
OWEN, WAIT. DON'T...
YOU'RE GOING TO LET ME WALK OUT OF HERE SO I CAN TAKE ON BLACKBIRD MYSELF.
YOU WON'T TRY TO STOP ME. YOU WON'T FOLLOW ME.
IN FACT, YOU'LL WISH ME GOOD LUCK.
GOOD LUCK, OWEN.
WAIT HERE AND COUNT DOWN FROM 100.
I ONLY HOPE YOU CAN FORGIVE ME.
100, 99, 98...

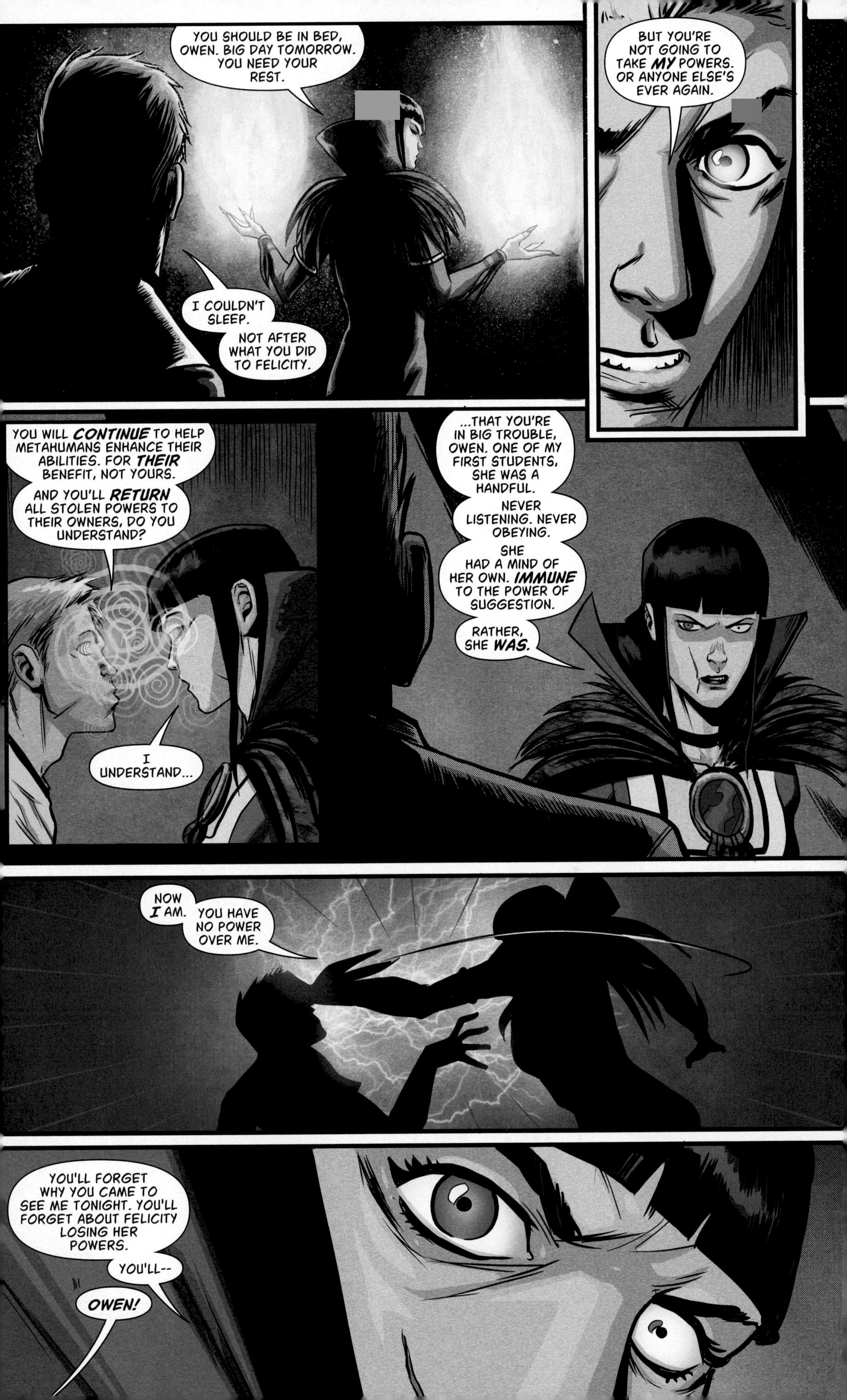
YOU SHOULD BE IN BED, OWEN. BIG DAY TOMORROW. YOU NEED YOUR REST.
I COULDN'T SLEEP.
NOT AFTER WHAT YOU DID TO FELICITY.
BUT YOU'RE NOT GOING TO TAKE MY POWERS. OR ANYONE ELSE'S EVER AGAIN.
YOU WILL CONTINUE TO HELP METAHUMANS ENHANCE THEIR ABILITIES. FOR THEIR BENEFIT, NOT YOURS.
AND YOU'LL RETURN ALL STOLEN POWERS TO THEIR OWNERS, DO YOU UNDERSTAND?
I UNDERSTAND...
...THAT YOU'RE IN BIG TROUBLE, OWEN. ONE OF MY FIRST STUDENTS, SHE WAS A HANDFUL.
NEVER LISTENING. NEVER OBEYING.
SHE HAD A MIND OF HER OWN. IMMUNE TO THE POWER OF SUGGESTION.
RATHER, SHE WAS.
NOW I AM.
YOU HAVE NO POWER OVER ME.
YOU'LL FORGET WHY YOU CAME TO SEE ME TONIGHT. YOU'LL FORGET ABOUT FELICITY LOSING HER POWERS.
YOU'LL--
OWEN!

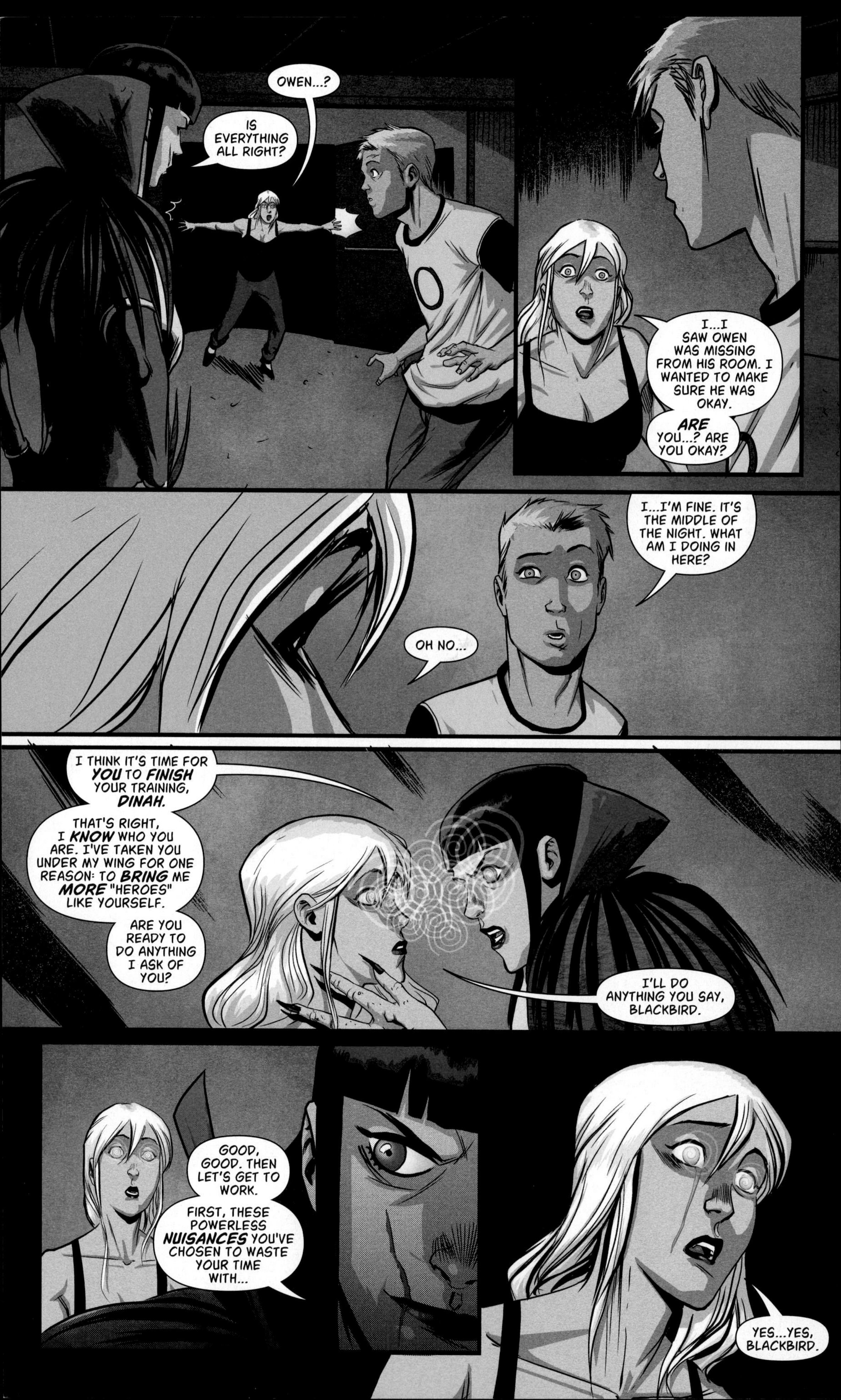
IS EVERYTHING ALL RIGHT?
OWEN...?
I...I SAW OWEN WAS MISSING FROM HIS ROOM. I WANTED TO MAKE SURE HE WAS OKAY.
ARE YOU...? ARE YOU OKAY?
I...I'M FINE. IT'S THE MIDDLE OF THE NIGHT. WHAT AM I DOING IN HERE?
OH NO...
I THINK IT'S TIME FOR YOU TO FINISH YOUR TRAINING, DINAH.
THAT'S RIGHT, I KNOW WHO YOU ARE. I'VE TAKEN YOU UNDER MY WING FOR ONE REASON: TO BRING ME MORE "HEROES" LIKE YOURSELF.
ARE YOU READY TO DO ANYTHING I ASK OF YOU?
I'LL DO ANYTHING YOU SAY, BLACKBIRD.
GOOD, GOOD. THEN LET'S GET TO WORK.
FIRST, THESE POWERLESS NUISANCES YOU'VE CHOSEN TO WASTE YOUR TIME WITH...
YES...YES, BLACKBIRD.

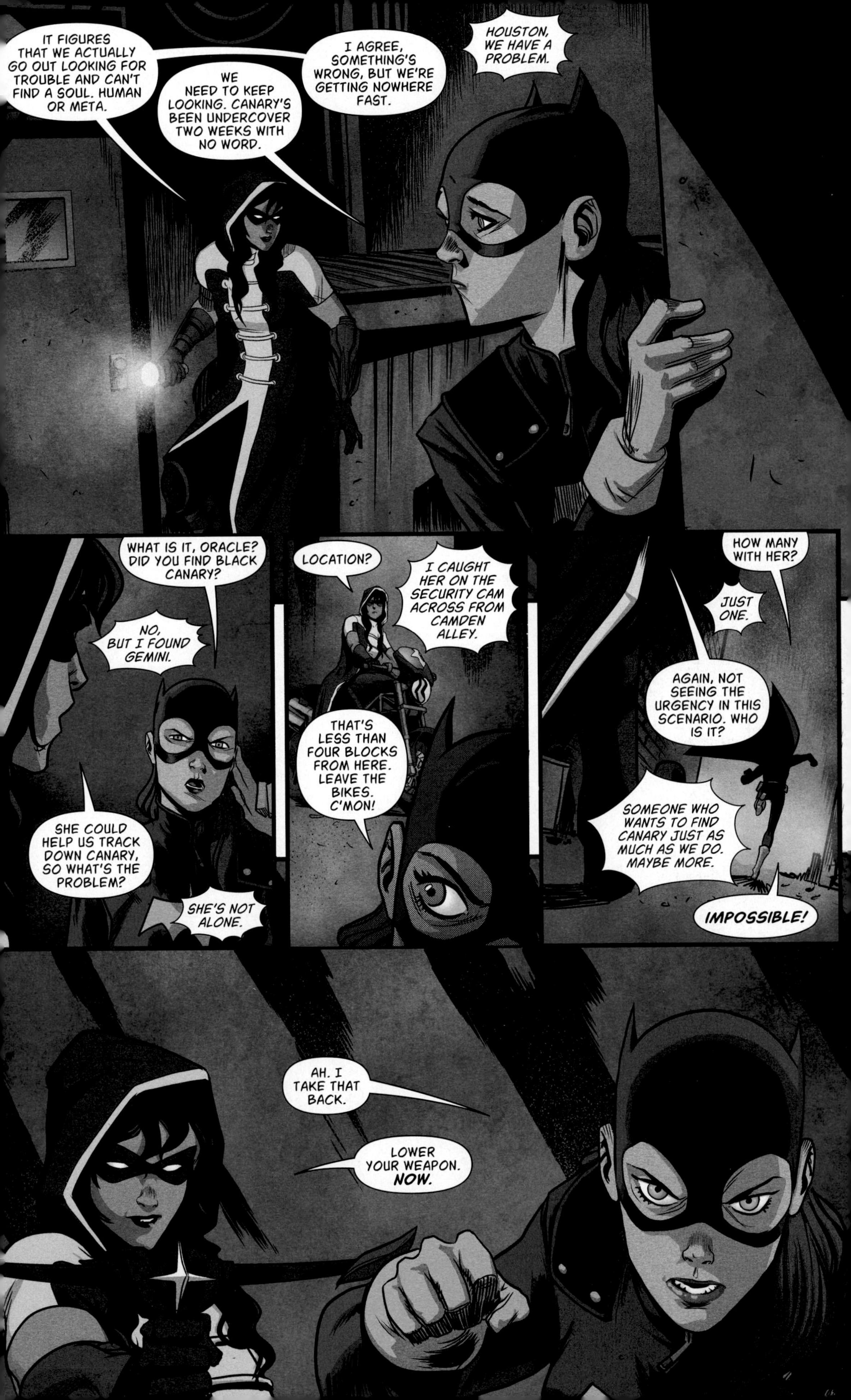

IT FIGURES THAT WE ACTUALLY GO OUT LOOKING FOR TROUBLE AND CAN'T FIND A SOUL. HUMAN OR META.
WE NEED TO KEEP LOOKING. CANARY'S BEEN UNDERCOVER TWO WEEKS WITH NO WORD.
I AGREE, SOMETHING'S WRONG, BUT WE'RE GETTING NOWHERE FAST.
HOUSTON, WE HAVE A PROBLEM.
WHAT IS IT, ORACLE? DID YOU FIND BLACK CANARY?
NO, BUT I FOUND GEMINI.
SHE COULD HELP US TRACK DOWN CANARY, SO WHAT'S THE PROBLEM?
SHE'S NOT ALONE.
LOCATION?
I CAUGHT HER ON THE SECURITY CAM ACROSS FROM CAMDEN ALLEY.
THAT'S LESS THAN FOUR BLOCKS FROM HERE. LEAVE THE BIKES. C'MON!
HOW MANY WITH HER?
JUST ONE.
AGAIN, NOT SEEING THE URGENCY IN THIS SCENARIO. WHO IS IT?
SOMEONE WHO WANTS TO FIND CANARY JUST AS MUCH AS WE DO. MAYBE MORE.
IMPOSSIBLE!
AH. I TAKE THAT BACK.
LOWER YOUR WEAPON. NOW.

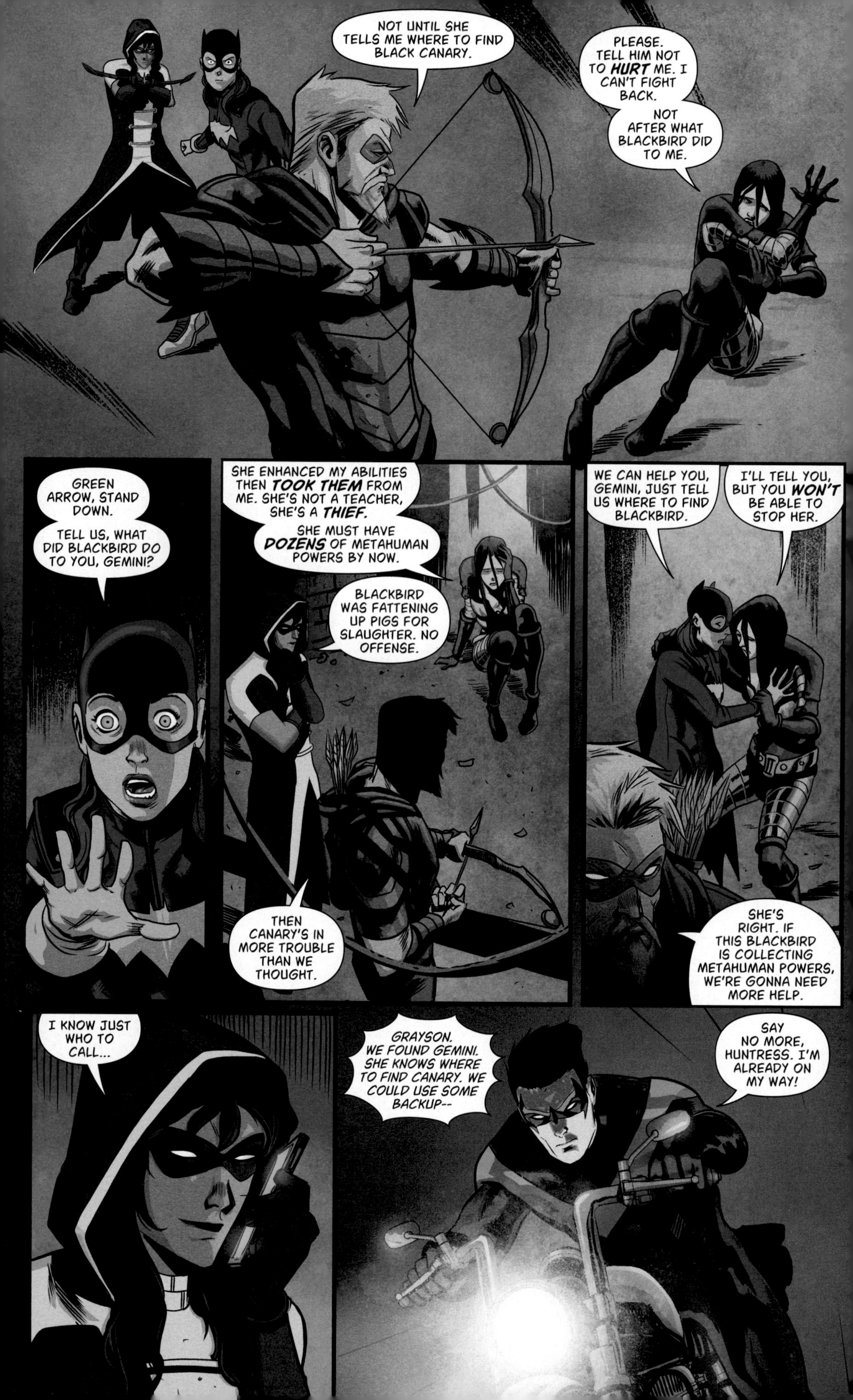
NOT UNTIL SHE TELLS ME WHERE TO FIND BLACK CANARY.
PLEASE. TELL HIM NOT TO HURT ME. I CAN'T FIGHT BACK.
NOT AFTER WHAT BLACKBIRD DID TO ME.
GREEN ARROW, STAND DOWN.
TELL US, WHAT DID BLACKBIRD DO TO YOU, GEMINI?
SHE ENHANCED MY ABILITIES THEN TOOK THEM FROM ME. SHE'S NOT A TEACHER, SHE'S A THIEF.
SHE MUST HAVE DOZENS OF METAHUMAN POWERS BY NOW.
BLACKBIRD WAS FATTENING UP PIGS FOR SLAUGHTER. NO OFFENSE.
THEN CANARY'S IN MORE TROUBLE THAN WE THOUGHT.
WE CAN HELP YOU, GEMINI, JUST TELL US WHERE TO FIND BLACKBIRD.
I'LL TELL YOU, BUT YOU WON'T BE ABLE TO STOP HER.
SHE'S RIGHT. IF THIS BLACKBIRD IS COLLECTING METAHUMAN POWERS, WE'RE GONNA NEED MORE HELP.
I KNOW JUST WHO TO CALL...
GRAYSON. WE FOUND GEMINI. SHE KNOWS WHERE TO FIND CANARY. WE COULD USE SOME BACKUP--
SAY NO MORE, HUNTRESS. I'M ALREADY ON MY WAY!

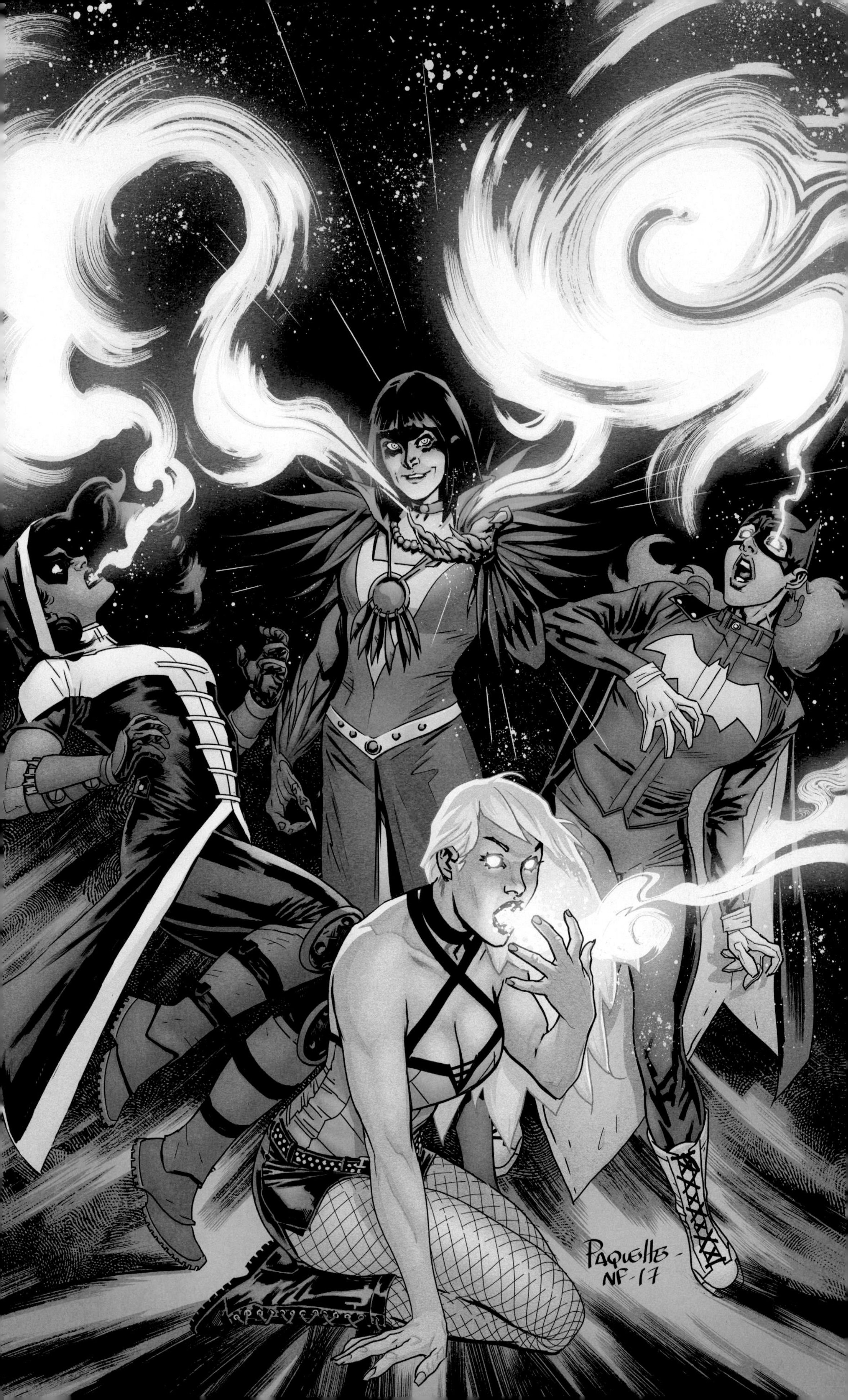
Paquette NF-17

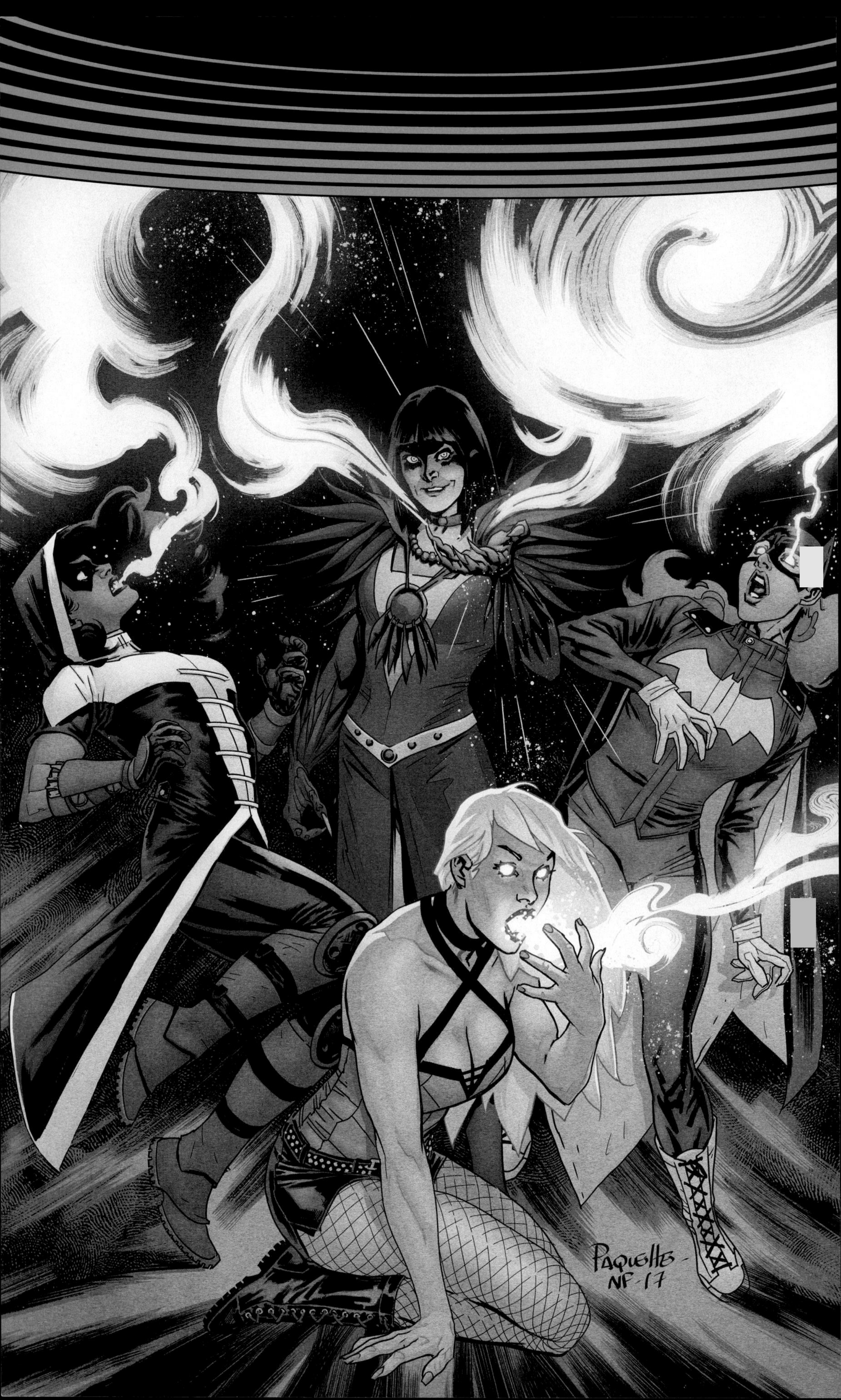
PAQUETTE NF-17

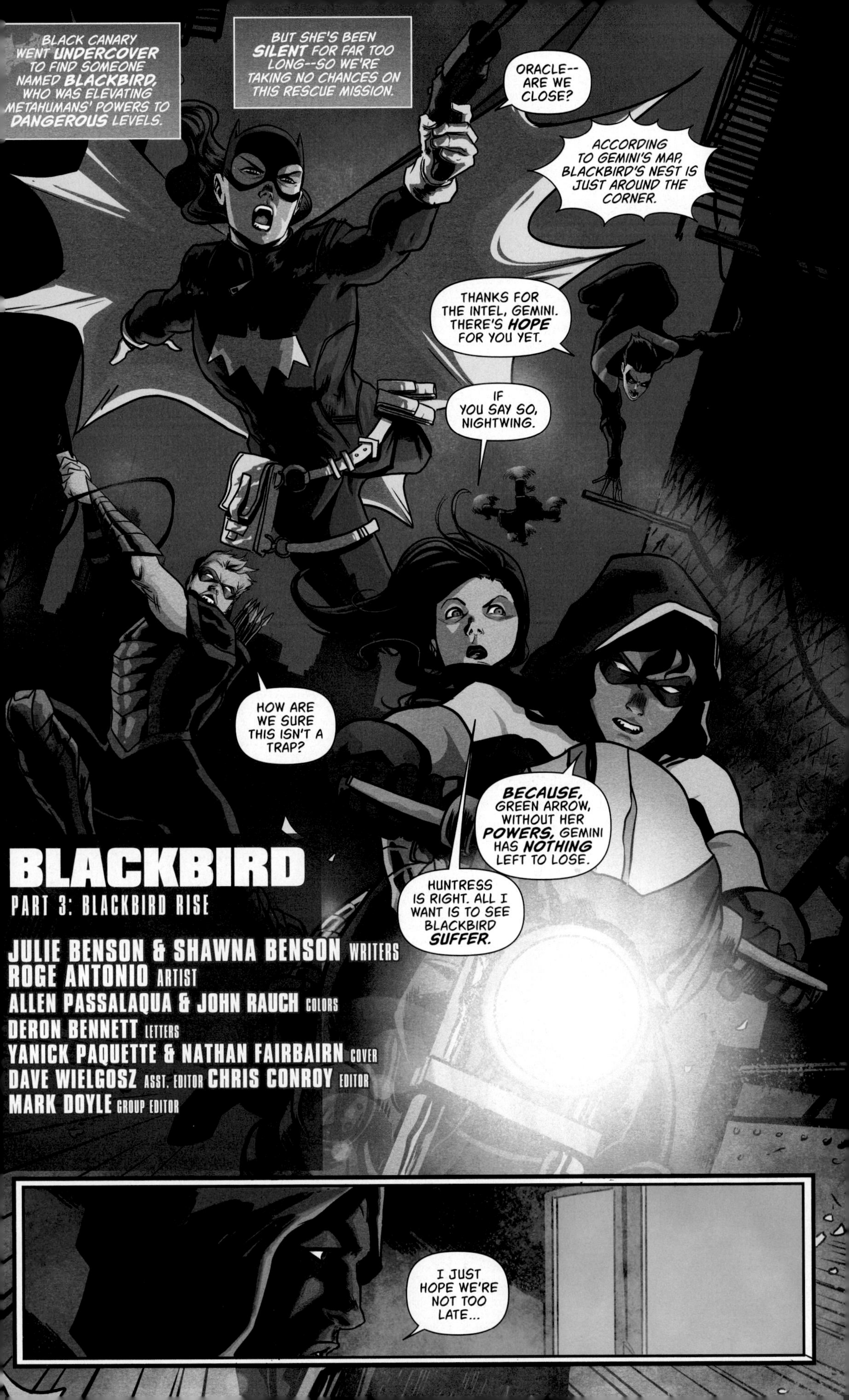
BLACK CANARY WENT UNDERCOVER TO FIND SOMEONE NAMED BLACKBIRD, WHO WAS ELEVATING METAHUMANS' POWERS TO DANGEROUS LEVELS.
BUT SHE'S BEEN SILENT FOR FAR TOO LONG--SO WE'RE TAKING NO CHANCES ON THIS RESCUE MISSION.
ORACLE-- ARE WE CLOSE?
ACCORDING TO GEMINI'S MAP, BLACKBIRD'S NEST IS JUST AROUND THE CORNER.
THANKS FOR THE INTEL, GEMINI. THERE'S HOPE FOR YOU YET.
IF YOU SAY SO, NIGHTWING.
HOW ARE WE SURE THIS ISN'T A TRAP?
BECAUSE, GREEN ARROW, WITHOUT HER POWERS, GEMINI HAS NOTHING LEFT TO LOSE.
HUNTRESS IS RIGHT. ALL I WANT IS TO SEE BLACKBIRD SUFFER.
BLACKBIRD
PART 3: BLACKBIRD RISE
JULIE BENSON & SHAWNA BENSON WRITERS
ROGE ANTONIO ARTIST
ALLEN PASSALAQUA & JOHN RAUCH COLORS
DERON BENNETT LETTERS
YANICK PAQUETTE & NATHAN FAIRBAIRN COVER
DAVE WIELGOSZ ASST. EDITOR CHRIS CONROY EDITOR
MARK DOYLE GROUP EDITOR
I JUST HOPE WE'RE NOT TOO LATE...

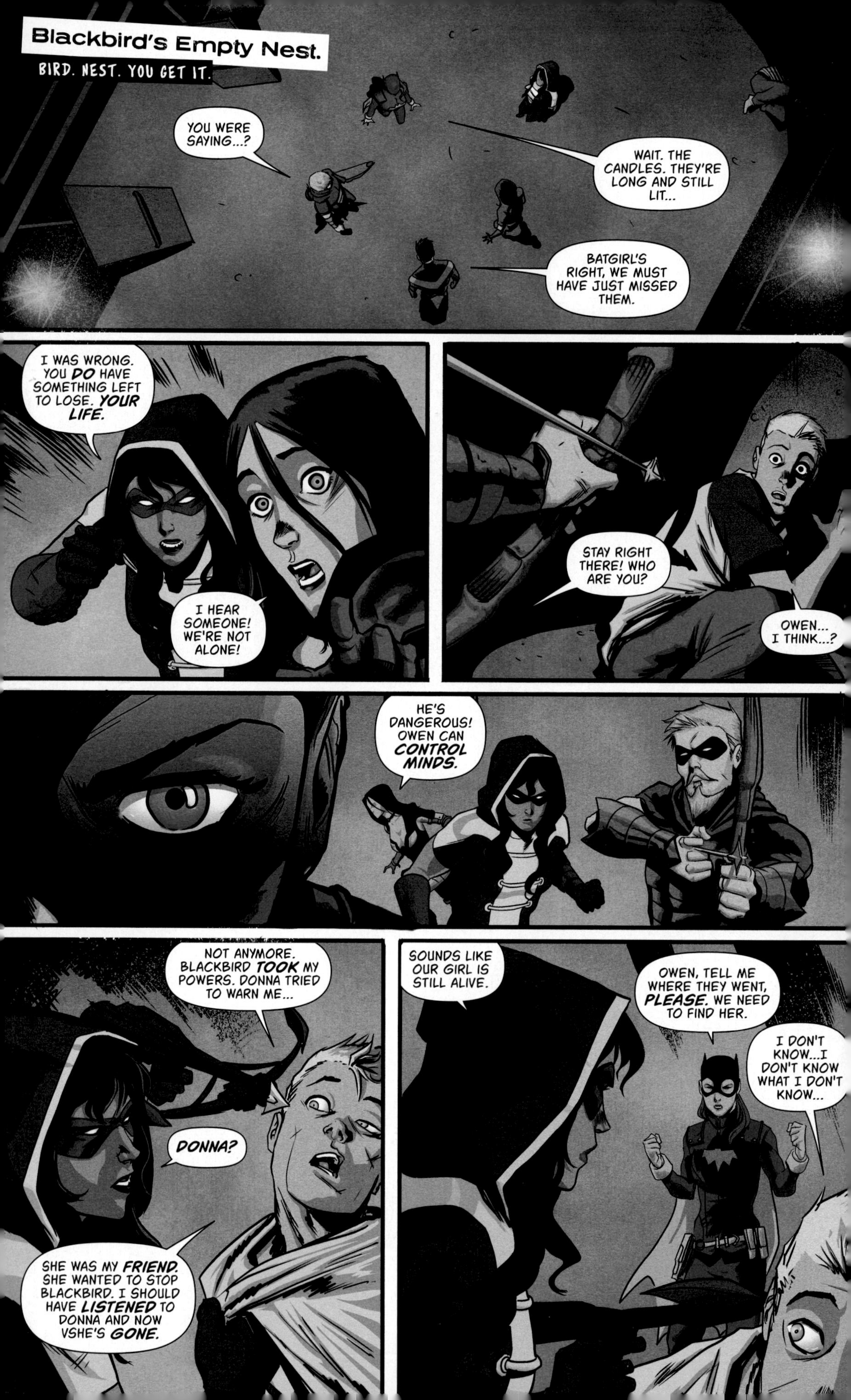
Blackbird's Empty Nest.
BIRD. NEST. YOU GET IT.
YOU WERE SAYING...?
WAIT. THE CANDLES. THEY'RE LONG AND STILL LIT...
BATGIRL'S RIGHT, WE MUST HAVE JUST MISSED THEM.
I WAS WRONG. YOU DO HAVE SOMETHING LEFT TO LOSE. YOUR LIFE.
I HEAR SOMEONE! WE'RE NOT ALONE!
STAY RIGHT THERE! WHO ARE YOU?
OWEN... I THINK...?
HE'S DANGEROUS! OWEN CAN CONTROL MINDS.
NOT ANYMORE. BLACKBIRD TOOK MY POWERS. DONNA TRIED TO WARN ME...
DONNA?
SHE WAS MY FRIEND. SHE WANTED TO STOP BLACKBIRD. I SHOULD HAVE LISTENED TO DONNA AND NOW VSHE'S GONE.
SOUNDS LIKE OUR GIRL IS STILL ALIVE.
OWEN, TELL ME WHERE THEY WENT, PLEASE. WE NEED TO FIND HER.
I DON'T KNOW...I DON'T KNOW WHAT I DON'T KNOW...

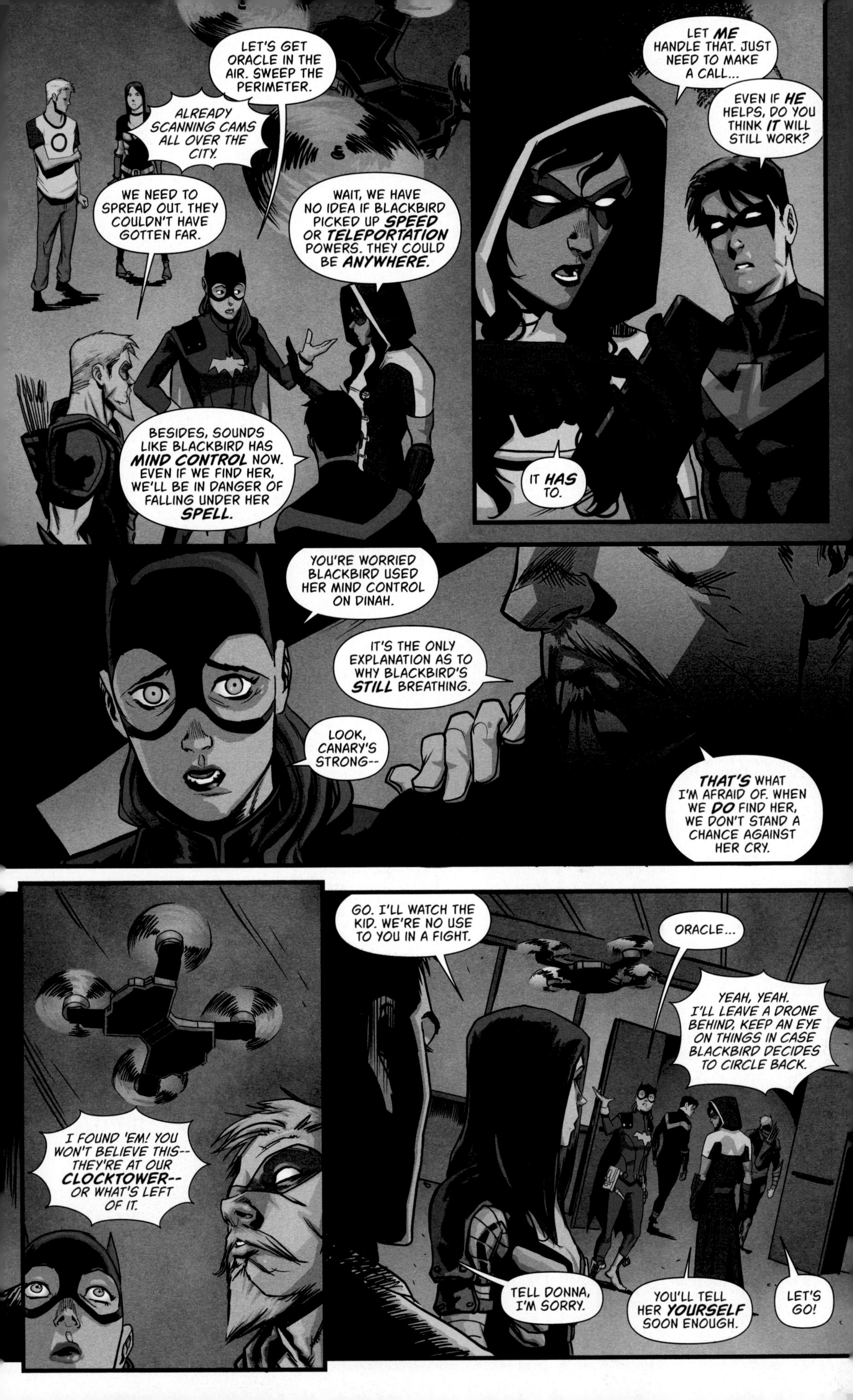

LET'S GET ORACLE IN THE AIR. SWEEP THE PERIMETER.
ALREADY SCANNING CAMS ALL OVER THE CITY.
WE NEED TO SPREAD OUT. THEY COULDN'T HAVE GOTTEN FAR.
WAIT, WE HAVE NO IDEA IF BLACKBIRD PICKED UP SPEED OR TELEPORTATION POWERS. THEY COULD BE ANYWHERE.
BESIDES, SOUNDS LIKE BLACKBIRD HAS MIND CONTROL NOW. EVEN IF WE FIND HER, WE'LL BE IN DANGER OF FALLING UNDER HER SPELL.
LET ME HANDLE THAT. JUST NEED TO MAKE A CALL...
EVEN IF HE HELPS, DO YOU THINK IT WILL STILL WORK?
IT HAS TO.
YOU'RE WORRIED BLACKBIRD USED HER MIND CONTROL ON DINAH.
IT'S THE ONLY EXPLANATION AS TO WHY BLACKBIRD'S STILL BREATHING.
LOOK, CANARY'S STRONG--
THAT'S WHAT I'M AFRAID OF. WHEN WE DO FIND HER, WE DON'T STAND A CHANCE AGAINST HER CRY.
I FOUND 'EM! YOU WON'T BELIEVE THIS-- THEY'RE AT OUR CLOCKTOWER-- OR WHAT'S LEFT OF IT.
GO. I'LL WATCH THE KID. WE'RE NO USE TO YOU IN A FIGHT.
ORACLE...
YEAH, YEAH. I'LL LEAVE A DRONE BEHIND, KEEP AN EYE ON THINGS IN CASE BLACKBIRD DECIDES TO CIRCLE BACK.
TELL DONNA, I'M SORRY.
YOU'LL TELL HER YOURSELF SOON ENOUGH.
LET'S GO!

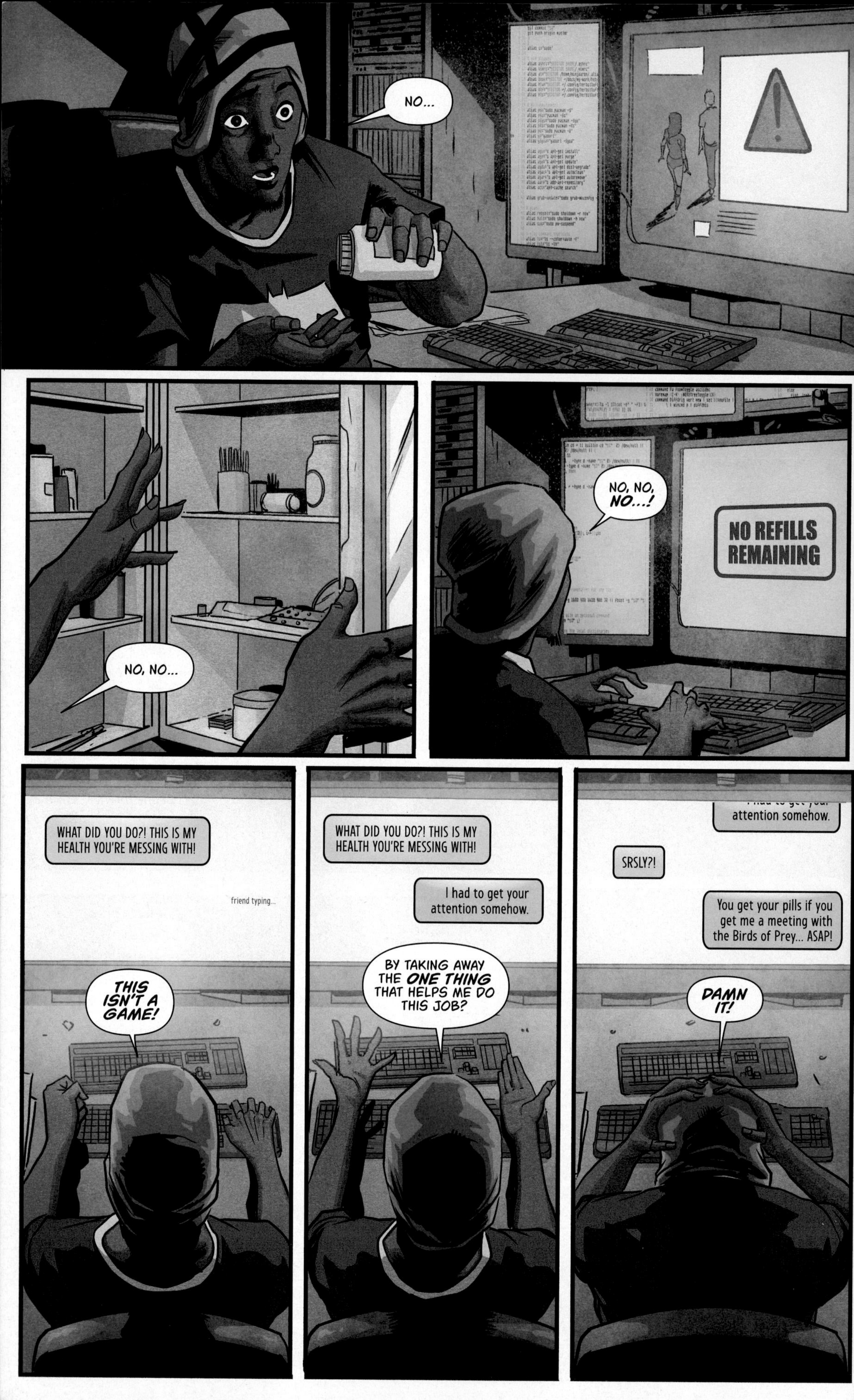
NO...
NO, NO...
NO, NO, NO...!
NO REFILLS REMAINING
WHAT DID YOU DO?! THIS IS MY HEALTH YOU'RE MESSING WITH!
friend typing...
THIS ISN'T A GAME!
WHAT DID YOU DO?! THIS IS MY HEALTH YOU'RE MESSING WITH!
I had to get your attention somehow.
BY TAKING AWAY THE ONE THING THAT HELPS ME DO THIS JOB?
attention somehow.
SRSLY?!
You get your pills if you get me a meeting with the Birds of Prey... ASAP!
DAMN IT!

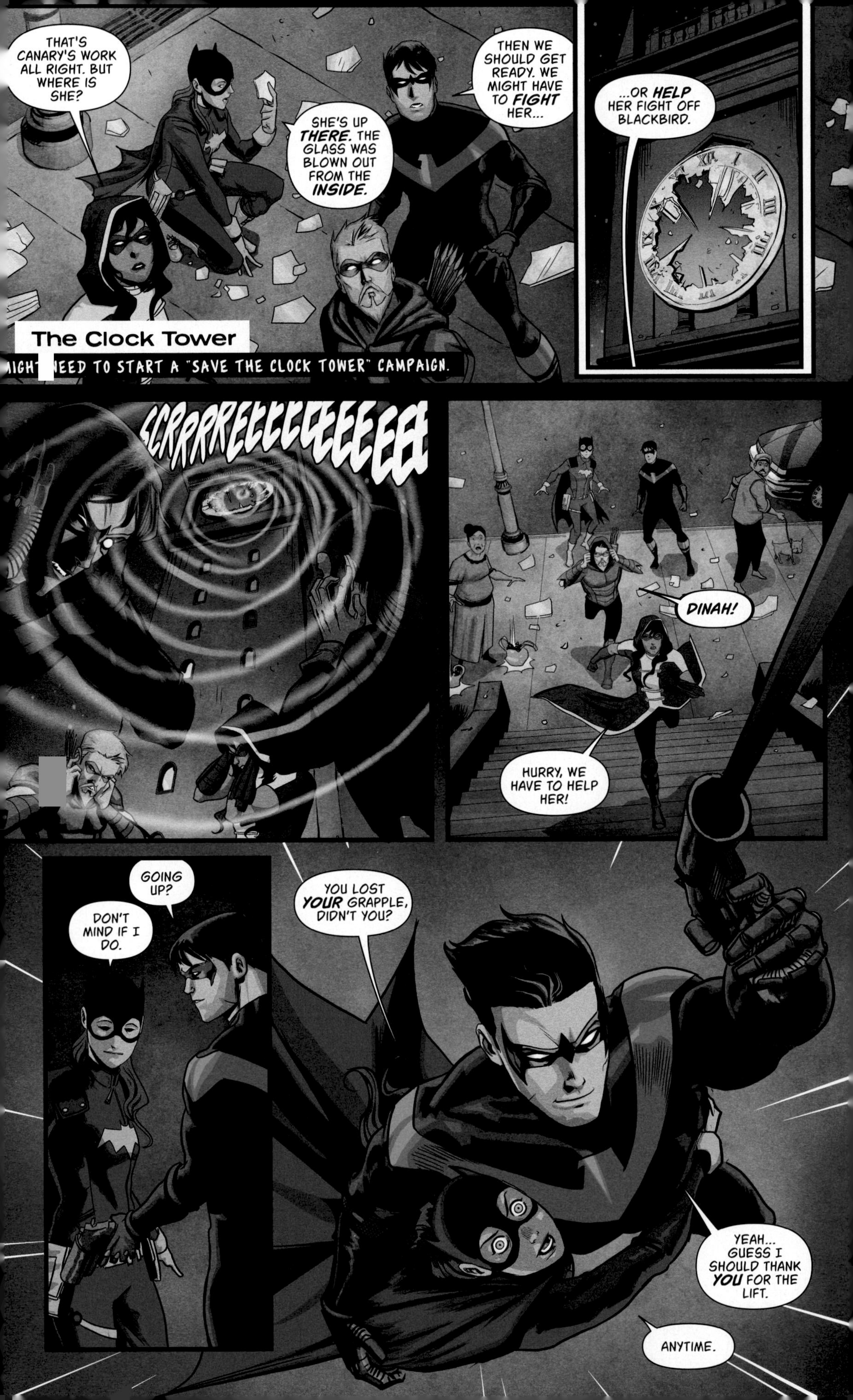

THAT'S CANARY'S WORK ALL RIGHT. BUT WHERE IS SHE?
SHE'S UP **THERE.** THE GLASS WAS BLOWN OUT FROM THE **INSIDE.**
THEN WE SHOULD GET READY. WE MIGHT HAVE TO **FIGHT** HER...
The Clock Tower
IGHT EED TO START A "SAVE THE CLOCK TOWER" CAMPAIGN.
...OR **HELP** HER FIGHT OFF BLACKBIRD.
SCRRRREEEEEEEEEEE
DINAH!
HURRY, WE HAVE TO HELP HER!
GOING UP?
DON'T MIND IF I DO.
YOU LOST **YOUR** GRAPPLE, DIDN'T YOU?
YEAH... GUESS I SHOULD THANK **YOU** FOR THE LIFT.
ANYTIME.

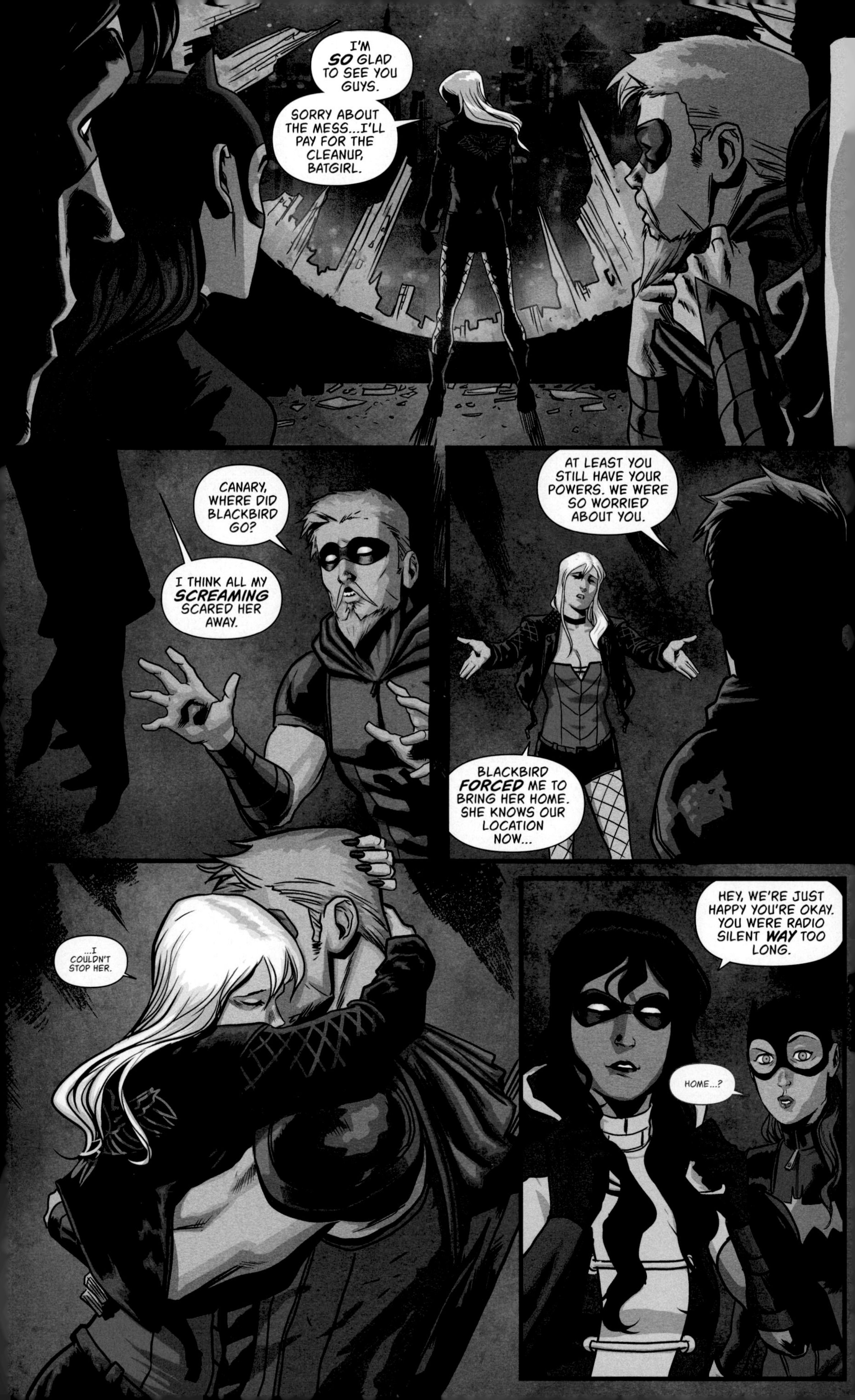
I'M SO GLAD TO SEE YOU GUYS.
SORRY ABOUT THE MESS...I'LL PAY FOR THE CLEANUP, BATGIRL.
CANARY, WHERE DID BLACKBIRD GO?
I THINK ALL MY SCREAMING SCARED HER AWAY.
AT LEAST YOU STILL HAVE YOUR POWERS. WE WERE SO WORRIED ABOUT YOU.
BLACKBIRD FORCED ME TO BRING HER HOME. SHE KNOWS OUR LOCATION NOW...
...I COULDN'T STOP HER.
HEY, WE'RE JUST HAPPY YOU'RE OKAY. YOU WERE RADIO SILENT WAY TOO LONG.
HOME...?

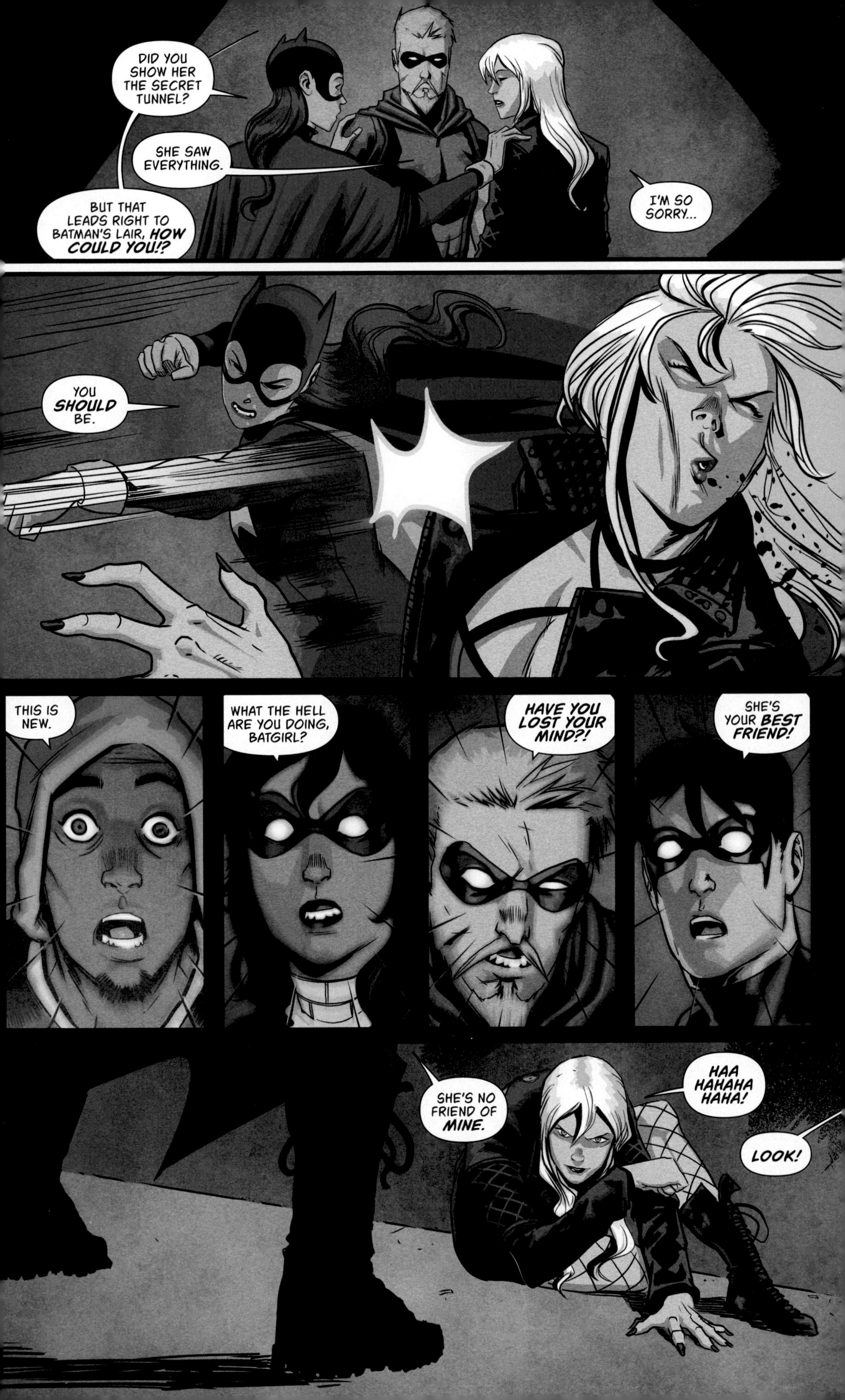
DID YOU SHOW HER THE SECRET TUNNEL?
SHE SAW EVERYTHING.
BUT THAT LEADS RIGHT TO BATMAN'S LAIR, HOW COULD YOU!?
I'M SO SORRY...
YOU SHOULD BE.
THIS IS NEW.
WHAT THE HELL ARE YOU DOING, BATGIRL?
HAVE YOU LOST YOUR MIND?!
SHE'S YOUR BEST FRIEND!
SHE'S NO FRIEND OF MINE.
HAA HAHAHA HAHA!
LOOK!

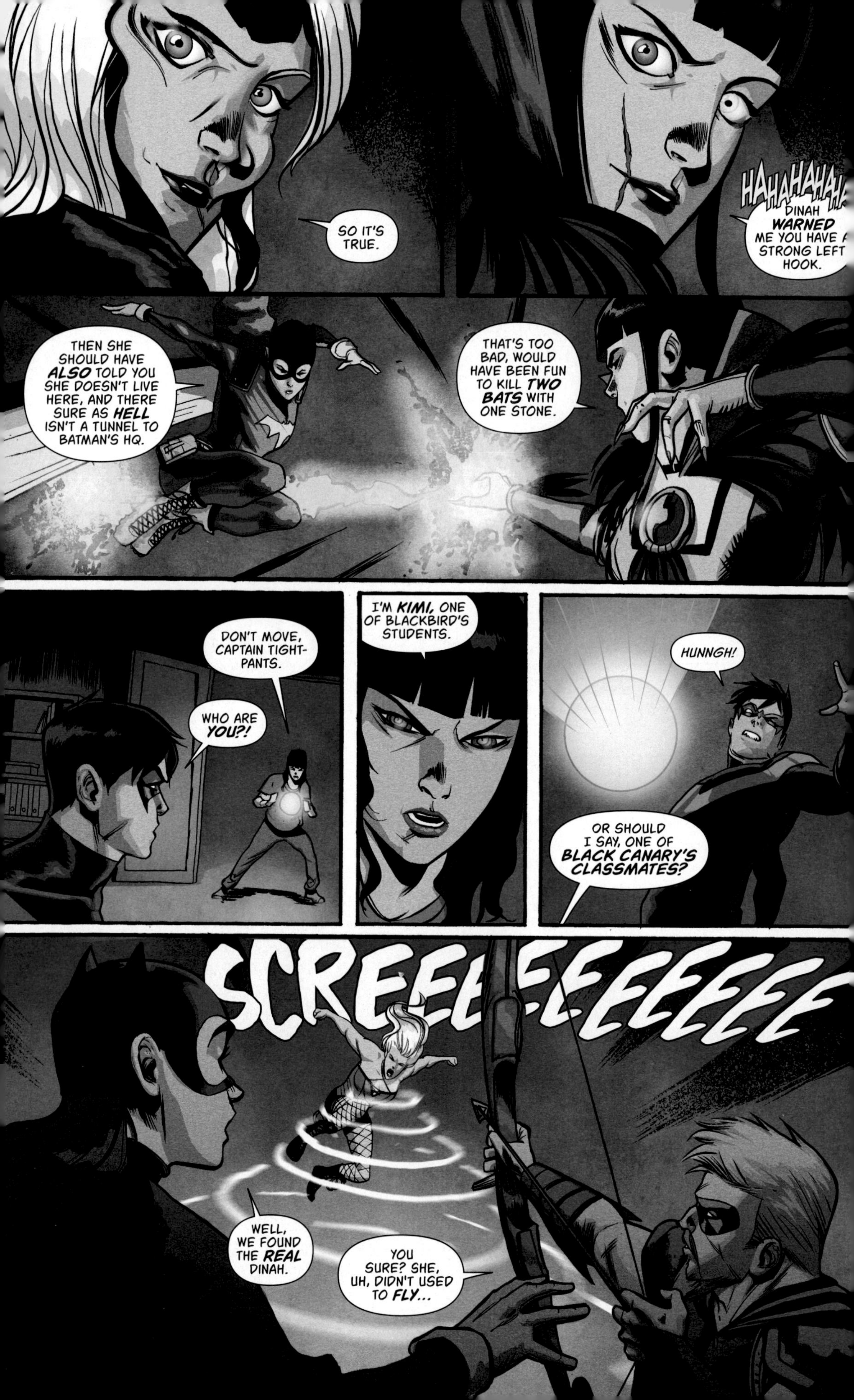
SO IT'S TRUE.
HAHAHAHAHAHA
DINAH WARNED ME YOU HAVE A STRONG LEFT HOOK.
THEN SHE SHOULD HAVE ALSO TOLD YOU SHE DOESN'T LIVE HERE, AND THERE SURE AS HELL ISN'T A TUNNEL TO BATMAN'S HQ.
THAT'S TOO BAD, WOULD HAVE BEEN FUN TO KILL TWO BATS WITH ONE STONE.
DON'T MOVE, CAPTAIN TIGHT-PANTS.
WHO ARE YOU?!
I'M KIMI, ONE OF BLACKBIRD'S STUDENTS.
HUNNGH!
OR SHOULD I SAY, ONE OF BLACK CANARY'S CLASSMATES?
SCREEEEEEEEEEE
WELL, WE FOUND THE REAL DINAH.
YOU SURE? SHE, UH, DIDN'T USED TO FLY...

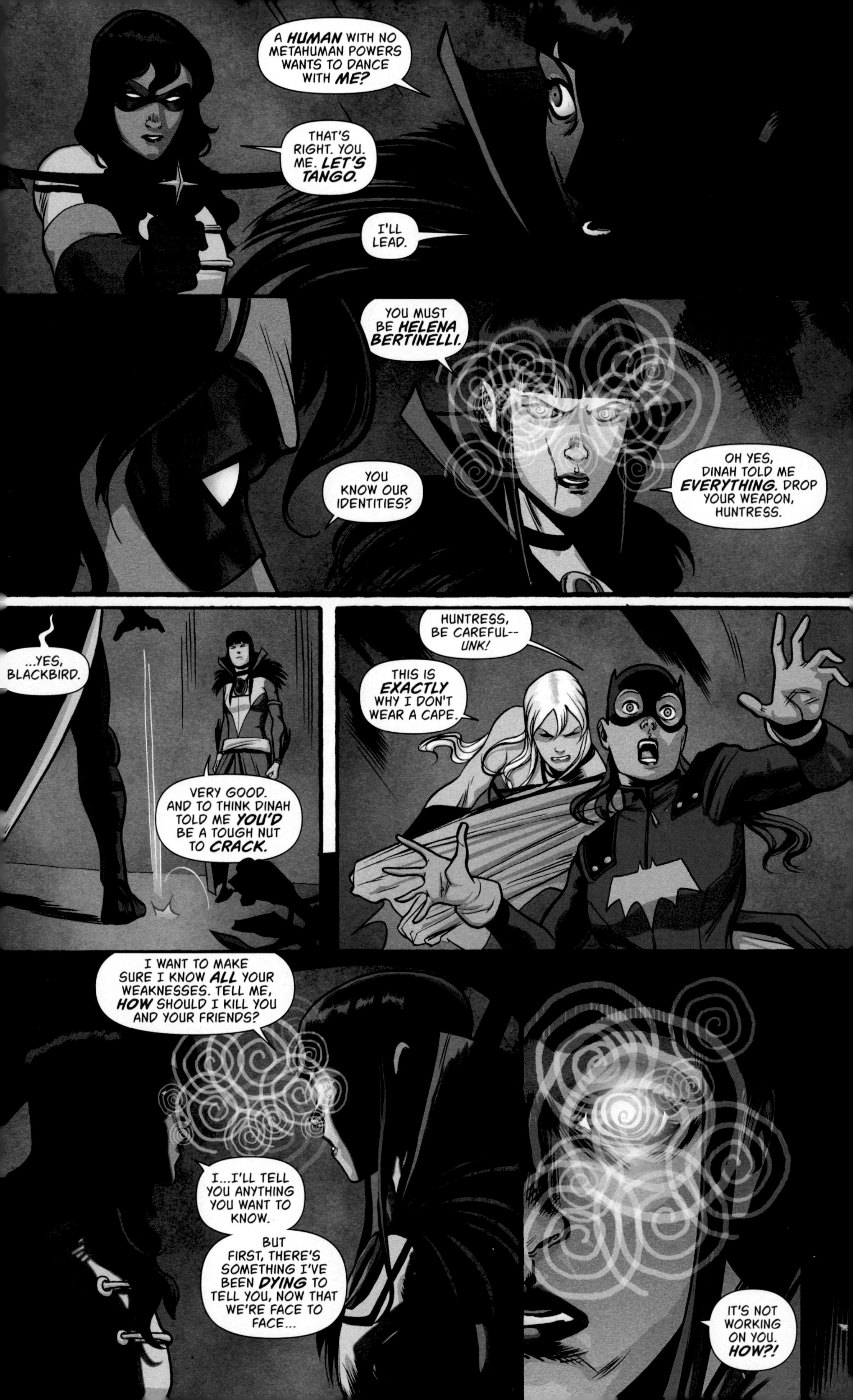

A HUMAN WITH NO METAHUMAN POWERS WANTS TO DANCE WITH ME?
THAT'S RIGHT. YOU. ME. LET'S TANGO.
I'LL LEAD.
YOU MUST BE HELENA BERTINELLI.
YOU KNOW OUR IDENTITIES?
OH YES, DINAH TOLD ME EVERYTHING. DROP YOUR WEAPON, HUNTRESS.
...YES, BLACKBIRD.
VERY GOOD. AND TO THINK DINAH TOLD ME YOU'D BE A TOUGH NUT TO CRACK.
HUNTRESS, BE CAREFUL-- UNK!
THIS IS EXACTLY WHY I DON'T WEAR A CAPE.
I WANT TO MAKE SURE I KNOW ALL YOUR WEAKNESSES. TELL ME, HOW SHOULD I KILL YOU AND YOUR FRIENDS?
I...I'LL TELL YOU ANYTHING YOU WANT TO KNOW.
BUT FIRST, THERE'S SOMETHING I'VE BEEN DYING TO TELL YOU, NOW THAT WE'RE FACE TO FACE...
IT'S NOT WORKING ON YOU. HOW?!

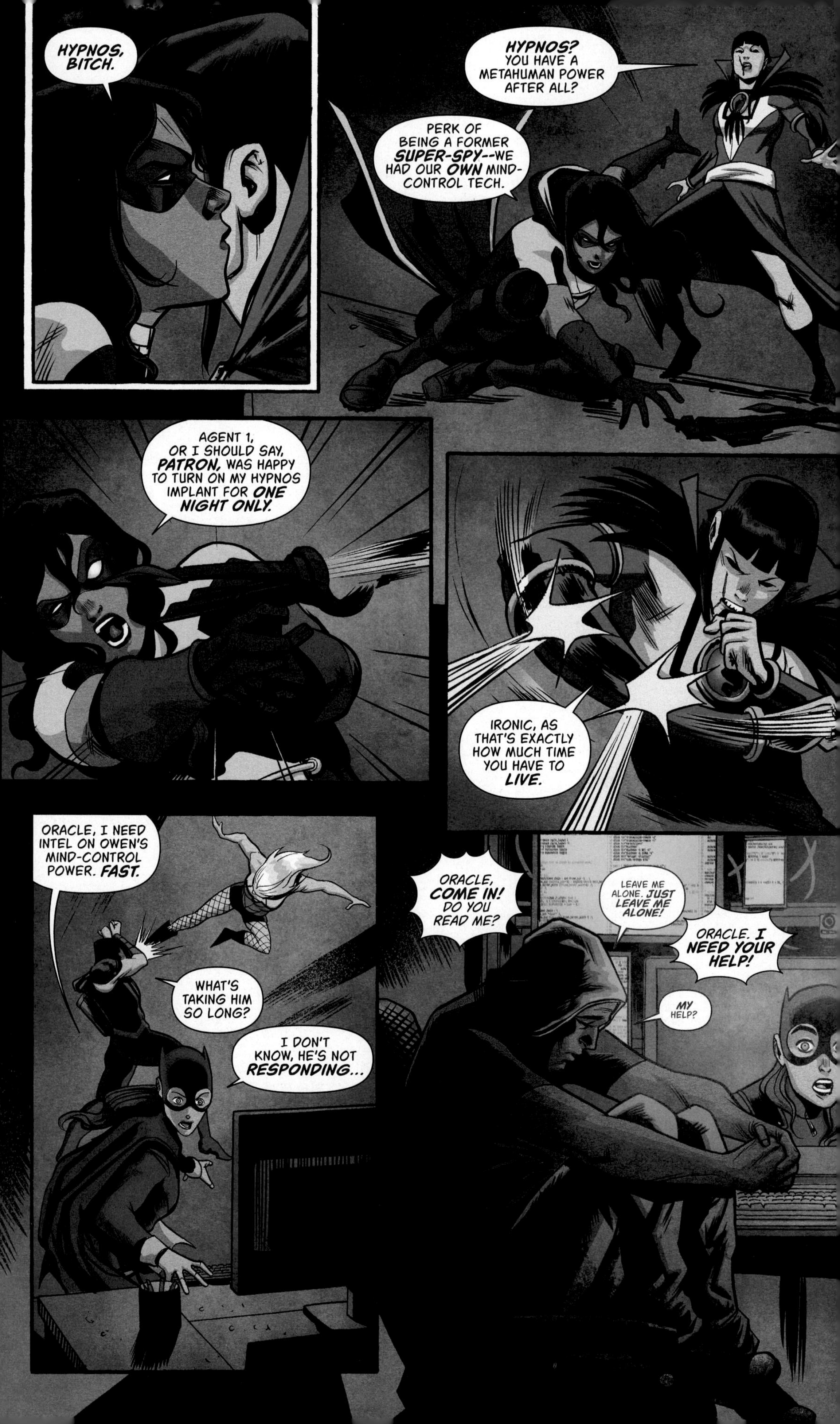
HYPNOS, BITCH.
HYPNOS? YOU HAVE A METAHUMAN POWER AFTER ALL?
PERK OF BEING A FORMER SUPER-SPY--WE HAD OUR OWN MIND-CONTROL TECH.
AGENT 1, OR I SHOULD SAY, PATRON, WAS HAPPY TO TURN ON MY HYPNOS IMPLANT FOR ONE NIGHT ONLY.
IRONIC, AS THAT'S EXACTLY HOW MUCH TIME YOU HAVE TO LIVE.
ORACLE, I NEED INTEL ON OWEN'S MIND-CONTROL POWER. FAST.
WHAT'S TAKING HIM SO LONG?
I DON'T KNOW, HE'S NOT RESPONDING...
ORACLE, COME IN! DO YOU READ ME?
LEAVE ME ALONE. JUST LEAVE ME ALONE!
ORACLE. I NEED YOUR HELP!
MY HELP?

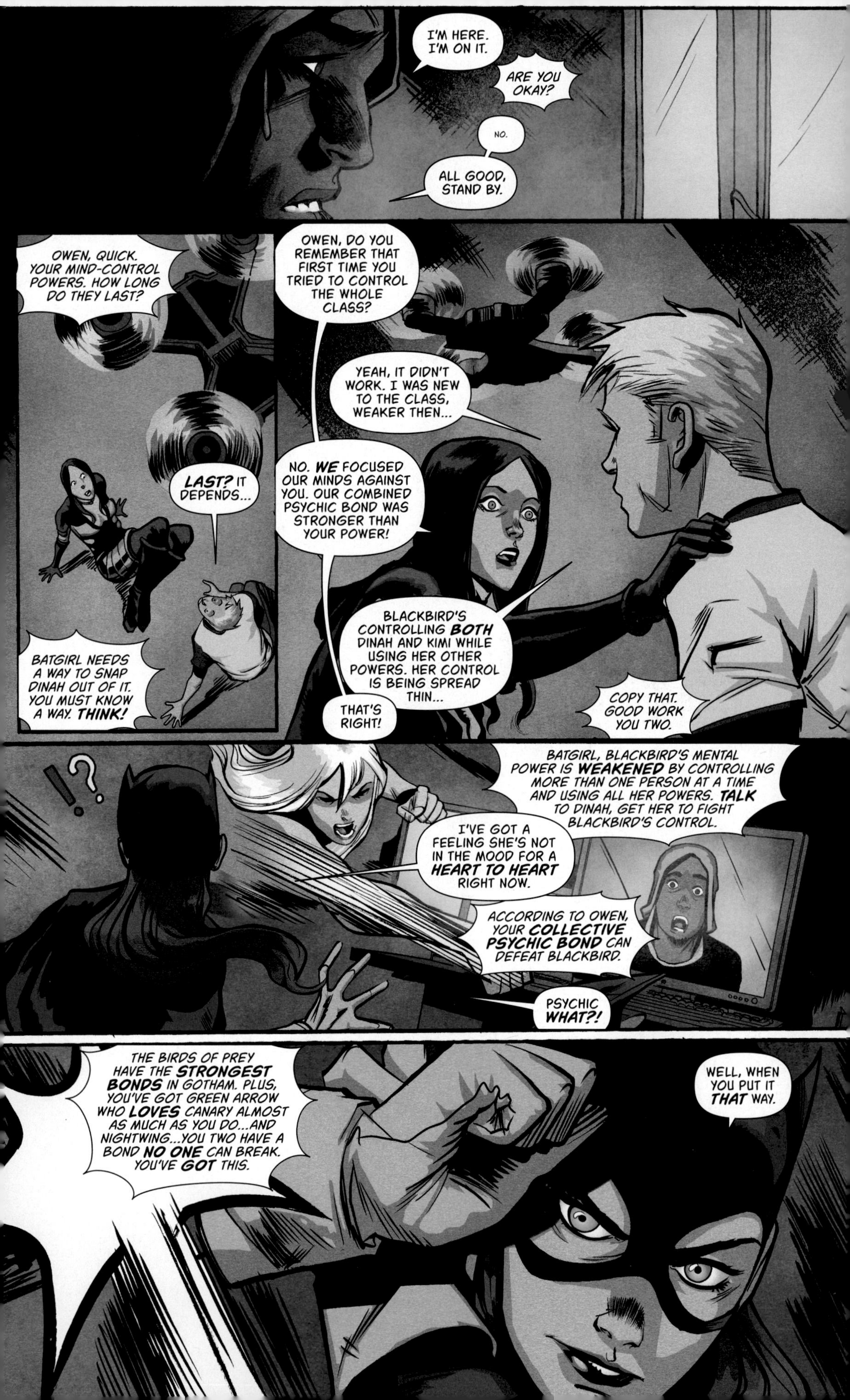

I'M HERE. I'M ON IT.
ARE YOU OKAY?
NO.
ALL GOOD, STAND BY.
OWEN, QUICK. YOUR MIND-CONTROL POWERS. HOW LONG DO THEY LAST?
LAST? IT DEPENDS...
BATGIRL NEEDS A WAY TO SNAP DINAH OUT OF IT. YOU MUST KNOW A WAY. THINK!
OWEN, DO YOU REMEMBER THAT FIRST TIME YOU TRIED TO CONTROL THE WHOLE CLASS?
YEAH, IT DIDN'T WORK. I WAS NEW TO THE CLASS, WEAKER THEN...
NO. WE FOCUSED OUR MINDS AGAINST YOU. OUR COMBINED PSYCHIC BOND WAS STRONGER THAN YOUR POWER!
THAT'S RIGHT!
BLACKBIRD'S CONTROLLING BOTH DINAH AND KIMI WHILE USING HER OTHER POWERS. HER CONTROL IS BEING SPREAD THIN...
COPY THAT. GOOD WORK YOU TWO.
!?
BATGIRL, BLACKBIRD'S MENTAL POWER IS WEAKENED BY CONTROLLING MORE THAN ONE PERSON AT A TIME AND USING ALL HER POWERS. TALK TO DINAH, GET HER TO FIGHT BLACKBIRD'S CONTROL.
I'VE GOT A FEELING SHE'S NOT IN THE MOOD FOR A HEART TO HEART RIGHT NOW.
ACCORDING TO OWEN, YOUR COLLECTIVE PSYCHIC BOND CAN DEFEAT BLACKBIRD.
PSYCHIC WHAT?!
THE BIRDS OF PREY HAVE THE STRONGEST BONDS IN GOTHAM. PLUS, YOU'VE GOT GREEN ARROW WHO LOVES CANARY ALMOST AS MUCH AS YOU DO...AND NIGHTWING...YOU TWO HAVE A BOND NO ONE CAN BREAK. YOU'VE GOT THIS.
WELL, WHEN YOU PUT IT THAT WAY.

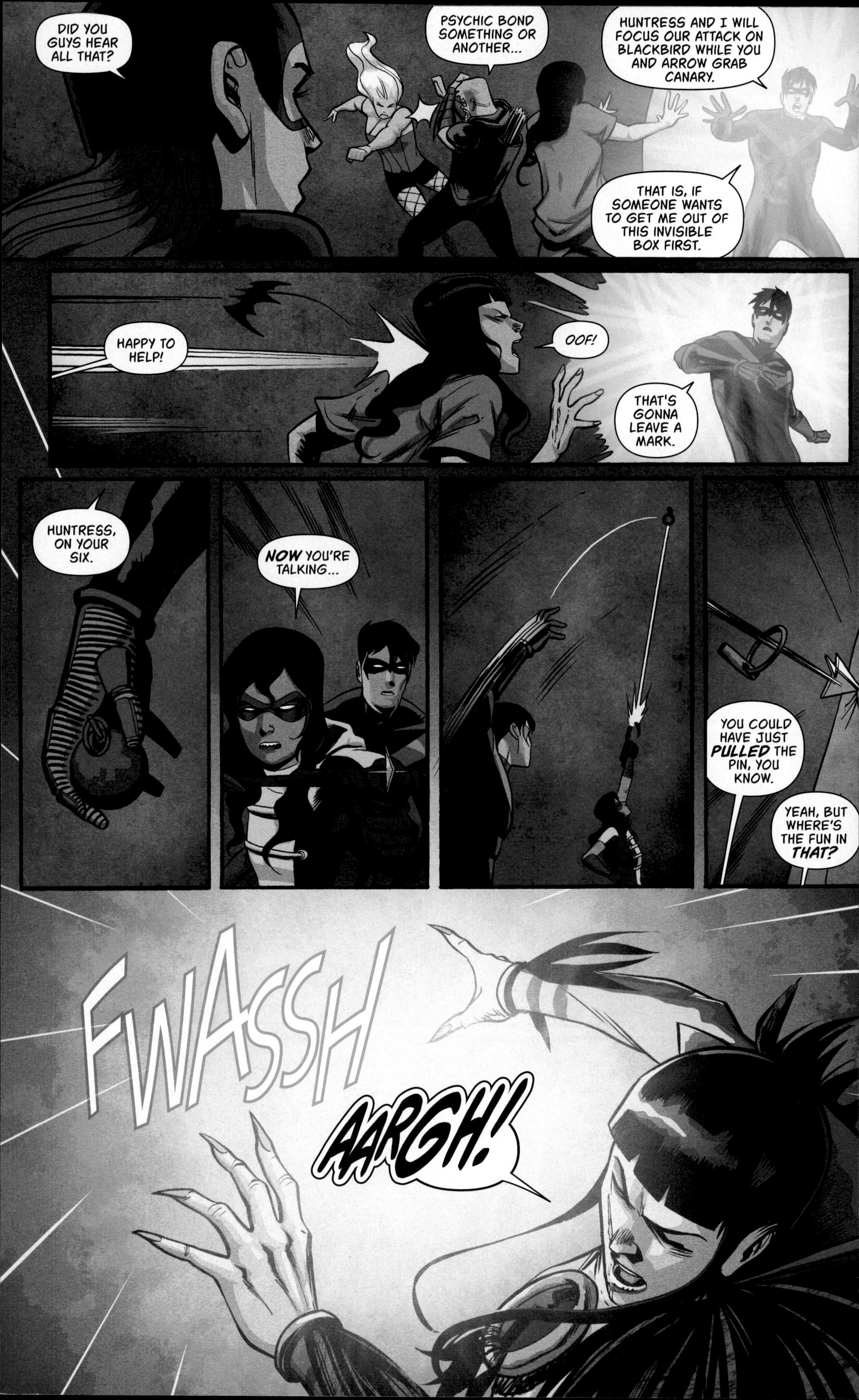
DID YOU GUYS HEAR ALL THAT?
PSYCHIC BOND SOMETHING OR ANOTHER...
HUNTRESS AND I WILL FOCUS OUR ATTACK ON BLACKBIRD WHILE YOU AND ARROW GRAB CANARY.
THAT IS, IF SOMEONE WANTS TO GET ME OUT OF THIS INVISIBLE BOX FIRST.
HAPPY TO HELP!
OOF!
THAT'S GONNA LEAVE A MARK.
HUNTRESS, ON YOUR SIX.
NOW YOU'RE TALKING...
YOU COULD HAVE JUST PULLED THE PIN, YOU KNOW.
YEAH, BUT WHERE'S THE FUN IN THAT?
FWASSH
AARGH!

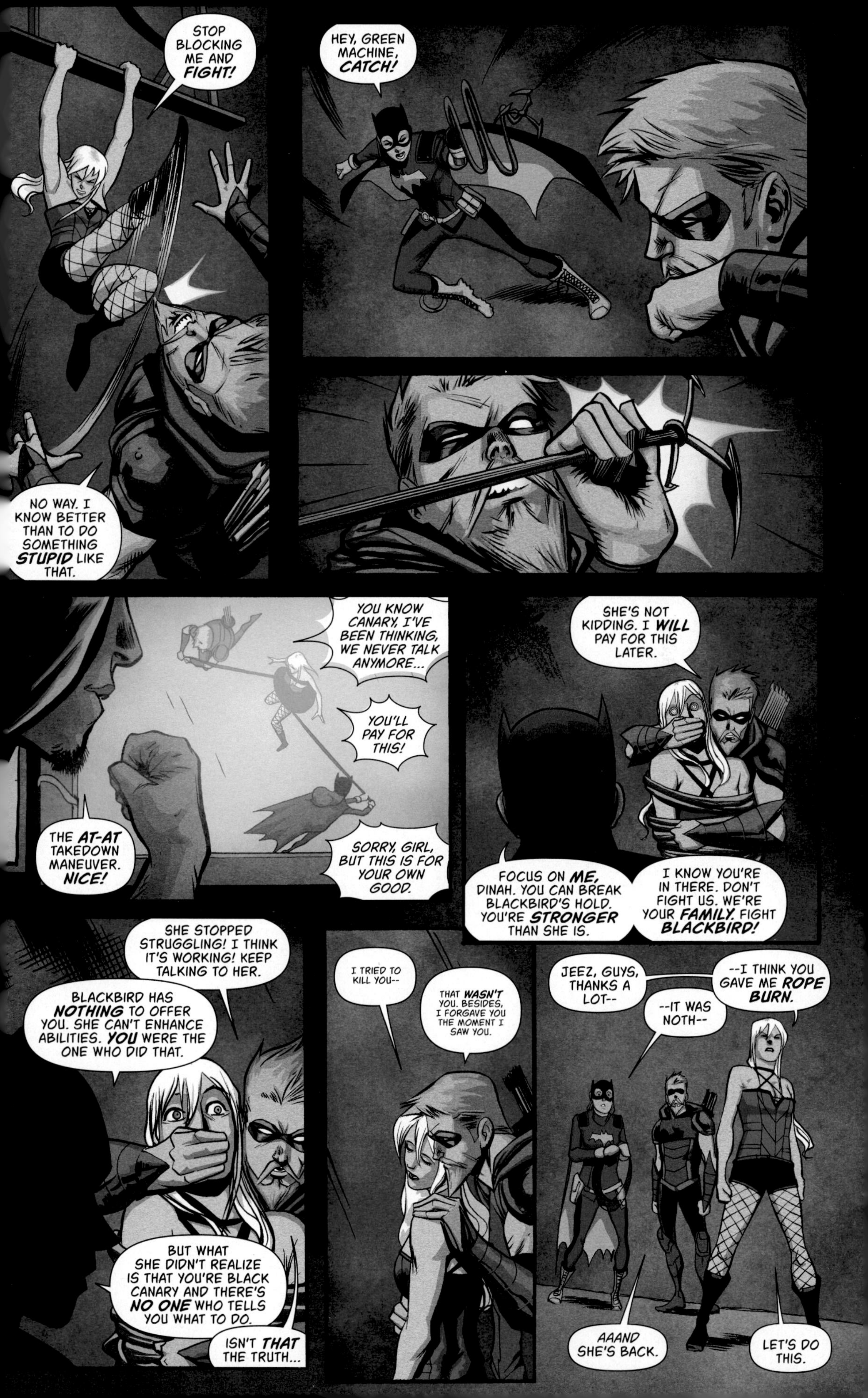
STOP BLOCKING ME AND FIGHT!
NO WAY. I KNOW BETTER THAN TO DO SOMETHING STUPID LIKE THAT.
HEY, GREEN MACHINE, CATCH!
YOU KNOW CANARY, I'VE BEEN THINKING, WE NEVER TALK ANYMORE...
YOU'LL PAY FOR THIS!
THE AT-AT TAKEDOWN MANEUVER. NICE!
SORRY, GIRL, BUT THIS IS FOR YOUR OWN GOOD.
SHE'S NOT KIDDING. I WILL PAY FOR THIS LATER.
FOCUS ON ME, DINAH. YOU CAN BREAK BLACKBIRD'S HOLD. YOU'RE STRONGER THAN SHE IS.
I KNOW YOU'RE IN THERE. DON'T FIGHT US. WE'RE YOUR FAMILY. FIGHT BLACKBIRD!
SHE STOPPED STRUGGLING! I THINK IT'S WORKING! KEEP TALKING TO HER.
BLACKBIRD HAS NOTHING TO OFFER YOU. SHE CAN'T ENHANCE ABILITIES. YOU WERE THE ONE WHO DID THAT.
BUT WHAT SHE DIDN'T REALIZE IS THAT YOU'RE BLACK CANARY AND THERE'S NO ONE WHO TELLS YOU WHAT TO DO.
ISN'T THAT THE TRUTH...
I TRIED TO KILL YOU--
THAT WASN'T YOU. BESIDES, I FORGAVE YOU THE MOMENT I SAW YOU.
JEEZ, GUYS, THANKS A LOT--
--IT WAS NOTH--
--I THINK YOU GAVE ME ROPE BURN.
AAAND SHE'S BACK.
LET'S DO THIS.

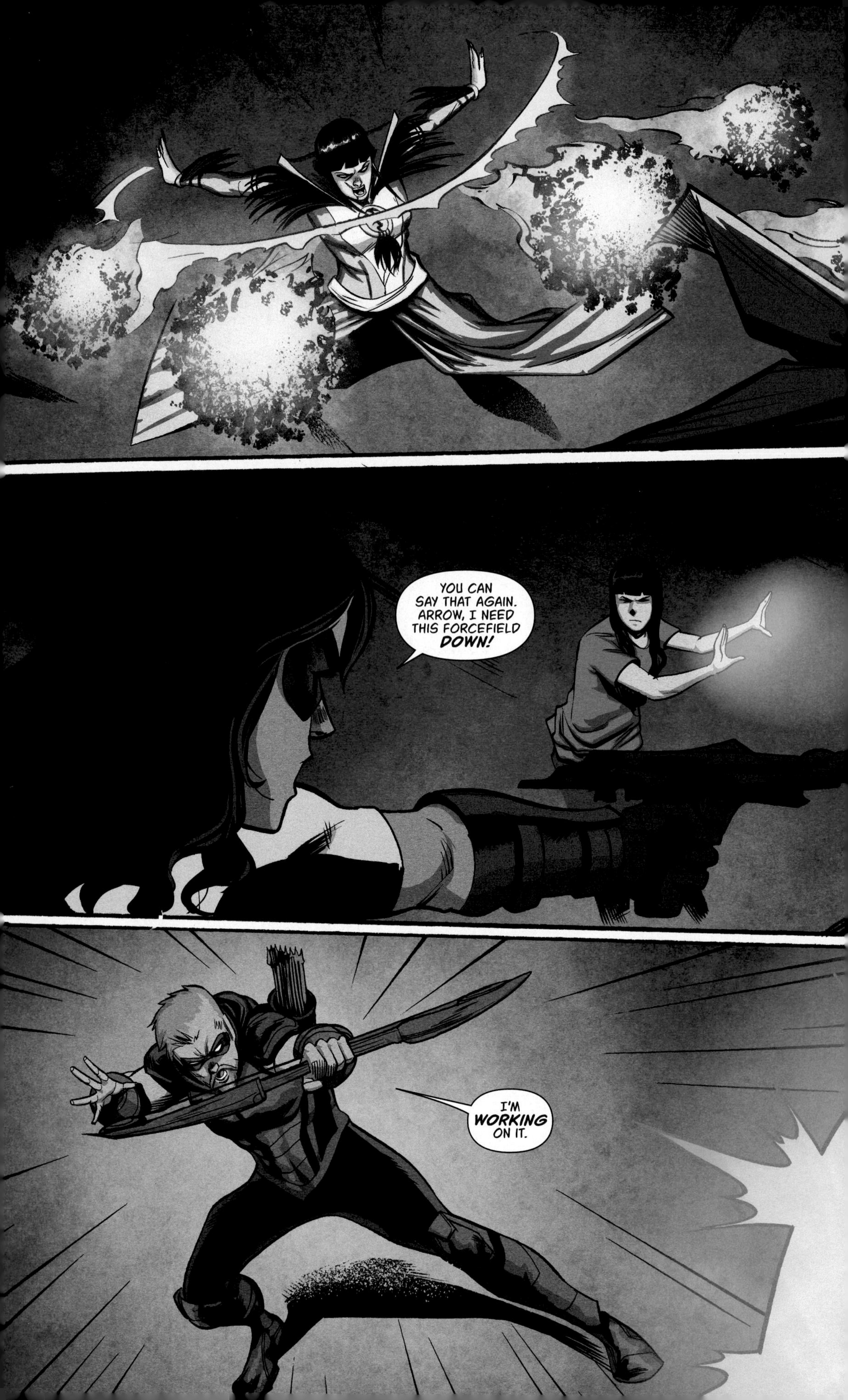
YOU CAN SAY THAT AGAIN. ARROW, I NEED THIS FORCEFIELD DOWN!
I'M WORKING ON IT.

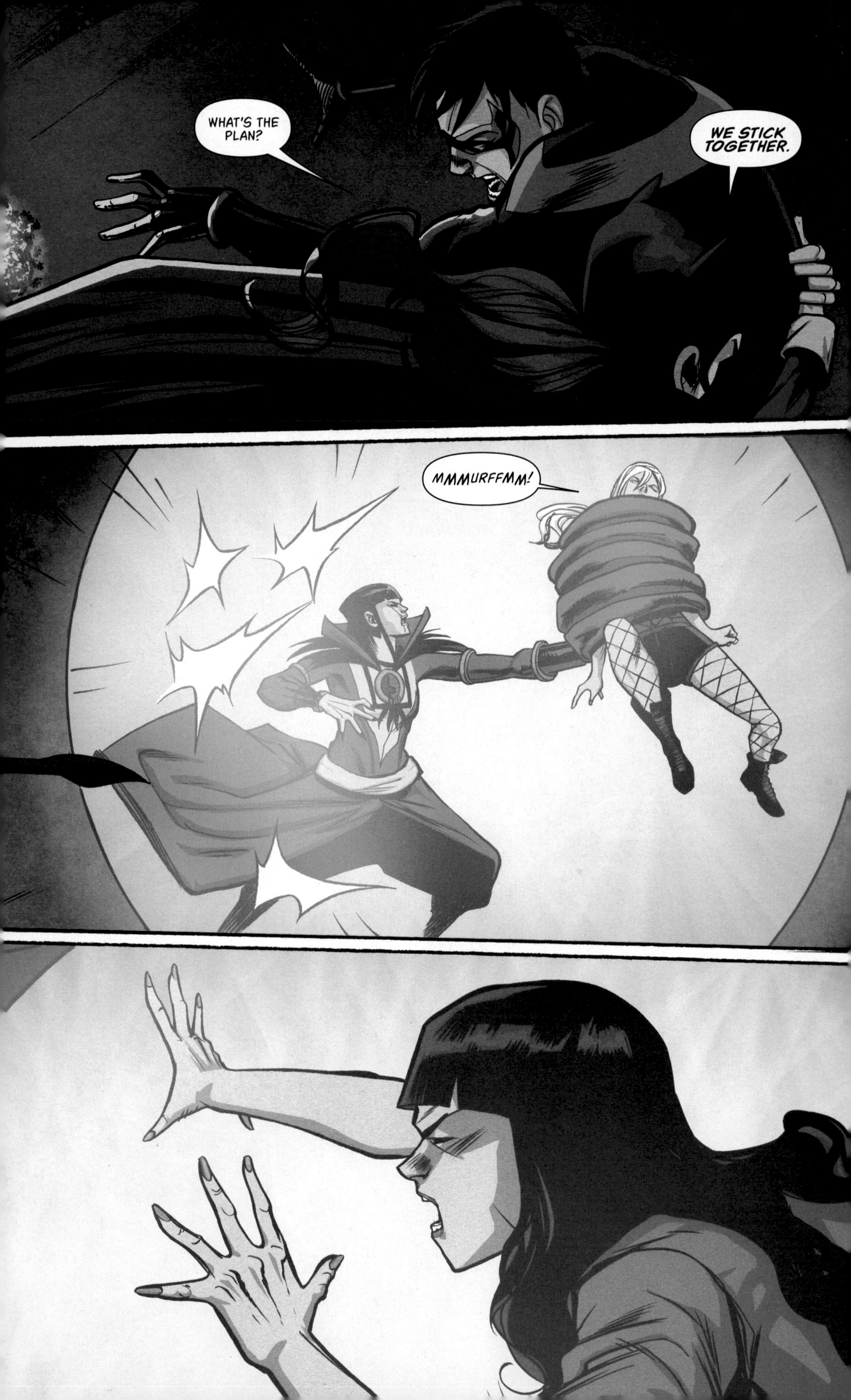
WHAT'S THE PLAN?
WE STICK TOGETHER.
MMMURFFMM!

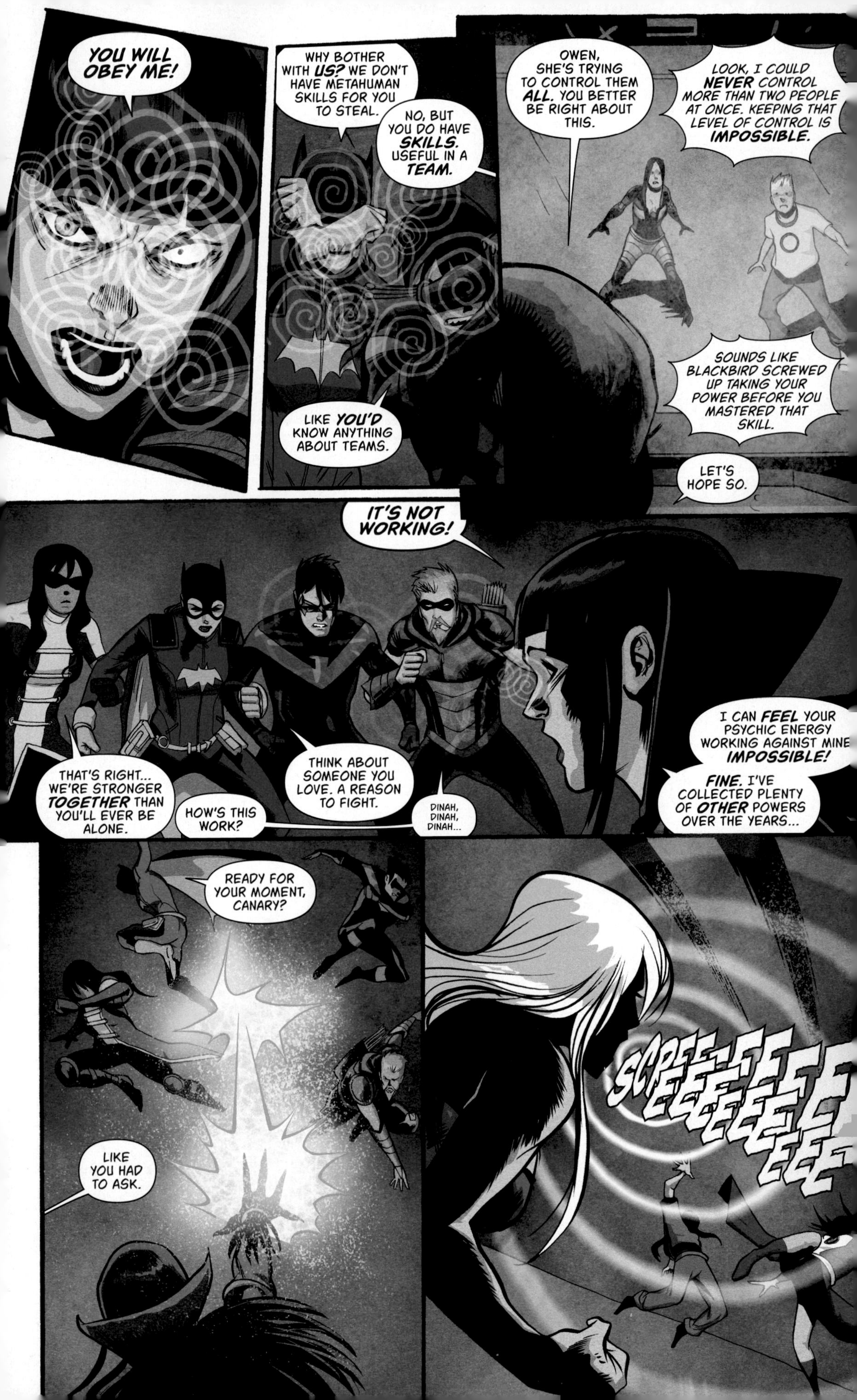

YOU WILL OBEY ME!
WHY BOTHER WITH US? WE DON'T HAVE METAHUMAN SKILLS FOR YOU TO STEAL.
NO, BUT YOU DO HAVE SKILLS. USEFUL IN A TEAM.
LIKE YOU'D KNOW ANYTHING ABOUT TEAMS.
OWEN, SHE'S TRYING TO CONTROL THEM ALL. YOU BETTER BE RIGHT ABOUT THIS.
LOOK, I COULD NEVER CONTROL MORE THAN TWO PEOPLE AT ONCE. KEEPING THAT LEVEL OF CONTROL IS IMPOSSIBLE.
SOUNDS LIKE BLACKBIRD SCREWED UP TAKING YOUR POWER BEFORE YOU MASTERED THAT SKILL.
LET'S HOPE SO.
IT'S NOT WORKING!
THAT'S RIGHT... WE'RE STRONGER TOGETHER THAN YOU'LL EVER BE ALONE.
HOW'S THIS WORK?
THINK ABOUT SOMEONE YOU LOVE. A REASON TO FIGHT.
DINAH, DINAH, DINAH...
I CAN FEEL YOUR PSYCHIC ENERGY WORKING AGAINST MINE. IMPOSSIBLE!
FINE. I'VE COLLECTED PLENTY OF OTHER POWERS OVER THE YEARS...
READY FOR YOUR MOMENT, CANARY?
LIKE YOU HAD TO ASK.
SCREEEEEEEEEEEEEEEEEEEEE

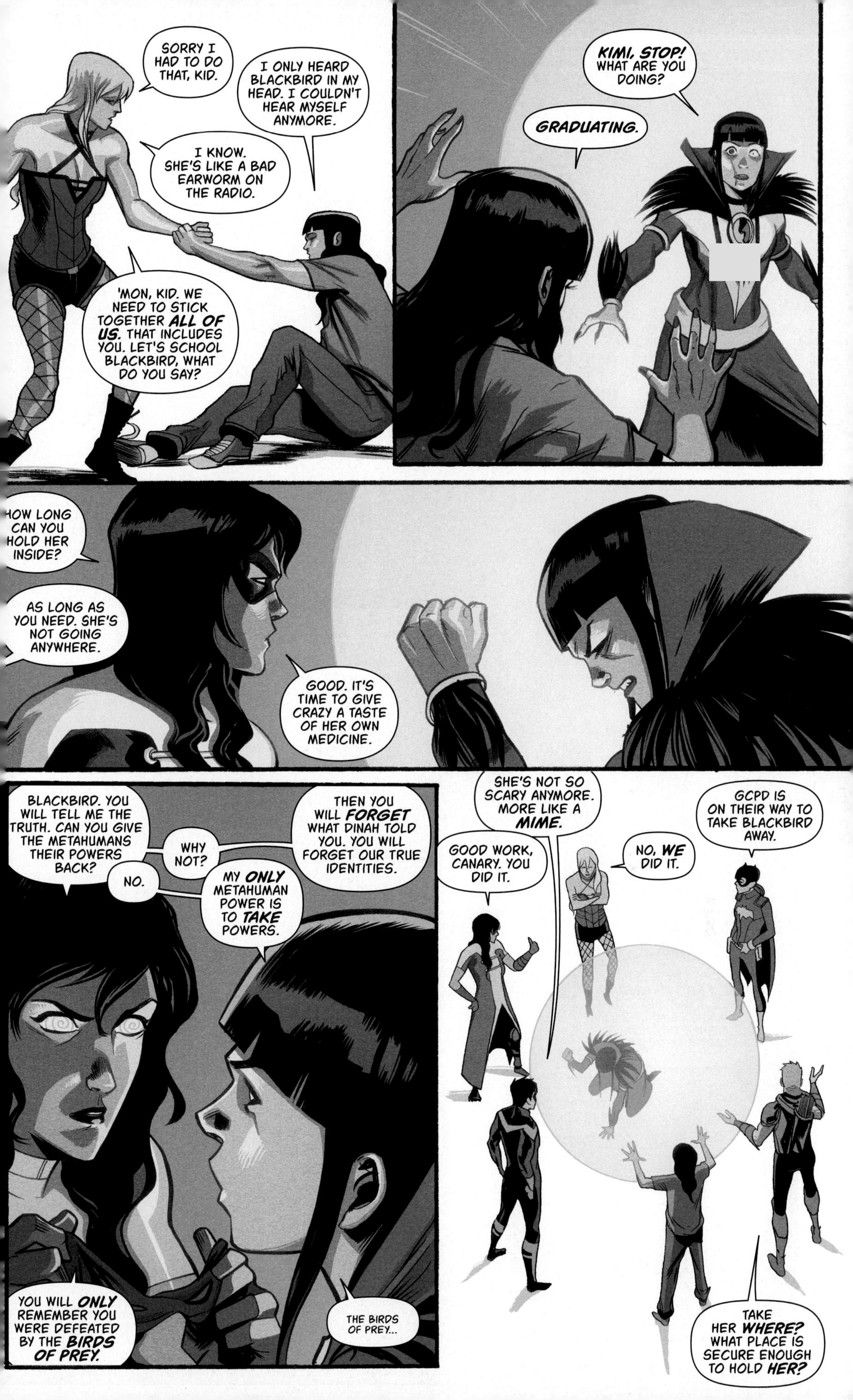
SORRY I HAD TO DO THAT, KID.
I ONLY HEARD BLACKBIRD IN MY HEAD. I COULDN'T HEAR MYSELF ANYMORE.
I KNOW. SHE'S LIKE A BAD EARWORM ON THE RADIO.
'MON, KID. WE NEED TO STICK TOGETHER ALL OF US. THAT INCLUDES YOU. LET'S SCHOOL BLACKBIRD, WHAT DO YOU SAY?
KIMI, STOP! WHAT ARE YOU DOING?
GRADUATING.
HOW LONG CAN YOU HOLD HER INSIDE?
AS LONG AS YOU NEED. SHE'S NOT GOING ANYWHERE.
GOOD. IT'S TIME TO GIVE CRAZY A TASTE OF HER OWN MEDICINE.
BLACKBIRD. YOU WILL TELL ME THE TRUTH. CAN YOU GIVE THE METAHUMANS THEIR POWERS BACK?
NO.
WHY NOT?
MY ONLY METAHUMAN POWER IS TO TAKE POWERS.
THEN YOU WILL FORGET WHAT DINAH TOLD YOU. YOU WILL FORGET OUR TRUE IDENTITIES.
YOU WILL ONLY REMEMBER YOU WERE DEFEATED BY THE BIRDS OF PREY.
THE BIRDS OF PREY...
SHE'S NOT SO SCARY ANYMORE. MORE LIKE A MIME.
GOOD WORK, CANARY. YOU DID IT.
NO, WE DID IT.
GCPD IS ON THEIR WAY TO TAKE BLACKBIRD AWAY.
TAKE HER WHERE? WHAT PLACE IS SECURE ENOUGH TO HOLD HER?

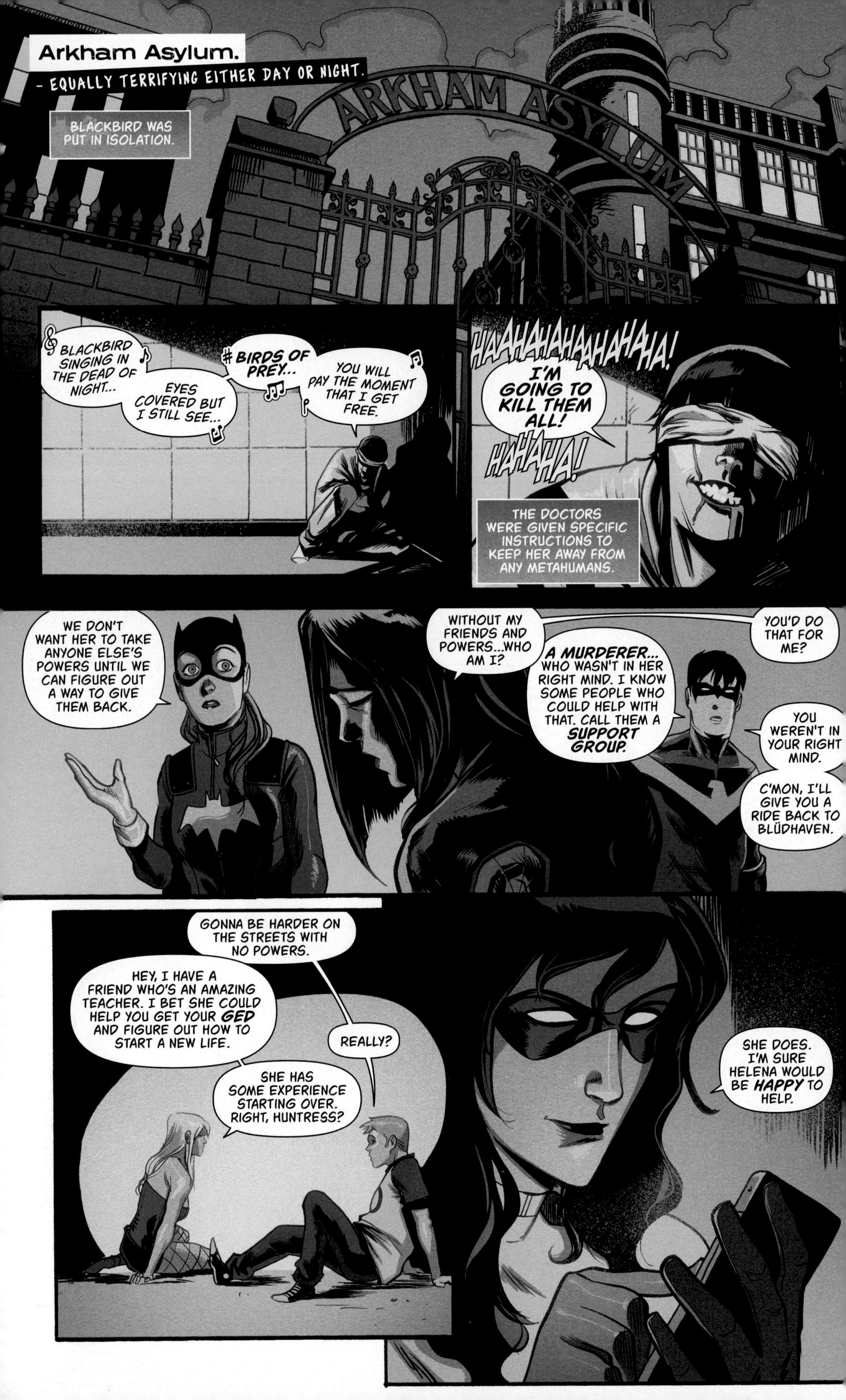
Arkham Asylum.
- EQUALLY TERRIFYING EITHER DAY OR NIGHT.
BLACKBIRD WAS PUT IN ISOLATION.
ARKHAM ASYLUM
BLACKBIRD SINGING IN THE DEAD OF NIGHT...
EYES COVERED BUT I STILL SEE...
#BIRDS OF PREY...
YOU WILL PAY THE MOMENT THAT I GET FREE.
HAAHAHAHAAHAHAHA!
I'M GOING TO KILL THEM ALL!
HAHAHA!
THE DOCTORS WERE GIVEN SPECIFIC INSTRUCTIONS TO KEEP HER AWAY FROM ANY METAHUMANS.
WE DON'T WANT HER TO TAKE ANYONE ELSE'S POWERS UNTIL WE CAN FIGURE OUT A WAY TO GIVE THEM BACK.
WITHOUT MY FRIENDS AND POWERS...WHO AM I?
A MURDERER... WHO WASN'T IN HER RIGHT MIND. I KNOW SOME PEOPLE WHO COULD HELP WITH THAT. CALL THEM A SUPPORT GROUP.
YOU'D DO THAT FOR ME?
YOU WEREN'T IN YOUR RIGHT MIND.
C'MON, I'LL GIVE YOU A RIDE BACK TO BLÜDHAVEN.
GONNA BE HARDER ON THE STREETS WITH NO POWERS.
HEY, I HAVE A FRIEND WHO'S AN AMAZING TEACHER. I BET SHE COULD HELP YOU GET YOUR GED AND FIGURE OUT HOW TO START A NEW LIFE.
REALLY?
SHE HAS SOME EXPERIENCE STARTING OVER. RIGHT, HUNTRESS?
SHE DOES. I'M SURE HELENA WOULD BE HAPPY TO HELP.

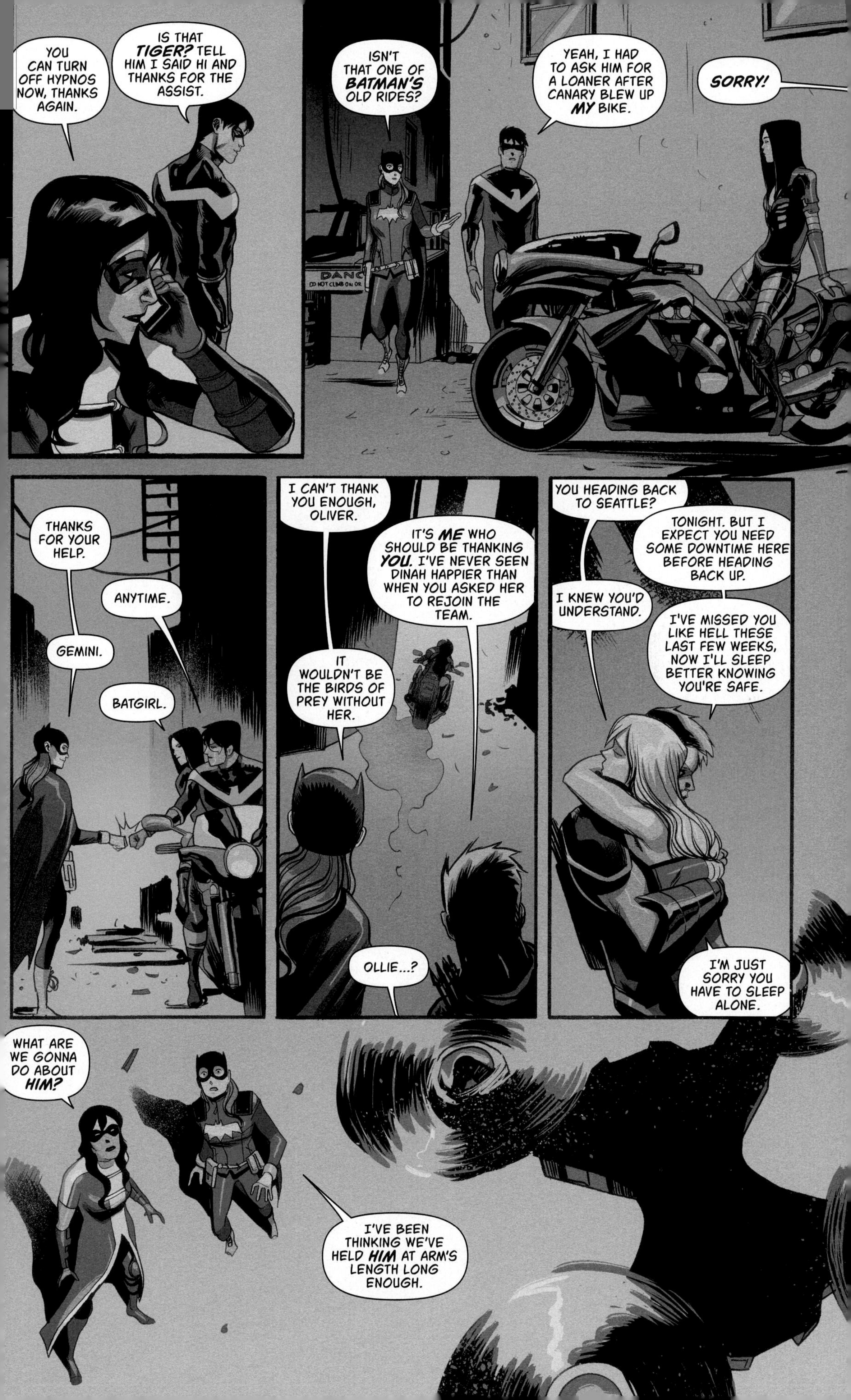

YOU CAN TURN OFF HYPNOS NOW, THANKS AGAIN.
IS THAT TIGER? TELL HIM I SAID HI AND THANKS FOR THE ASSIST.
ISN'T THAT ONE OF BATMAN'S OLD RIDES?
YEAH, I HAD TO ASK HIM FOR A LOANER AFTER CANARY BLEW UP MY BIKE.
SORRY!
DANG
DO NOT CLIMB ON OR
THANKS FOR YOUR HELP.
ANYTIME.
GEMINI.
BATGIRL.
I CAN'T THANK YOU ENOUGH, OLIVER.
IT'S ME WHO SHOULD BE THANKING YOU. I'VE NEVER SEEN DINAH HAPPIER THAN WHEN YOU ASKED HER TO REJOIN THE TEAM.
IT WOULDN'T BE THE BIRDS OF PREY WITHOUT HER.
OLLIE...?
YOU HEADING BACK TO SEATTLE?
TONIGHT. BUT I EXPECT YOU NEED SOME DOWNTIME HERE BEFORE HEADING BACK UP.
I KNEW YOU'D UNDERSTAND.
I'VE MISSED YOU LIKE HELL THESE LAST FEW WEEKS, NOW I'LL SLEEP BETTER KNOWING YOU'RE SAFE.
I'M JUST SORRY YOU HAVE TO SLEEP ALONE.
WHAT ARE WE GONNA DO ABOUT HIM?
I'VE BEEN THINKING WE'VE HELD HIM AT ARM'S LENGTH LONG ENOUGH.

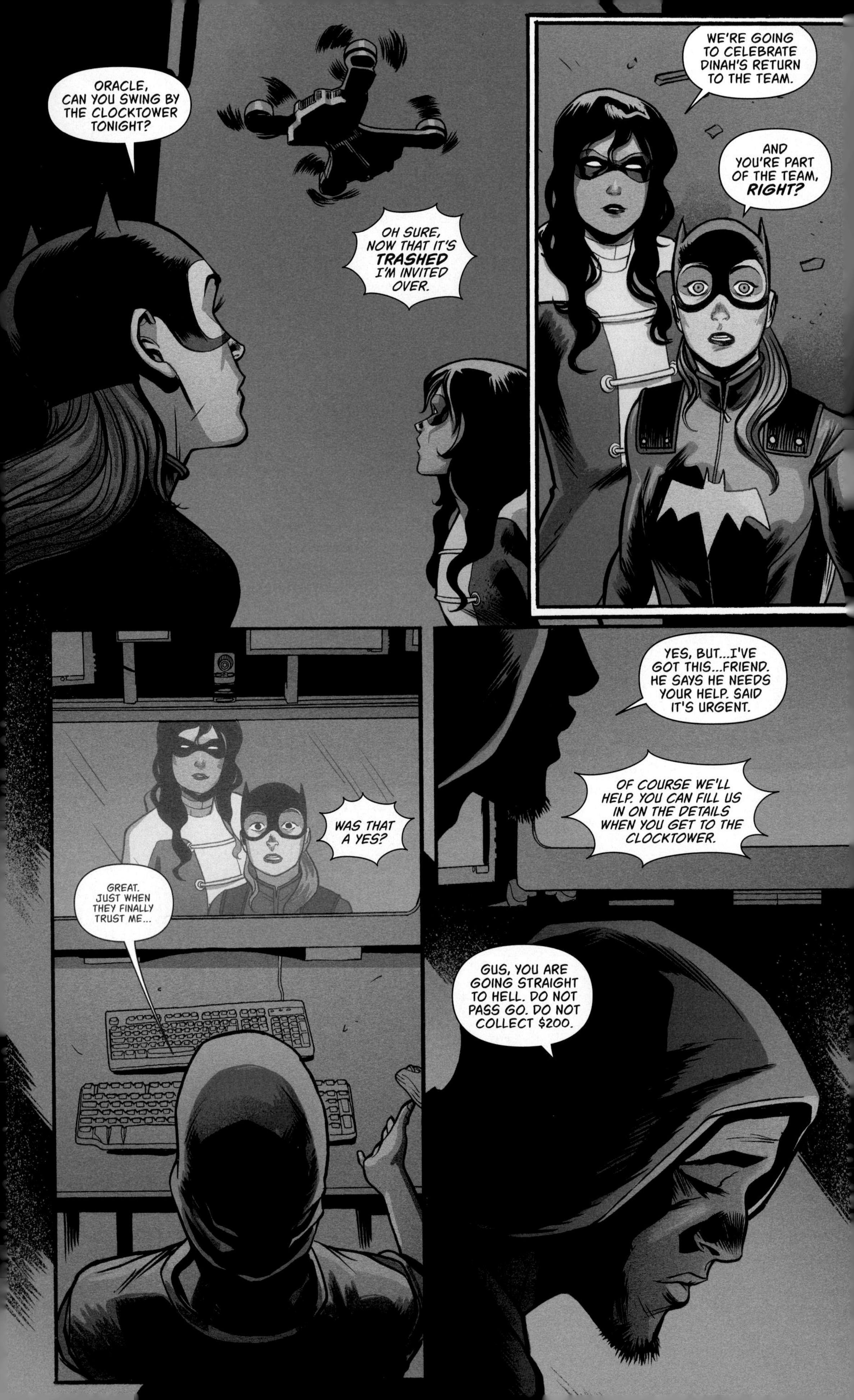
ORACLE, CAN YOU SWING BY THE CLOCKTOWER TONIGHT?
OH SURE, NOW THAT IT'S TRASHED I'M INVITED OVER.
WE'RE GOING TO CELEBRATE DINAH'S RETURN TO THE TEAM.
AND YOU'RE PART OF THE TEAM, RIGHT?
WAS THAT A YES?
GREAT. JUST WHEN THEY FINALLY TRUST ME...
YES, BUT...I'VE GOT THIS...FRIEND. HE SAYS HE NEEDS YOUR HELP. SAID IT'S URGENT.
OF COURSE WE'LL HELP. YOU CAN FILL US IN ON THE DETAILS WHEN YOU GET TO THE CLOCKTOWER.
GUS, YOU ARE GOING STRAIGHT TO HELL. DO NOT PASS GO. DO NOT COLLECT $200.

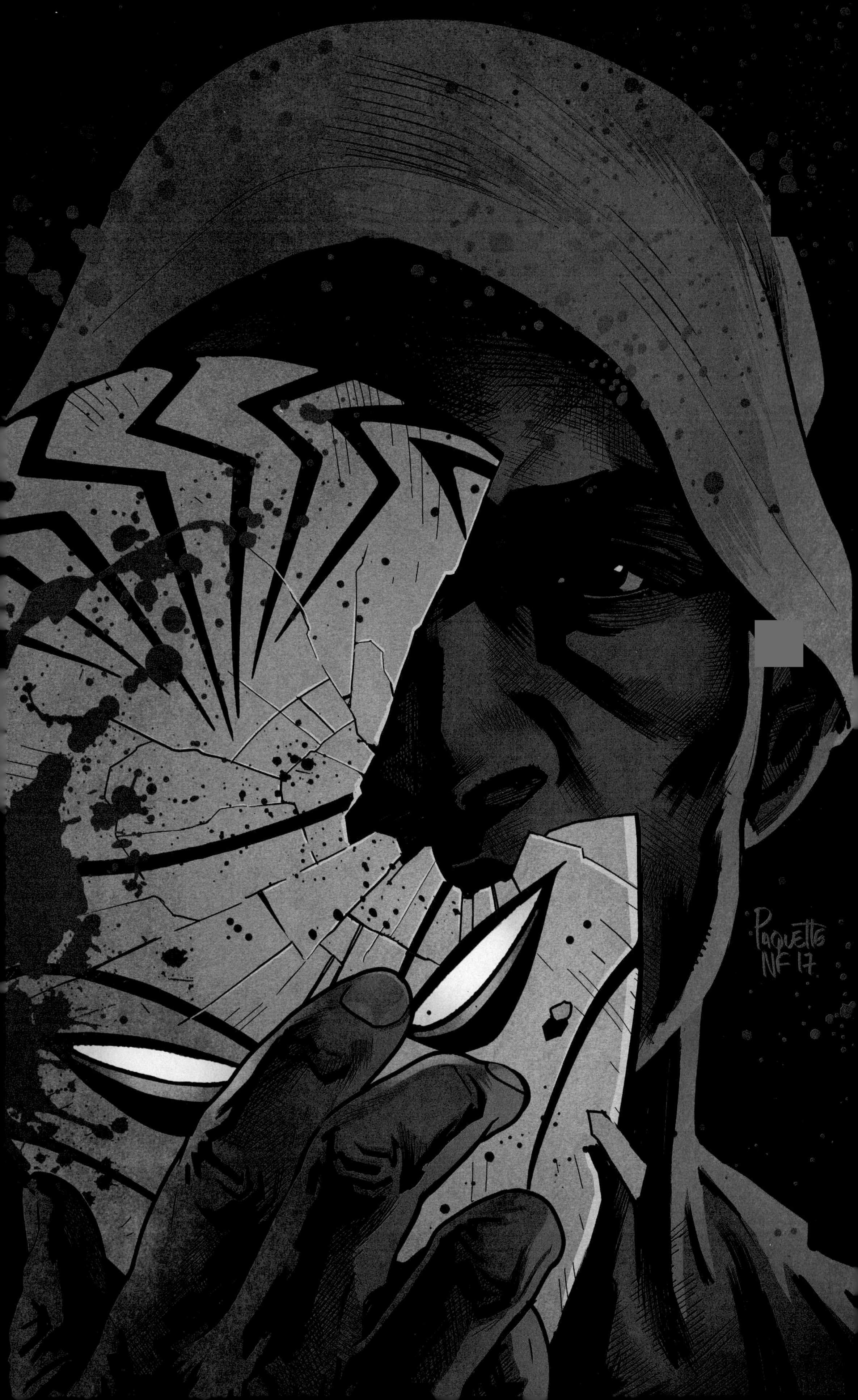
PAQUETTE
NF 17

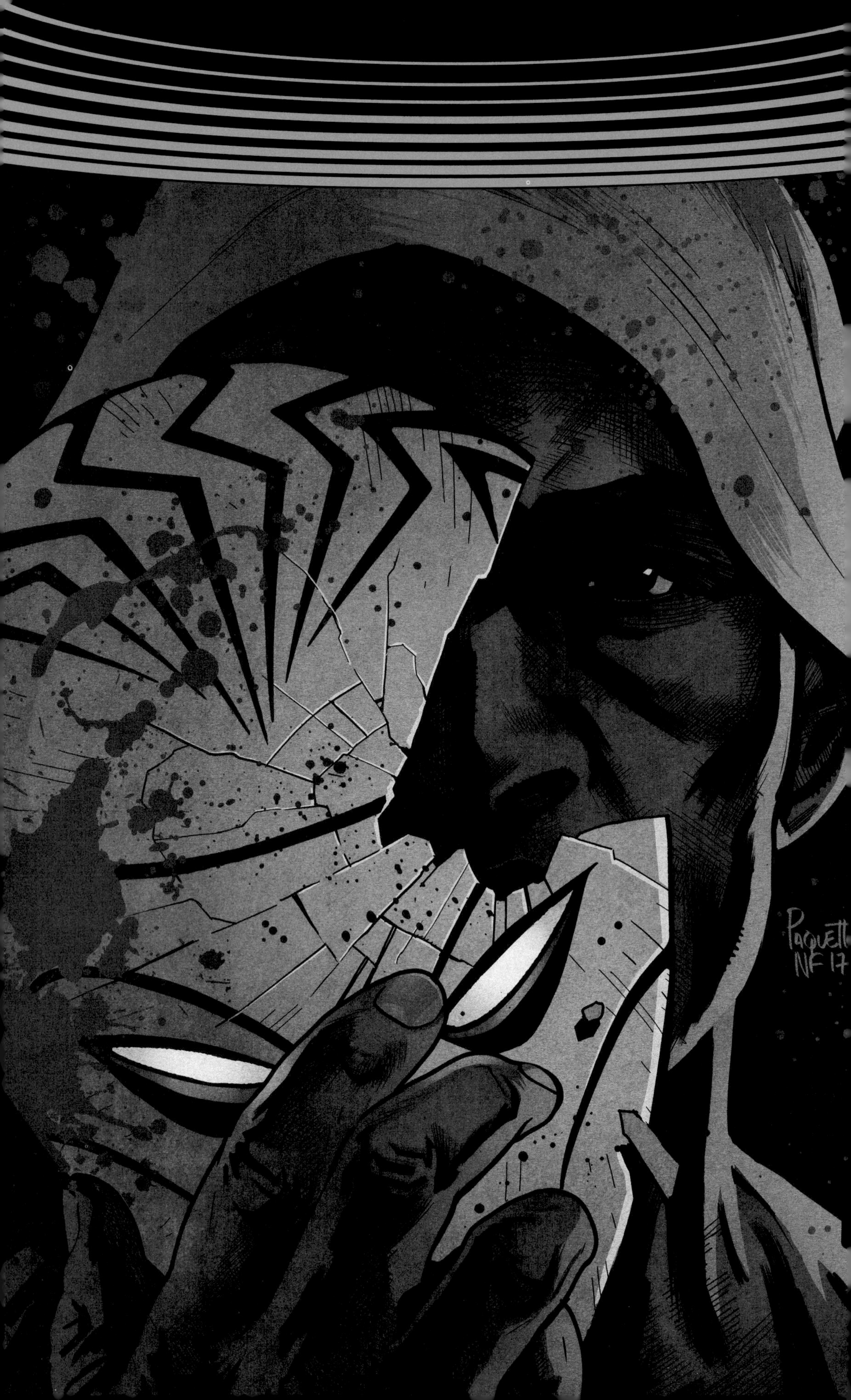
Paquett
NF 17

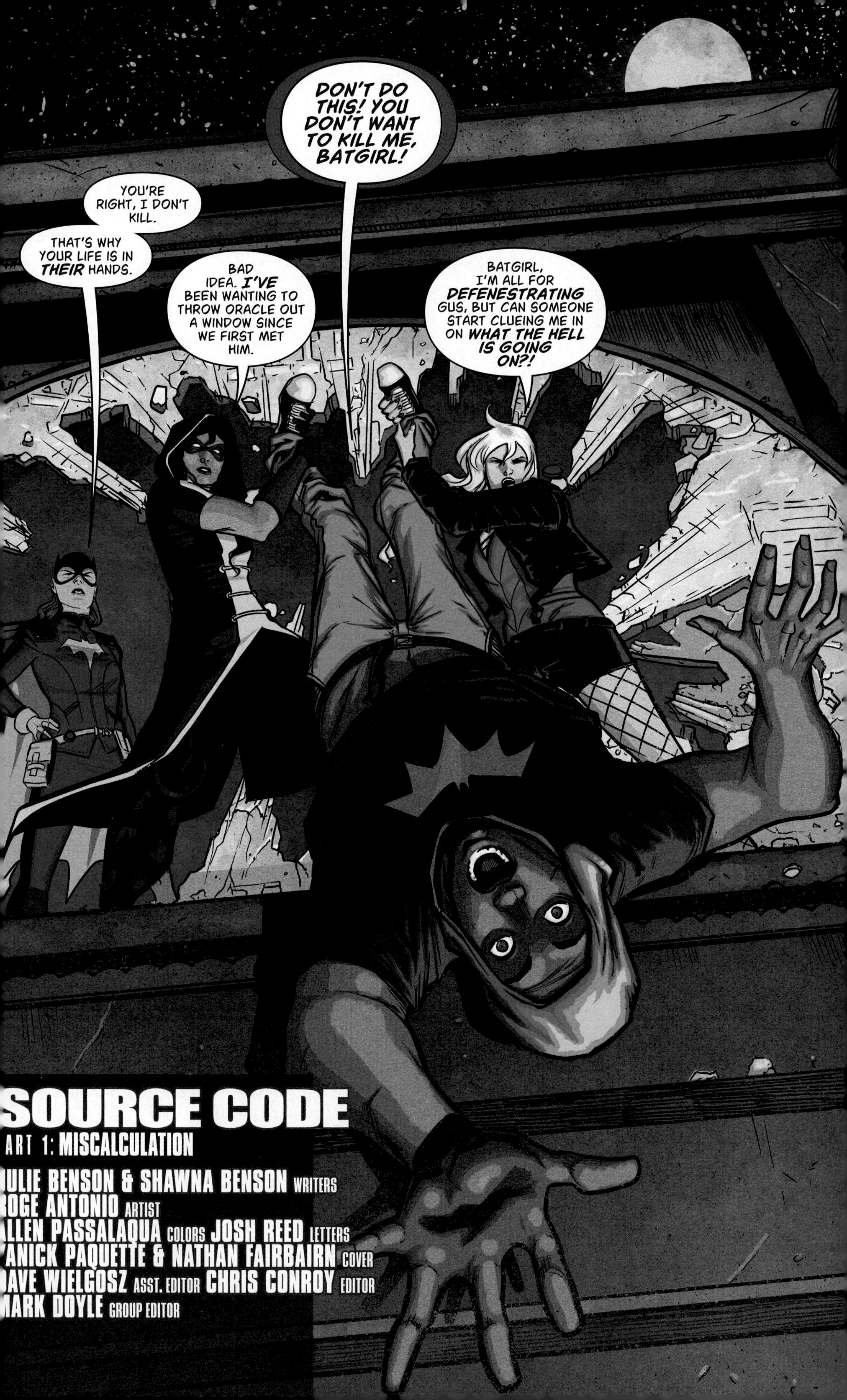
DON'T DO THIS! YOU DON'T WANT TO KILL ME, BATGIRL!
YOU'RE RIGHT, I DON'T KILL.
THAT'S WHY YOUR LIFE IS IN *THEIR* HANDS.
BAD IDEA. *I'VE* BEEN WANTING TO THROW ORACLE OUT A WINDOW SINCE WE FIRST MET HIM.
BATGIRL, I'M ALL FOR *DEFENESTRATING* GUS, BUT CAN SOMEONE START CLUEING ME IN ON *WHAT THE HELL IS GOING ON?!*

SOURCE CODE

ART 1: MISCALCULATION

ULIE BENSON & SHAWNA BENSON WRITERS
OGE ANTONIO ARTIST
LLEN PASSALAQUA COLORS JOSH REED LETTERS
ANICK PAQUETTE & NATHAN FAIRBAIRN COVER
AVE WIELGOSZ ASST. EDITOR CHRIS CONROY EDITOR
ARK DOYLE GROUP EDITOR

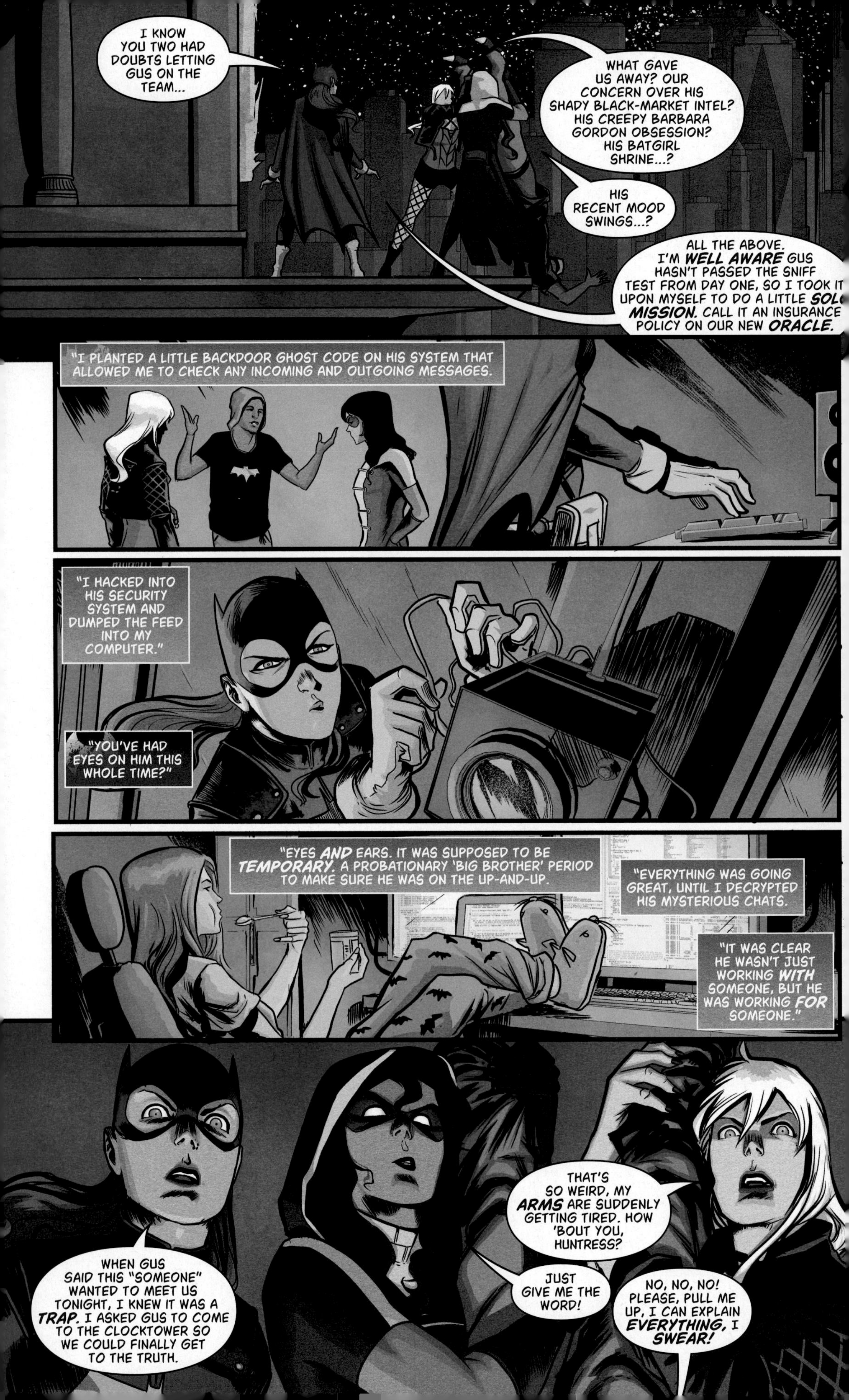
I KNOW YOU TWO HAD DOUBTS LETTING GUS ON THE TEAM...
WHAT GAVE US AWAY? OUR CONCERN OVER HIS SHADY BLACK-MARKET INTEL? HIS CREEPY BARBARA GORDON OBSESSION? HIS BATGIRL SHRINE...?
HIS RECENT MOOD SWINGS...?
ALL THE ABOVE. I'M WELL AWARE GUS HASN'T PASSED THE SNIFF TEST FROM DAY ONE, SO I TOOK IT UPON MYSELF TO DO A LITTLE SOLO MISSION. CALL IT AN INSURANCE POLICY ON OUR NEW ORACLE.
"I PLANTED A LITTLE BACKDOOR GHOST CODE ON HIS SYSTEM THAT ALLOWED ME TO CHECK ANY INCOMING AND OUTGOING MESSAGES.
"I HACKED INTO HIS SECURITY SYSTEM AND DUMPED THE FEED INTO MY COMPUTER."
"YOU'VE HAD EYES ON HIM THIS WHOLE TIME?"
"EYES AND EARS. IT WAS SUPPOSED TO BE TEMPORARY. A PROBATIONARY 'BIG BROTHER' PERIOD TO MAKE SURE HE WAS ON THE UP-AND-UP.
"EVERYTHING WAS GOING GREAT, UNTIL I DECRYPTED HIS MYSTERIOUS CHATS.
"IT WAS CLEAR HE WASN'T JUST WORKING WITH SOMEONE, BUT HE WAS WORKING FOR SOMEONE."
WHEN GUS SAID THIS "SOMEONE" WANTED TO MEET US TONIGHT, I KNEW IT WAS A TRAP. I ASKED GUS TO COME TO THE CLOCKTOWER SO WE COULD FINALLY GET TO THE TRUTH.
THAT'S SO WEIRD, MY ARMS ARE SUDDENLY GETTING TIRED. HOW 'BOUT YOU, HUNTRESS?
JUST GIVE ME THE WORD!
NO, NO, NO! PLEASE, PULL ME UP, I CAN EXPLAIN EVERYTHING, I SWEAR!

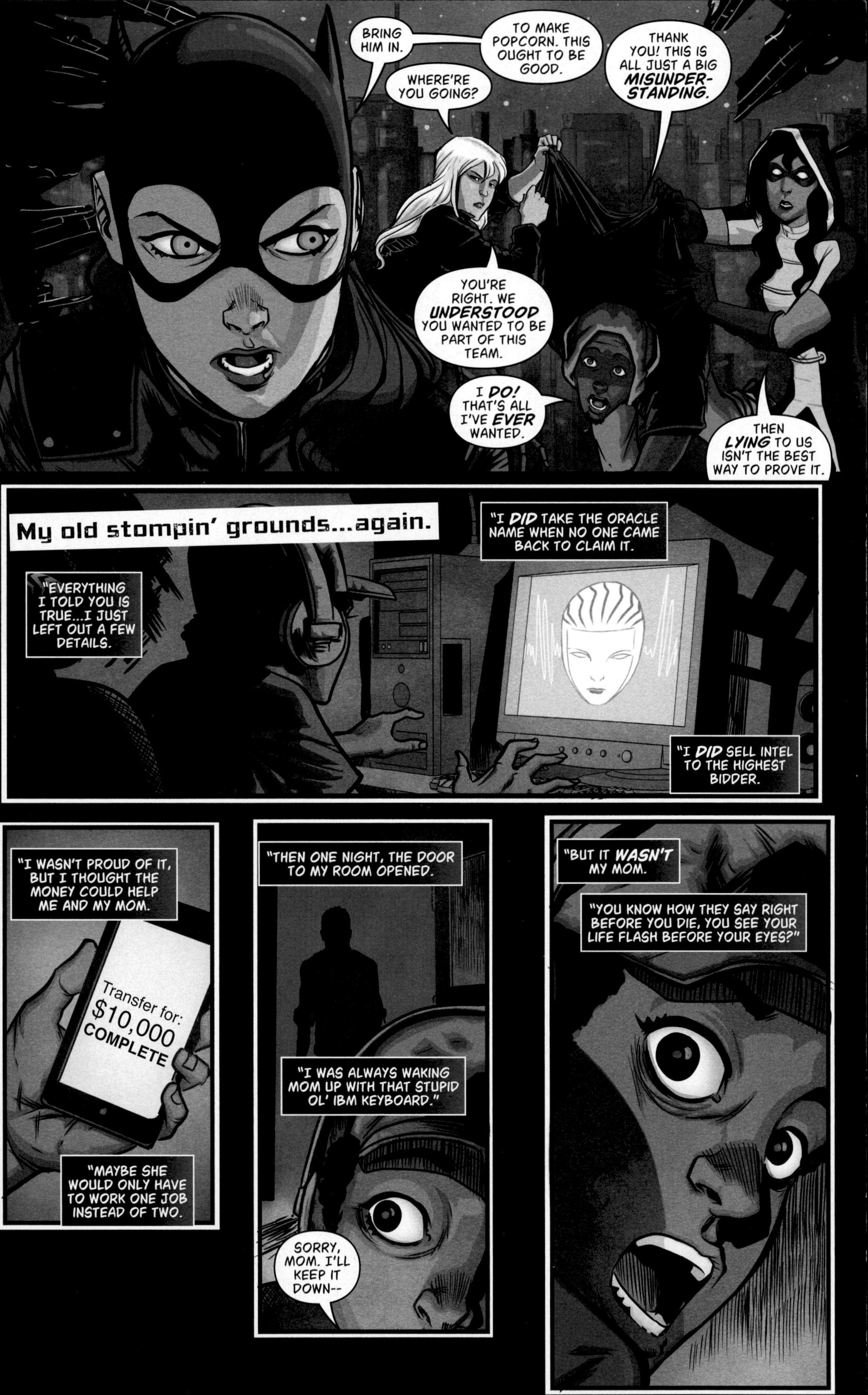
BRING HIM IN.
WHERE'RE YOU GOING?
TO MAKE POPCORN. THIS OUGHT TO BE GOOD.
THANK YOU! THIS IS ALL JUST A BIG MISUNDER-STANDING.
YOU'RE RIGHT. WE UNDERSTOOD YOU WANTED TO BE PART OF THIS TEAM.
I DO! THAT'S ALL I'VE EVER WANTED.
THEN LYING TO US ISN'T THE BEST WAY TO PROVE IT.
My old stompin' grounds...again.
"EVERYTHING I TOLD YOU IS TRUE...I JUST LEFT OUT A FEW DETAILS.
"I DID TAKE THE ORACLE NAME WHEN NO ONE CAME BACK TO CLAIM IT.
"I DID SELL INTEL TO THE HIGHEST BIDDER.
"I WASN'T PROUD OF IT, BUT I THOUGHT THE MONEY COULD HELP ME AND MY MOM.
Transfer for: $10,000 COMPLETE
"MAYBE SHE WOULD ONLY HAVE TO WORK ONE JOB INSTEAD OF TWO.
"THEN ONE NIGHT, THE DOOR TO MY ROOM OPENED.
"I WAS ALWAYS WAKING MOM UP WITH THAT STUPID OL' IBM KEYBOARD."
SORRY, MOM. I'LL KEEP IT DOWN--
"BUT IT WASN'T MY MOM.
"YOU KNOW HOW THEY SAY RIGHT BEFORE YOU DIE, YOU SEE YOUR LIFE FLASH BEFORE YOUR EYES?"

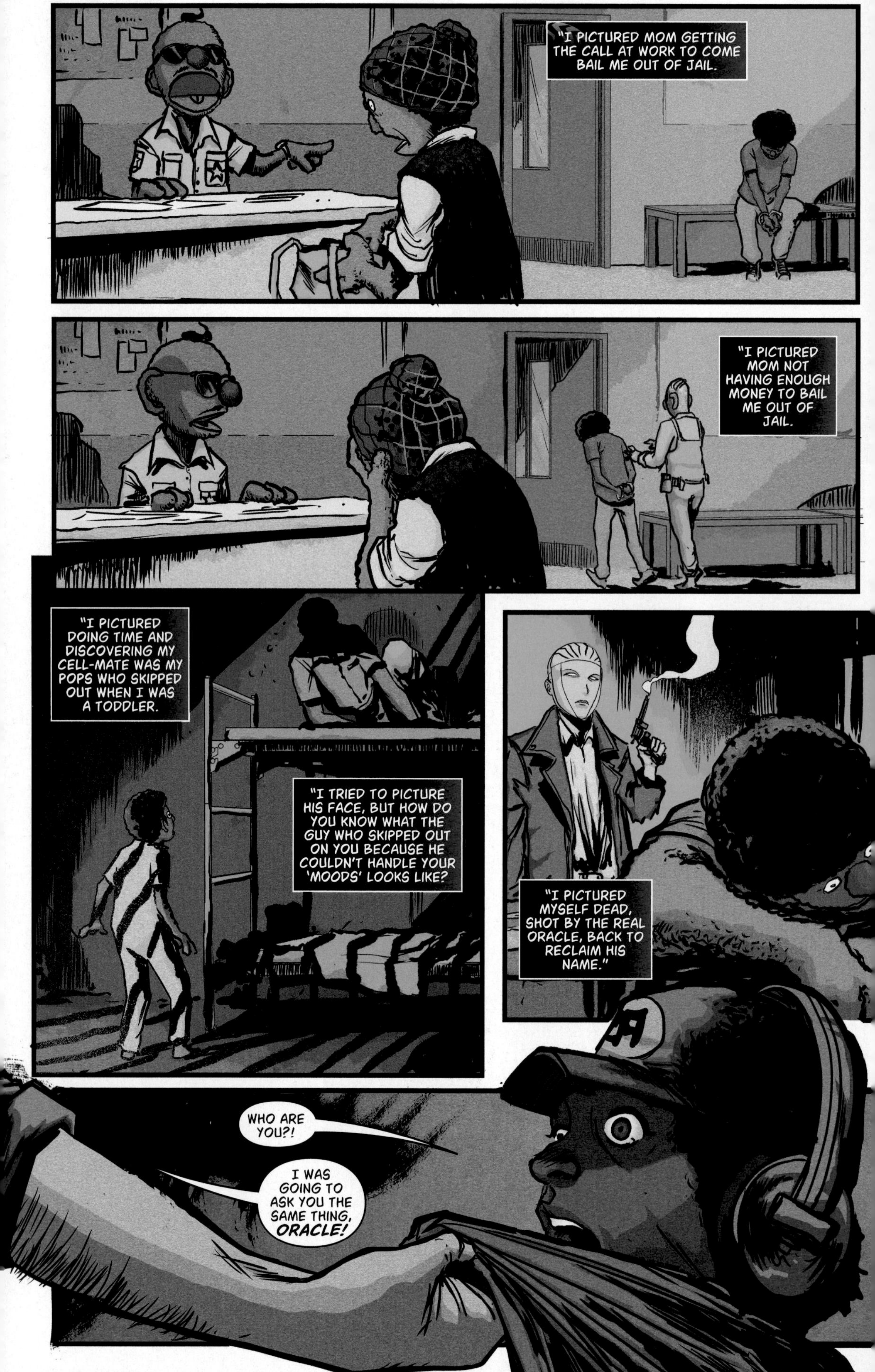
"I PICTURED MOM GETTING THE CALL AT WORK TO COME BAIL ME OUT OF JAIL.
"I PICTURED MOM NOT HAVING ENOUGH MONEY TO BAIL ME OUT OF JAIL.
"I PICTURED DOING TIME AND DISCOVERING MY CELL-MATE WAS MY POPS WHO SKIPPED OUT WHEN I WAS A TODDLER.
"I TRIED TO PICTURE HIS FACE, BUT HOW DO YOU KNOW WHAT THE GUY WHO SKIPPED OUT ON YOU BECAUSE HE COULDN'T HANDLE YOUR 'MOODS' LOOKS LIKE?
"I PICTURED MYSELF DEAD, SHOT BY THE REAL ORACLE, BACK TO RECLAIM HIS NAME."
WHO ARE YOU?!
I WAS GOING TO ASK YOU THE SAME THING, ORACLE!

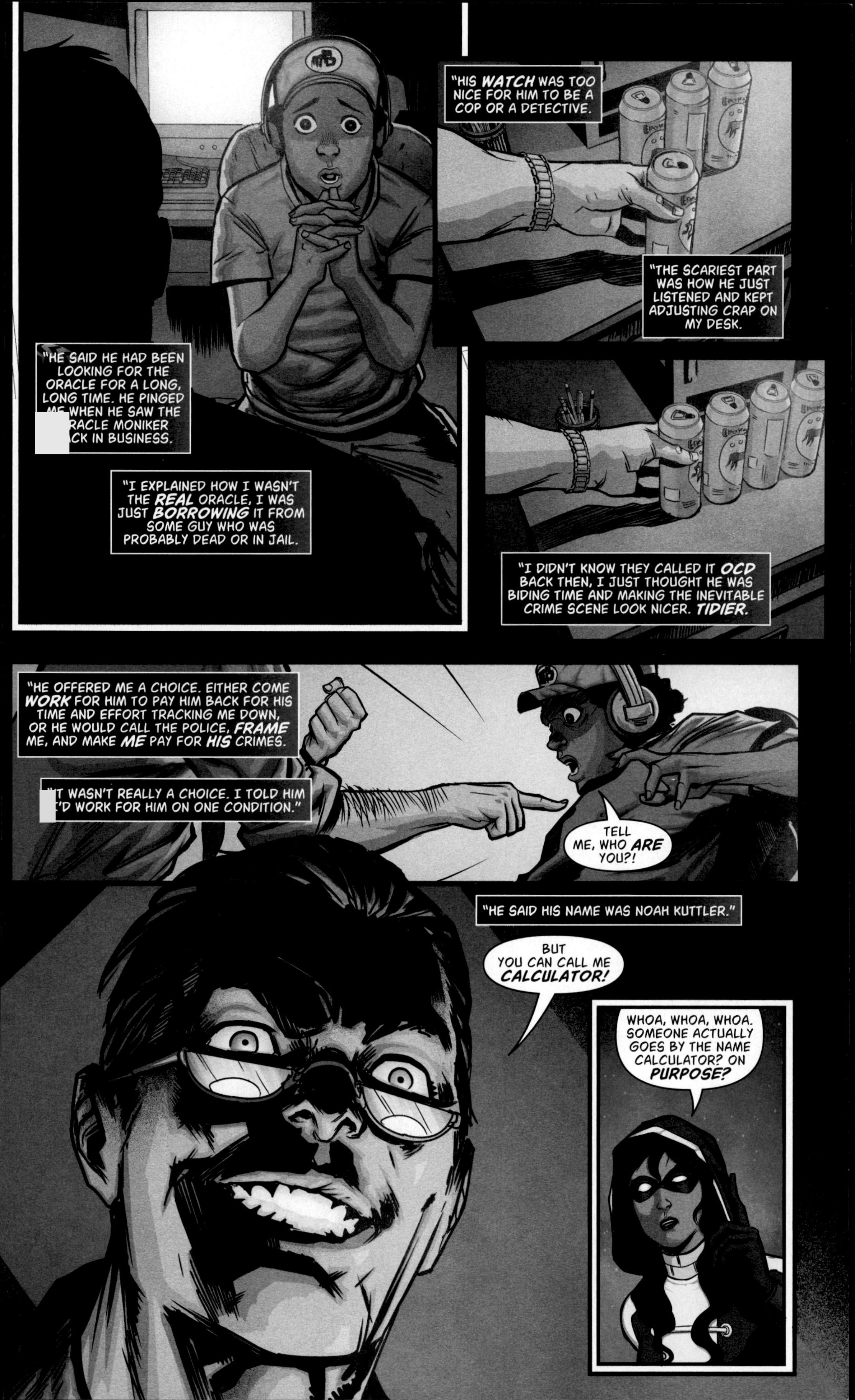
"HIS WATCH WAS TOO NICE FOR HIM TO BE A COP OR A DETECTIVE.
"THE SCARIEST PART WAS HOW HE JUST LISTENED AND KEPT ADJUSTING CRAP ON MY DESK.
"HE SAID HE HAD BEEN LOOKING FOR THE ORACLE FOR A LONG, LONG TIME. HE PINGED ME WHEN HE SAW THE RACLE MONIKER CK IN BUSINESS.
"I EXPLAINED HOW I WASN'T THE REAL ORACLE, I WAS JUST BORROWING IT FROM SOME GUY WHO WAS PROBABLY DEAD OR IN JAIL.
"I DIDN'T KNOW THEY CALLED IT OCD BACK THEN, I JUST THOUGHT HE WAS BIDING TIME AND MAKING THE INEVITABLE CRIME SCENE LOOK NICER. TIDIER.
"HE OFFERED ME A CHOICE. EITHER COME WORK FOR HIM TO PAY HIM BACK FOR HIS TIME AND EFFORT TRACKING ME DOWN, OR HE WOULD CALL THE POLICE, FRAME ME, AND MAKE ME PAY FOR HIS CRIMES.
"T WASN'T REALLY A CHOICE. I TOLD HIM 'D WORK FOR HIM ON ONE CONDITION."
TELL ME, WHO ARE YOU?!
"HE SAID HIS NAME WAS NOAH KUTTLER."
BUT YOU CAN CALL ME CALCULATOR!
WHOA, WHOA, WHOA. SOMEONE ACTUALLY GOES BY THE NAME CALCULATOR? ON PURPOSE?

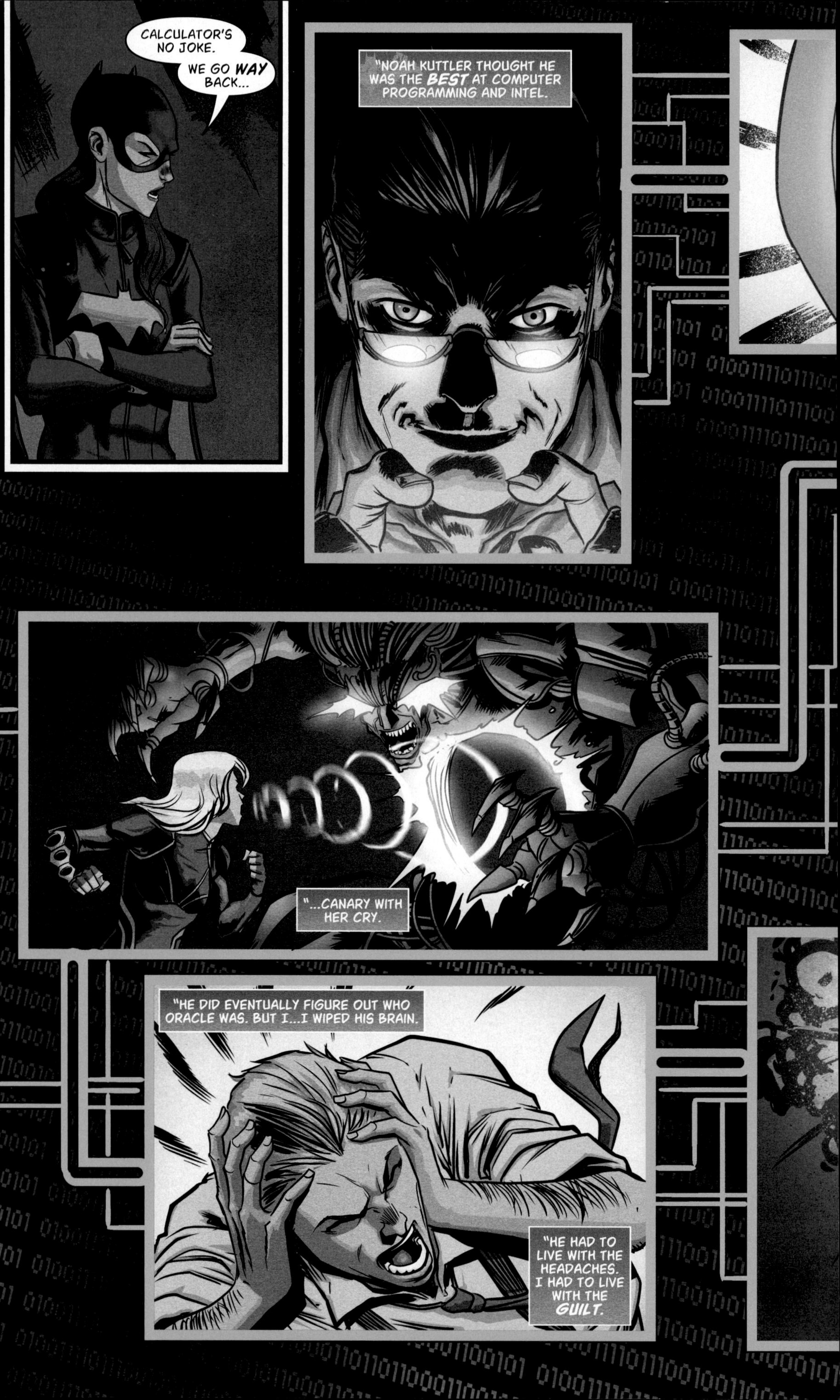
CALCULATOR'S NO JOKE.
WE GO WAY BACK...
"NOAH KUTTLER THOUGHT HE WAS THE BEST AT COMPUTER PROGRAMMING AND INTEL.
"...CANARY WITH HER CRY.
"HE DID EVENTUALLY FIGURE OUT WHO ORACLE WAS. BUT I...I WIPED HIS BRAIN.
"HE HAD TO LIVE WITH THE HEADACHES. I HAD TO LIVE WITH THE GUILT.

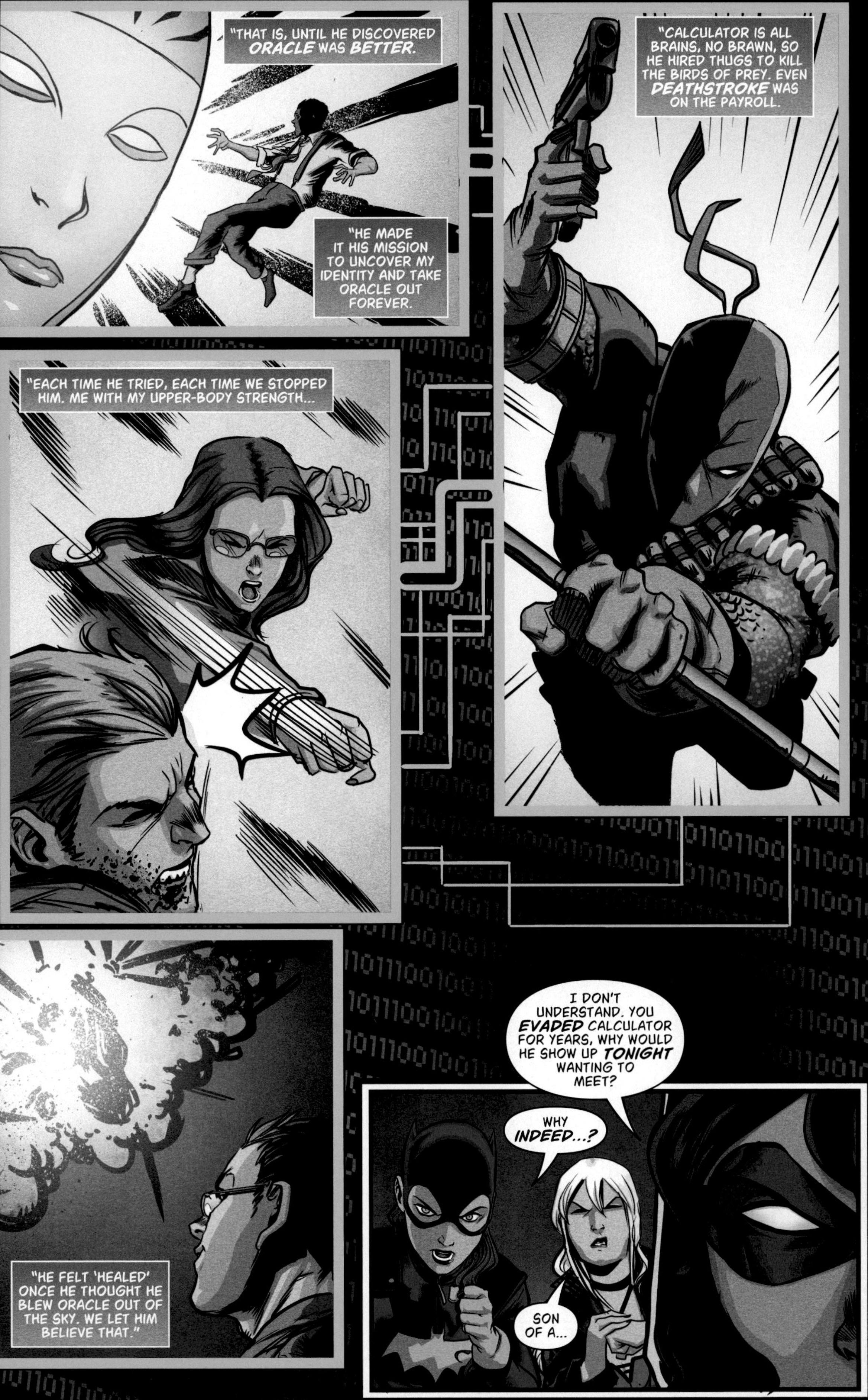
"THAT IS, UNTIL HE DISCOVERED ORACLE WAS BETTER.
"HE MADE IT HIS MISSION TO UNCOVER MY IDENTITY AND TAKE ORACLE OUT FOREVER.
"CALCULATOR IS ALL BRAINS, NO BRAWN, SO HE HIRED THUGS TO KILL THE BIRDS OF PREY. EVEN DEATHSTROKE WAS ON THE PAYROLL.
"EACH TIME HE TRIED, EACH TIME WE STOPPED HIM. ME WITH MY UPPER-BODY STRENGTH...
"HE FELT 'HEALED' ONCE HE THOUGHT HE BLEW ORACLE OUT OF THE SKY. WE LET HIM BELIEVE THAT."
I DON'T UNDERSTAND. YOU EVADED CALCULATOR FOR YEARS, WHY WOULD HE SHOW UP TONIGHT WANTING TO MEET?
WHY INDEED...?
SON OF A...

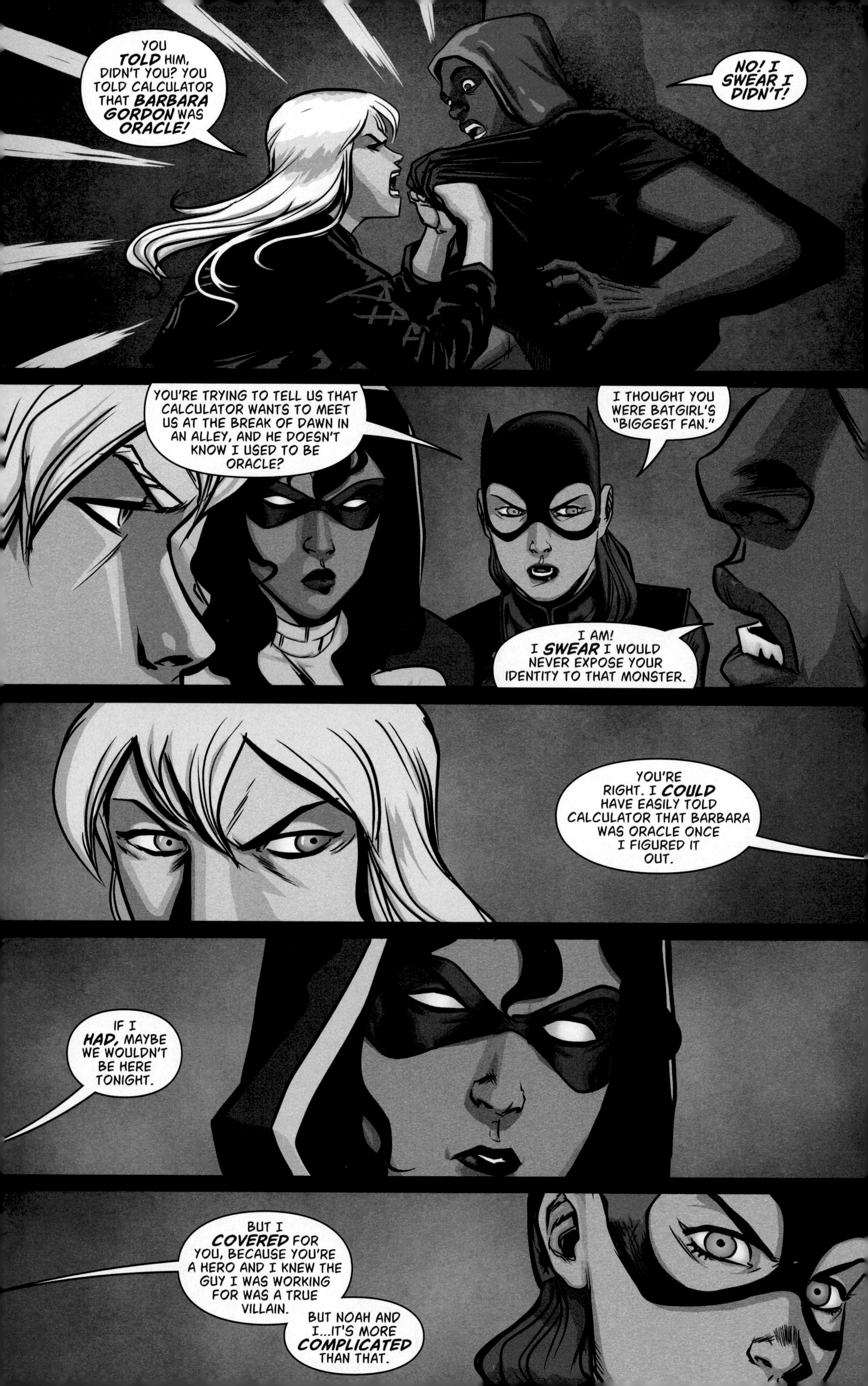
YOU TOLD HIM, DIDN'T YOU? YOU TOLD CALCULATOR THAT BARBARA GORDON WAS ORACLE!
NO! I SWEAR I DIDN'T!
YOU'RE TRYING TO TELL US THAT CALCULATOR WANTS TO MEET US AT THE BREAK OF DAWN IN AN ALLEY, AND HE DOESN'T KNOW I USED TO BE ORACLE?
I THOUGHT YOU WERE BATGIRL'S "BIGGEST FAN."
I AM! I SWEAR I WOULD NEVER EXPOSE YOUR IDENTITY TO THAT MONSTER.
YOU'RE RIGHT. I COULD HAVE EASILY TOLD CALCULATOR THAT BARBARA WAS ORACLE ONCE I FIGURED IT OUT.
IF I HAD, MAYBE WE WOULDN'T BE HERE TONIGHT.
BUT I COVERED FOR YOU, BECAUSE YOU'RE A HERO AND I KNEW THE GUY I WAS WORKING FOR WAS A TRUE VILLAIN.
BUT NOAH AND I...IT'S MORE COMPLICATED THAN THAT.

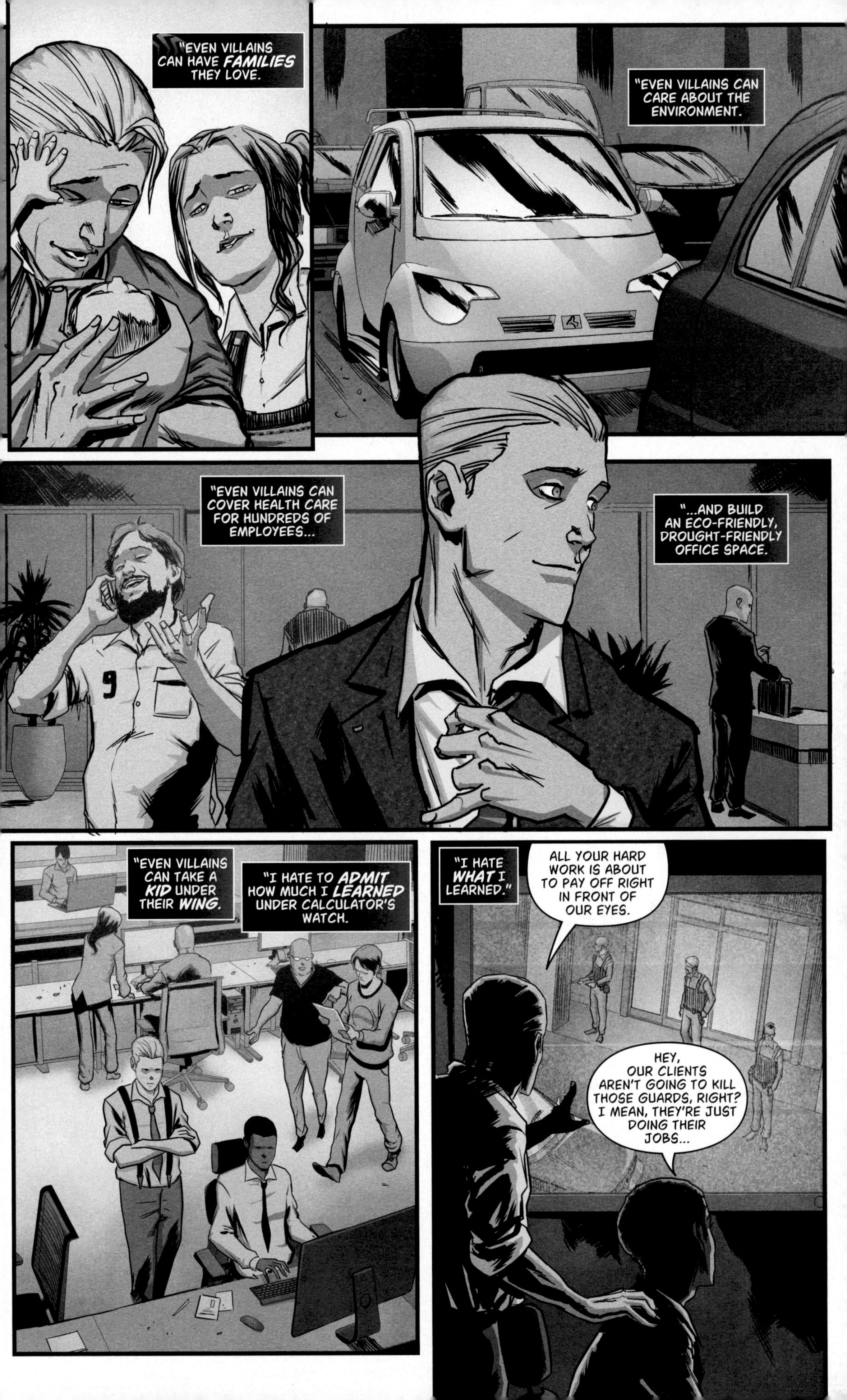
"EVEN VILLAINS CAN HAVE FAMILIES THEY LOVE.
"EVEN VILLAINS CAN CARE ABOUT THE ENVIRONMENT.
"EVEN VILLAINS CAN COVER HEALTH CARE FOR HUNDREDS OF EMPLOYEES...
"...AND BUILD AN ECO-FRIENDLY, DROUGHT-FRIENDLY OFFICE SPACE.
9
"EVEN VILLAINS CAN TAKE A KID UNDER THEIR WING.
"I HATE TO ADMIT HOW MUCH I LEARNED UNDER CALCULATOR'S WATCH.
"I HATE WHAT I LEARNED."
ALL YOUR HARD WORK IS ABOUT TO PAY OFF RIGHT IN FRONT OF OUR EYES.
HEY, OUR CLIENTS AREN'T GOING TO KILL THOSE GUARDS, RIGHT? I MEAN, THEY'RE JUST DOING THEIR JOBS...

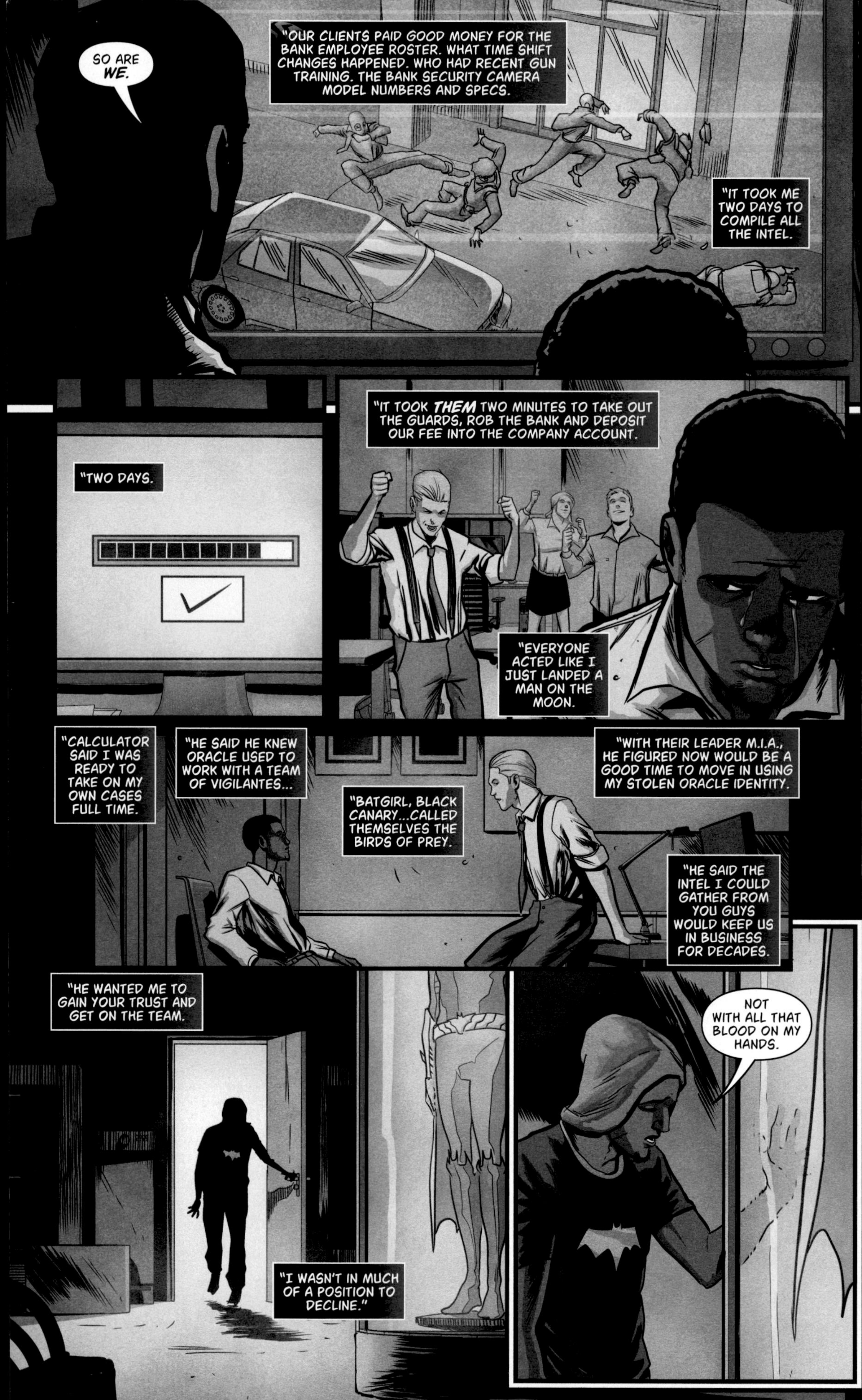
SO ARE WE.
"OUR CLIENTS PAID GOOD MONEY FOR THE BANK EMPLOYEE ROSTER. WHAT TIME SHIFT CHANGES HAPPENED. WHO HAD RECENT GUN TRAINING. THE BANK SECURITY CAMERA MODEL NUMBERS AND SPECS.
"IT TOOK ME TWO DAYS TO COMPILE ALL THE INTEL.
"TWO DAYS.
"IT TOOK THEM TWO MINUTES TO TAKE OUT THE GUARDS, ROB THE BANK AND DEPOSIT OUR FEE INTO THE COMPANY ACCOUNT.
"EVERYONE ACTED LIKE I JUST LANDED A MAN ON THE MOON.
"CALCULATOR SAID I WAS READY TO TAKE ON MY OWN CASES FULL TIME.
"HE SAID HE KNEW ORACLE USED TO WORK WITH A TEAM OF VIGILANTES...
"BATGIRL, BLACK CANARY...CALLED THEMSELVES THE BIRDS OF PREY.
"WITH THEIR LEADER M.I.A., HE FIGURED NOW WOULD BE A GOOD TIME TO MOVE IN USING MY STOLEN ORACLE IDENTITY.
"HE SAID THE INTEL I COULD GATHER FROM YOU GUYS WOULD KEEP US IN BUSINESS FOR DECADES.
"HE WANTED ME TO GAIN YOUR TRUST AND GET ON THE TEAM.
"I WASN'T IN MUCH OF A POSITION TO DECLINE."
NOT WITH ALL THAT BLOOD ON MY HANDS.

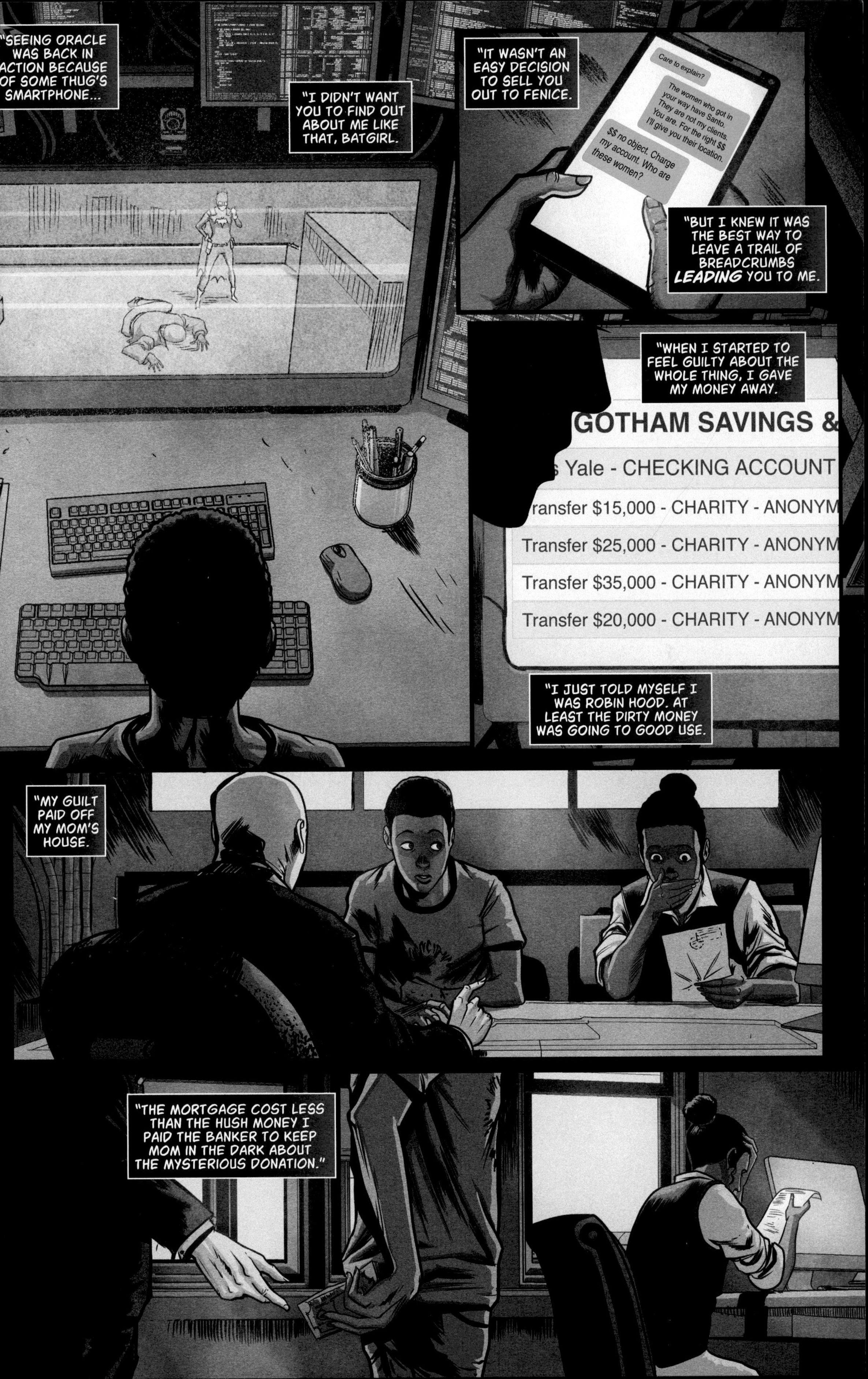

"SEEING ORACLE WAS BACK IN ACTION BECAUSE OF SOME THUG'S SMARTPHONE...
"I DIDN'T WANT YOU TO FIND OUT ABOUT ME LIKE THAT, BATGIRL.
"IT WASN'T AN EASY DECISION TO SELL YOU OUT TO FENICE.
Care to explain?
The women who got in your way have Santo. They are not my clients. You are. For the right $$ I'll give you their location.
$$ no object. Charge my account. Who are these women?
"BUT I KNEW IT WAS THE BEST WAY TO LEAVE A TRAIL OF BREADCRUMBS LEADING YOU TO ME.
"WHEN I STARTED TO FEEL GUILTY ABOUT THE WHOLE THING, I GAVE MY MONEY AWAY.
GOTHAM SAVINGS &
Yale - CHECKING ACCOUNT
Transfer $15,000 - CHARITY - ANONYM
Transfer $25,000 - CHARITY - ANONYM
Transfer $35,000 - CHARITY - ANONYM
Transfer $20,000 - CHARITY - ANONYM
"I JUST TOLD MYSELF I WAS ROBIN HOOD. AT LEAST THE DIRTY MONEY WAS GOING TO GOOD USE.
"MY GUILT PAID OFF MY MOM'S HOUSE.
"THE MORTGAGE COST LESS THAN THE HUSH MONEY I PAID THE BANKER TO KEEP MOM IN THE DARK ABOUT THE MYSTERIOUS DONATION."

"I KNEW I COULDN'T KEEP LYING TO MOM IF I STILL LIVED AT HOME, SO I BOUGHT THE GOTHAM TOWER AND TOLD HER I HAD A JOB OPPORTUNITY.

"I DIDN'T TELL HER THE JOB WAS WORKING FOR A GUY **BLACKMAILING** ME. SHE WOULDN'T UNDERSTAND. HELL, I BARELY DID.

"WE STILL TALK ON THE PHONE. SHE QUIT ONE OF HER JOBS, BUT KEPT THE OTHER, EVEN THOUGH I SEND HER MONEY EVERY WEEK.

"SHE BEGS ME TO VISIT HER, BUT I CAN'T RISK IT. CAN'T GET HER INVOLVED.

"I HAVEN'T SEEN HER IN PERSON IN MONTHS.

"IF I'M BEING HONEST, IT'S BECAUSE I CAN'T STAND LYING TO HER FACE.

"AND I'D **HAVE** TO LIE, SO LONG AS I WAS WORKING FOR CALCULATOR.

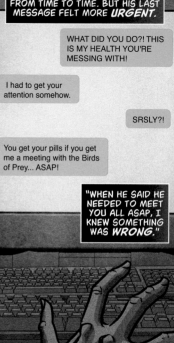

"CALCULATOR CHECKS IN ON ME FROM TIME TO TIME. BUT HIS LAST MESSAGE FELT MORE **URGENT**.

WHAT DID YOU DO?! THIS IS MY HEALTH YOU'RE MESSING WITH!

I had to get your attention somehow.

SRSLY?!

You get your pills if you get me a meeting with the Birds of Prey... ASAP!

"WHEN HE SAID HE NEEDED TO MEET YOU ALL ASAP, I KNEW SOMETHING WAS **WRONG**."

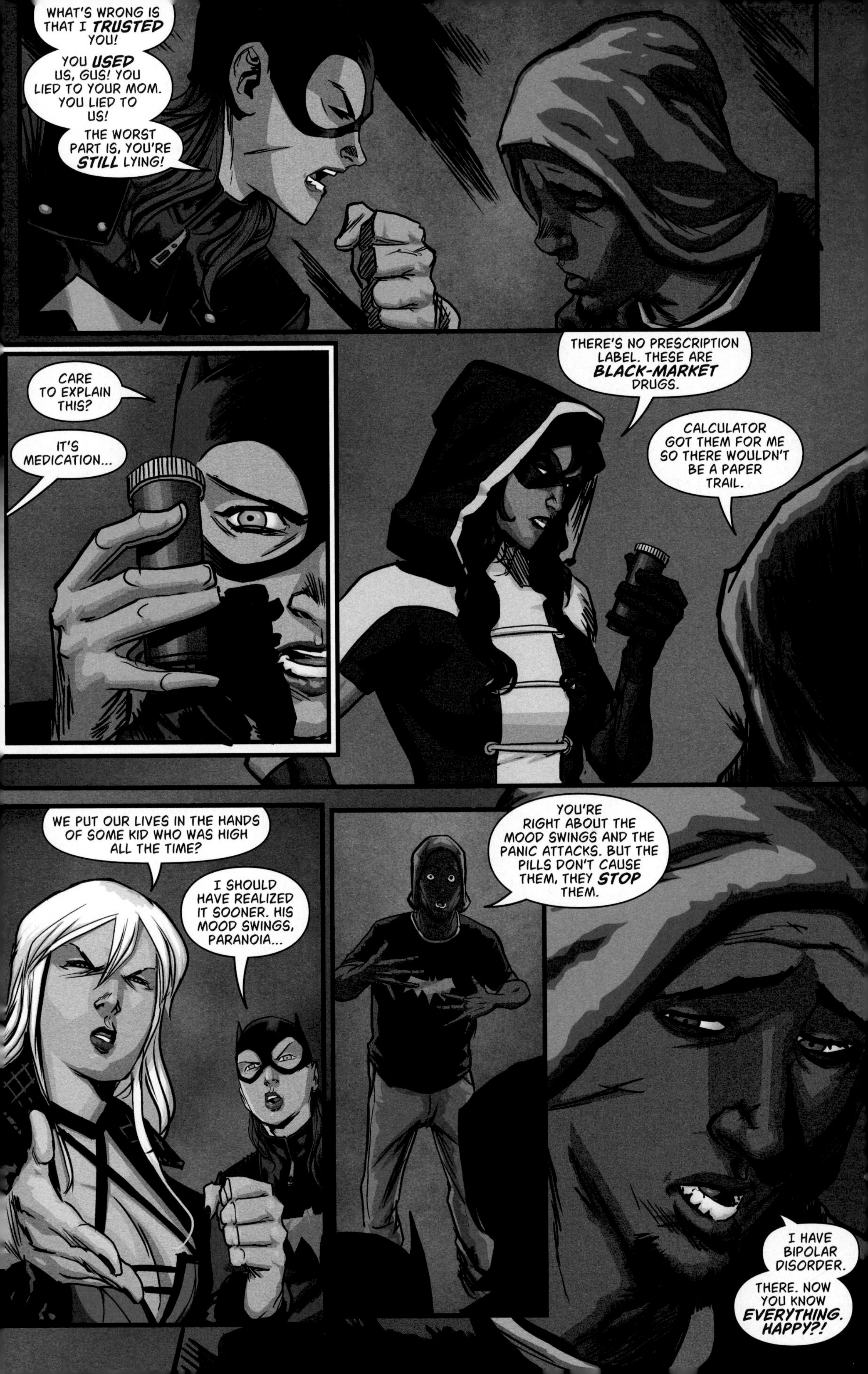
WHAT'S WRONG IS THAT I TRUSTED YOU!
YOU USED US, GUS! YOU LIED TO YOUR MOM. YOU LIED TO US!
THE WORST PART IS, YOU'RE STILL LYING!
CARE TO EXPLAIN THIS?
IT'S MEDICATION...
THERE'S NO PRESCRIPTION LABEL. THESE ARE BLACK-MARKET DRUGS.
CALCULATOR GOT THEM FOR ME SO THERE WOULDN'T BE A PAPER TRAIL.
WE PUT OUR LIVES IN THE HANDS OF SOME KID WHO WAS HIGH ALL THE TIME?
I SHOULD HAVE REALIZED IT SOONER. HIS MOOD SWINGS, PARANOIA...
YOU'RE RIGHT ABOUT THE MOOD SWINGS AND THE PANIC ATTACKS. BUT THE PILLS DON'T CAUSE THEM, THEY STOP THEM.
I HAVE BIPOLAR DISORDER.
THERE. NOW YOU KNOW EVERYTHING. HAPPY?!

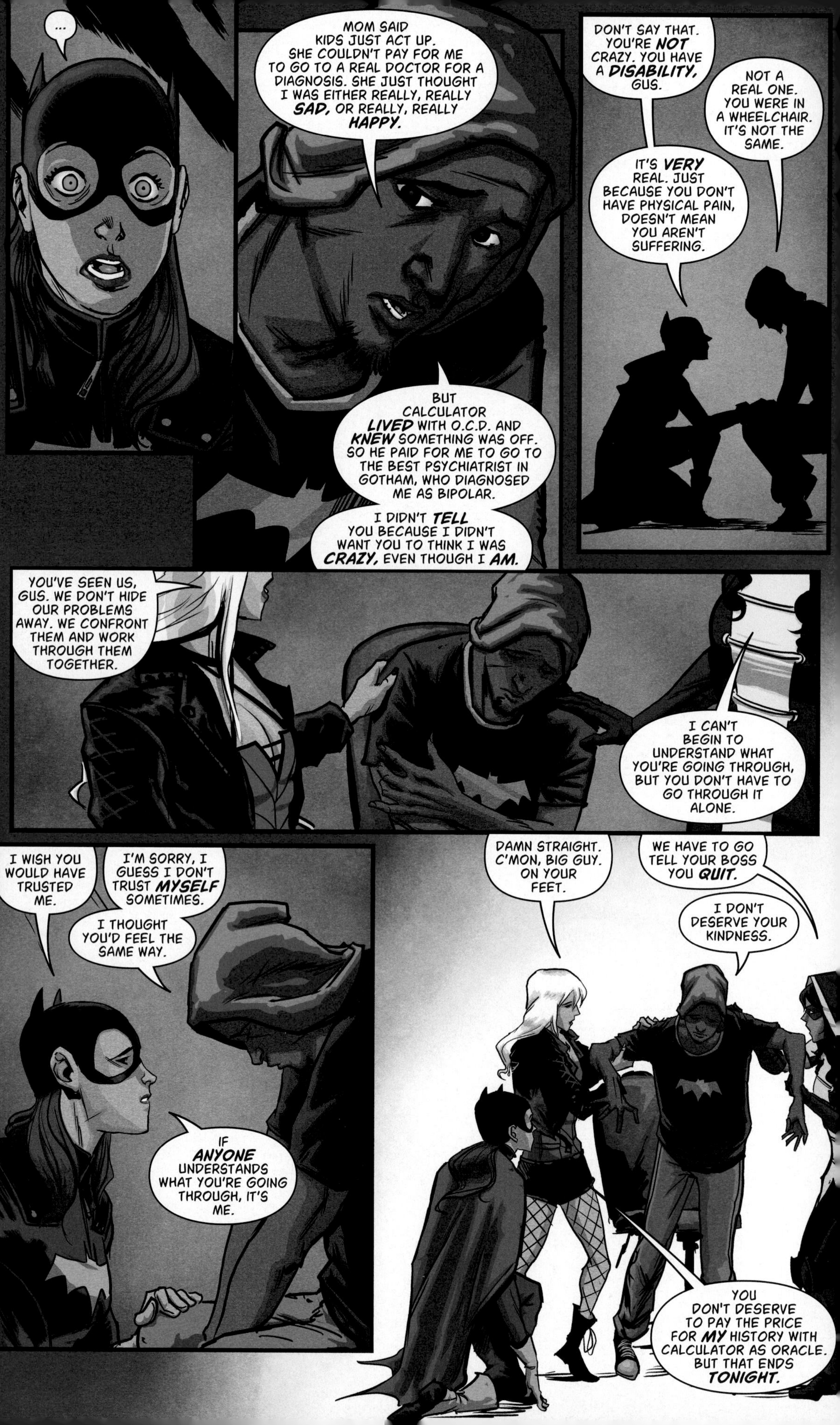
...
MOM SAID KIDS JUST ACT UP. SHE COULDN'T PAY FOR ME TO GO TO A REAL DOCTOR FOR A DIAGNOSIS. SHE JUST THOUGHT I WAS EITHER REALLY, REALLY SAD, OR REALLY, REALLY HAPPY.
BUT CALCULATOR LIVED WITH O.C.D. AND KNEW SOMETHING WAS OFF. SO HE PAID FOR ME TO GO TO THE BEST PSYCHIATRIST IN GOTHAM, WHO DIAGNOSED ME AS BIPOLAR.
I DIDN'T TELL YOU BECAUSE I DIDN'T WANT YOU TO THINK I WAS CRAZY, EVEN THOUGH I AM.
DON'T SAY THAT. YOU'RE NOT CRAZY. YOU HAVE A DISABILITY, GUS.
NOT A REAL ONE. YOU WERE IN A WHEELCHAIR. IT'S NOT THE SAME.
IT'S VERY REAL. JUST BECAUSE YOU DON'T HAVE PHYSICAL PAIN, DOESN'T MEAN YOU AREN'T SUFFERING.
YOU'VE SEEN US, GUS. WE DON'T HIDE OUR PROBLEMS AWAY. WE CONFRONT THEM AND WORK THROUGH THEM TOGETHER.
I CAN'T BEGIN TO UNDERSTAND WHAT YOU'RE GOING THROUGH, BUT YOU DON'T HAVE TO GO THROUGH IT ALONE.
I WISH YOU WOULD HAVE TRUSTED ME.
I'M SORRY, I GUESS I DON'T TRUST MYSELF SOMETIMES.
I THOUGHT YOU'D FEEL THE SAME WAY.
IF ANYONE UNDERSTANDS WHAT YOU'RE GOING THROUGH, IT'S ME.
DAMN STRAIGHT. C'MON, BIG GUY. ON YOUR FEET.
WE HAVE TO GO TELL YOUR BOSS YOU QUIT.
I DON'T DESERVE YOUR KINDNESS.
YOU DON'T DESERVE TO PAY THE PRICE FOR MY HISTORY WITH CALCULATOR AS ORACLE. BUT THAT ENDS TONIGHT.

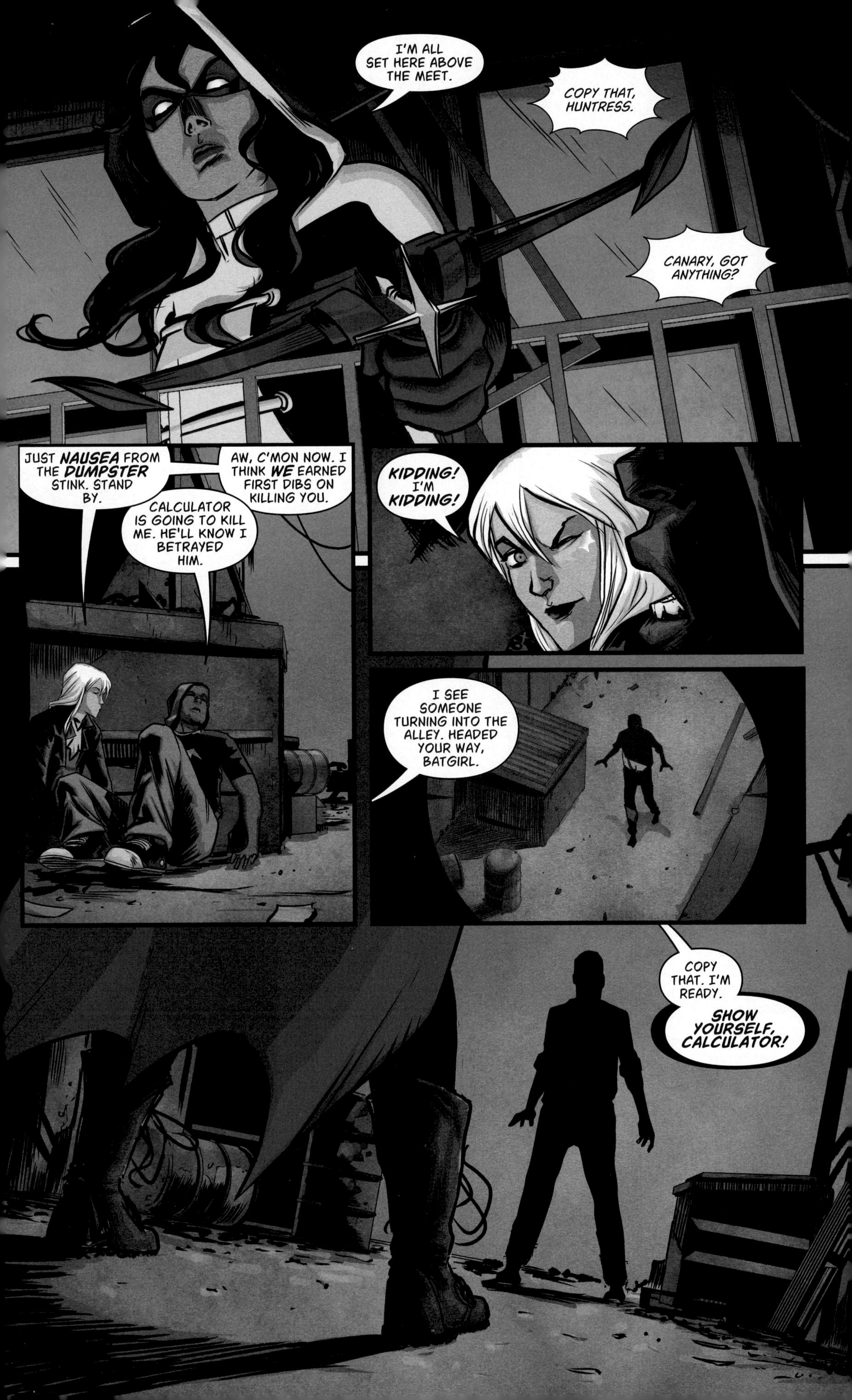

I'M ALL SET HERE ABOVE THE MEET.
COPY THAT, HUNTRESS.
CANARY, GOT ANYTHING?
JUST NAUSEA FROM THE DUMPSTER STINK. STAND BY.
CALCULATOR IS GOING TO KILL ME. HE'LL KNOW I BETRAYED HIM.
AW, C'MON NOW. I THINK WE EARNED FIRST DIBS ON KILLING YOU.
KIDDING! I'M KIDDING!
I SEE SOMEONE TURNING INTO THE ALLEY. HEADED YOUR WAY, BATGIRL.
COPY THAT. I'M READY.
SHOW YOURSELF, CALCULATOR!

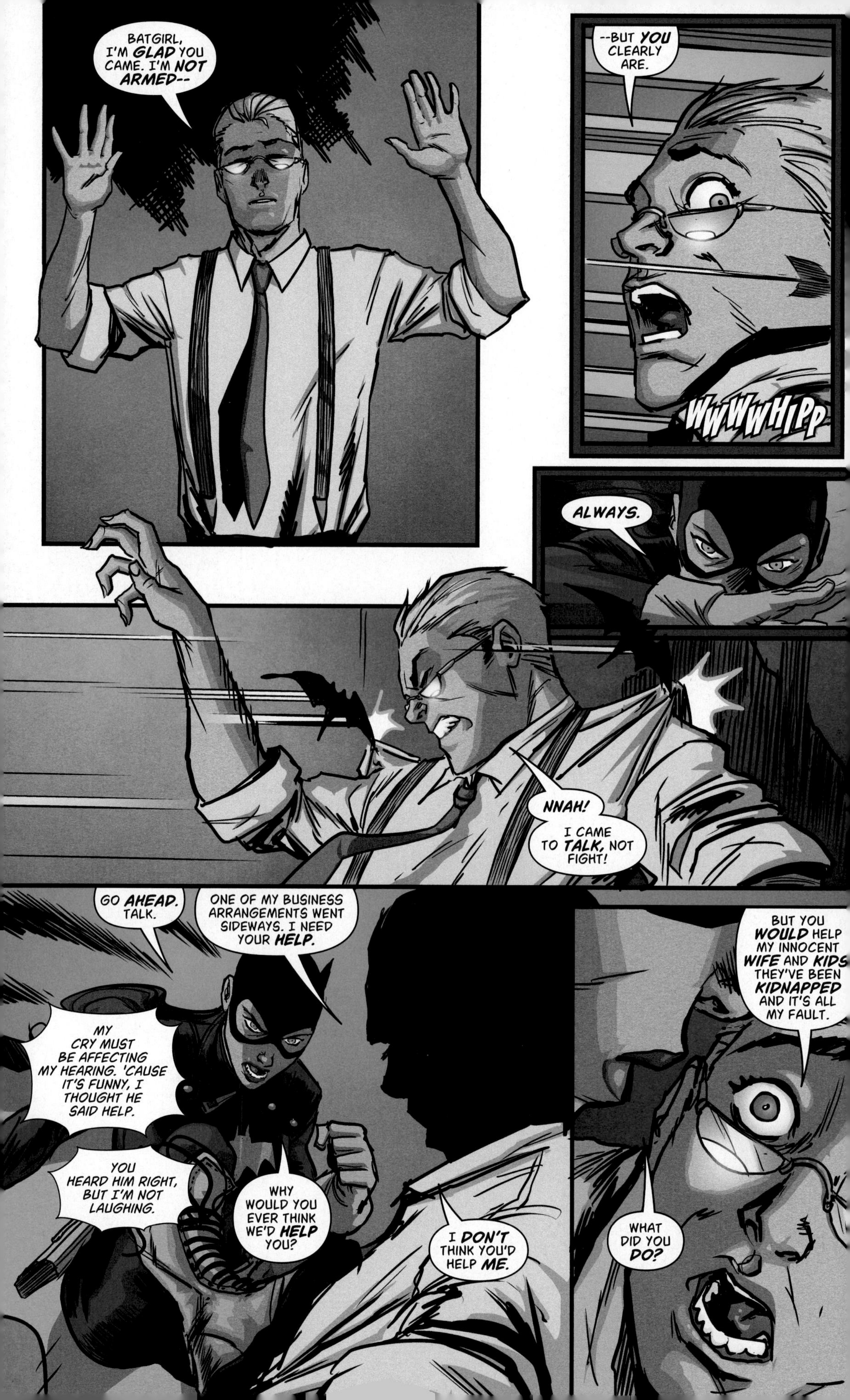
BATGIRL, I'M GLAD YOU CAME. I'M NOT ARMED--
--BUT YOU CLEARLY ARE.
WWWWHIPP
ALWAYS.
NNAH!
I CAME TO TALK, NOT FIGHT!
GO AHEAD. TALK.
ONE OF MY BUSINESS ARRANGEMENTS WENT SIDEWAYS. I NEED YOUR HELP.
MY CRY MUST BE AFFECTING MY HEARING. 'CAUSE IT'S FUNNY, I THOUGHT HE SAID HELP.
YOU HEARD HIM RIGHT, BUT I'M NOT LAUGHING.
WHY WOULD YOU EVER THINK WE'D HELP YOU?
I DON'T THINK YOU'D HELP ME.
BUT YOU WOULD HELP MY INNOCENT WIFE AND KIDS. THEY'VE BEEN KIDNAPPED AND IT'S ALL MY FAULT.
WHAT DID YOU DO?

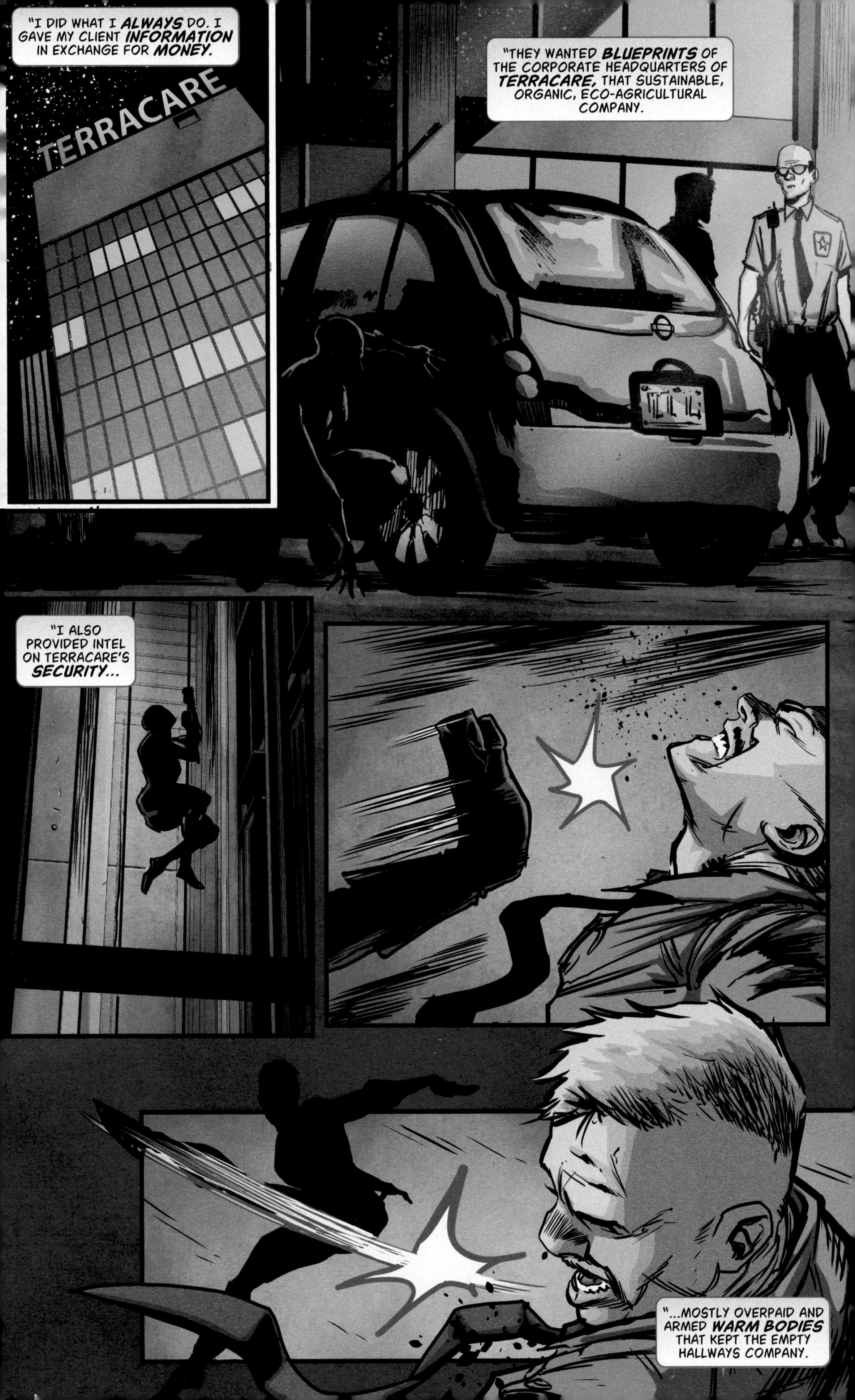
"I DID WHAT I ALWAYS DO. I GAVE MY CLIENT INFORMATION IN EXCHANGE FOR MONEY.
TERRACARE
"THEY WANTED BLUEPRINTS OF THE CORPORATE HEADQUARTERS OF TERRACARE, THAT SUSTAINABLE, ORGANIC, ECO-AGRICULTURAL COMPANY.
"I ALSO PROVIDED INTEL ON TERRACARE'S SECURITY...
"...MOSTLY OVERPAID AND ARMED WARM BODIES THAT KEPT THE EMPTY HALLWAYS COMPANY.

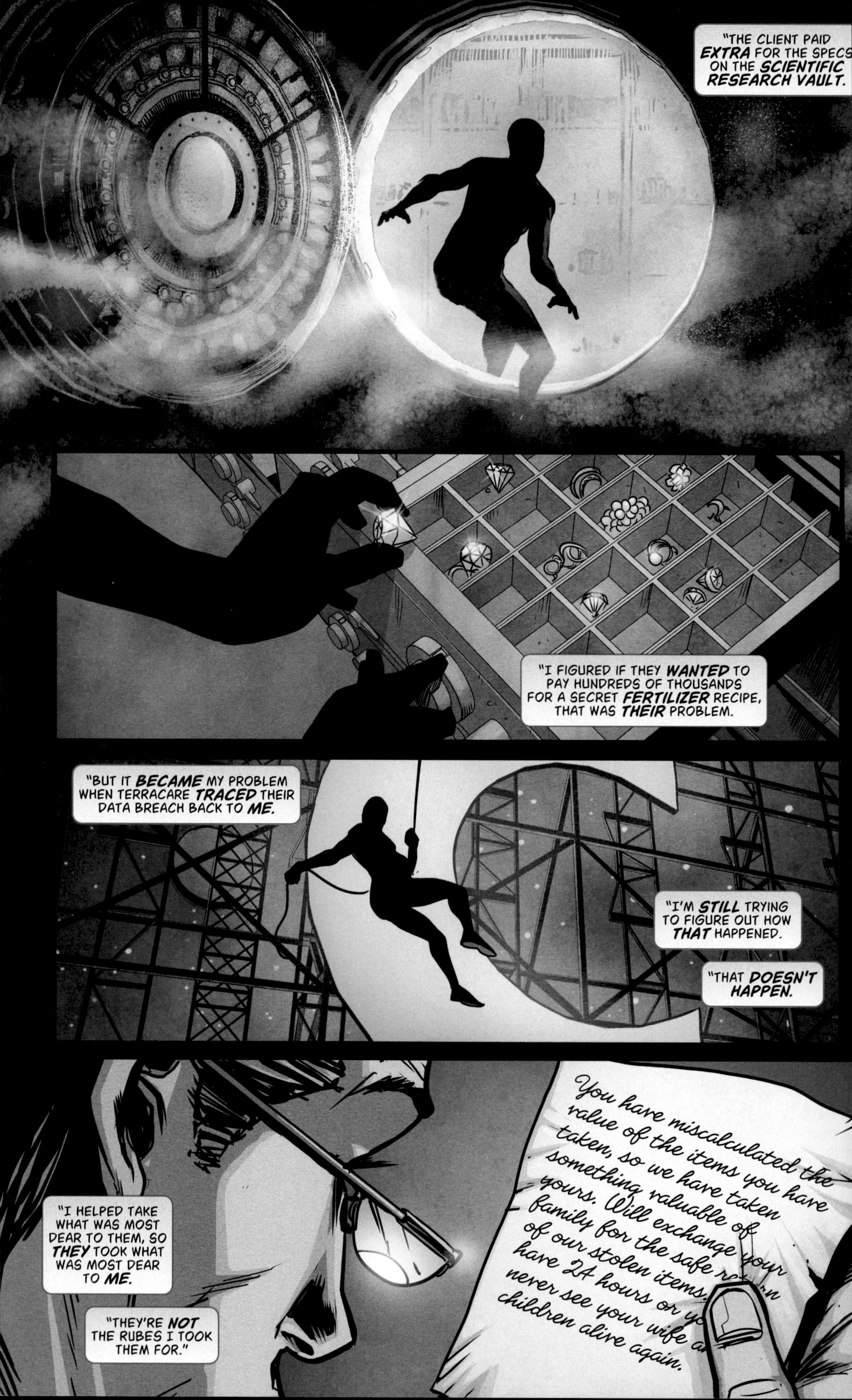
"THE CLIENT PAID EXTRA FOR THE SPECS ON THE SCIENTIFIC RESEARCH VAULT.
"I FIGURED IF THEY WANTED TO PAY HUNDREDS OF THOUSANDS FOR A SECRET FERTILIZER RECIPE, THAT WAS THEIR PROBLEM.
"BUT IT BECAME MY PROBLEM WHEN TERRACARE TRACED THEIR DATA BREACH BACK TO ME.
"I'M STILL TRYING TO FIGURE OUT HOW THAT HAPPENED.
"THAT DOESN'T HAPPEN.
You have miscalculated the
value of the items you have
taken, so we have taken
something valuable of
yours. Will exchange your
family for the safe r
of our stolen items.
have 24 hours or yo
never see your wife a
children alive again.
"I HELPED TAKE WHAT WAS MOST DEAR TO THEM, SO THEY TOOK WHAT WAS MOST DEAR TO ME.
"THEY'RE NOT THE RUBES I TOOK THEM FOR."

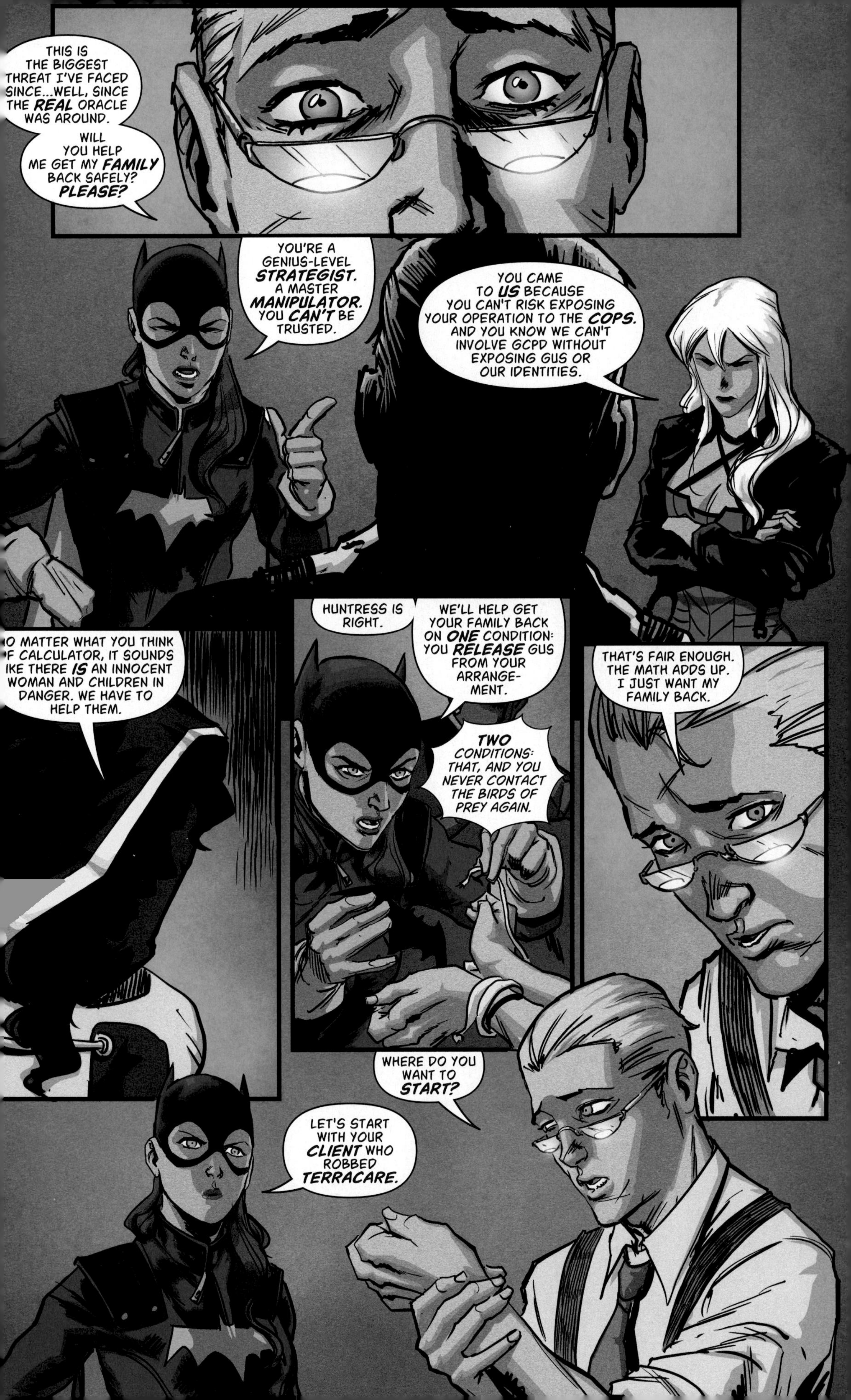
THIS IS THE BIGGEST THREAT I'VE FACED SINCE...WELL, SINCE THE REAL ORACLE WAS AROUND.
WILL YOU HELP ME GET MY FAMILY BACK SAFELY? PLEASE?
YOU'RE A GENIUS-LEVEL STRATEGIST. A MASTER MANIPULATOR. YOU CAN'T BE TRUSTED.
YOU CAME TO US BECAUSE YOU CAN'T RISK EXPOSING YOUR OPERATION TO THE COPS. AND YOU KNOW WE CAN'T INVOLVE GCPD WITHOUT EXPOSING GUS OR OUR IDENTITIES.
O MATTER WHAT YOU THINK F CALCULATOR, IT SOUNDS IKE THERE IS AN INNOCENT WOMAN AND CHILDREN IN DANGER. WE HAVE TO HELP THEM.
HUNTRESS IS RIGHT.
WE'LL HELP GET YOUR FAMILY BACK ON ONE CONDITION: YOU RELEASE GUS FROM YOUR ARRANGE-MENT.
TWO CONDITIONS: THAT, AND YOU NEVER CONTACT THE BIRDS OF PREY AGAIN.
THAT'S FAIR ENOUGH. THE MATH ADDS UP. I JUST WANT MY FAMILY BACK.
WHERE DO YOU WANT TO START?
LET'S START WITH YOUR CLIENT WHO ROBBED TERRACARE.

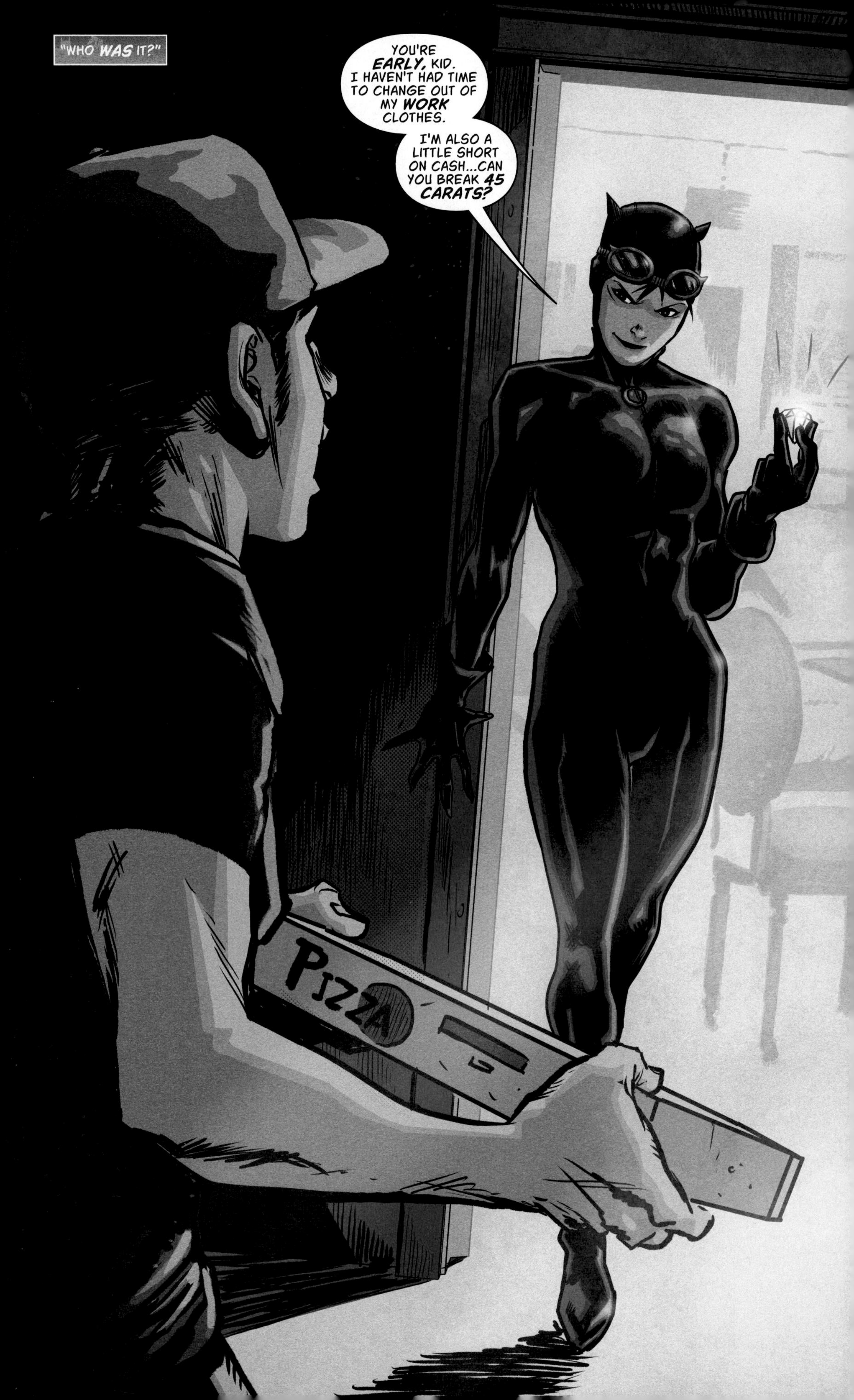
"WHO WAS IT?"
YOU'RE EARLY, KID. I HAVEN'T HAD TIME TO CHANGE OUT OF MY WORK CLOTHES.
I'M ALSO A LITTLE SHORT ON CASH...CAN YOU BREAK 45 CARATS?
PIZZA

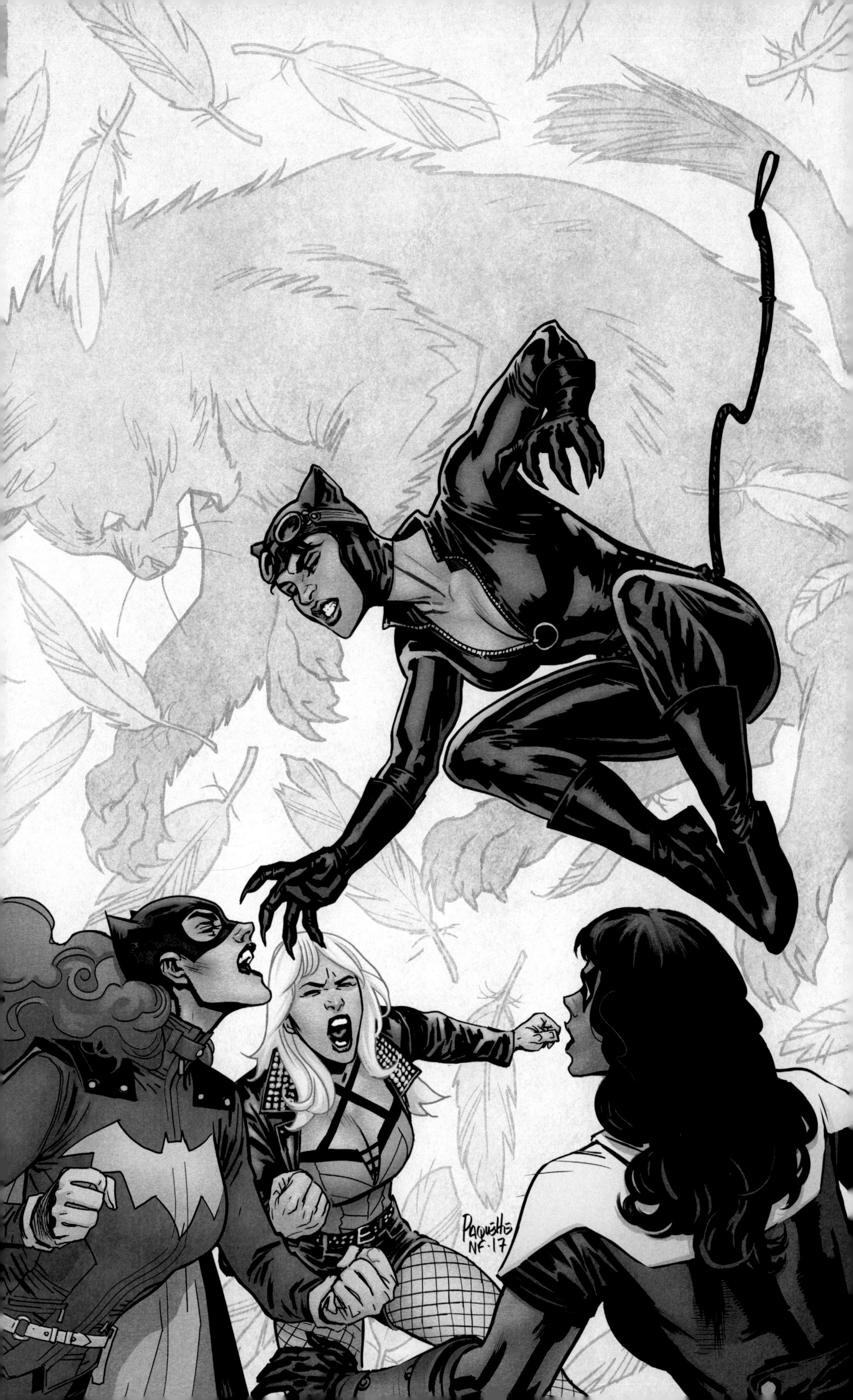

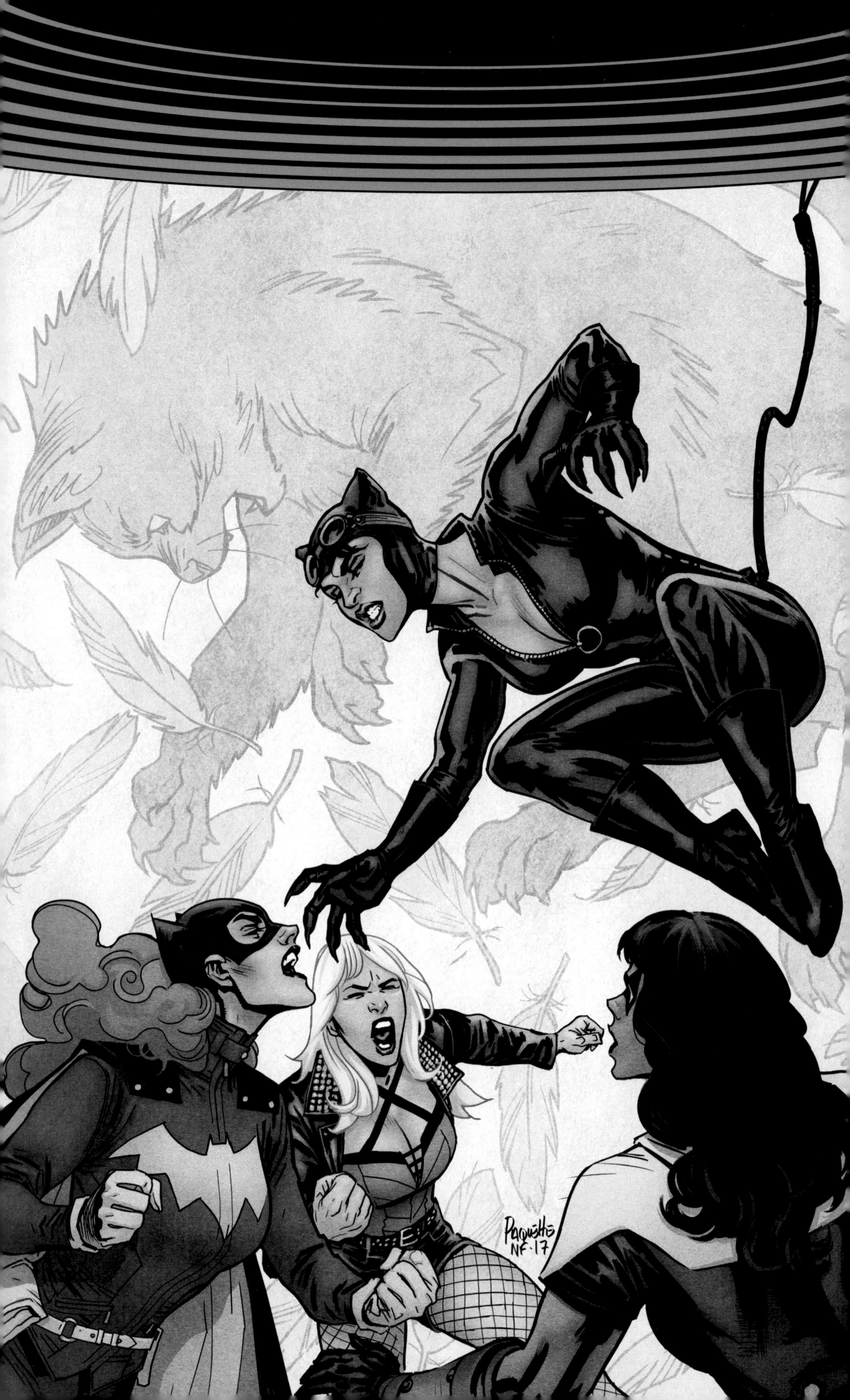

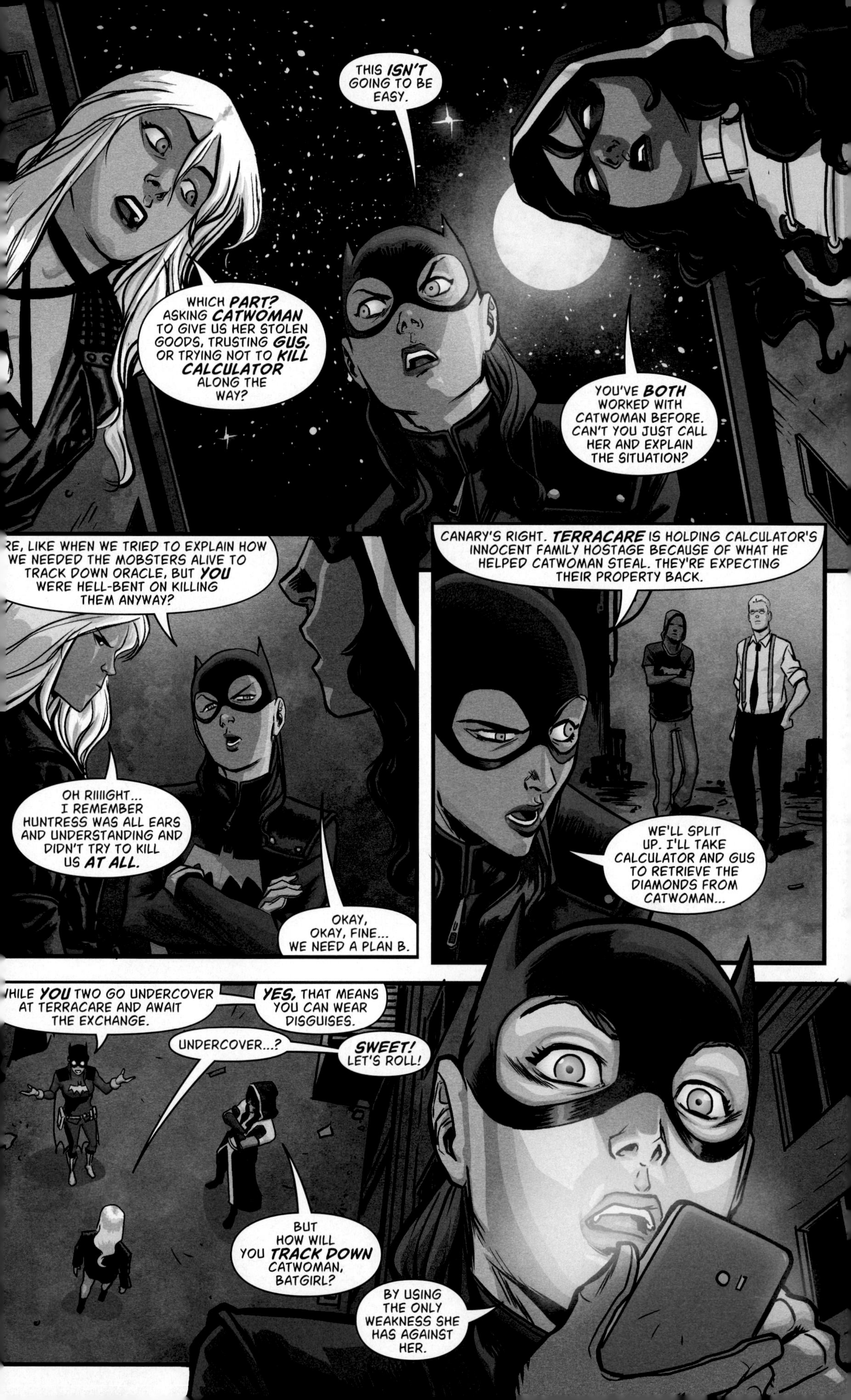
THIS ISN'T GOING TO BE EASY.
WHICH PART? ASKING CATWOMAN TO GIVE US HER STOLEN GOODS, TRUSTING GUS, OR TRYING NOT TO KILL CALCULATOR ALONG THE WAY?
YOU'VE BOTH WORKED WITH CATWOMAN BEFORE. CAN'T YOU JUST CALL HER AND EXPLAIN THE SITUATION?
RE, LIKE WHEN WE TRIED TO EXPLAIN HOW WE NEEDED THE MOBSTERS ALIVE TO TRACK DOWN ORACLE, BUT YOU WERE HELL-BENT ON KILLING THEM ANYWAY?
OH RIIIGHT... I REMEMBER HUNTRESS WAS ALL EARS AND UNDERSTANDING AND DIDN'T TRY TO KILL US AT ALL.
OKAY, OKAY, FINE... WE NEED A PLAN B.
CANARY'S RIGHT. TERRACARE IS HOLDING CALCULATOR'S INNOCENT FAMILY HOSTAGE BECAUSE OF WHAT HE HELPED CATWOMAN STEAL. THEY'RE EXPECTING THEIR PROPERTY BACK.
WE'LL SPLIT UP. I'LL TAKE CALCULATOR AND GUS TO RETRIEVE THE DIAMONDS FROM CATWOMAN...
HILE YOU TWO GO UNDERCOVER AT TERRACARE AND AWAIT THE EXCHANGE.
YES, THAT MEANS YOU CAN WEAR DISGUISES.
UNDERCOVER...?
SWEET! LET'S ROLL!
BUT HOW WILL YOU TRACK DOWN CATWOMAN, BATGIRL?
BY USING THE ONLY WEAKNESS SHE HAS AGAINST HER.

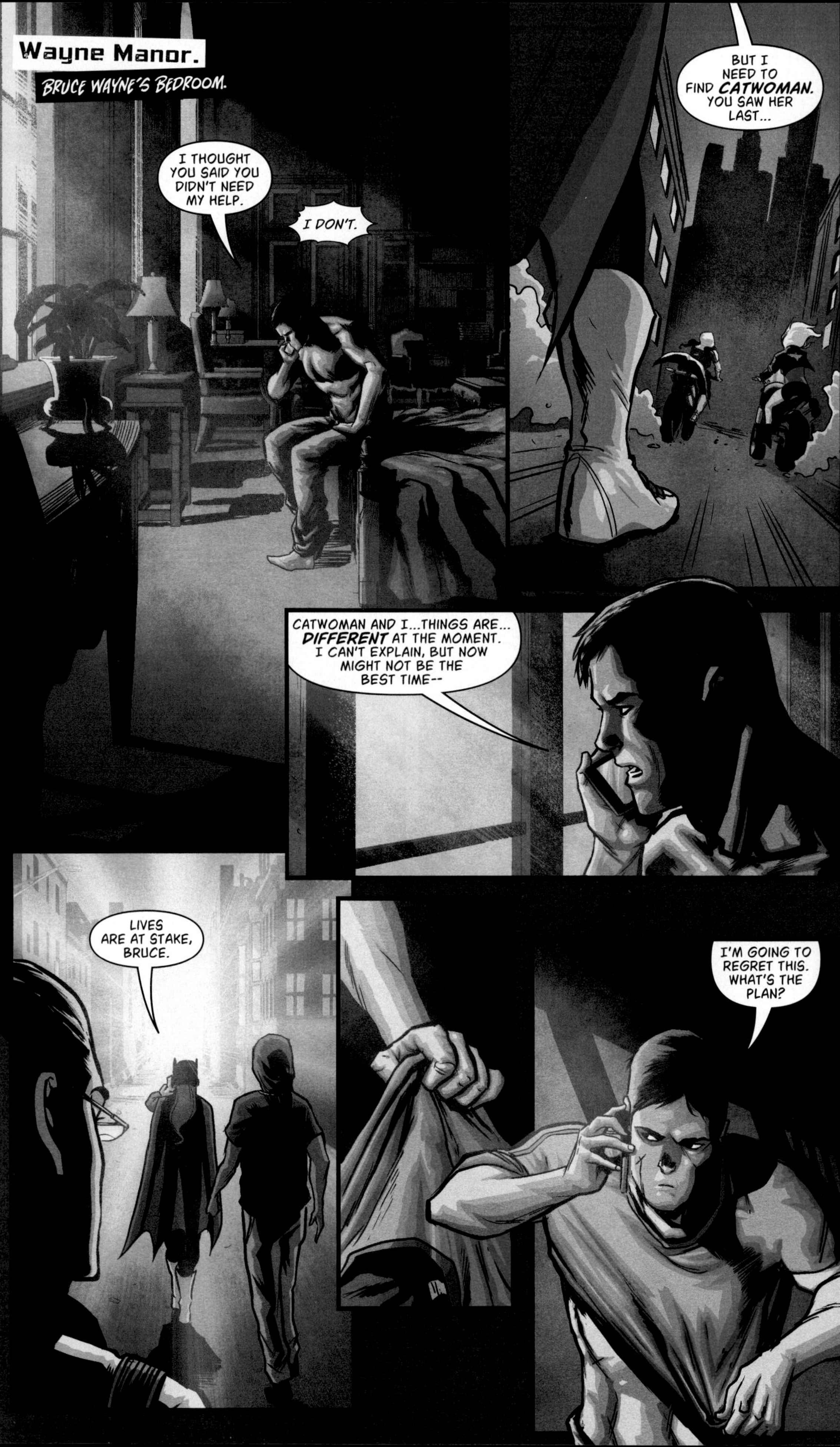
Wayne Manor.
BRUCE WAYNE'S BEDROOM.
I THOUGHT YOU SAID YOU DIDN'T NEED MY HELP.
I DON'T.
BUT I NEED TO FIND CATWOMAN. YOU SAW HER LAST...
CATWOMAN AND I...THINGS ARE... DIFFERENT AT THE MOMENT. I CAN'T EXPLAIN, BUT NOW MIGHT NOT BE THE BEST TIME--
LIVES ARE AT STAKE, BRUCE.
I'M GOING TO REGRET THIS. WHAT'S THE PLAN?

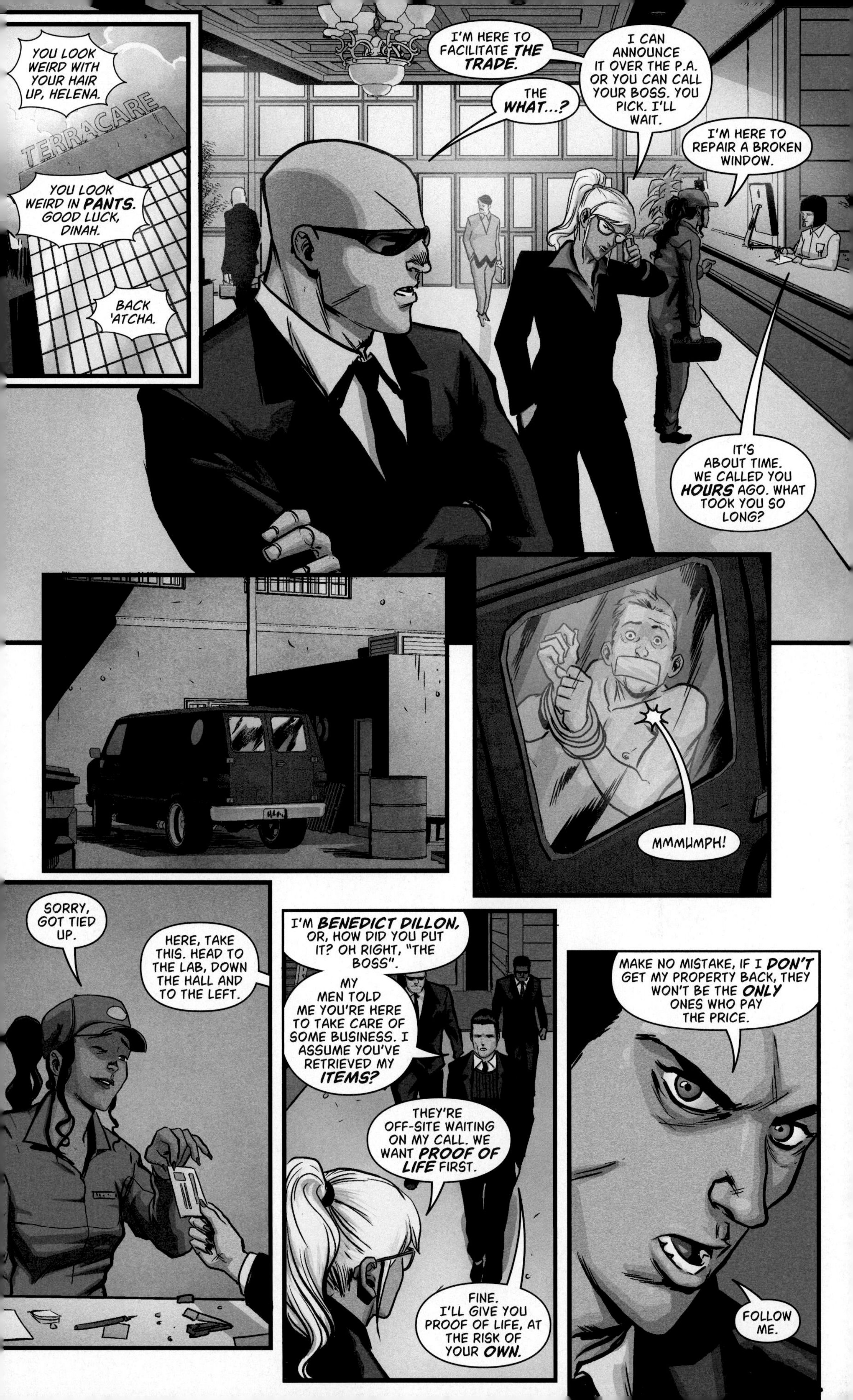

YOU LOOK WEIRD WITH YOUR HAIR UP, HELENA.
TERRACARE
YOU LOOK WEIRD IN PANTS. GOOD LUCK, DINAH.
BACK 'ATCHA.
I'M HERE TO FACILITATE THE TRADE.
THE WHAT...?
I CAN ANNOUNCE IT OVER THE P.A. OR YOU CAN CALL YOUR BOSS. YOU PICK. I'LL WAIT.
I'M HERE TO REPAIR A BROKEN WINDOW.
IT'S ABOUT TIME. WE CALLED YOU HOURS AGO. WHAT TOOK YOU SO LONG?
MMMUMPH!
SORRY, GOT TIED UP.
HERE, TAKE THIS. HEAD TO THE LAB, DOWN THE HALL AND TO THE LEFT.
I'M BENEDICT DILLON, OR, HOW DID YOU PUT IT? OH RIGHT, "THE BOSS".
MY MEN TOLD ME YOU'RE HERE TO TAKE CARE OF SOME BUSINESS. I ASSUME YOU'VE RETRIEVED MY ITEMS?
THEY'RE OFF-SITE WAITING ON MY CALL. WE WANT PROOF OF LIFE FIRST.
FINE. I'LL GIVE YOU PROOF OF LIFE, AT THE RISK OF YOUR OWN.
MAKE NO MISTAKE, IF I DON'T GET MY PROPERTY BACK, THEY WON'T BE THE ONLY ONES WHO PAY THE PRICE.
FOLLOW ME.

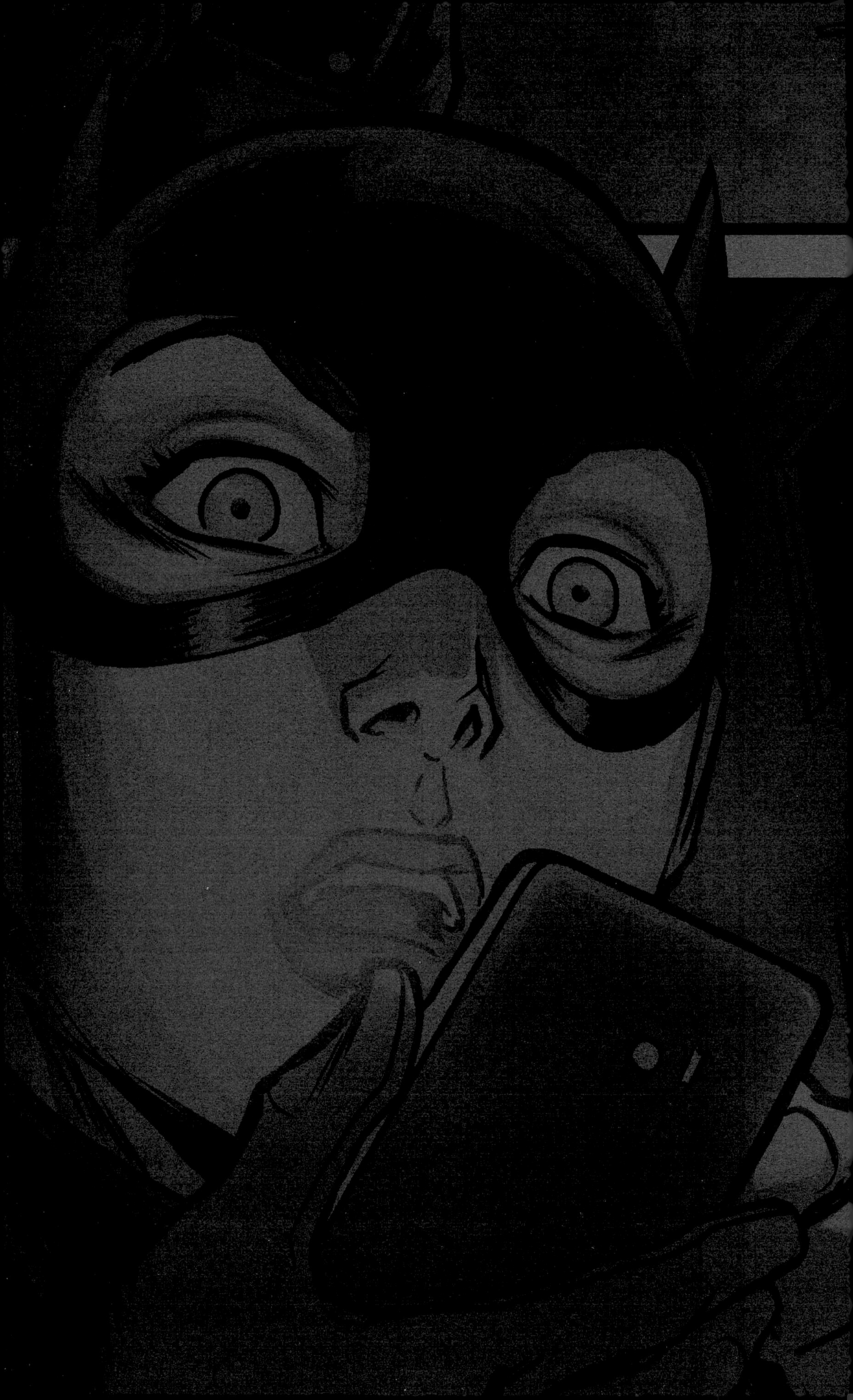

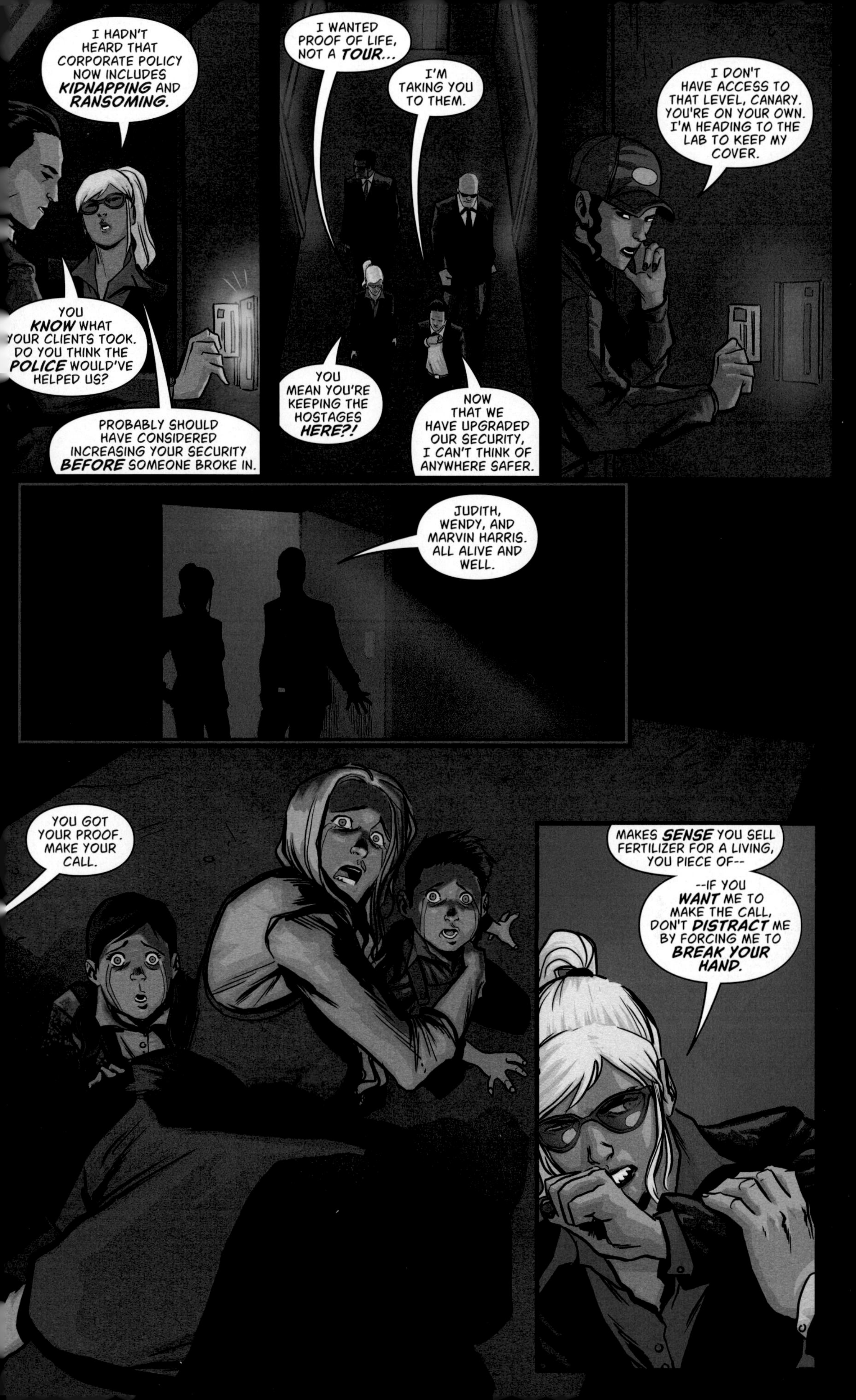
I HADN'T HEARD THAT CORPORATE POLICY NOW INCLUDES **KIDNAPPING** AND **RANSOMING.**
YOU **KNOW** WHAT YOUR CLIENTS TOOK. DO YOU THINK THE **POLICE** WOULD'VE HELPED US?
PROBABLY SHOULD HAVE CONSIDERED INCREASING YOUR SECURITY **BEFORE** SOMEONE BROKE IN.
I WANTED PROOF OF LIFE, NOT A **TOUR...**
I'M TAKING YOU TO THEM.
YOU MEAN YOU'RE KEEPING THE HOSTAGES **HERE?!**
NOW THAT WE HAVE UPGRADED OUR SECURITY, I CAN'T THINK OF ANYWHERE SAFER.
I DON'T HAVE ACCESS TO THAT LEVEL, CANARY. YOU'RE ON YOUR OWN. I'M HEADING TO THE LAB TO KEEP MY COVER.
JUDITH, WENDY, AND MARVIN HARRIS. ALL ALIVE AND WELL.
YOU GOT YOUR PROOF. MAKE YOUR CALL.
MAKES **SENSE** YOU SELL FERTILIZER FOR A LIVING, YOU PIECE OF--
--IF YOU **WANT** ME TO MAKE THE CALL, DON'T **DISTRACT** ME BY FORCING ME TO **BREAK YOUR HAND.**

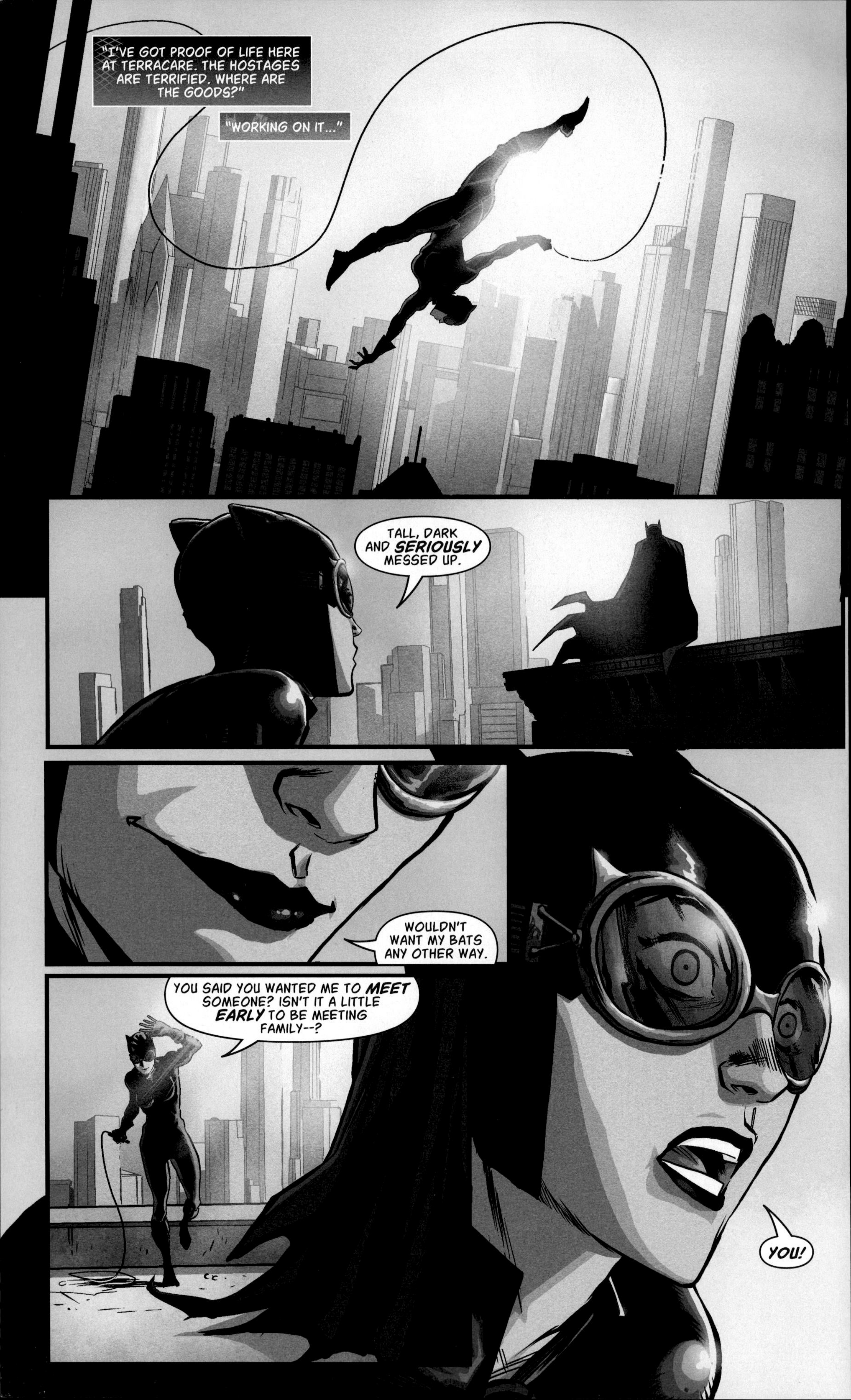
"I'VE GOT PROOF OF LIFE HERE AT TERRACARE. THE HOSTAGES ARE TERRIFIED. WHERE ARE THE GOODS?"
"WORKING ON IT..."
TALL, DARK AND SERIOUSLY MESSED UP.
WOULDN'T WANT MY BATS ANY OTHER WAY.
YOU SAID YOU WANTED ME TO MEET SOMEONE? ISN'T IT A LITTLE EARLY TO BE MEETING FAMILY--?
YOU!

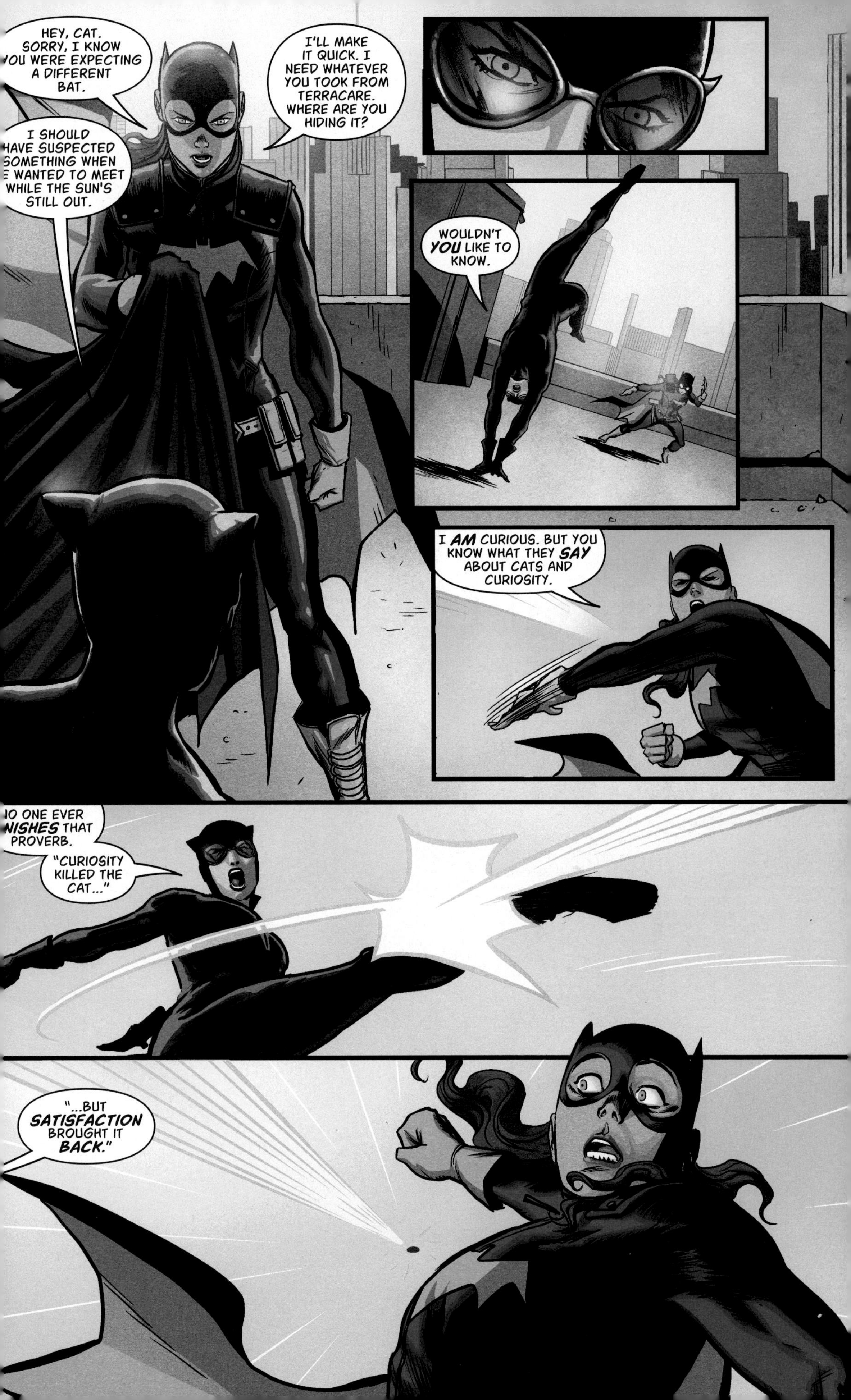
HEY, CAT. SORRY, I KNOW YOU WERE EXPECTING A DIFFERENT BAT.
I SHOULD HAVE SUSPECTED SOMETHING WHEN WANTED TO MEET WHILE THE SUN'S STILL OUT.
I'LL MAKE IT QUICK. I NEED WHATEVER YOU TOOK FROM TERRACARE. WHERE ARE YOU HIDING IT?
WOULDN'T YOU LIKE TO KNOW.
I AM CURIOUS. BUT YOU KNOW WHAT THEY SAY ABOUT CATS AND CURIOSITY.
NO ONE EVER FINISHES THAT PROVERB.
"CURIOSITY KILLED THE CAT..."
"...BUT SATISFACTION BROUGHT IT BACK."

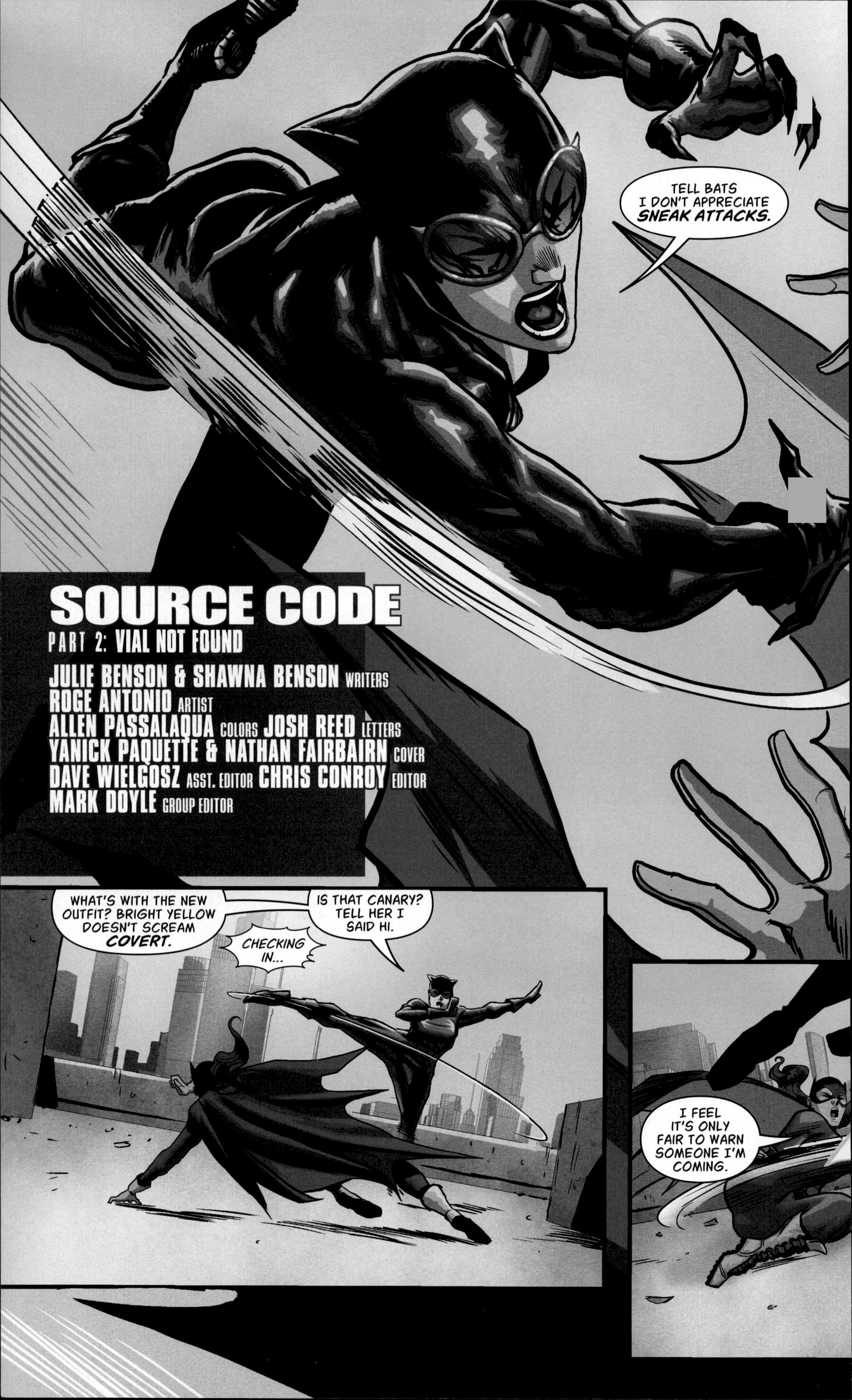
TELL BATS
I DON'T APPRECIATE
SNEAK ATTACKS.
SOURCE CODE
PART 2: VIAL NOT FOUND
JULIE BENSON & SHAWNA BENSON WRITERS
ROGE ANTONIO ARTIST
ALLEN PASSALAQUA COLORS JOSH REED LETTERS
YANICK PAQUETTE & NATHAN FAIRBAIRN COVER
DAVE WIELGOSZ ASST. EDITOR CHRIS CONROY EDITOR
MARK DOYLE GROUP EDITOR
WHAT'S WITH THE NEW OUTFIT? BRIGHT YELLOW DOESN'T SCREAM COVERT.
CHECKING IN...
IS THAT CANARY? TELL HER I SAID HI.
I FEEL IT'S ONLY FAIR TO WARN SOMEONE I'M COMING.

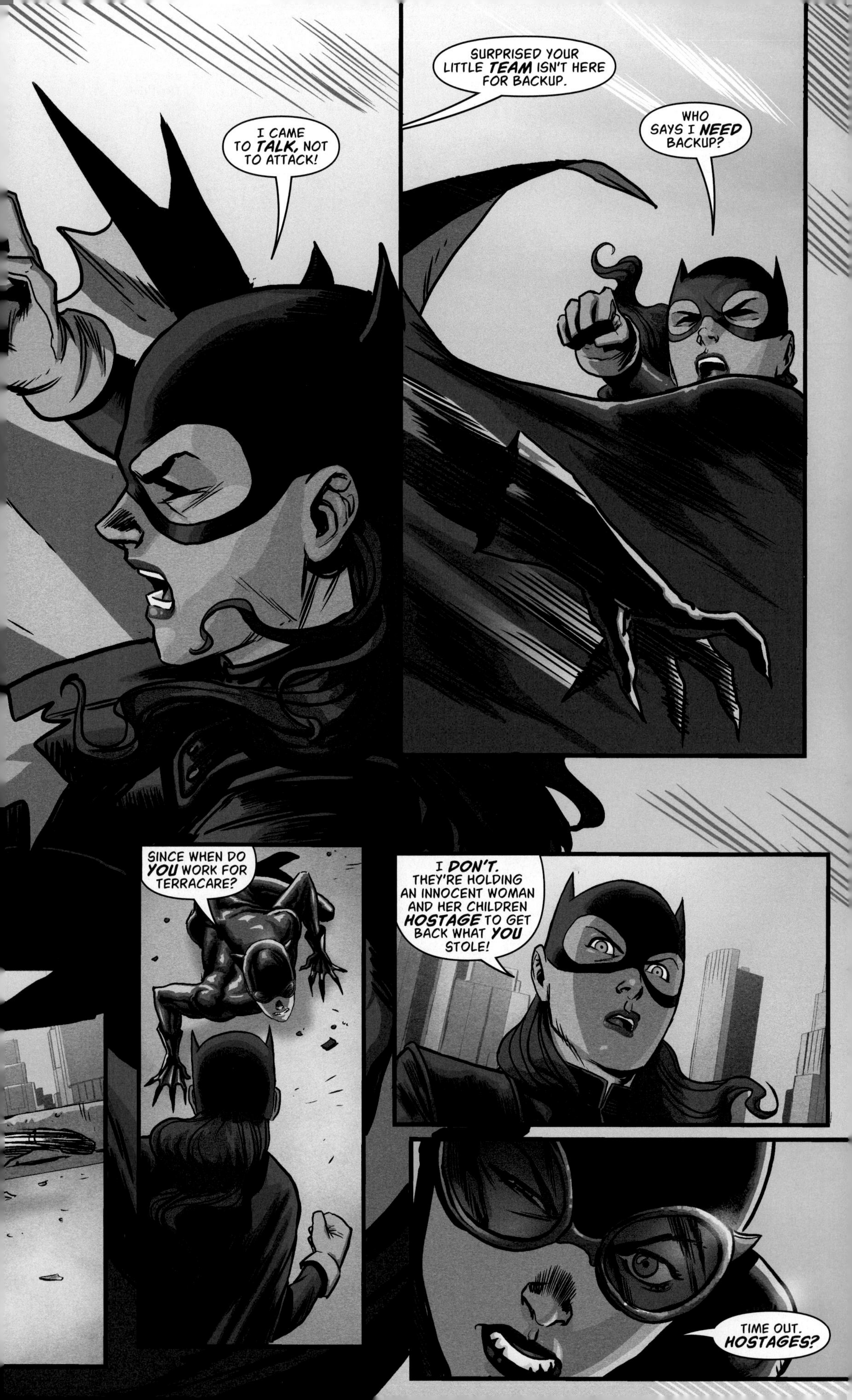
I CAME TO TALK, NOT TO ATTACK!
SURPRISED YOUR LITTLE TEAM ISN'T HERE FOR BACKUP.
WHO SAYS I NEED BACKUP?
SINCE WHEN DO YOU WORK FOR TERRACARE?
I DON'T. THEY'RE HOLDING AN INNOCENT WOMAN AND HER CHILDREN HOSTAGE TO GET BACK WHAT YOU STOLE!
TIME OUT. HOSTAGES?

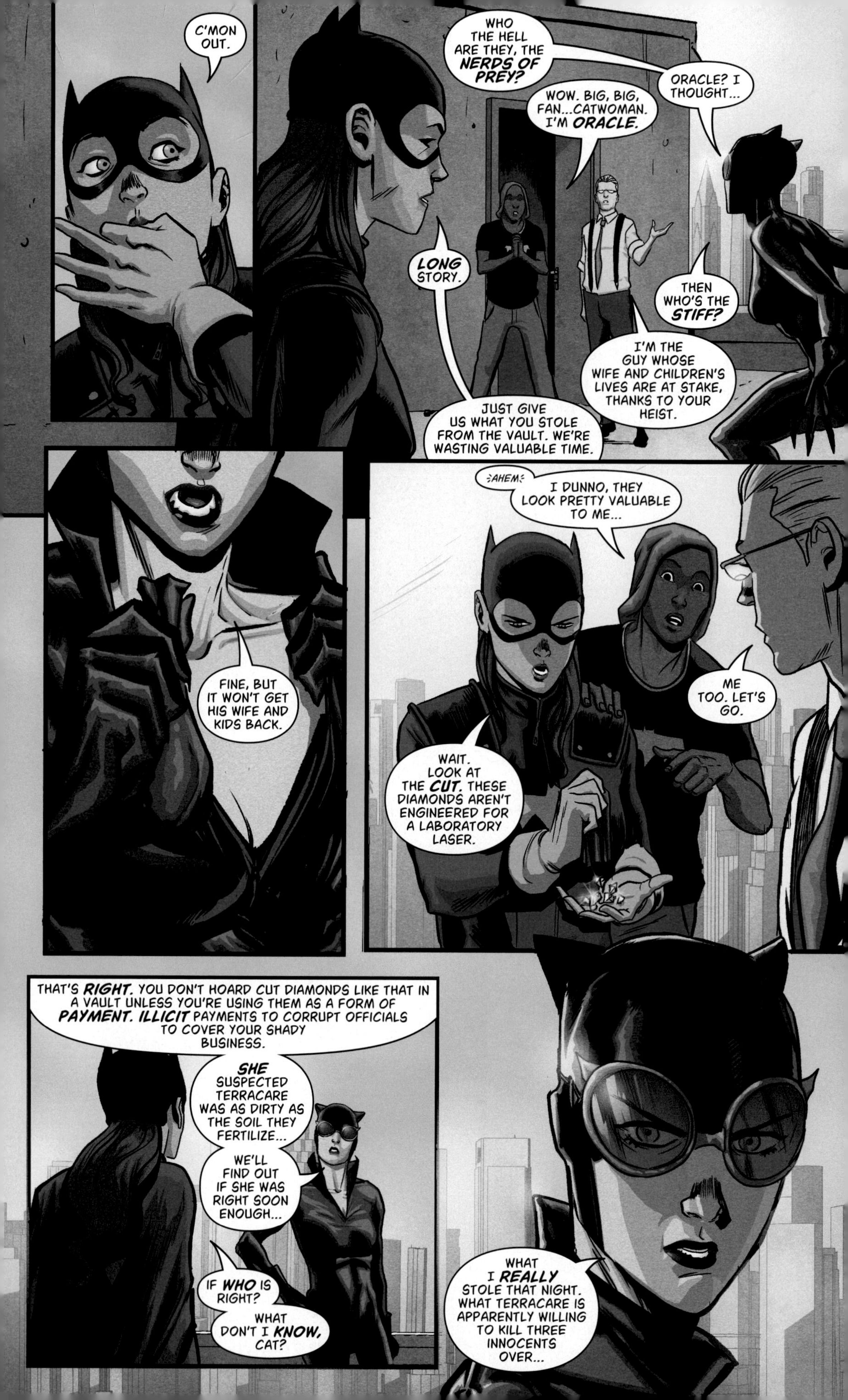
C'MON OUT.
WHO THE HELL ARE THEY, THE NERDS OF PREY?
ORACLE? I THOUGHT...
WOW. BIG, BIG, FAN...CATWOMAN. I'M ORACLE.
LONG STORY.
THEN WHO'S THE STIFF?
I'M THE GUY WHOSE WIFE AND CHILDREN'S LIVES ARE AT STAKE, THANKS TO YOUR HEIST.
JUST GIVE US WHAT YOU STOLE FROM THE VAULT. WE'RE WASTING VALUABLE TIME.
FINE, BUT IT WON'T GET HIS WIFE AND KIDS BACK.
AHEM
I DUNNO, THEY LOOK PRETTY VALUABLE TO ME...
ME TOO. LET'S GO.
WAIT. LOOK AT THE CUT. THESE DIAMONDS AREN'T ENGINEERED FOR A LABORATORY LASER.
THAT'S RIGHT. YOU DON'T HOARD CUT DIAMONDS LIKE THAT IN A VAULT UNLESS YOU'RE USING THEM AS A FORM OF PAYMENT. ILLICIT PAYMENTS TO CORRUPT OFFICIALS TO COVER YOUR SHADY BUSINESS.
SHE SUSPECTED TERRACARE WAS AS DIRTY AS THE SOIL THEY FERTILIZE...
WE'LL FIND OUT IF SHE WAS RIGHT SOON ENOUGH...
IF WHO IS RIGHT?
WHAT DON'T I KNOW, CAT?
WHAT I REALLY STOLE THAT NIGHT. WHAT TERRACARE IS APPARENTLY WILLING TO KILL THREE INNOCENTS OVER...

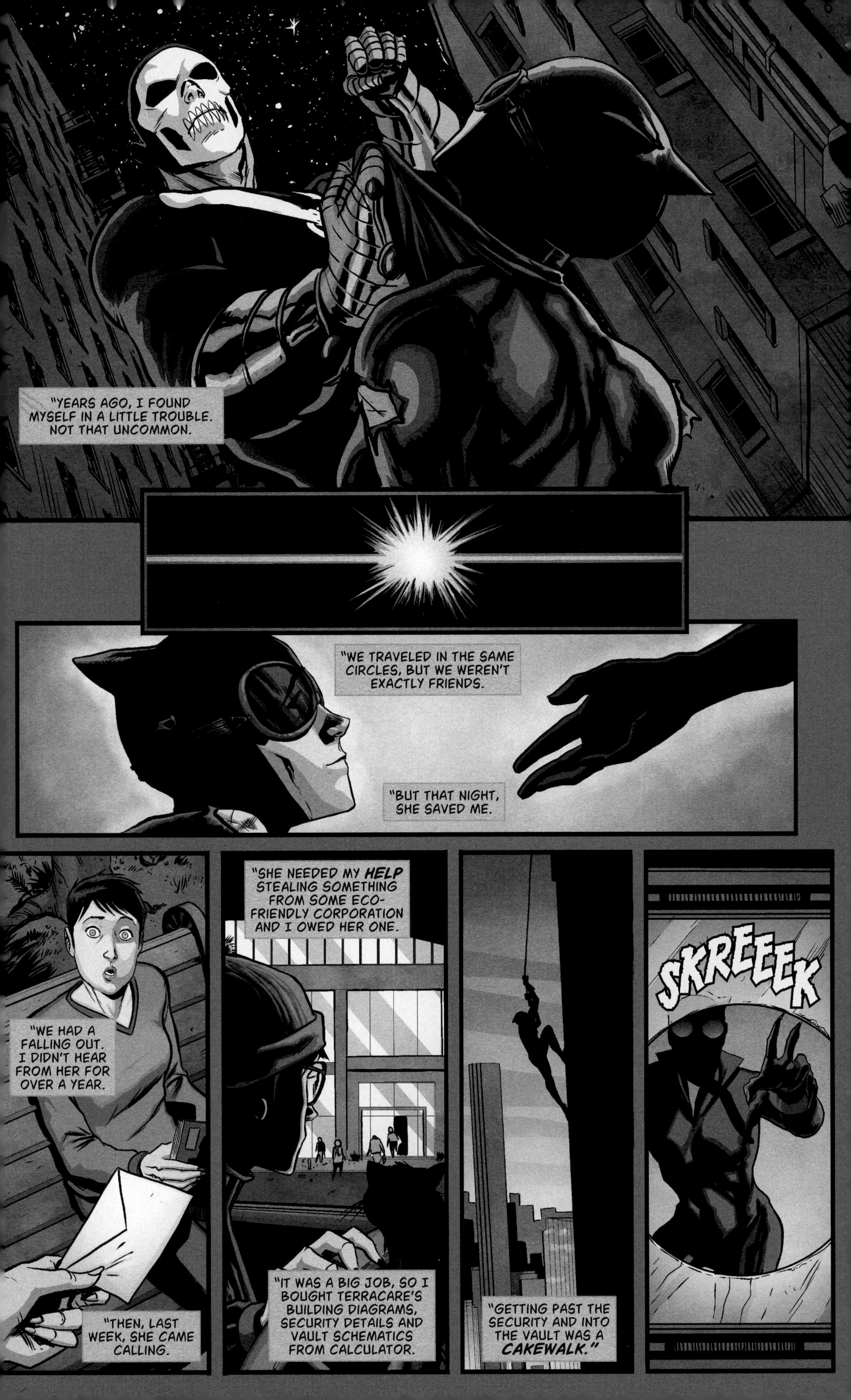
"YEARS AGO, I FOUND MYSELF IN A LITTLE TROUBLE. NOT THAT UNCOMMON.
"WE TRAVELED IN THE SAME CIRCLES, BUT WE WEREN'T EXACTLY FRIENDS.
"BUT THAT NIGHT, SHE SAVED ME.
"WE HAD A FALLING OUT. I DIDN'T HEAR FROM HER FOR OVER A YEAR.
"THEN, LAST WEEK, SHE CAME CALLING.
"SHE NEEDED MY HELP STEALING SOMETHING FROM SOME ECO-FRIENDLY CORPORATION AND I OWED HER ONE.
"IT WAS A BIG JOB, SO I BOUGHT TERRACARE'S BUILDING DIAGRAMS, SECURITY DETAILS AND VAULT SCHEMATICS FROM CALCULATOR.
"GETTING PAST THE SECURITY AND INTO THE VAULT WAS A CAKEWALK."
SKREEEK

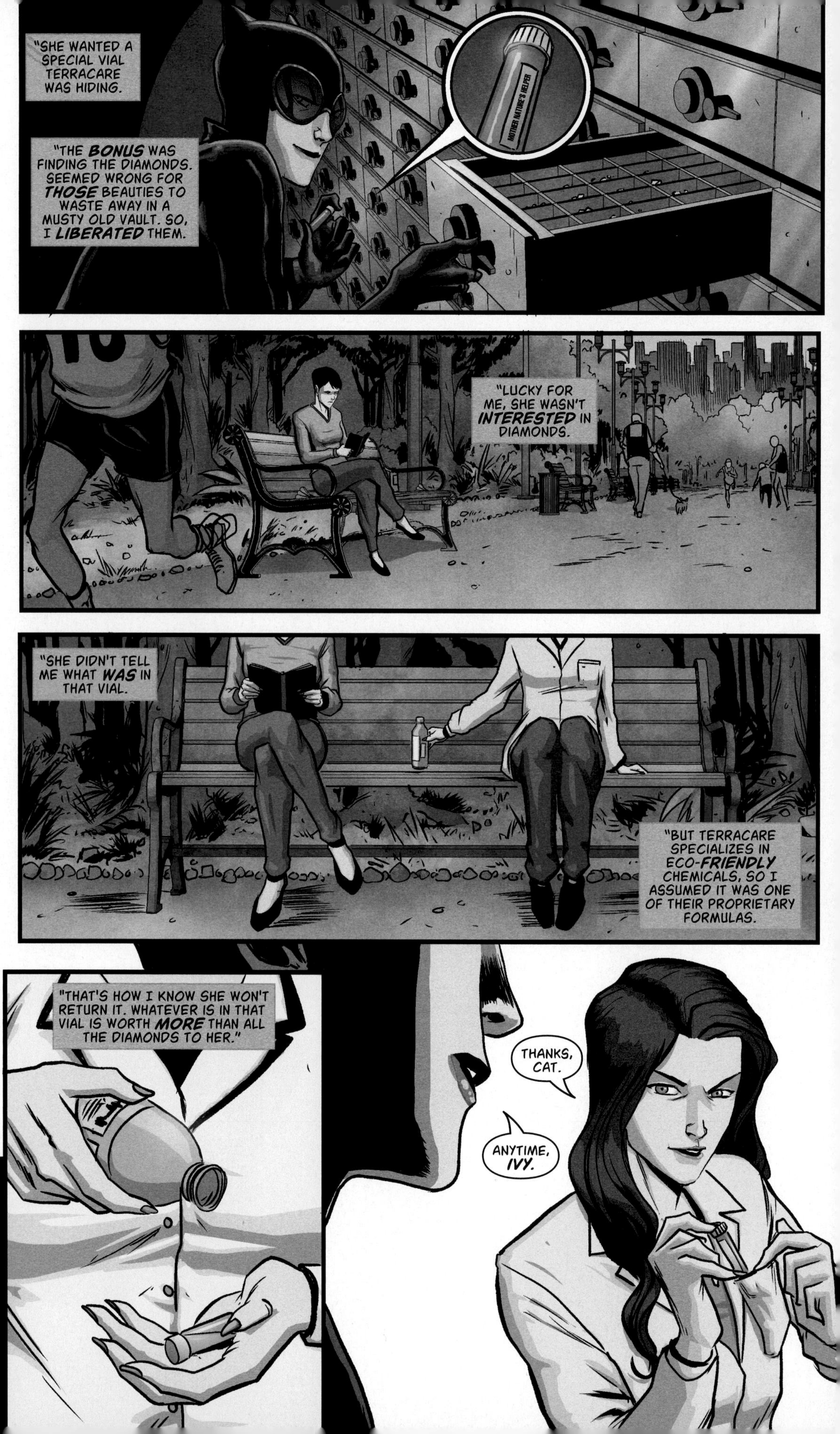
"SHE WANTED A SPECIAL VIAL TERRACARE WAS HIDING.
MOTHER NATURE'S HELPER
"THE BONUS WAS FINDING THE DIAMONDS. SEEMED WRONG FOR THOSE BEAUTIES TO WASTE AWAY IN A MUSTY OLD VAULT. SO, I LIBERATED THEM.
"LUCKY FOR ME, SHE WASN'T INTERESTED IN DIAMONDS.
"SHE DIDN'T TELL ME WHAT WAS IN THAT VIAL.
"BUT TERRACARE SPECIALIZES IN ECO-FRIENDLY CHEMICALS, SO I ASSUMED IT WAS ONE OF THEIR PROPRIETARY FORMULAS.
"THAT'S HOW I KNOW SHE WON'T RETURN IT. WHATEVER IS IN THAT VIAL IS WORTH MORE THAN ALL THE DIAMONDS TO HER."
THANKS, CAT.
ANYTIME, IVY.

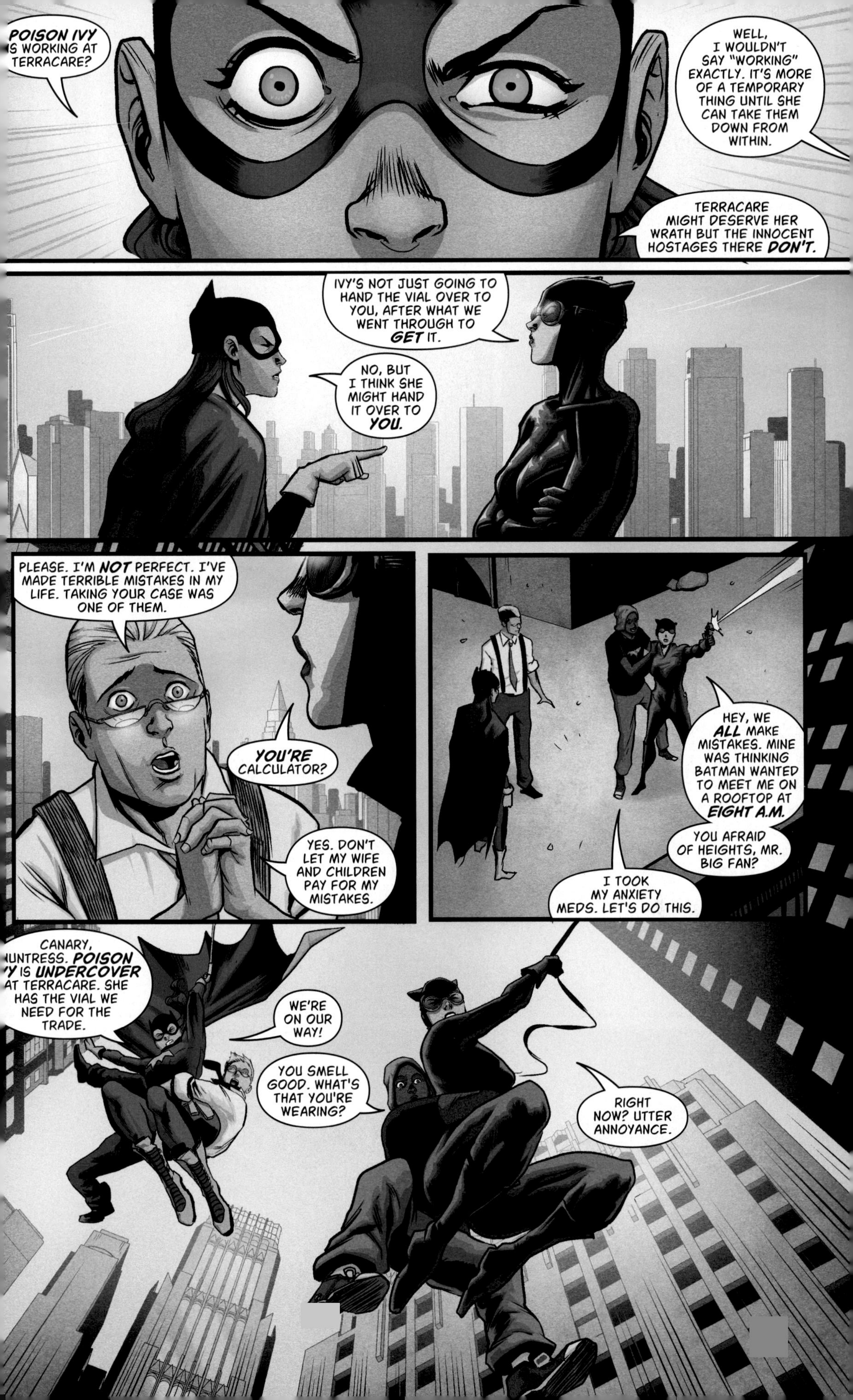
POISON IVY IS WORKING AT TERRACARE?
WELL, I WOULDN'T SAY "WORKING" EXACTLY. IT'S MORE OF A TEMPORARY THING UNTIL SHE CAN TAKE THEM DOWN FROM WITHIN.
TERRACARE MIGHT DESERVE HER WRATH BUT THE INNOCENT HOSTAGES THERE DON'T.
IVY'S NOT JUST GOING TO HAND THE VIAL OVER TO YOU, AFTER WHAT WE WENT THROUGH TO GET IT.
NO, BUT I THINK SHE MIGHT HAND IT OVER TO YOU.
PLEASE. I'M NOT PERFECT. I'VE MADE TERRIBLE MISTAKES IN MY LIFE. TAKING YOUR CASE WAS ONE OF THEM.
YOU'RE CALCULATOR?
YES. DON'T LET MY WIFE AND CHILDREN PAY FOR MY MISTAKES.
HEY, WE ALL MAKE MISTAKES. MINE WAS THINKING BATMAN WANTED TO MEET ME ON A ROOFTOP AT EIGHT A.M.
YOU AFRAID OF HEIGHTS, MR. BIG FAN?
I TOOK MY ANXIETY MEDS. LET'S DO THIS.
CANARY, HUNTRESS. POISON IVY IS UNDERCOVER AT TERRACARE. SHE HAS THE VIAL WE NEED FOR THE TRADE.
WE'RE ON OUR WAY!
YOU SMELL GOOD. WHAT'S THAT YOU'RE WEARING?
RIGHT NOW? UTTER ANNOYANCE.

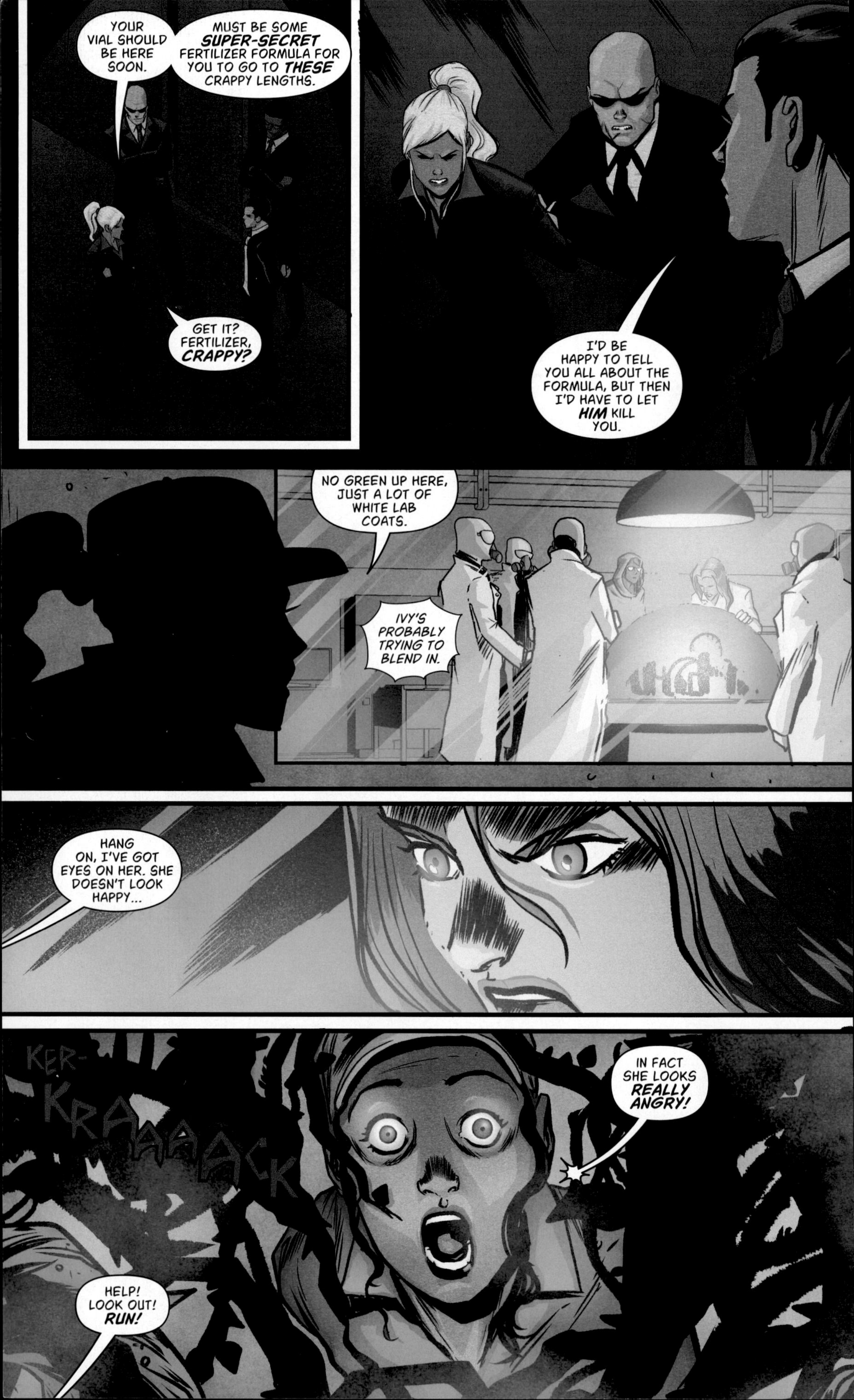
YOUR VIAL SHOULD BE HERE SOON.
MUST BE SOME SUPER-SECRET FERTILIZER FORMULA FOR YOU TO GO TO THESE CRAPPY LENGTHS.
GET IT? FERTILIZER, CRAPPY?
I'D BE HAPPY TO TELL YOU ALL ABOUT THE FORMULA, BUT THEN I'D HAVE TO LET HIM KILL YOU.
NO GREEN UP HERE, JUST A LOT OF WHITE LAB COATS.
IVY'S PROBABLY TRYING TO BLEND IN.
HANG ON, I'VE GOT EYES ON HER. SHE DOESN'T LOOK HAPPY...
KER-KRAAAACK
IN FACT SHE LOOKS REALLY ANGRY!
HELP! LOOK OUT! RUN!

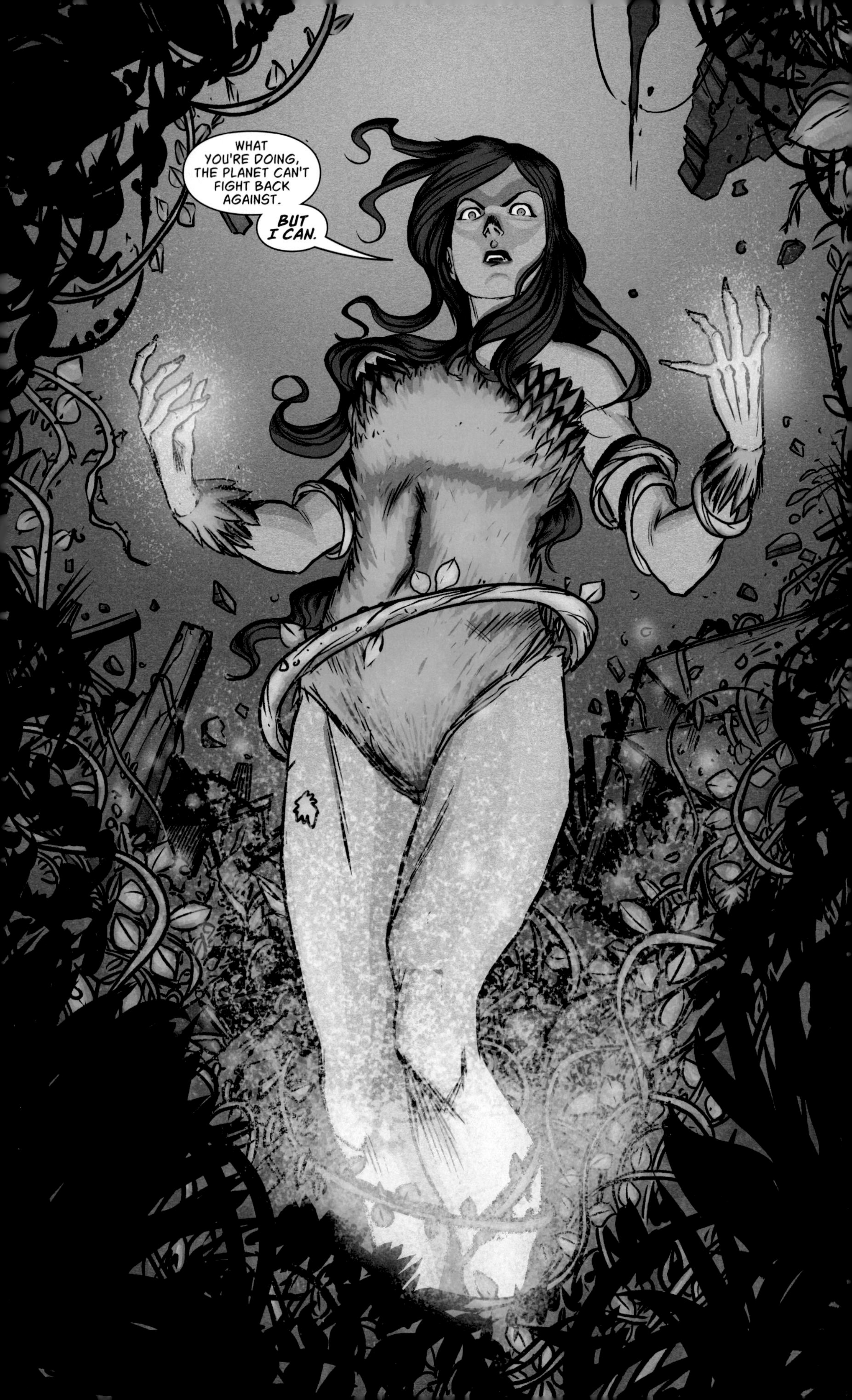
WHAT YOU'RE DOING, THE PLANET CAN'T FIGHT BACK AGAINST.
BUT I CAN.

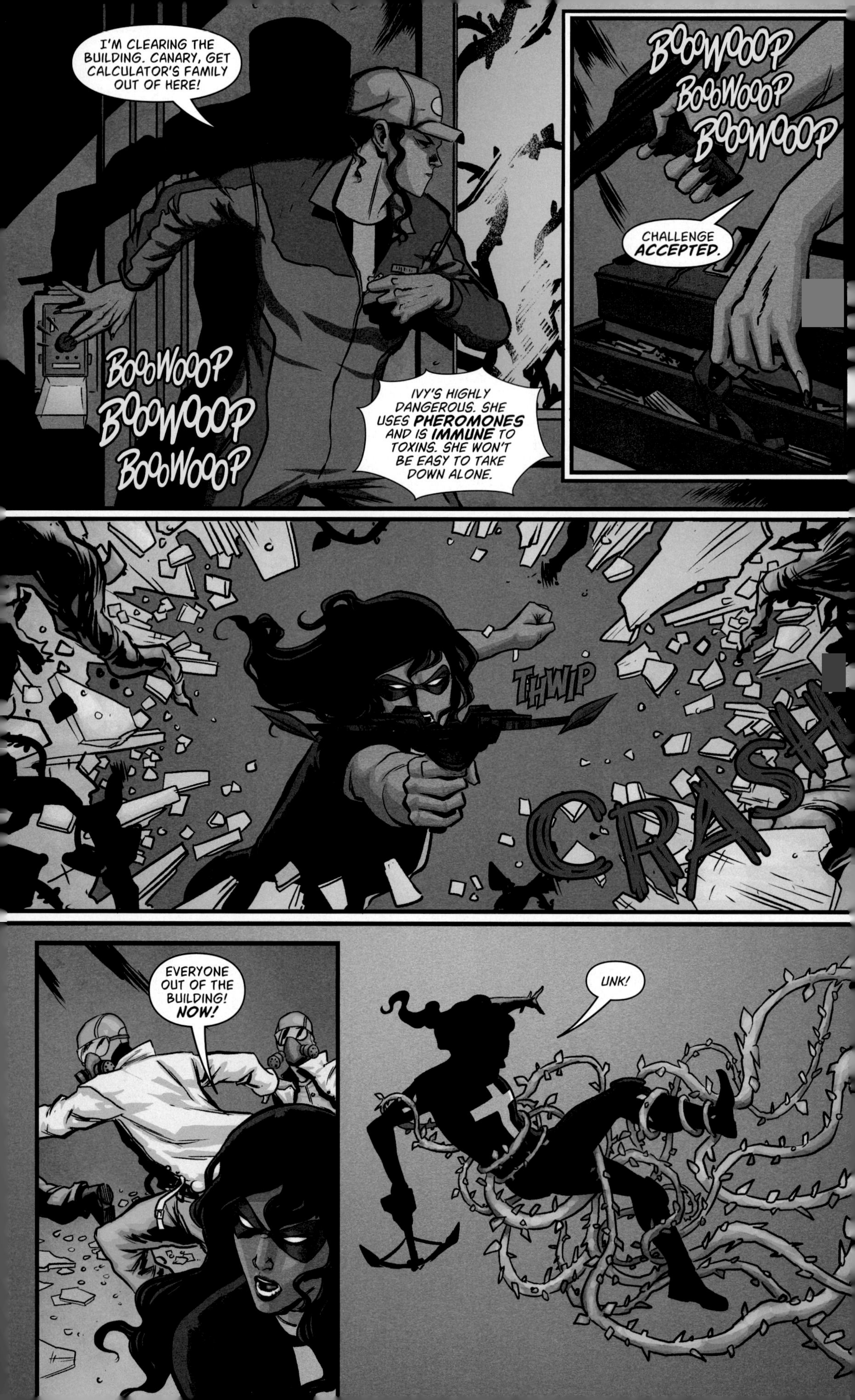
I'M CLEARING THE BUILDING. CANARY, GET CALCULATOR'S FAMILY OUT OF HERE!
BOOOWOOOP
BOOOWOOOP
BOOOWOOOP
IVY'S HIGHLY DANGEROUS. SHE USES PHEROMONES AND IS IMMUNE TO TOXINS. SHE WON'T BE EASY TO TAKE DOWN ALONE.
BOOOWOOOP
BOOOWOOOP
BOOOWOOOP
CHALLENGE ACCEPTED.
THWIP
CRASH
EVERYONE OUT OF THE BUILDING! NOW!
UNK!

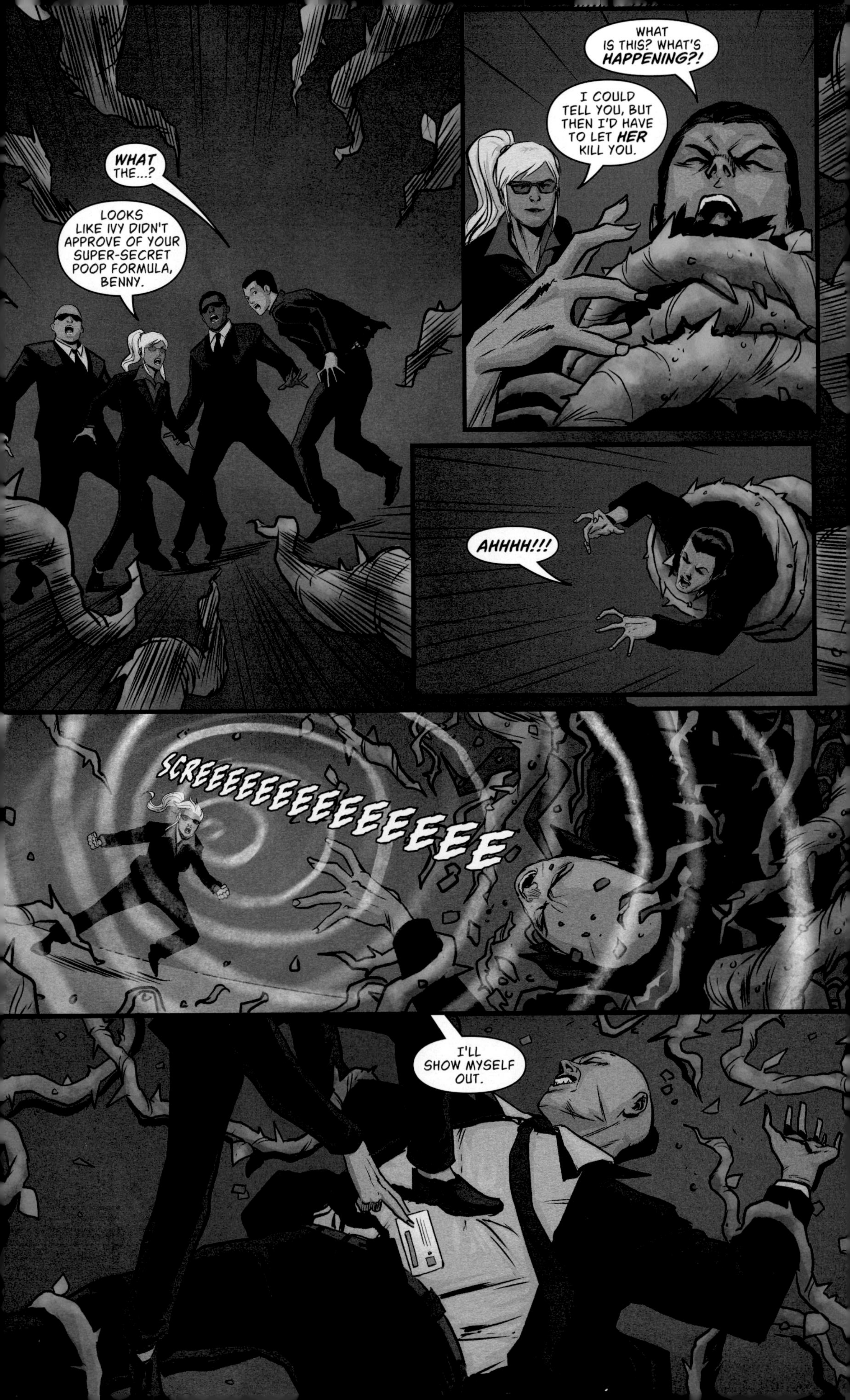
WHAT THE...?
LOOKS LIKE IVY DIDN'T APPROVE OF YOUR SUPER-SECRET POOP FORMULA, BENNY.
WHAT IS THIS? WHAT'S HAPPENING?!
I COULD TELL YOU, BUT THEN I'D HAVE TO LET HER KILL YOU.
AHHHH!!!
SCREEEEEEEEEEEEEEE
I'LL SHOW MYSELF OUT.

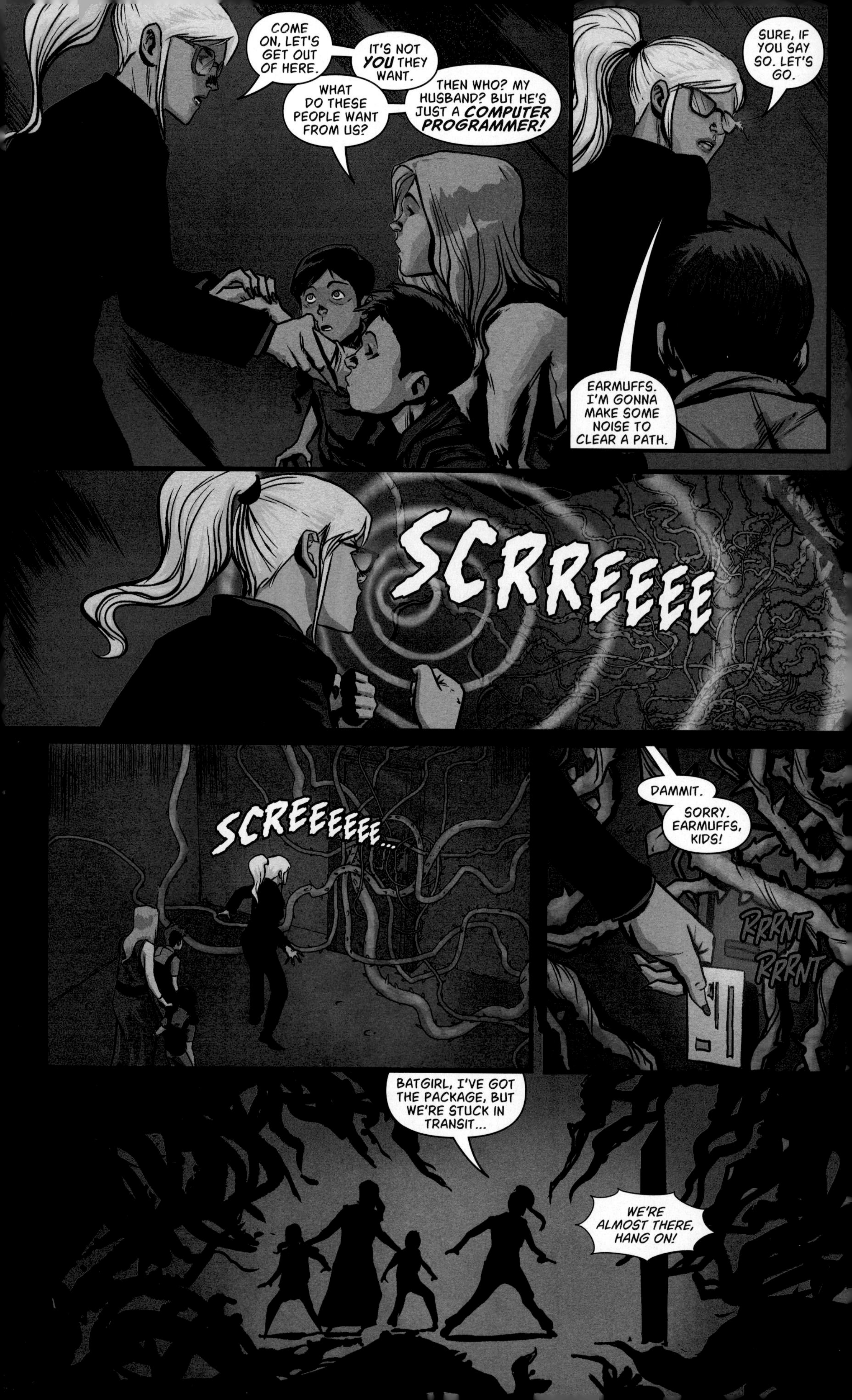
COME ON, LET'S GET OUT OF HERE.
IT'S NOT YOU THEY WANT.
WHAT DO THESE PEOPLE WANT FROM US?
THEN WHO? MY HUSBAND? BUT HE'S JUST A COMPUTER PROGRAMMER!
SURE, IF YOU SAY SO. LET'S GO.
EARMUFFS. I'M GONNA MAKE SOME NOISE TO CLEAR A PATH.
SCRREEEEE
SCREEEEEEE...
DAMMIT.
SORRY. EARMUFFS, KIDS!
RRRNT RRRNT
BATGIRL, I'VE GOT THE PACKAGE, BUT WE'RE STUCK IN TRANSIT...
WE'RE ALMOST THERE, HANG ON!

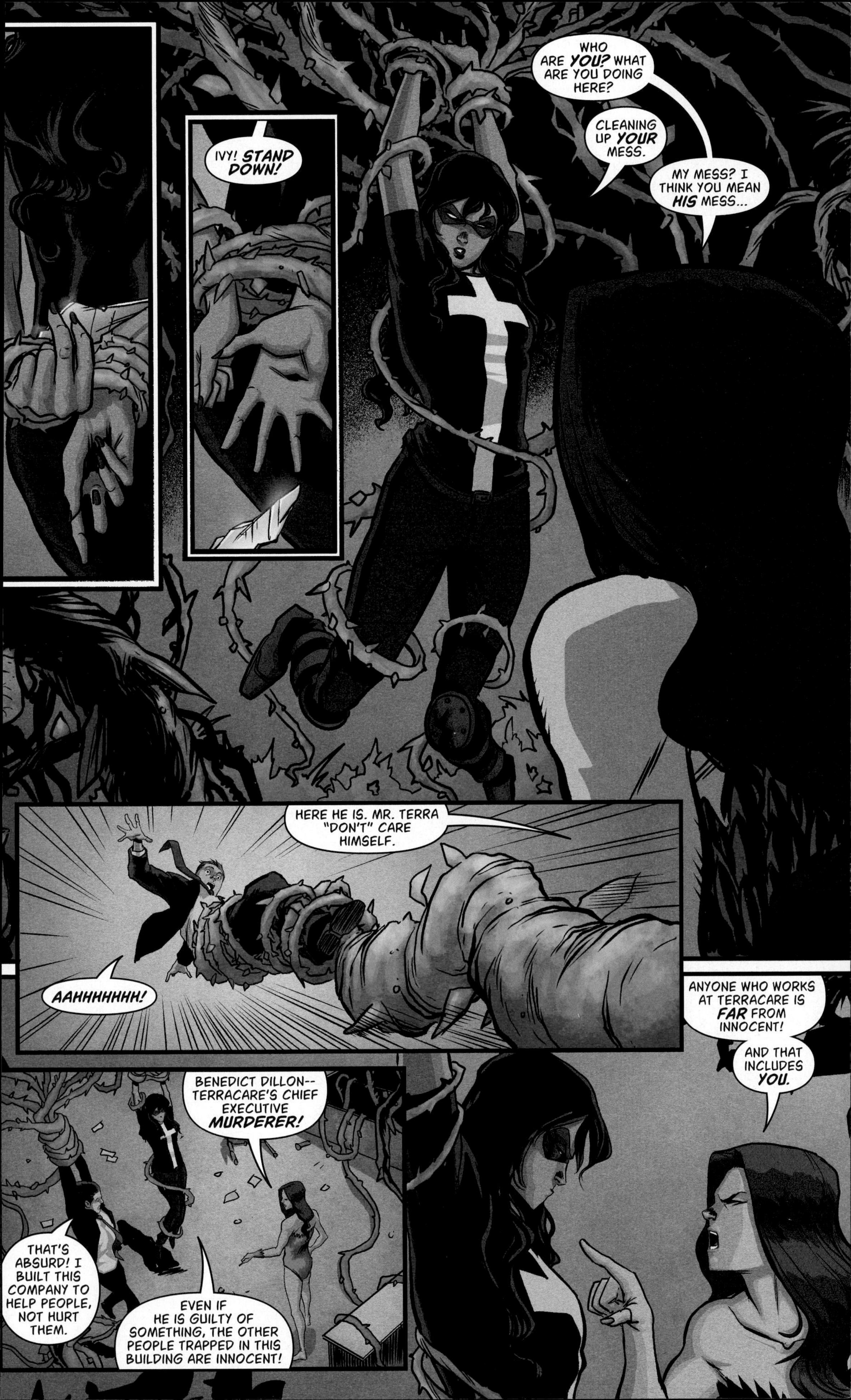
IVY! STAND DOWN!
WHO ARE YOU? WHAT ARE YOU DOING HERE?
CLEANING UP YOUR MESS.
MY MESS? I THINK YOU MEAN HIS MESS...
HERE HE IS. MR. TERRA "DON'T" CARE HIMSELF.
AAHHHHHHH!
BENEDICT DILLON-- TERRACARE'S CHIEF EXECUTIVE MURDERER!
THAT'S ABSURD! I BUILT THIS COMPANY TO HELP PEOPLE, NOT HURT THEM.
EVEN IF HE IS GUILTY OF SOMETHING, THE OTHER PEOPLE TRAPPED IN THIS BUILDING ARE INNOCENT!
ANYONE WHO WORKS AT TERRACARE IS FAR FROM INNOCENT!
AND THAT INCLUDES YOU.

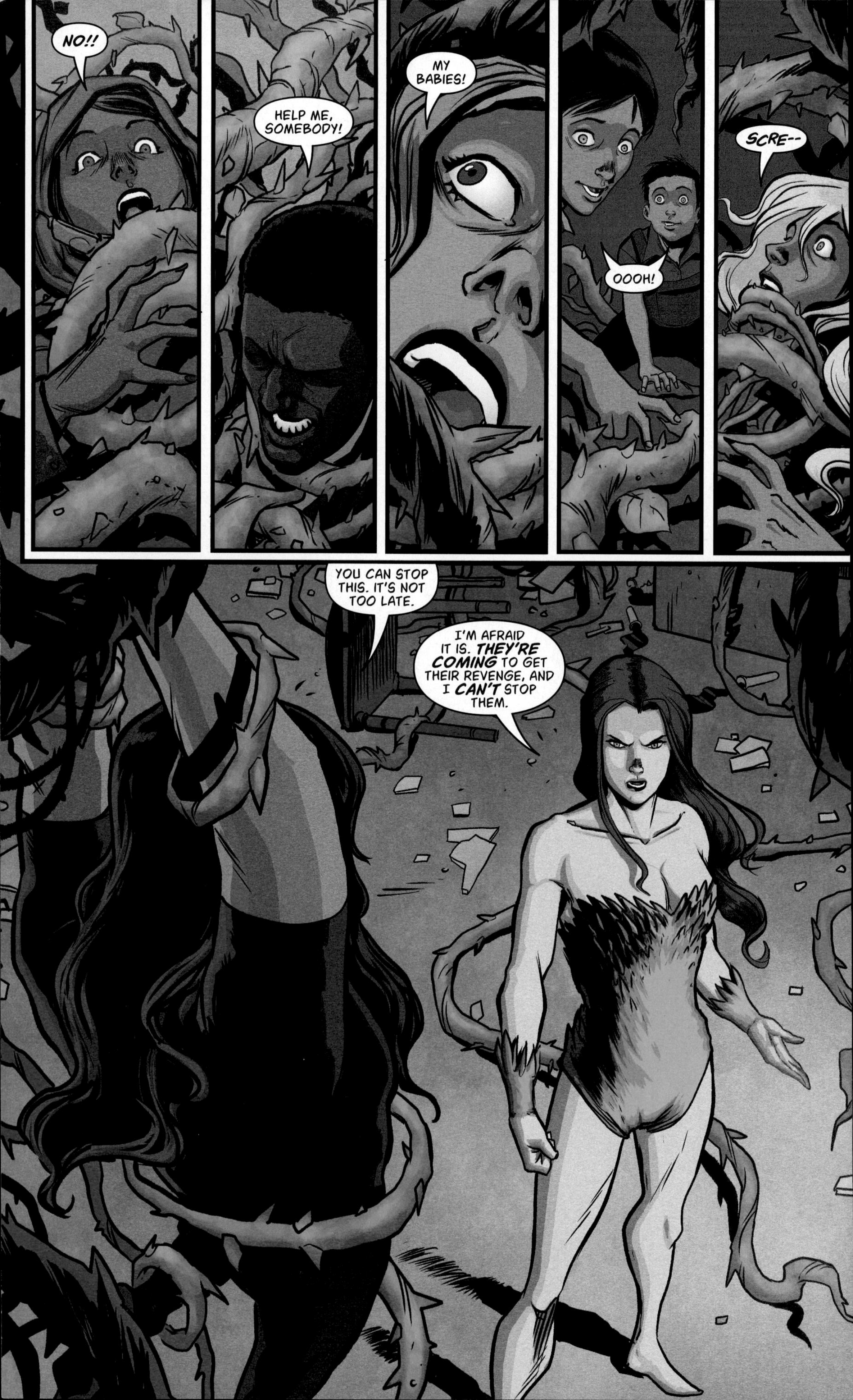
NO!!
HELP ME, SOMEBODY!
MY BABIES!
OOOH!
SCRE--
YOU CAN STOP THIS. IT'S NOT TOO LATE.
I'M AFRAID IT IS. THEY'RE COMING TO GET THEIR REVENGE, AND I CAN'T STOP THEM.

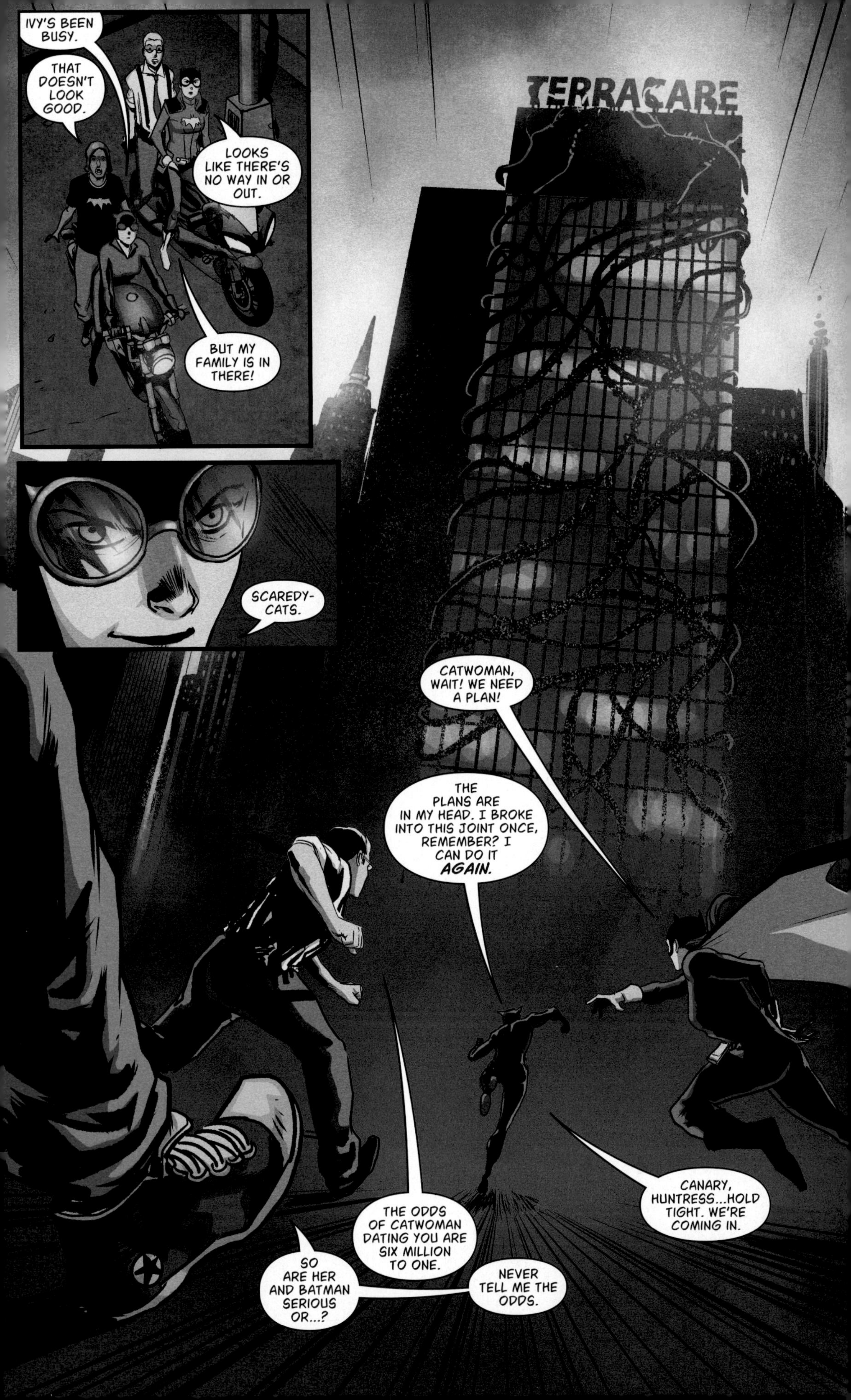
IVY'S BEEN BUSY.
THAT DOESN'T LOOK GOOD.
LOOKS LIKE THERE'S NO WAY IN OR OUT.
BUT MY FAMILY IS IN THERE!
SCAREDY-CATS.
TERRACARE
CATWOMAN, WAIT! WE NEED A PLAN!
THE PLANS ARE IN MY HEAD. I BROKE INTO THIS JOINT ONCE, REMEMBER? I CAN DO IT AGAIN.
CANARY, HUNTRESS...HOLD TIGHT. WE'RE COMING IN.
THE ODDS OF CATWOMAN DATING YOU ARE SIX MILLION TO ONE.
SO ARE HER AND BATMAN SERIOUS OR...?
NEVER TELL ME THE ODDS.

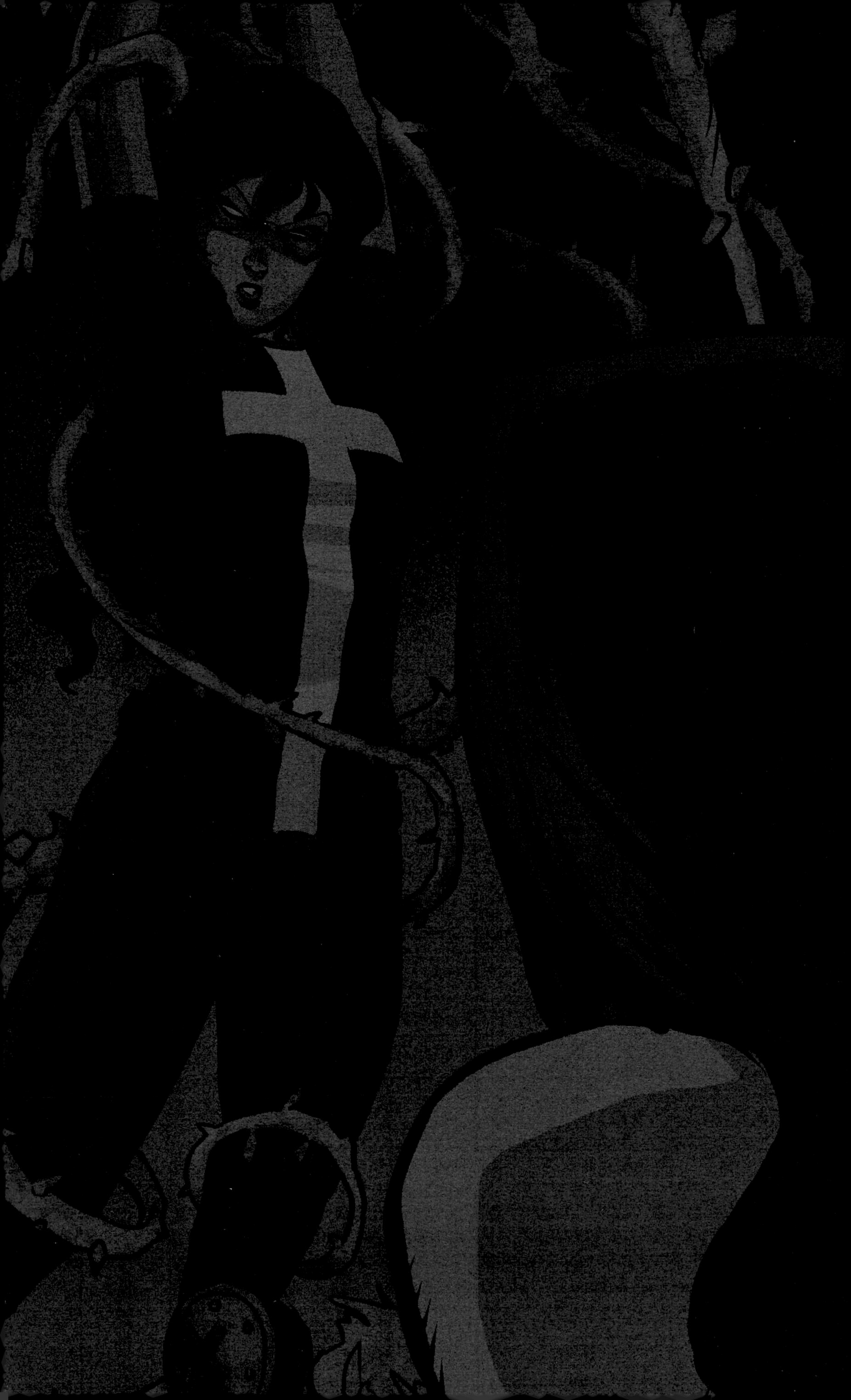

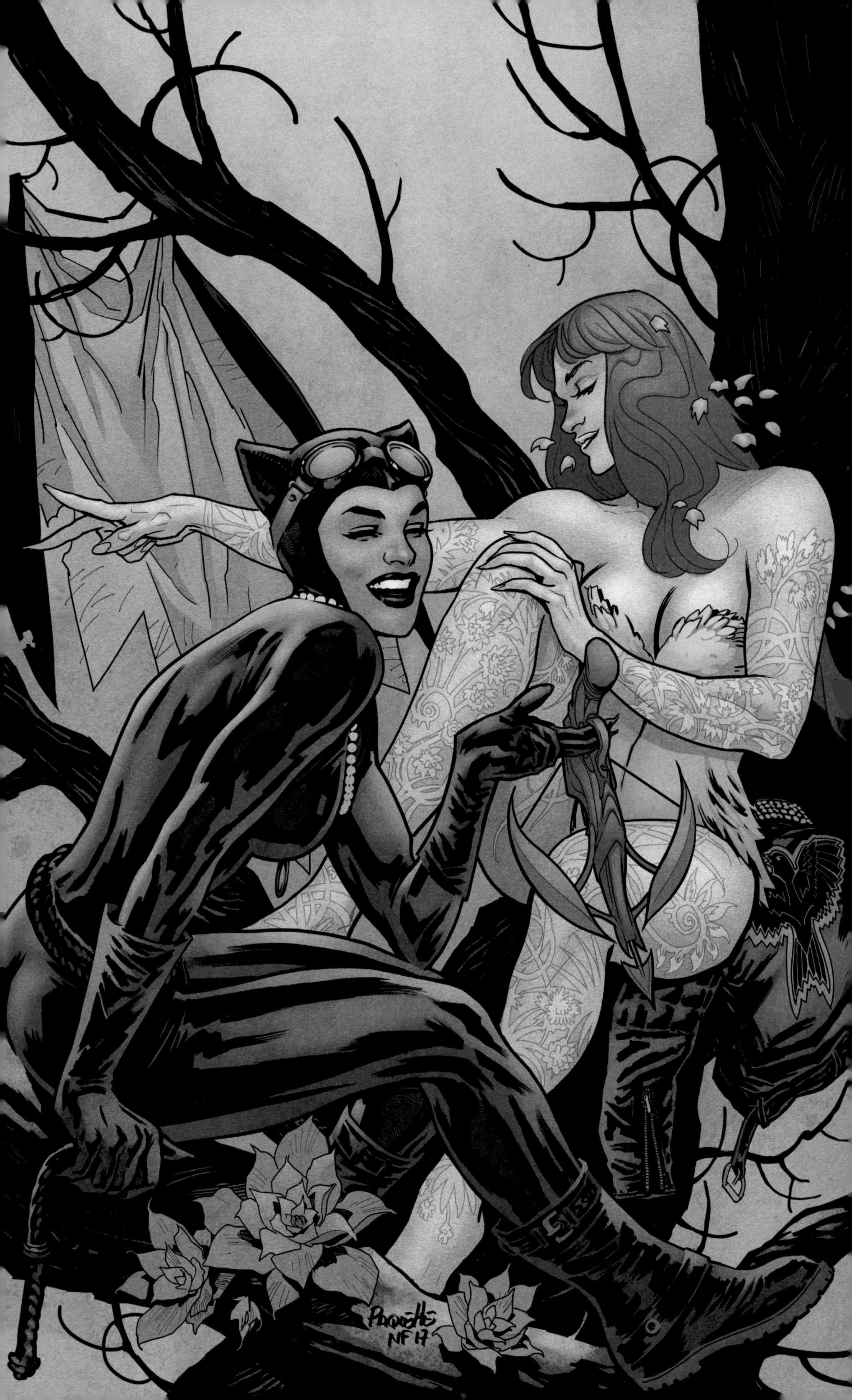

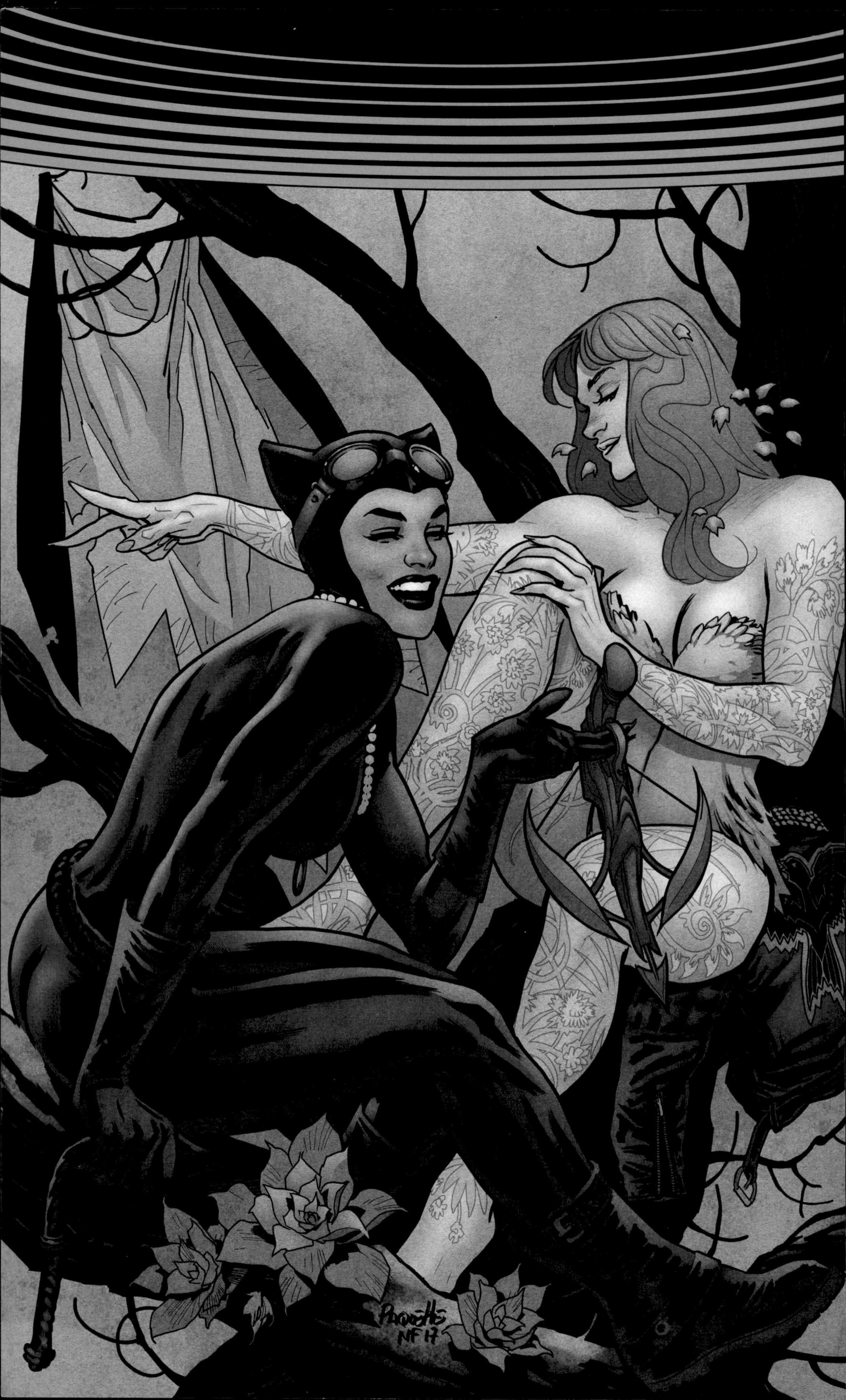

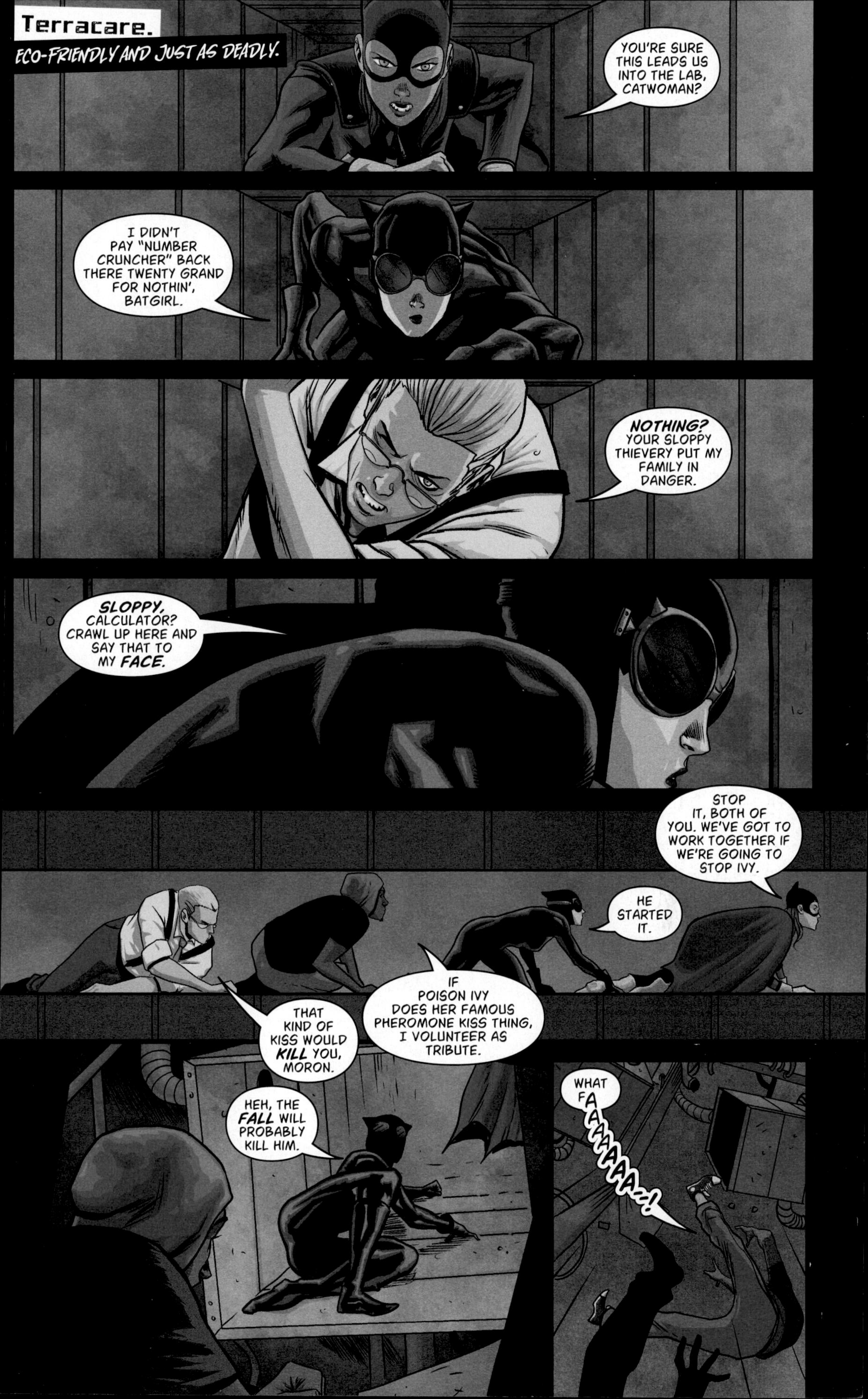
Terracare.
ECO-FRIENDLY AND JUST AS DEADLY.
YOU'RE SURE THIS LEADS US INTO THE LAB, CATWOMAN?
I DIDN'T PAY "NUMBER CRUNCHER" BACK THERE TWENTY GRAND FOR NOTHIN', BATGIRL.
NOTHING? YOUR SLOPPY THIEVERY PUT MY FAMILY IN DANGER.
SLOPPY, CALCULATOR? CRAWL UP HERE AND SAY THAT TO MY FACE.
STOP IT, BOTH OF YOU. WE'VE GOT TO WORK TOGETHER IF WE'RE GOING TO STOP IVY.
HE STARTED IT.
IF POISON IVY DOES HER FAMOUS PHEROMONE KISS THING, I VOLUNTEER AS TRIBUTE.
THAT KIND OF KISS WOULD KILL YOU, MORON.
HEH, THE FALL WILL PROBABLY KILL HIM.
WHAT
FAAAAAAA--!

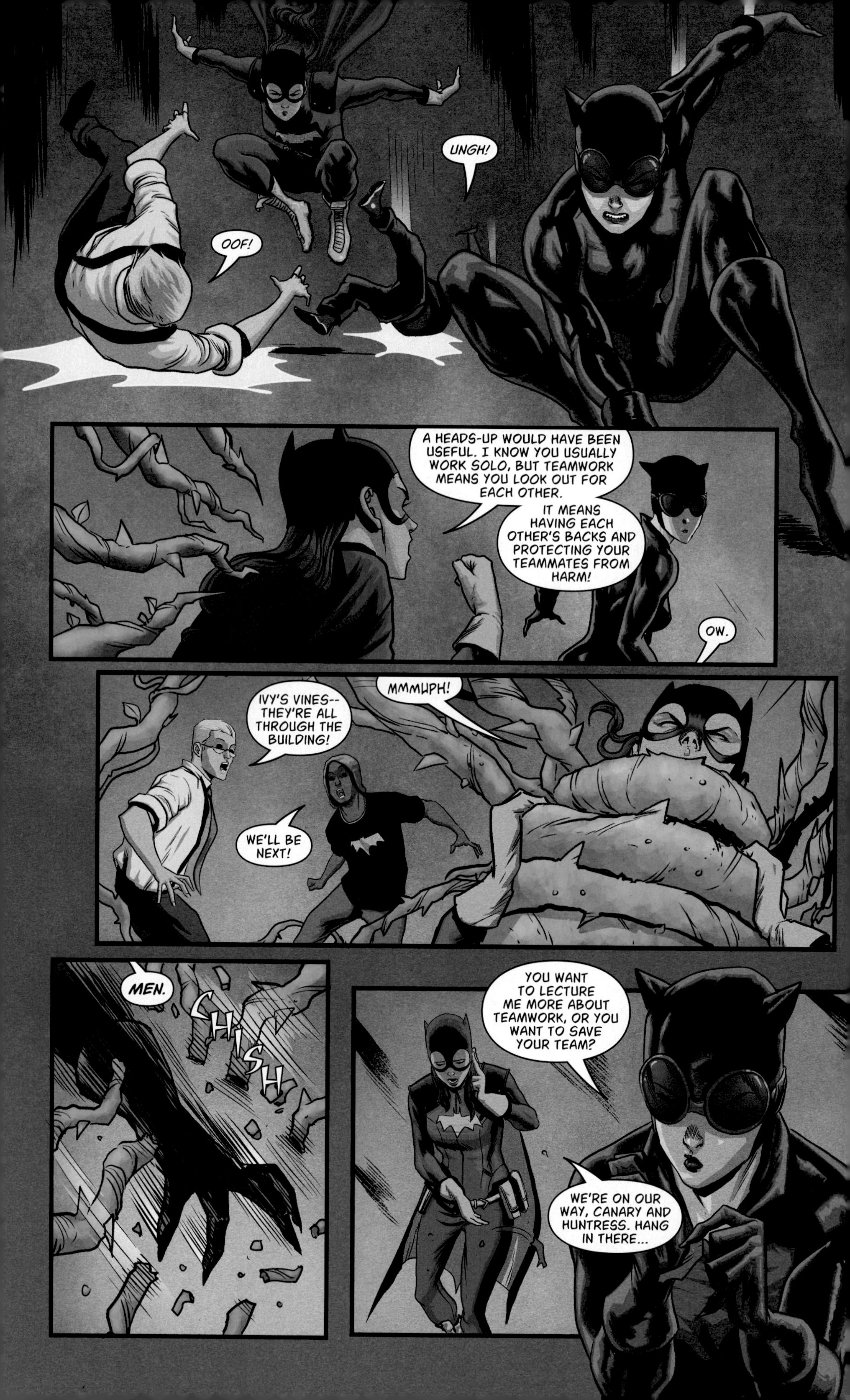
UNGH!
OOF!
A HEADS-UP WOULD HAVE BEEN USEFUL. I KNOW YOU USUALLY WORK SOLO, BUT TEAMWORK MEANS YOU LOOK OUT FOR EACH OTHER.
IT MEANS HAVING EACH OTHER'S BACKS AND PROTECTING YOUR TEAMMATES FROM HARM!
OW.
IVY'S VINES-- THEY'RE ALL THROUGH THE BUILDING!
MMMUPH!
WE'LL BE NEXT!
MEN.
CHISH
YOU WANT TO LECTURE ME MORE ABOUT TEAMWORK, OR YOU WANT TO SAVE YOUR TEAM?
WE'RE ON OUR WAY, CANARY AND HUNTRESS. HANG IN THERE...

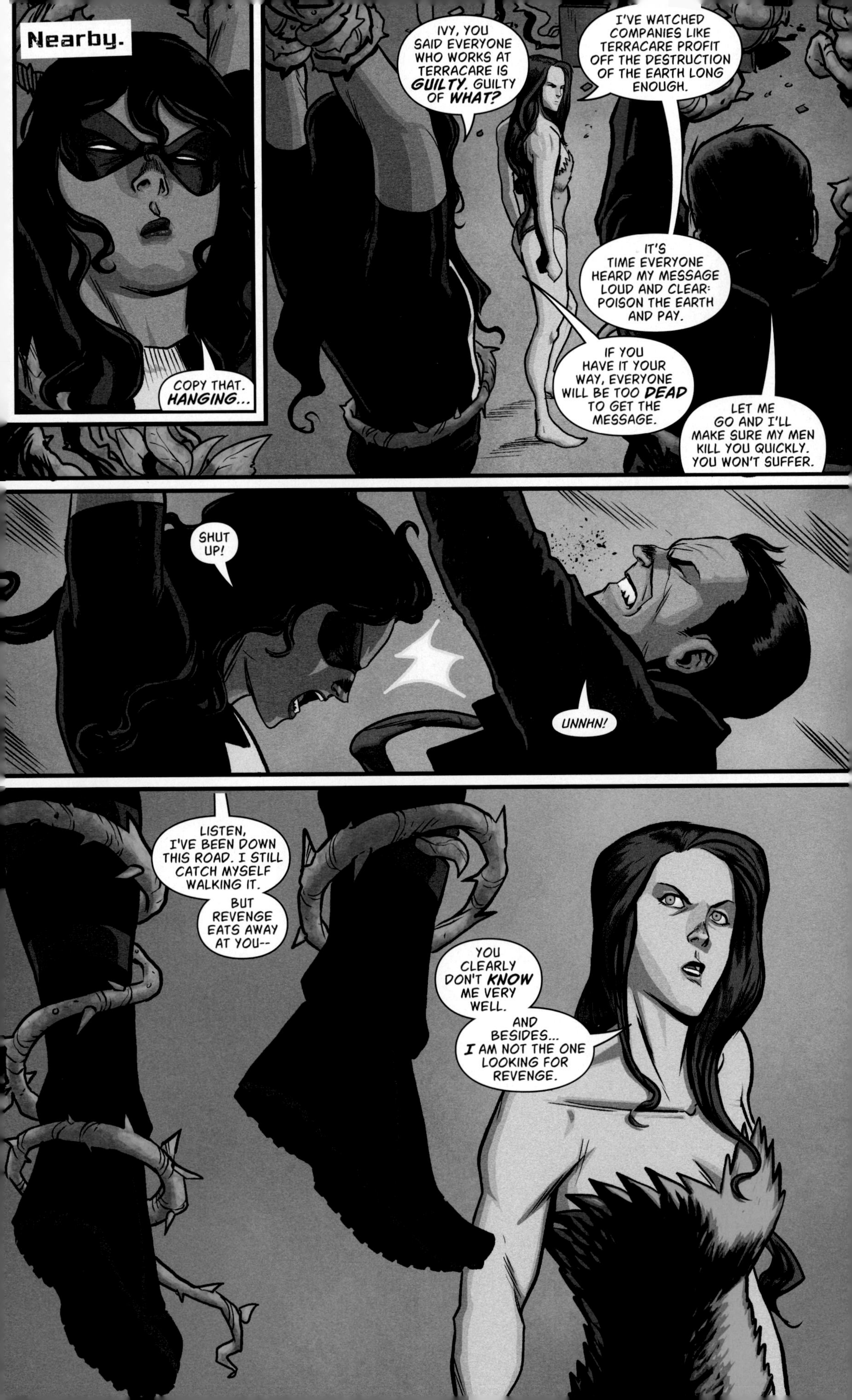
Nearby.
COPY THAT. HANGING...
IVY, YOU SAID EVERYONE WHO WORKS AT TERRACARE IS GUILTY. GUILTY OF WHAT?
I'VE WATCHED COMPANIES LIKE TERRACARE PROFIT OFF THE DESTRUCTION OF THE EARTH LONG ENOUGH.
IT'S TIME EVERYONE HEARD MY MESSAGE LOUD AND CLEAR: POISON THE EARTH AND PAY.
IF YOU HAVE IT YOUR WAY, EVERYONE WILL BE TOO DEAD TO GET THE MESSAGE.
LET ME GO AND I'LL MAKE SURE MY MEN KILL YOU QUICKLY. YOU WON'T SUFFER.
SHUT UP!
UNNHN!
LISTEN, I'VE BEEN DOWN THIS ROAD. I STILL CATCH MYSELF WALKING IT.
BUT REVENGE EATS AWAY AT YOU--
YOU CLEARLY DON'T KNOW ME VERY WELL.
AND BESIDES... I AM NOT THE ONE LOOKING FOR REVENGE.

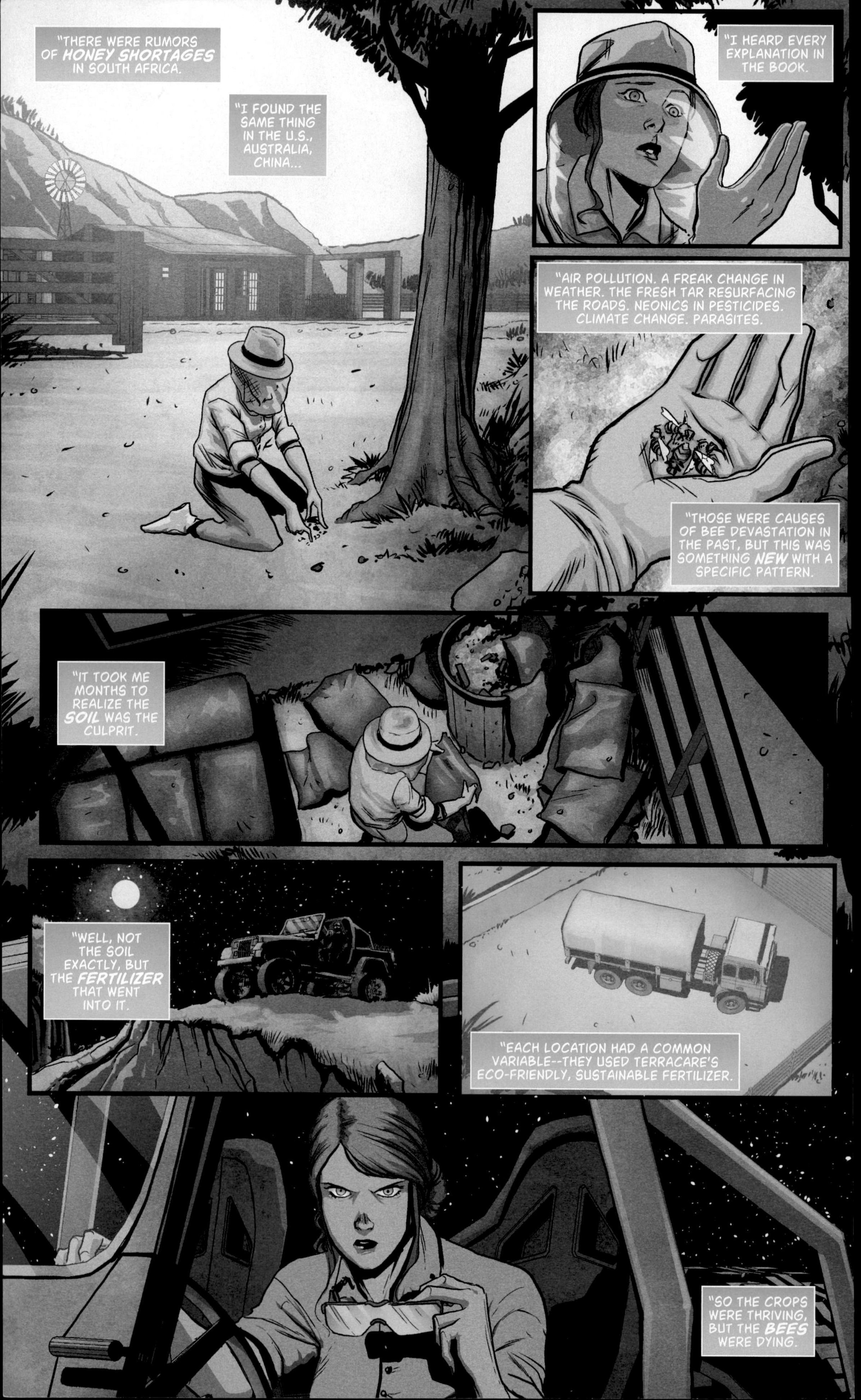
"THERE WERE RUMORS OF HONEY SHORTAGES IN SOUTH AFRICA.
"I FOUND THE SAME THING IN THE U.S., AUSTRALIA, CHINA...
"I HEARD EVERY EXPLANATION IN THE BOOK.
"AIR POLLUTION. A FREAK CHANGE IN WEATHER. THE FRESH TAR RESURFACING THE ROADS. NEONICS IN PESTICIDES. CLIMATE CHANGE. PARASITES.
"THOSE WERE CAUSES OF BEE DEVASTATION IN THE PAST, BUT THIS WAS SOMETHING NEW WITH A SPECIFIC PATTERN.
"IT TOOK ME MONTHS TO REALIZE THE SOIL WAS THE CULPRIT.
"WELL, NOT THE SOIL EXACTLY, BUT THE FERTILIZER THAT WENT INTO IT.
"EACH LOCATION HAD A COMMON VARIABLE--THEY USED TERRACARE'S ECO-FRIENDLY, SUSTAINABLE FERTILIZER.
"SO THE CROPS WERE THRIVING, BUT THE BEES WERE DYING.

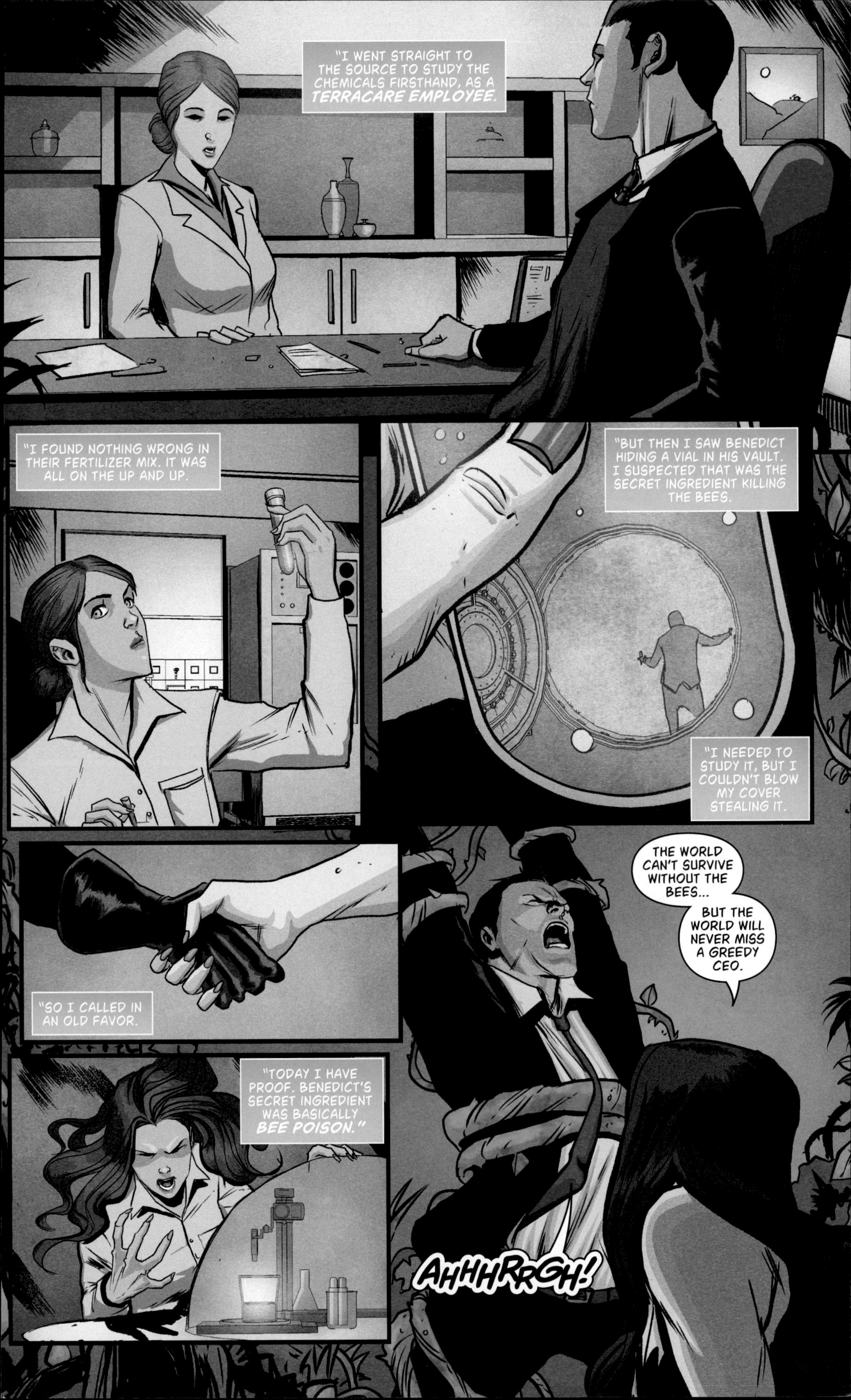
"I WENT STRAIGHT TO THE SOURCE TO STUDY THE CHEMICALS FIRSTHAND, AS A TERRACARE EMPLOYEE.
"I FOUND NOTHING WRONG IN THEIR FERTILIZER MIX. IT WAS ALL ON THE UP AND UP.
"BUT THEN I SAW BENEDICT HIDING A VIAL IN HIS VAULT. I SUSPECTED THAT WAS THE SECRET INGREDIENT KILLING THE BEES.
"I NEEDED TO STUDY IT, BUT I COULDN'T BLOW MY COVER STEALING IT.
"SO I CALLED IN AN OLD FAVOR.
"TODAY I HAVE PROOF. BENEDICT'S SECRET INGREDIENT WAS BASICALLY BEE POISON."
THE WORLD CAN'T SURVIVE WITHOUT THE BEES...
BUT THE WORLD WILL NEVER MISS A GREEDY CEO.
AHHHRRGH!

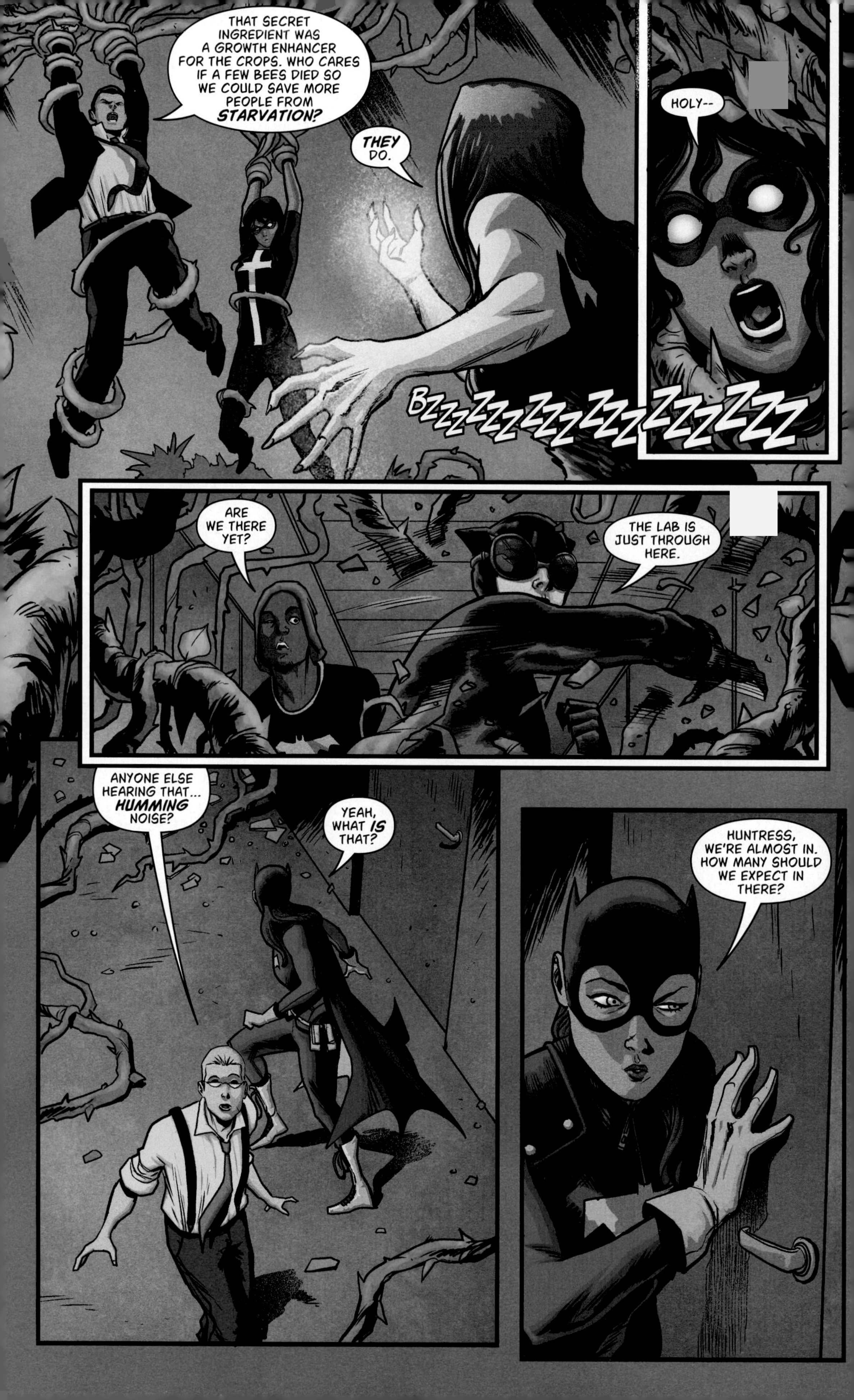
THAT SECRET INGREDIENT WAS A GROWTH ENHANCER FOR THE CROPS. WHO CARES IF A FEW BEES DIED SO WE COULD SAVE MORE PEOPLE FROM STARVATION?
THEY DO.
HOLY--
BZZZZZZZZZZZZZZZZ
ARE WE THERE YET?
THE LAB IS JUST THROUGH HERE.
ANYONE ELSE HEARING THAT... HUMMING NOISE?
YEAH, WHAT IS THAT?
HUNTRESS, WE'RE ALMOST IN. HOW MANY SHOULD WE EXPECT IN THERE?

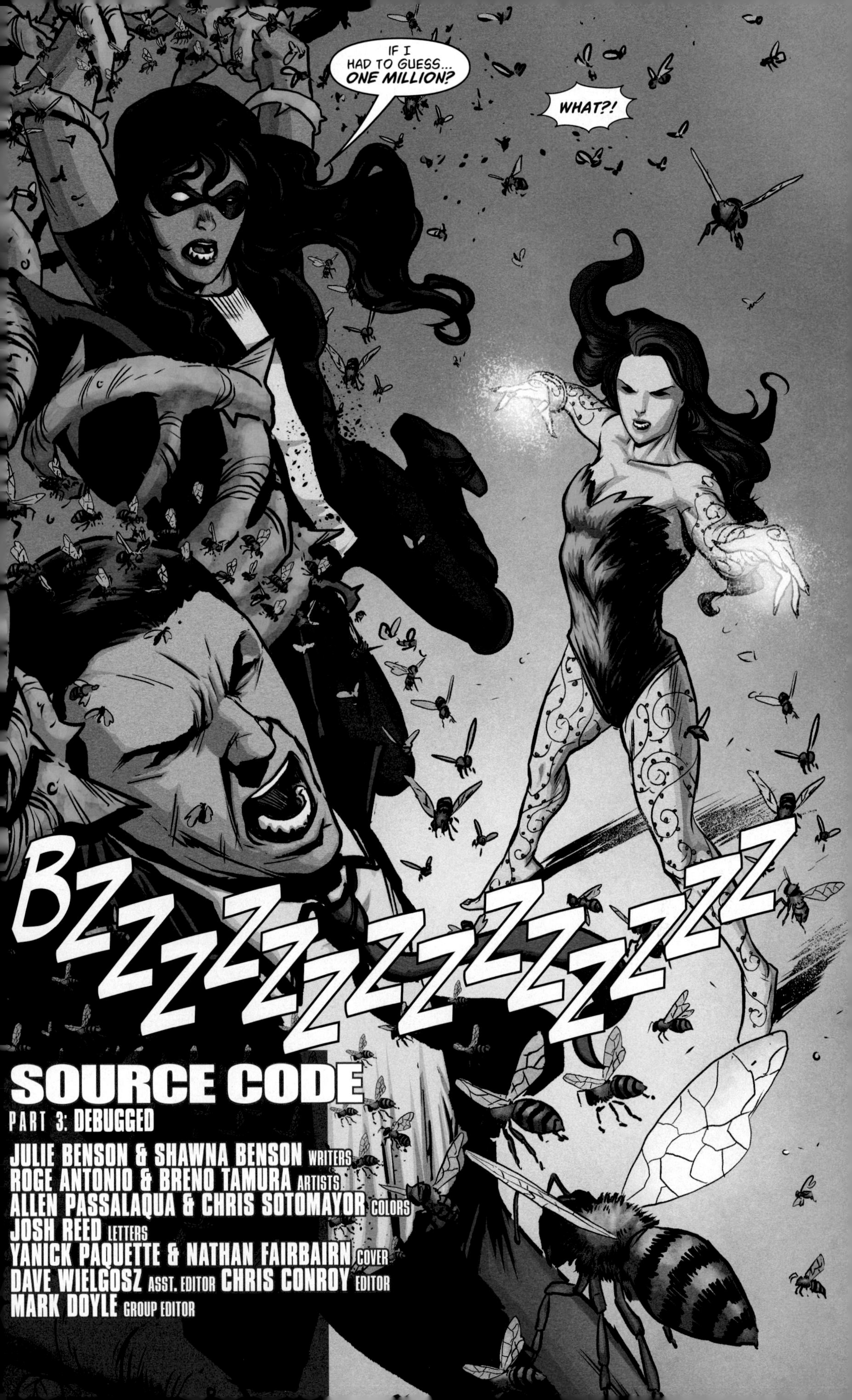
IF I HAD TO GUESS... ONE MILLION?
WHAT?!
BZZZZZZZZZZZZZZ
SOURCE CODE
PART 3: DEBUGGED
JULIE BENSON & SHAWNA BENSON WRITERS
ROGE ANTONIO & BRENO TAMURA ARTISTS
ALLEN PASSALAQUA & CHRIS SOTOMAYOR COLORS
JOSH REED LETTERS
YANICK PAQUETTE & NATHAN FAIRBAIRN COVER
DAVE WIELGOSZ ASST. EDITOR CHRIS CONROY EDITOR
MARK DOYLE GROUP EDITOR

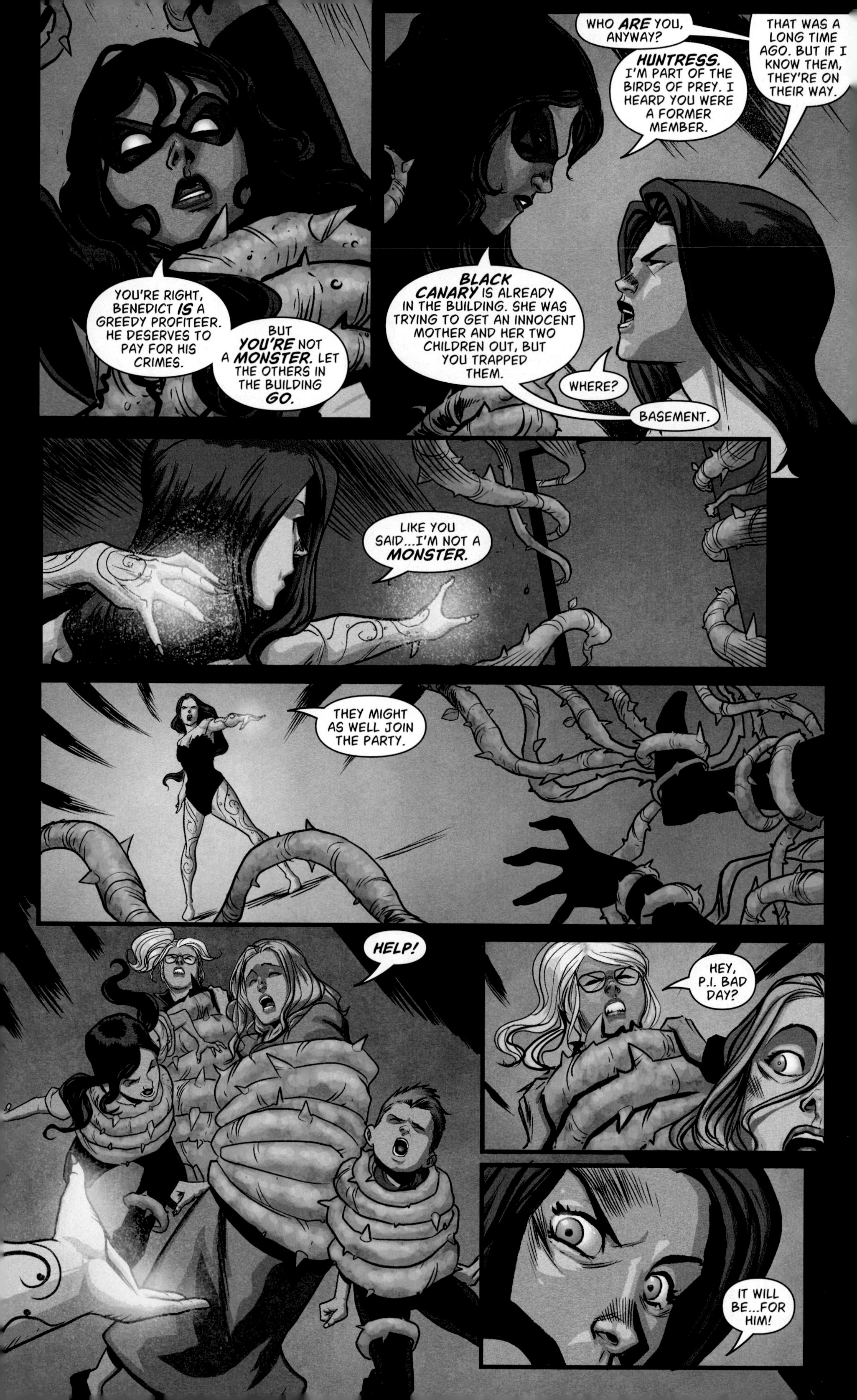
YOU'RE RIGHT, BENEDICT IS A GREEDY PROFITEER. HE DESERVES TO PAY FOR HIS CRIMES.
BUT YOU'RE NOT A MONSTER. LET THE OTHERS IN THE BUILDING GO.
WHO ARE YOU, ANYWAY?
HUNTRESS. I'M PART OF THE BIRDS OF PREY. I HEARD YOU WERE A FORMER MEMBER.
THAT WAS A LONG TIME AGO. BUT IF I KNOW THEM, THEY'RE ON THEIR WAY.
BLACK CANARY IS ALREADY IN THE BUILDING. SHE WAS TRYING TO GET AN INNOCENT MOTHER AND HER TWO CHILDREN OUT, BUT YOU TRAPPED THEM.
WHERE?
BASEMENT.
LIKE YOU SAID...I'M NOT A MONSTER.
THEY MIGHT AS WELL JOIN THE PARTY.
HELP!
HEY, P.I. BAD DAY?
IT WILL BE...FOR HIM!

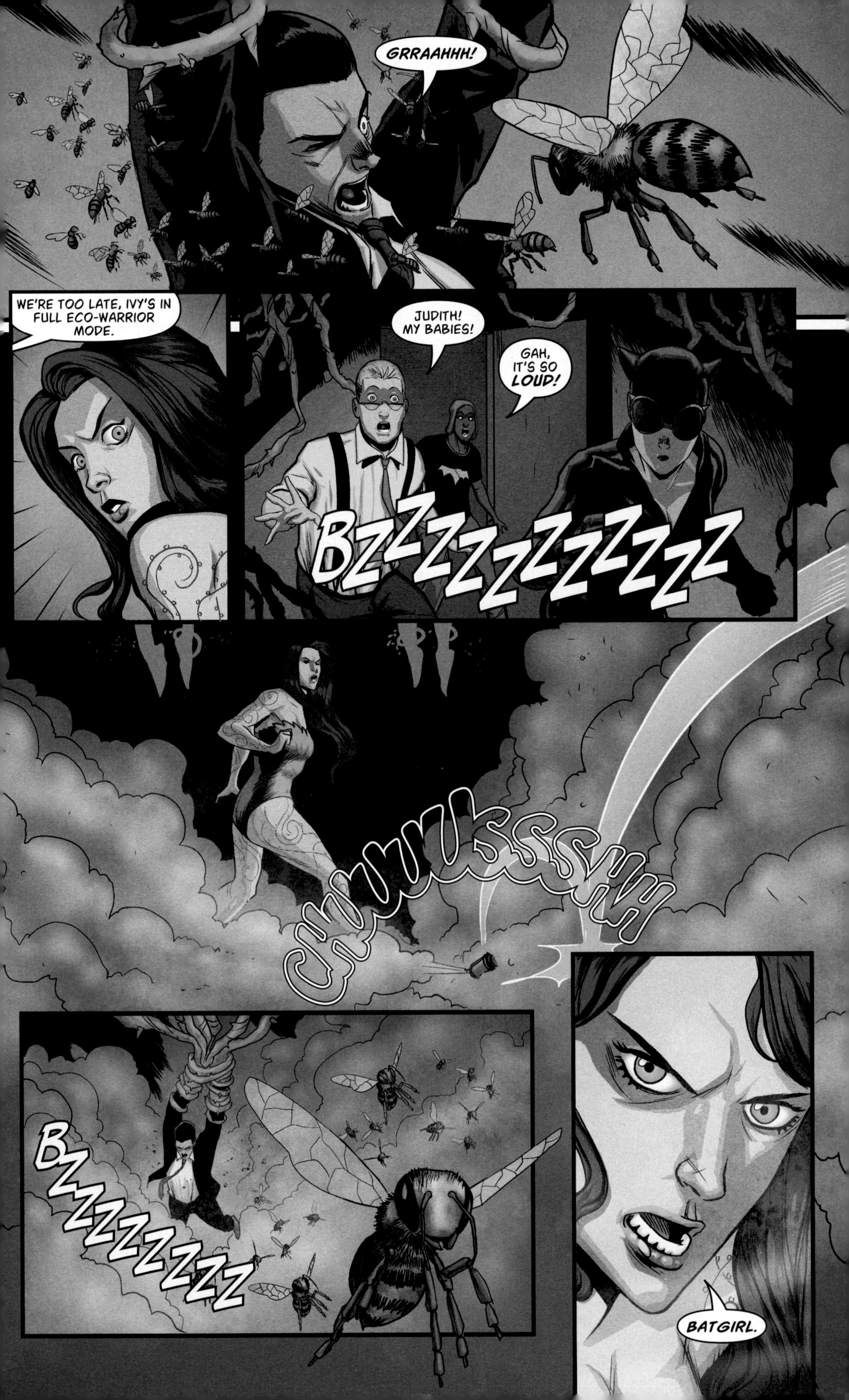
GRRAAHHH!
WE'RE TOO LATE, IVY'S IN FULL ECO-WARRIOR MODE.
JUDITH! MY BABIES!
GAH, IT'S SO LOUD!
BZZZZZZZZZZ
CHRUUKSSSHH
BZZZZZZZZZ
BATGIRL.

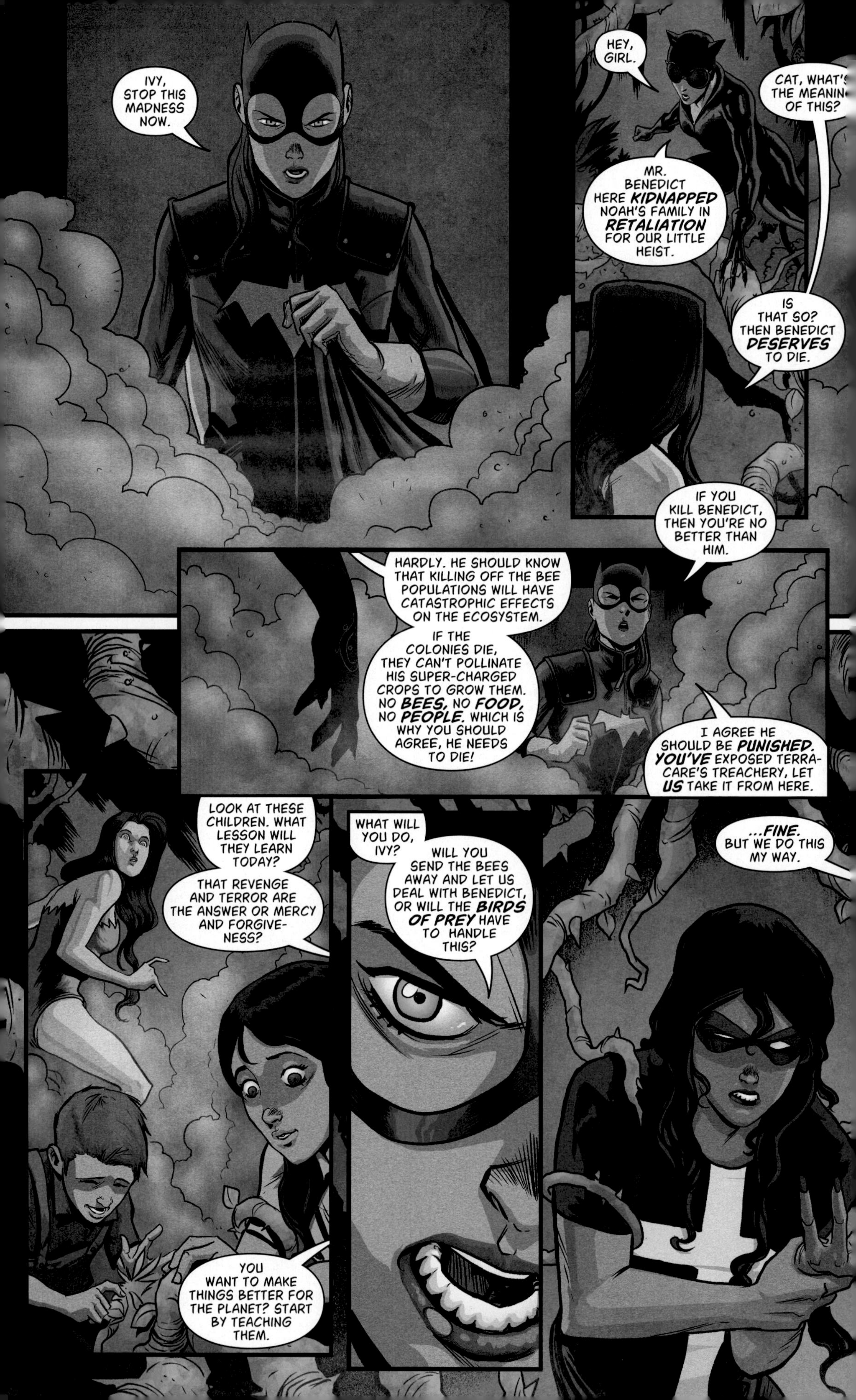
IVY, STOP THIS MADNESS NOW.
HEY, GIRL.
CAT, WHAT'S THE MEANING OF THIS?
MR. BENEDICT HERE KIDNAPPED NOAH'S FAMILY IN RETALIATION FOR OUR LITTLE HEIST.
IS THAT SO? THEN BENEDICT DESERVES TO DIE.
IF YOU KILL BENEDICT, THEN YOU'RE NO BETTER THAN HIM.
HARDLY. HE SHOULD KNOW THAT KILLING OFF THE BEE POPULATIONS WILL HAVE CATASTROPHIC EFFECTS ON THE ECOSYSTEM.
IF THE COLONIES DIE, THEY CAN'T POLLINATE HIS SUPER-CHARGED CROPS TO GROW THEM. NO BEES, NO FOOD, NO PEOPLE. WHICH IS WHY YOU SHOULD AGREE, HE NEEDS TO DIE!
I AGREE HE SHOULD BE PUNISHED. YOU'VE EXPOSED TERRA-CARE'S TREACHERY, LET US TAKE IT FROM HERE.
LOOK AT THESE CHILDREN. WHAT LESSON WILL THEY LEARN TODAY?
THAT REVENGE AND TERROR ARE THE ANSWER OR MERCY AND FORGIVE-NESS?
YOU WANT TO MAKE THINGS BETTER FOR THE PLANET? START BY TEACHING THEM.
WHAT WILL YOU DO, IVY?
WILL YOU SEND THE BEES AWAY AND LET US DEAL WITH BENEDICT, OR WILL THE BIRDS OF PREY HAVE TO HANDLE THIS?
...FINE. BUT WE DO THIS MY WAY.

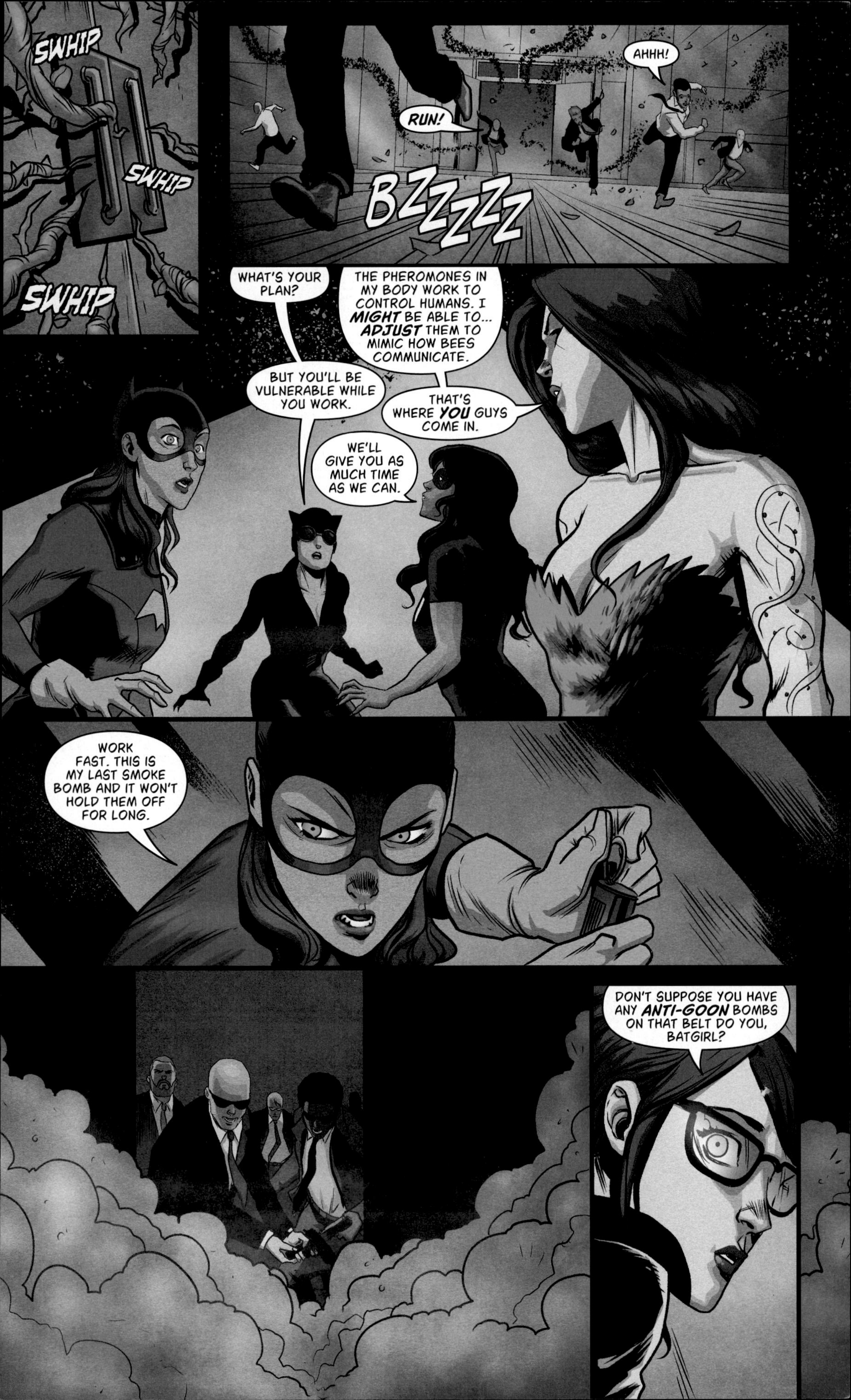
SWHIP
SWHIP
SWHIP
AHHH!
RUN!
BZZZZZ
WHAT'S YOUR PLAN?
THE PHEROMONES IN MY BODY WORK TO CONTROL HUMANS. I MIGHT BE ABLE TO... ADJUST THEM TO MIMIC HOW BEES COMMUNICATE.
BUT YOU'LL BE VULNERABLE WHILE YOU WORK.
THAT'S WHERE YOU GUYS COME IN.
WE'LL GIVE YOU AS MUCH TIME AS WE CAN.
WORK FAST. THIS IS MY LAST SMOKE BOMB AND IT WON'T HOLD THEM OFF FOR LONG.
DON'T SUPPOSE YOU HAVE ANY ANTI-GOON BOMBS ON THAT BELT DO YOU, BATGIRL?

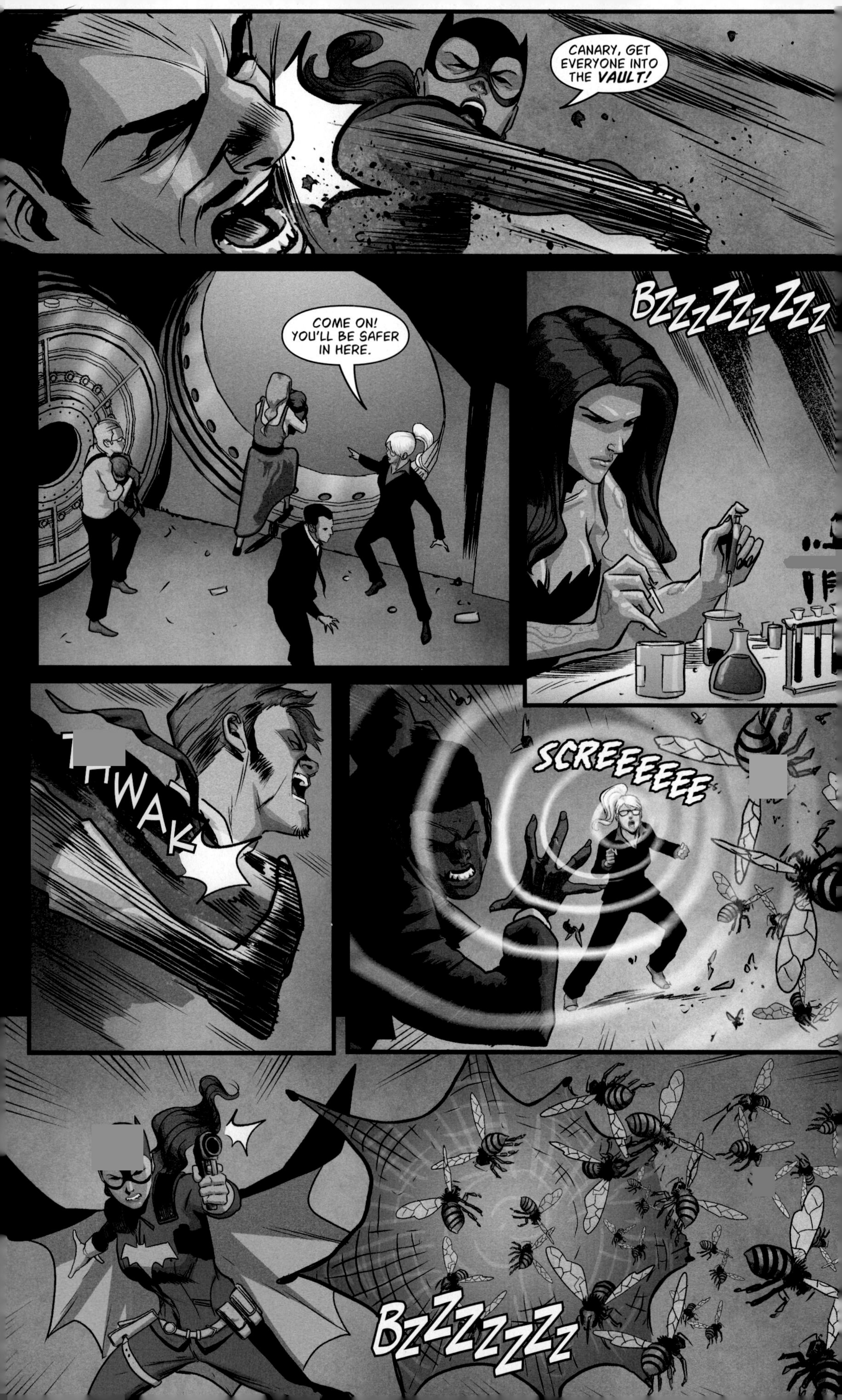
CANARY, GET EVERYONE INTO THE VAULT!
COME ON! YOU'LL BE SAFER IN HERE.
BZZZZZZZZZ
HWAK
SCREEEEEEE
BZZZZZZZZ

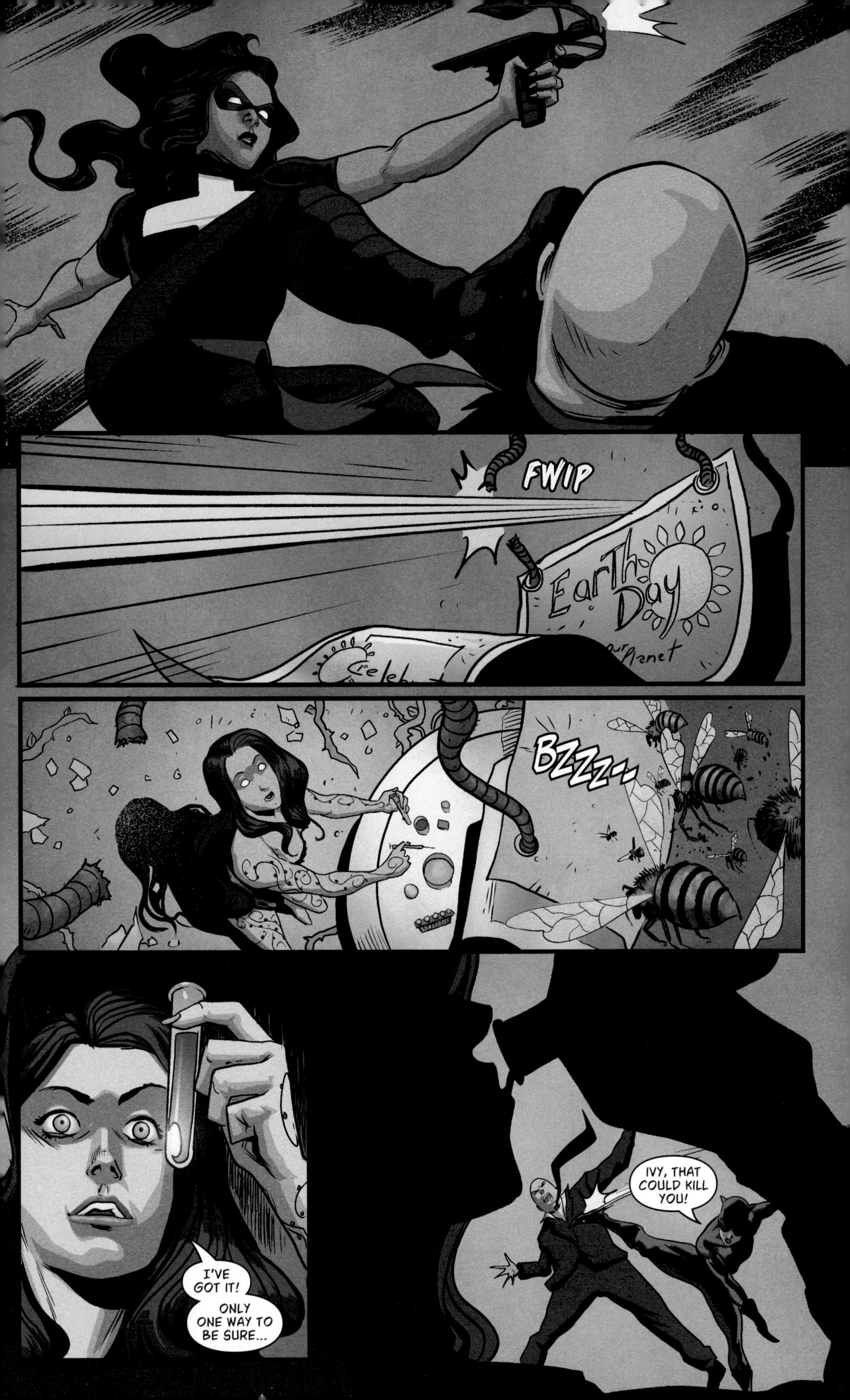
FWIP
Earth Day
BZZZ--
I'VE GOT IT!
ONLY ONE WAY TO BE SURE...
IVY, THAT COULD KILL YOU!

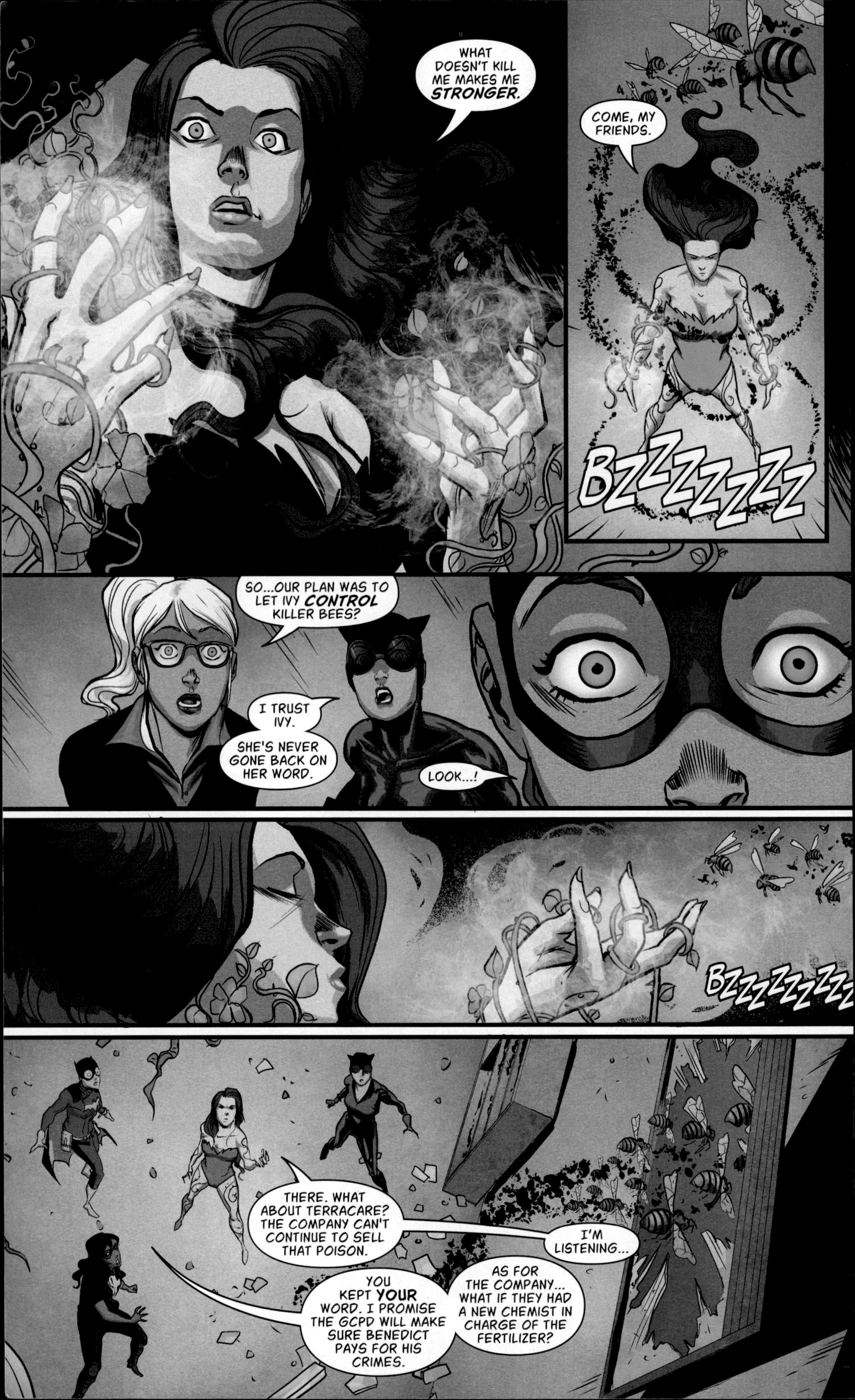
WHAT DOESN'T KILL ME MAKES ME STRONGER.
COME, MY FRIENDS.
BZZZZZZZZ
SO...OUR PLAN WAS TO LET IVY CONTROL KILLER BEES?
I TRUST IVY.
SHE'S NEVER GONE BACK ON HER WORD.
LOOK...!
BZZZZZZZZZ
THERE. WHAT ABOUT TERRACARE? THE COMPANY CAN'T CONTINUE TO SELL THAT POISON.
I'M LISTENING...
YOU KEPT YOUR WORD. I PROMISE THE GCPD WILL MAKE SURE BENEDICT PAYS FOR HIS CRIMES.
AS FOR THE COMPANY... WHAT IF THEY HAD A NEW CHEMIST IN CHARGE OF THE FERTILIZER?

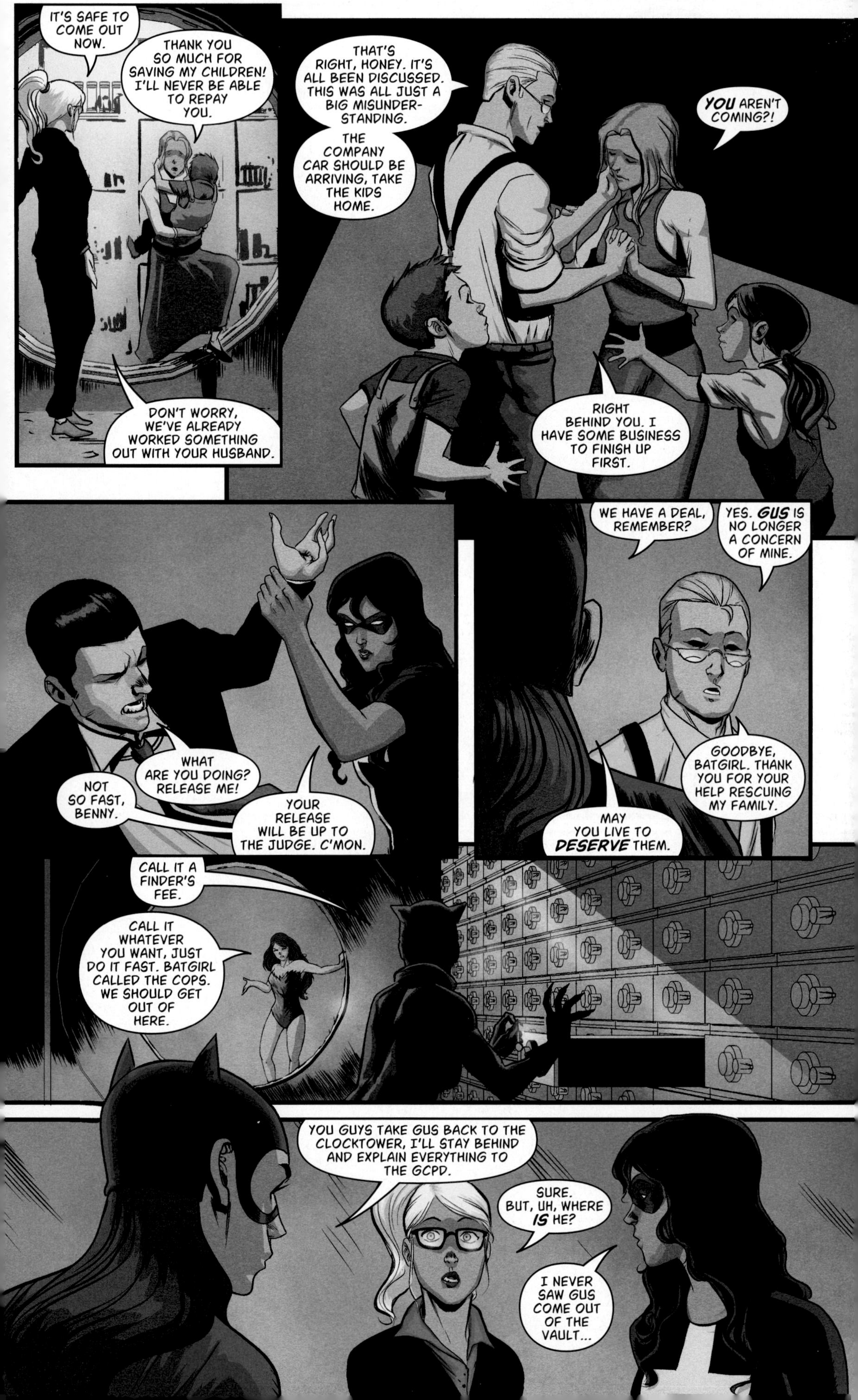
IT'S SAFE TO COME OUT NOW.
THANK YOU SO MUCH FOR SAVING MY CHILDREN! I'LL NEVER BE ABLE TO REPAY YOU.
DON'T WORRY, WE'VE ALREADY WORKED SOMETHING OUT WITH YOUR HUSBAND.
THAT'S RIGHT, HONEY. IT'S ALL BEEN DISCUSSED. THIS WAS ALL JUST A BIG MISUNDER-STANDING.
THE COMPANY CAR SHOULD BE ARRIVING, TAKE THE KIDS HOME.
YOU AREN'T COMING?!
RIGHT BEHIND YOU. I HAVE SOME BUSINESS TO FINISH UP FIRST.
WHAT ARE YOU DOING? RELEASE ME!
NOT SO FAST, BENNY.
YOUR RELEASE WILL BE UP TO THE JUDGE. C'MON.
WE HAVE A DEAL, REMEMBER?
YES. GUS IS NO LONGER A CONCERN OF MINE.
GOODBYE, BATGIRL. THANK YOU FOR YOUR HELP RESCUING MY FAMILY.
MAY YOU LIVE TO DESERVE THEM.
CALL IT A FINDER'S FEE.
CALL IT WHATEVER YOU WANT, JUST DO IT FAST. BATGIRL CALLED THE COPS. WE SHOULD GET OUT OF HERE.
YOU GUYS TAKE GUS BACK TO THE CLOCKTOWER, I'LL STAY BEHIND AND EXPLAIN EVERYTHING TO THE GCPD.
SURE. BUT, UH, WHERE IS HE?
I NEVER SAW GUS COME OUT OF THE VAULT...

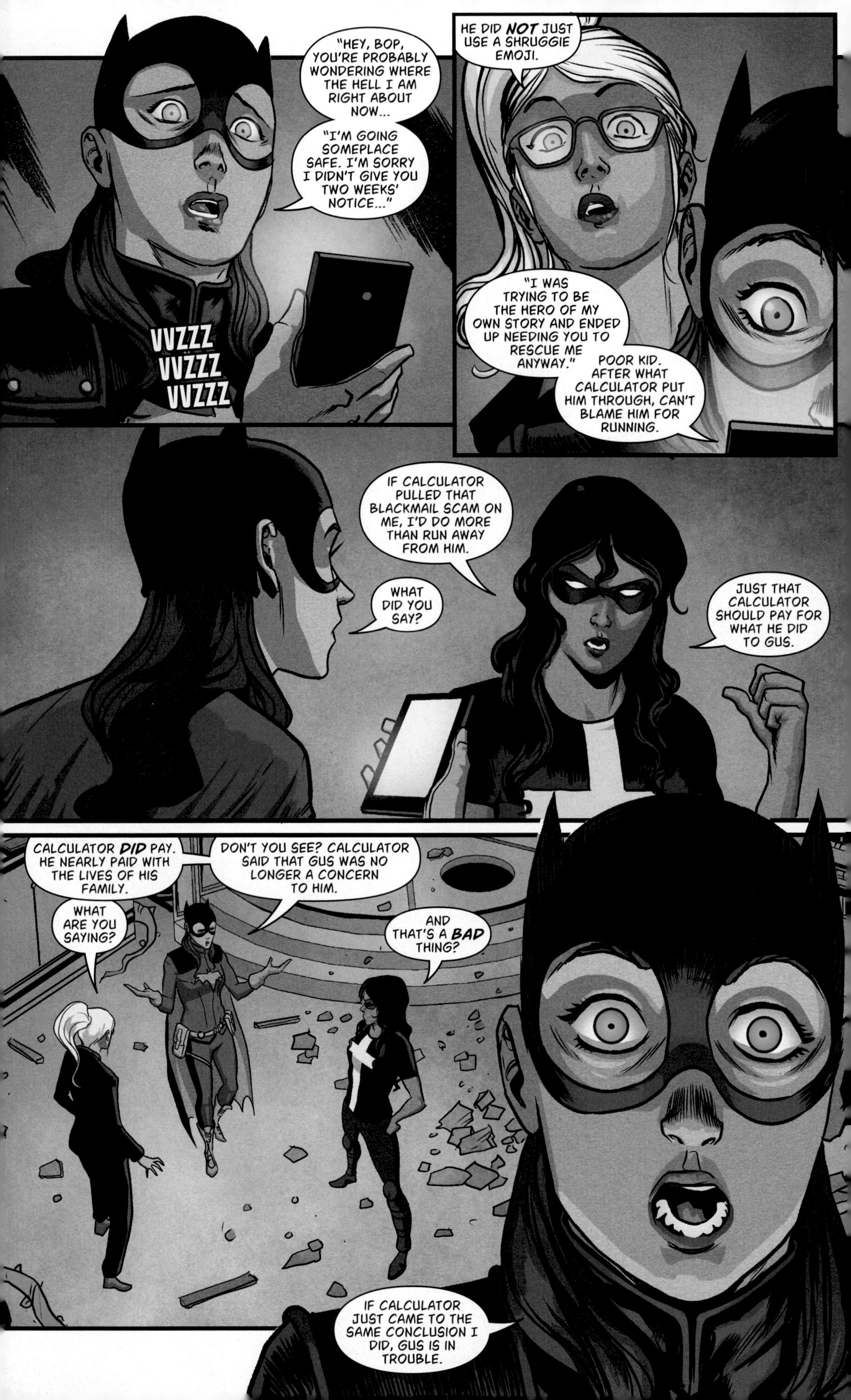
"HEY, BOP, YOU'RE PROBABLY WONDERING WHERE THE HELL I AM RIGHT ABOUT NOW...
"I'M GOING SOMEPLACE SAFE. I'M SORRY I DIDN'T GIVE YOU TWO WEEKS' NOTICE..."
VVZZZ VVZZZ VVZZZ
HE DID *NOT* JUST USE A SHRUGGIE EMOJI.
"I WAS TRYING TO BE THE HERO OF MY OWN STORY AND ENDED UP NEEDING YOU TO RESCUE ME ANYWAY."
POOR KID. AFTER WHAT CALCULATOR PUT HIM THROUGH, CAN'T BLAME HIM FOR RUNNING.
IF CALCULATOR PULLED THAT BLACKMAIL SCAM ON ME, I'D DO MORE THAN RUN AWAY FROM HIM.
WHAT DID YOU SAY?
JUST THAT CALCULATOR SHOULD PAY FOR WHAT HE DID TO GUS.
CALCULATOR *DID* PAY. HE NEARLY PAID WITH THE LIVES OF HIS FAMILY.
WHAT ARE YOU SAYING?
DON'T YOU SEE? CALCULATOR SAID THAT GUS WAS NO LONGER A CONCERN TO HIM.
AND THAT'S A *BAD* THING?
IF CALCULATOR JUST CAME TO THE SAME CONCLUSION I DID, GUS IS IN TROUBLE.

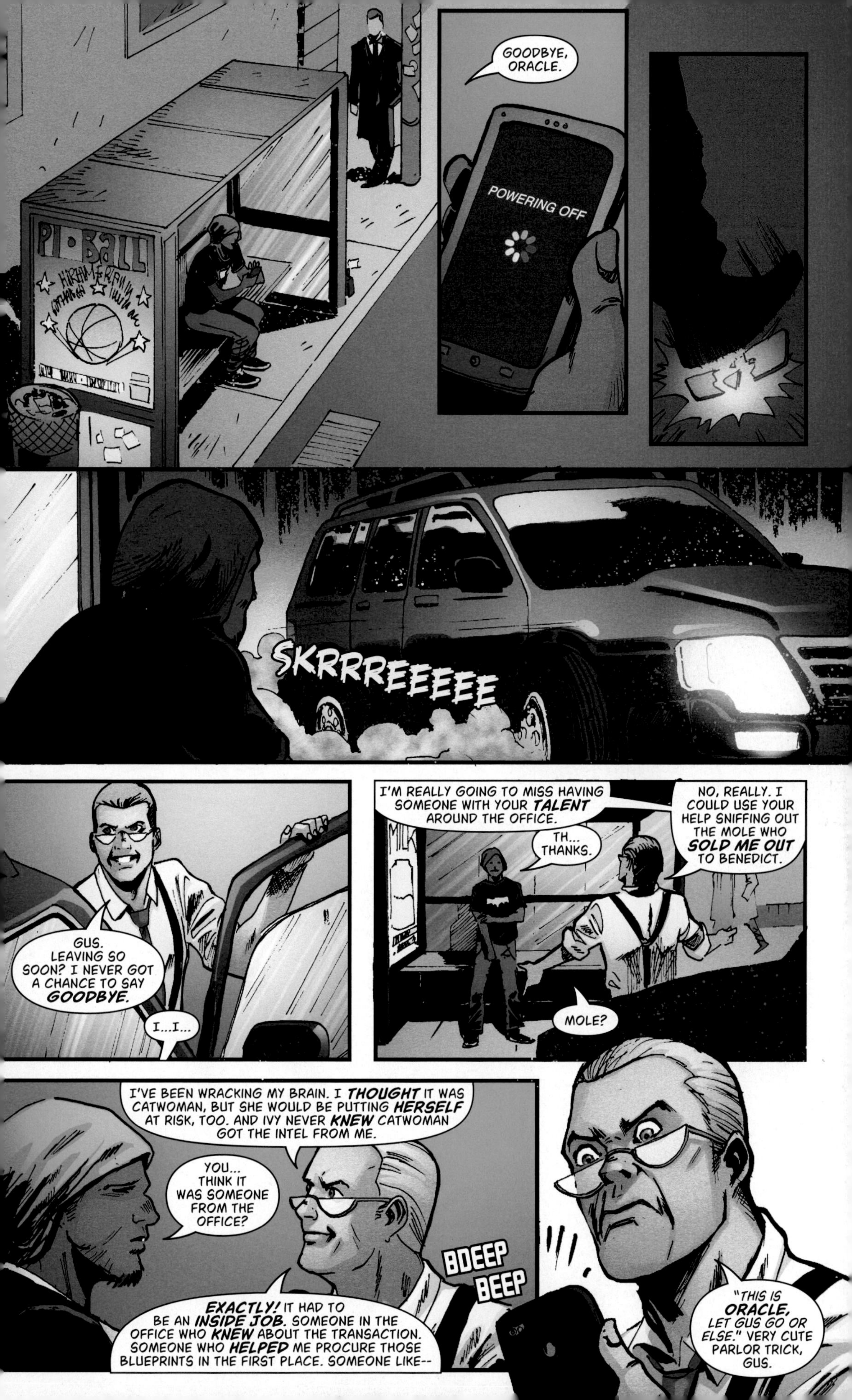

PI • BALL
GOODBYE, ORACLE.
POWERING OFF
SKRRREEEEEE
GUS. LEAVING SO SOON? I NEVER GOT A CHANCE TO SAY GOODBYE.
I...I...
I'M REALLY GOING TO MISS HAVING SOMEONE WITH YOUR TALENT AROUND THE OFFICE.
TH... THANKS.
NO, REALLY. I COULD USE YOUR HELP SNIFFING OUT THE MOLE WHO SOLD ME OUT TO BENEDICT.
MOLE?
I'VE BEEN WRACKING MY BRAIN. I THOUGHT IT WAS CATWOMAN, BUT SHE WOULD BE PUTTING HERSELF AT RISK, TOO. AND IVY NEVER KNEW CATWOMAN GOT THE INTEL FROM ME.
YOU... THINK IT WAS SOMEONE FROM THE OFFICE?
EXACTLY! IT HAD TO BE AN INSIDE JOB. SOMEONE IN THE OFFICE WHO KNEW ABOUT THE TRANSACTION. SOMEONE WHO HELPED ME PROCURE THOSE BLUEPRINTS IN THE FIRST PLACE. SOMEONE LIKE--
BDEEP BEEP
"THIS IS ORACLE, LET GUS GO OR ELSE." VERY CUTE PARLOR TRICK, GUS.

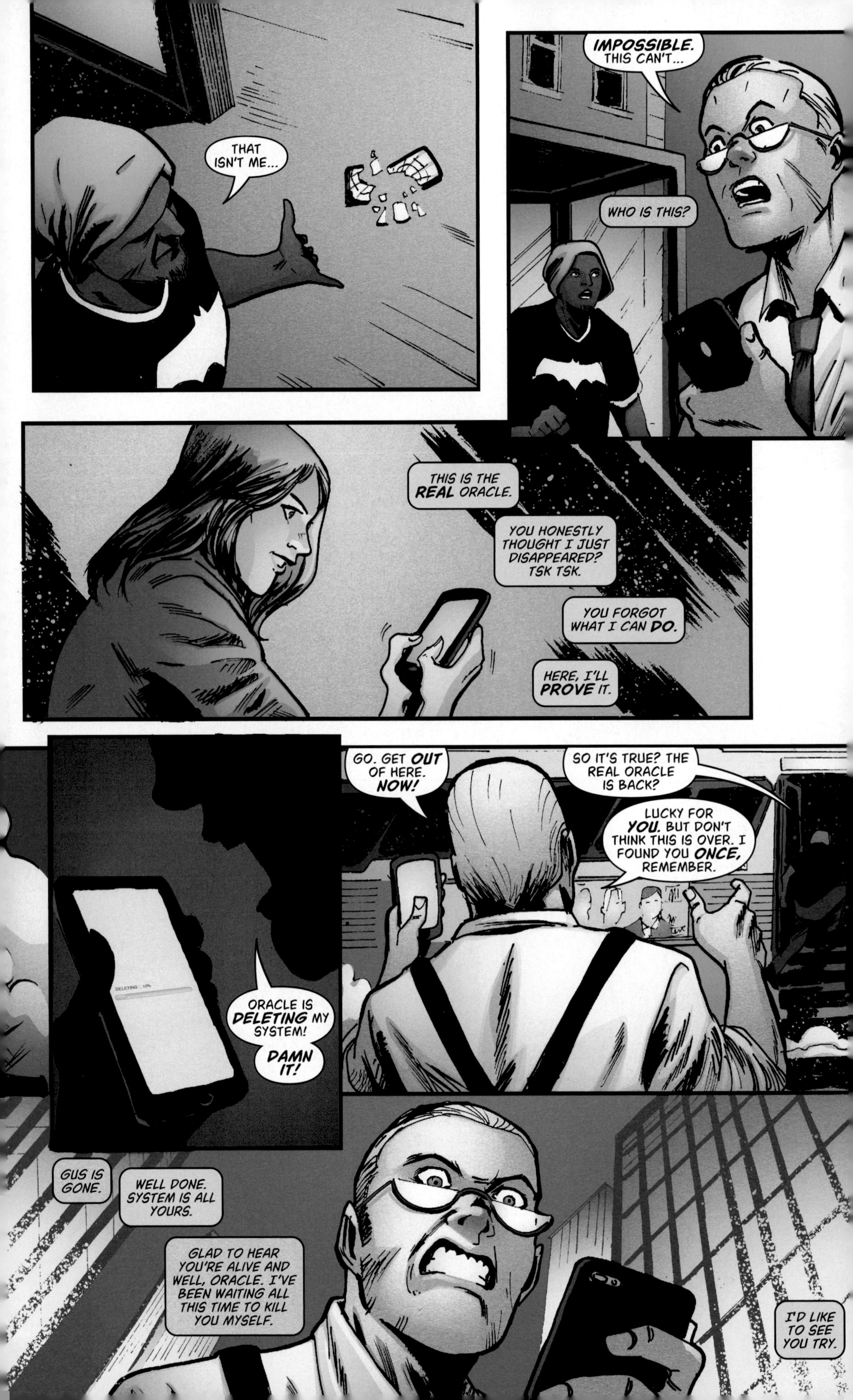
THAT ISN'T ME...
IMPOSSIBLE. THIS CAN'T...
WHO IS THIS?
THIS IS THE REAL ORACLE.
YOU HONESTLY THOUGHT I JUST DISAPPEARED? TSK TSK.
YOU FORGOT WHAT I CAN DO.
HERE, I'LL PROVE IT.
ORACLE IS DELETING MY SYSTEM!
DAMN IT!
GO. GET OUT OF HERE. NOW!
SO IT'S TRUE? THE REAL ORACLE IS BACK?
LUCKY FOR YOU. BUT DON'T THINK THIS IS OVER. I FOUND YOU ONCE, REMEMBER.
GUS IS GONE.
WELL DONE. SYSTEM IS ALL YOURS.
GLAD TO HEAR YOU'RE ALIVE AND WELL, ORACLE. I'VE BEEN WAITING ALL THIS TIME TO KILL YOU MYSELF.
I'D LIKE TO SEE YOU TRY.

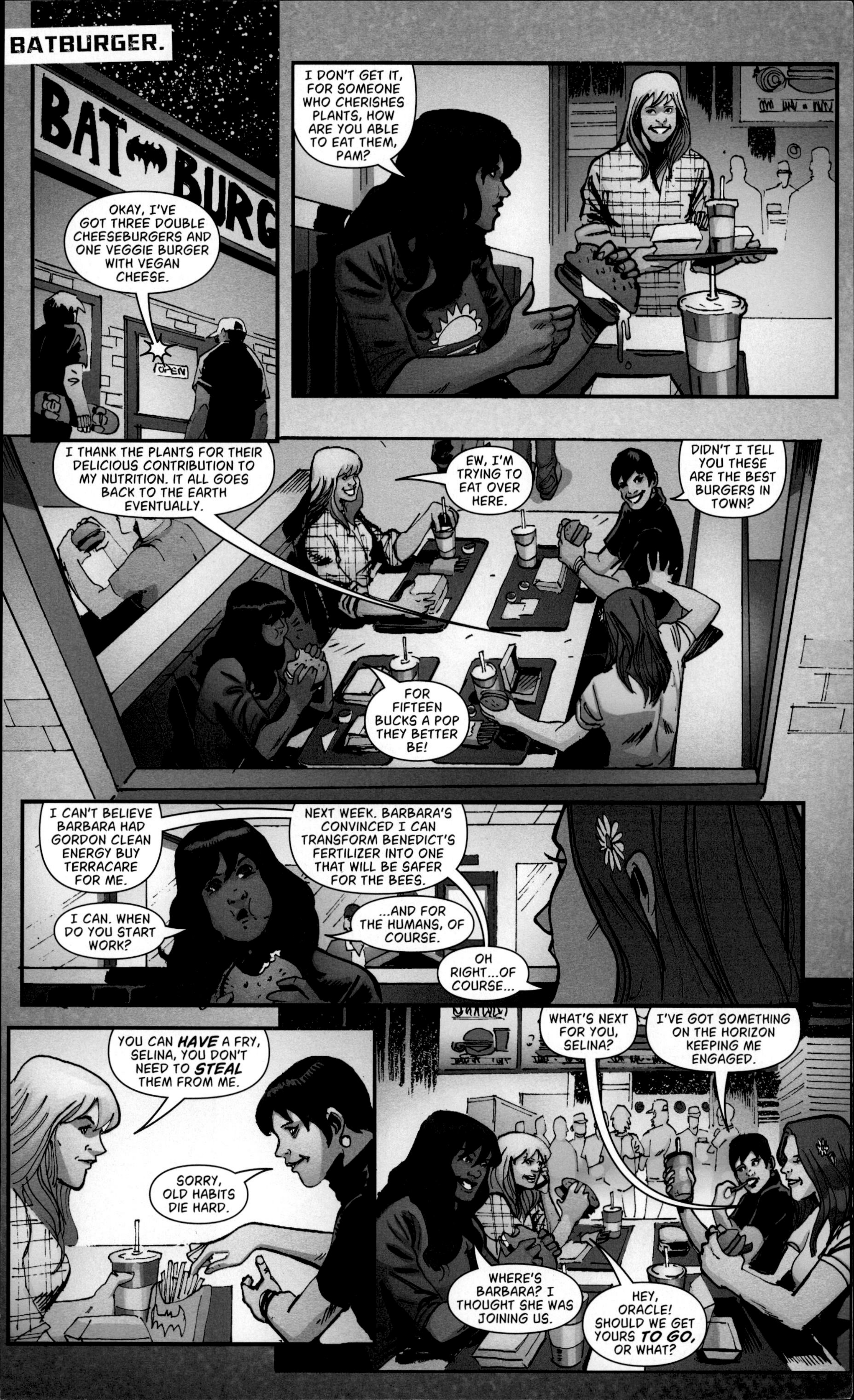
BATBURGER.
BAT BURG
OKAY, I'VE GOT THREE DOUBLE CHEESEBURGERS AND ONE VEGGIE BURGER WITH VEGAN CHEESE.
OPEN
I DON'T GET IT, FOR SOMEONE WHO CHERISHES PLANTS, HOW ARE YOU ABLE TO EAT THEM, PAM?
I THANK THE PLANTS FOR THEIR DELICIOUS CONTRIBUTION TO MY NUTRITION. IT ALL GOES BACK TO THE EARTH EVENTUALLY.
EW, I'M TRYING TO EAT OVER HERE.
DIDN'T I TELL YOU THESE ARE THE BEST BURGERS IN TOWN?
FOR FIFTEEN BUCKS A POP THEY BETTER BE!
I CAN'T BELIEVE BARBARA HAD GORDON CLEAN ENERGY BUY TERRACARE FOR ME.
NEXT WEEK. BARBARA'S CONVINCED I CAN TRANSFORM BENEDICT'S FERTILIZER INTO ONE THAT WILL BE SAFER FOR THE BEES.
I CAN. WHEN DO YOU START WORK?
...AND FOR THE HUMANS, OF COURSE.
OH RIGHT...OF COURSE...
YOU CAN ***HAVE*** A FRY, SELINA, YOU DON'T NEED TO ***STEAL*** THEM FROM ME.
SORRY, OLD HABITS DIE HARD.
WHAT'S NEXT FOR YOU, SELINA?
I'VE GOT SOMETHING ON THE HORIZON KEEPING ME ENGAGED.
WHERE'S BARBARA? I THOUGHT SHE WAS JOINING US.
HEY, ORACLE! SHOULD WE GET YOURS ***TO GO,*** OR WHAT?

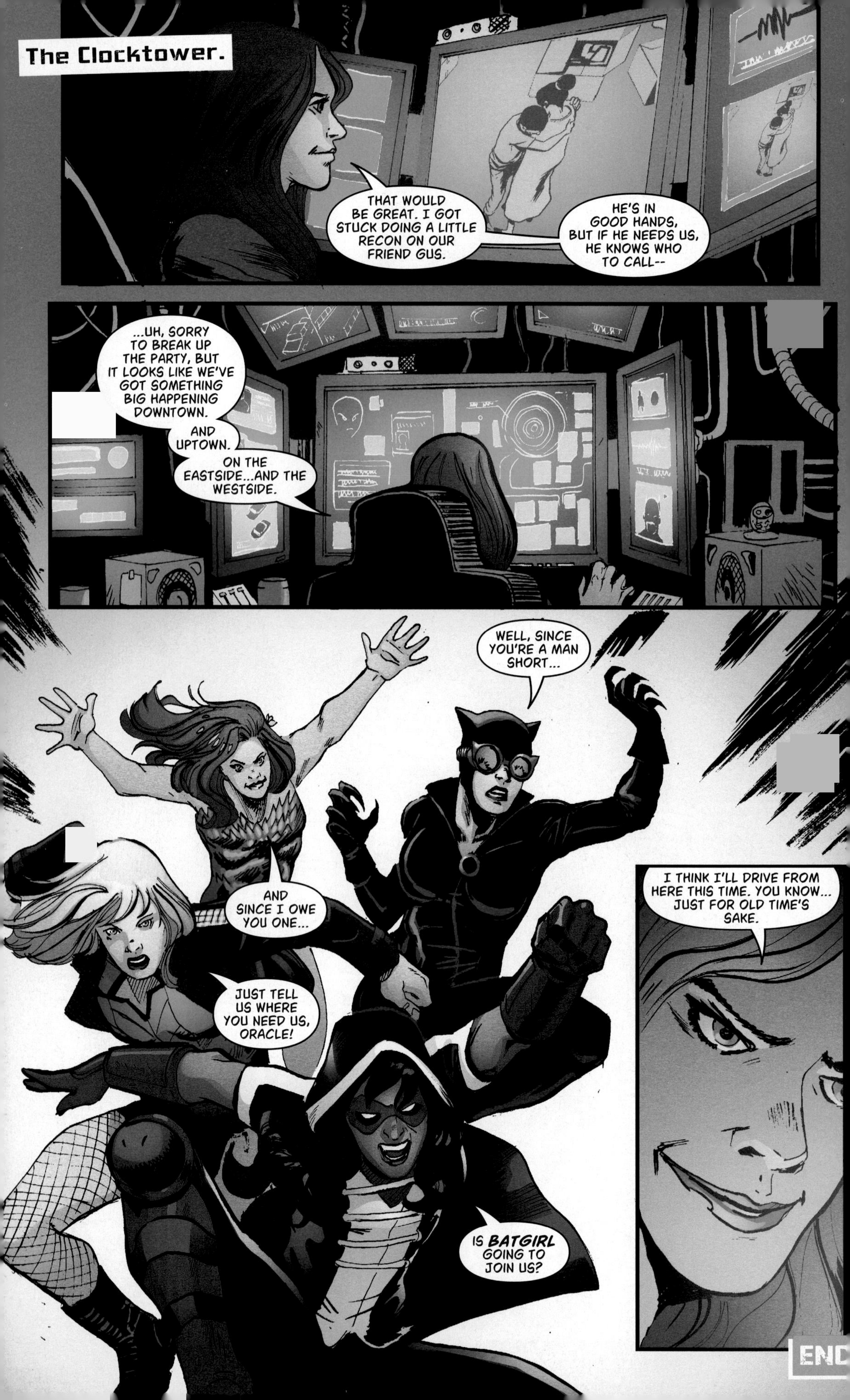

The Clocktower.
THAT WOULD BE GREAT. I GOT STUCK DOING A LITTLE RECON ON OUR FRIEND GUS.
HE'S IN GOOD HANDS, BUT IF HE NEEDS US, HE KNOWS WHO TO CALL--
...UH, SORRY TO BREAK UP THE PARTY, BUT IT LOOKS LIKE WE'VE GOT SOMETHING BIG HAPPENING DOWNTOWN.
AND UPTOWN.
ON THE EASTSIDE...AND THE WESTSIDE.
WELL, SINCE YOU'RE A MAN SHORT...
AND SINCE I OWE YOU ONE...
JUST TELL US WHERE YOU NEED US, ORACLE!
IS BATGIRL GOING TO JOIN US?
I THINK I'LL DRIVE FROM HERE THIS TIME. YOU KNOW... JUST FOR OLD TIME'S SAKE.
END

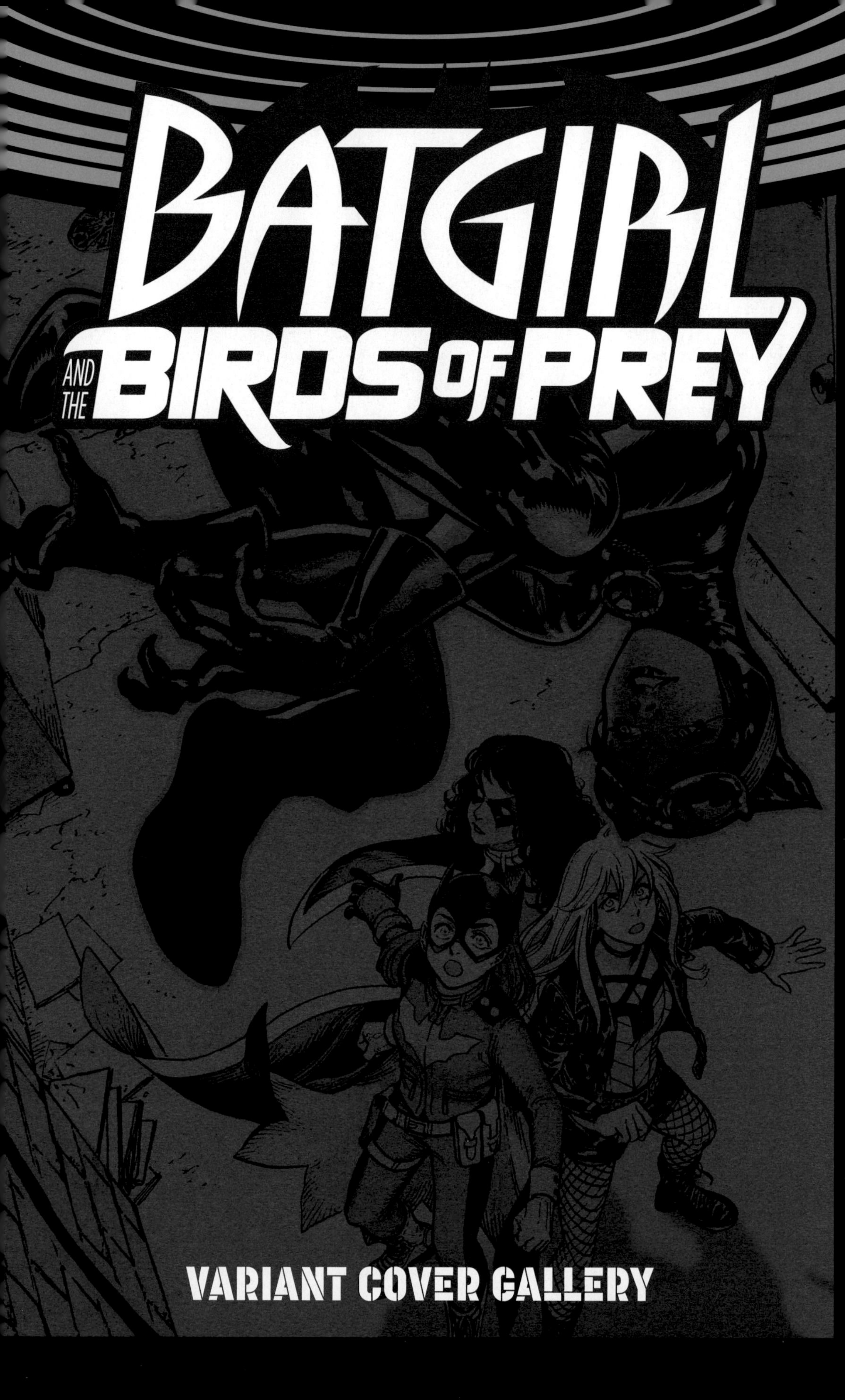
BATGIRL
AND THE BIRDS OF PREY
VARIANT COVER GALLERY

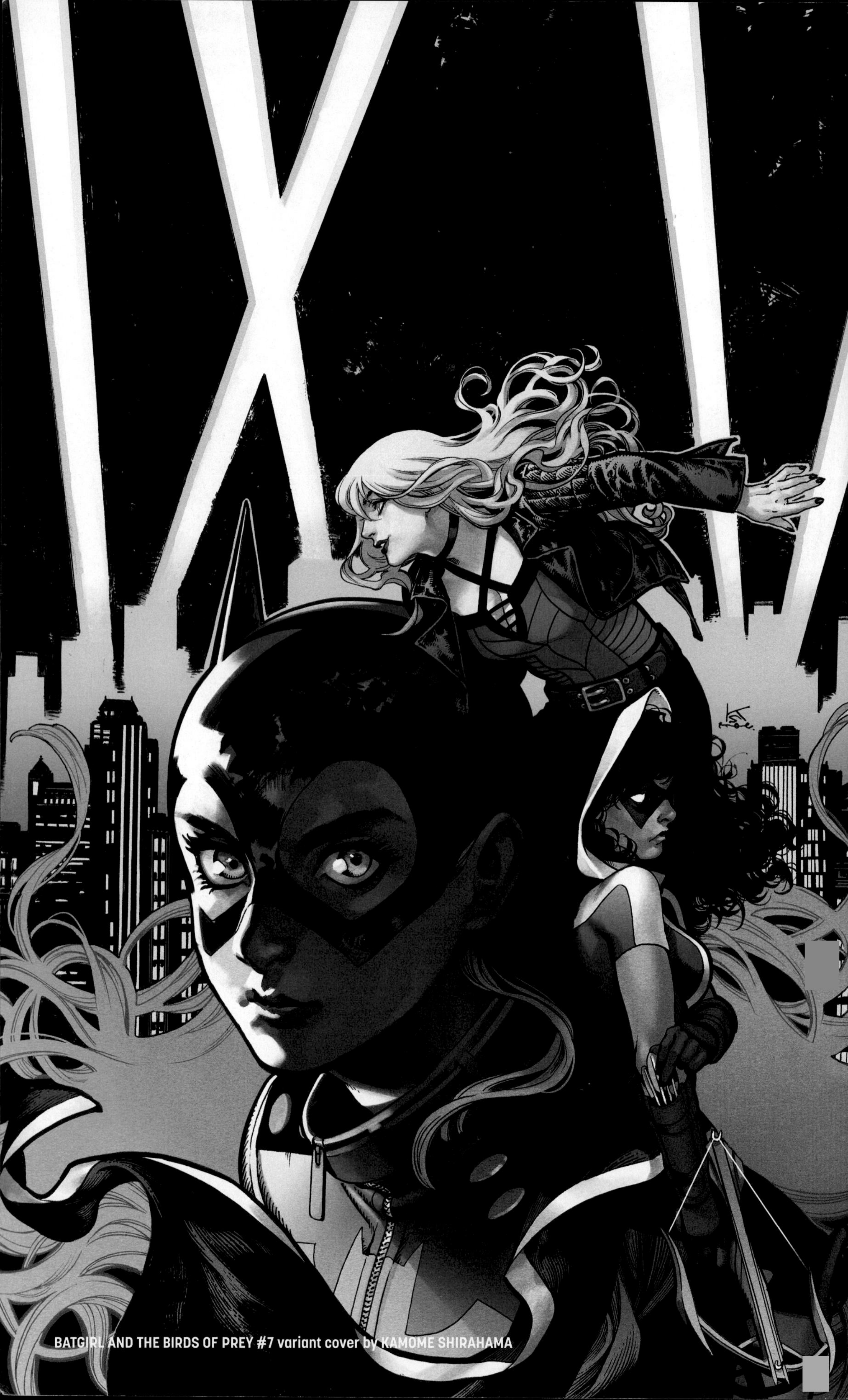

BATGIRL AND THE BIRDS OF PREY #7 variant cover by KAMOME SHIRAHAMA

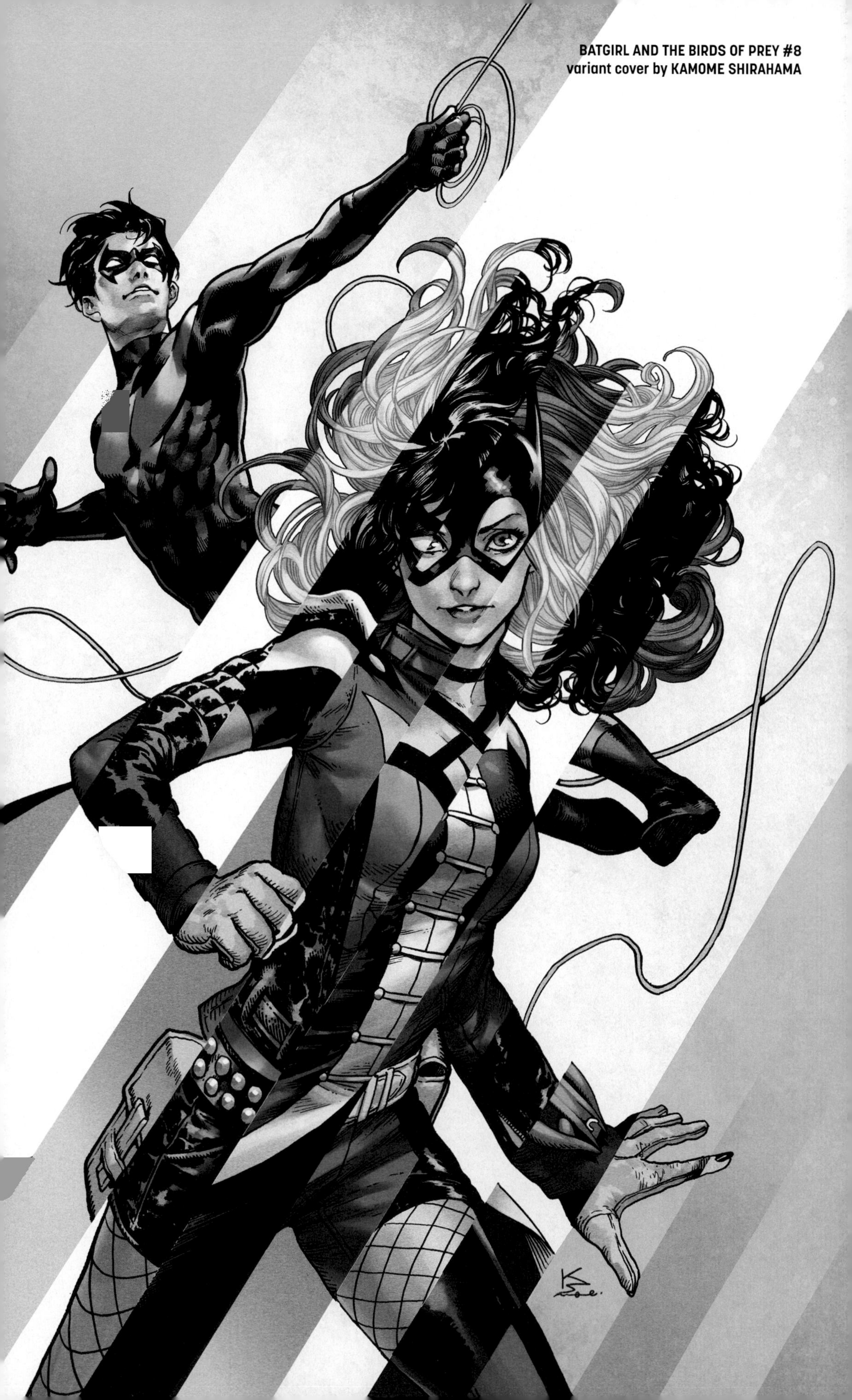

BATGIRL AND THE BIRDS OF PREY #8
variant cover by KAMOME SHIRAHAMA

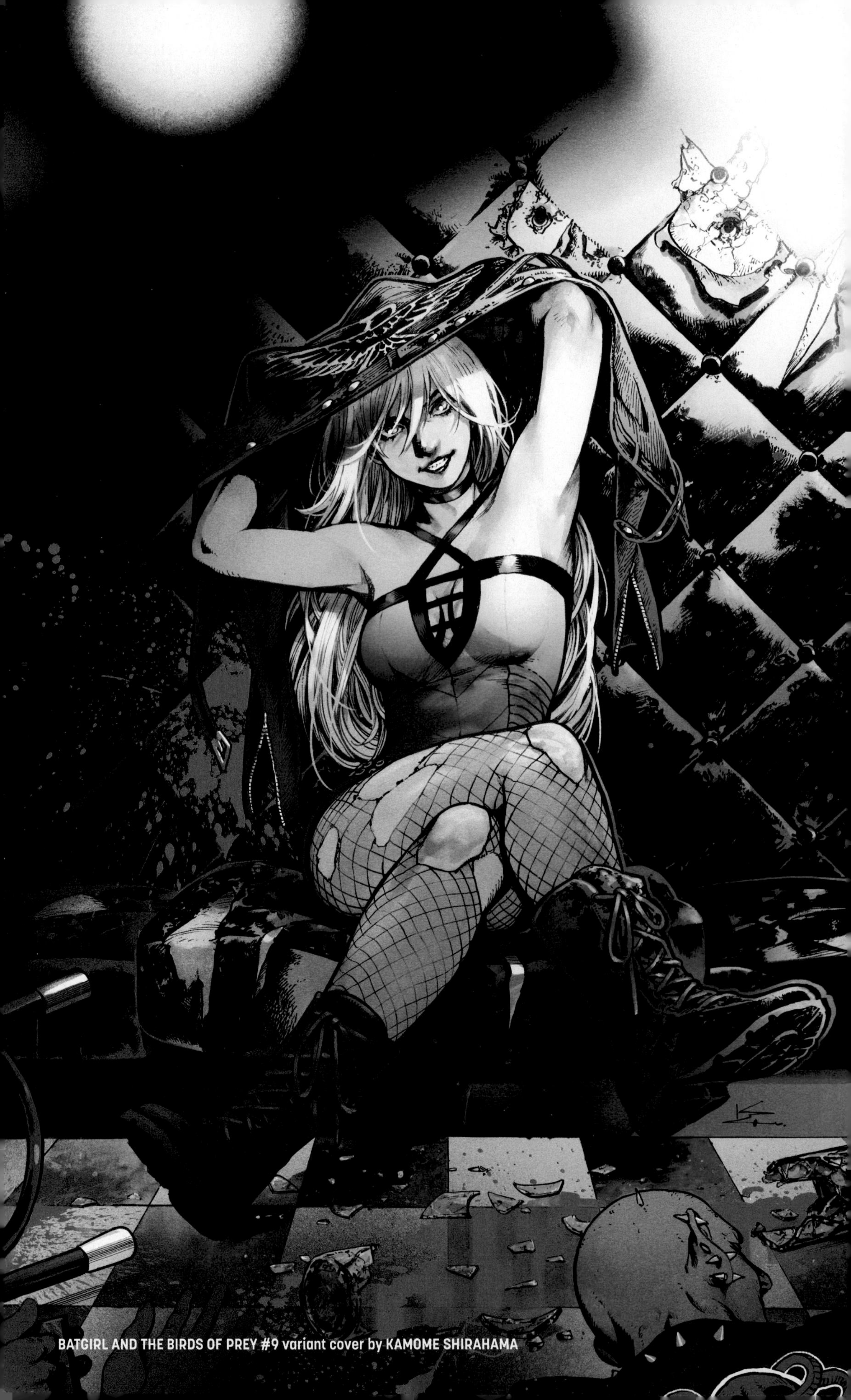

BATGIRL AND THE BIRDS OF PREY #9 variant cover by KAMOME SHIRAHAMA

BATGIRL AND THE BIRDS OF PREY #10 variant cover by KAMOME SHIRAHAMA

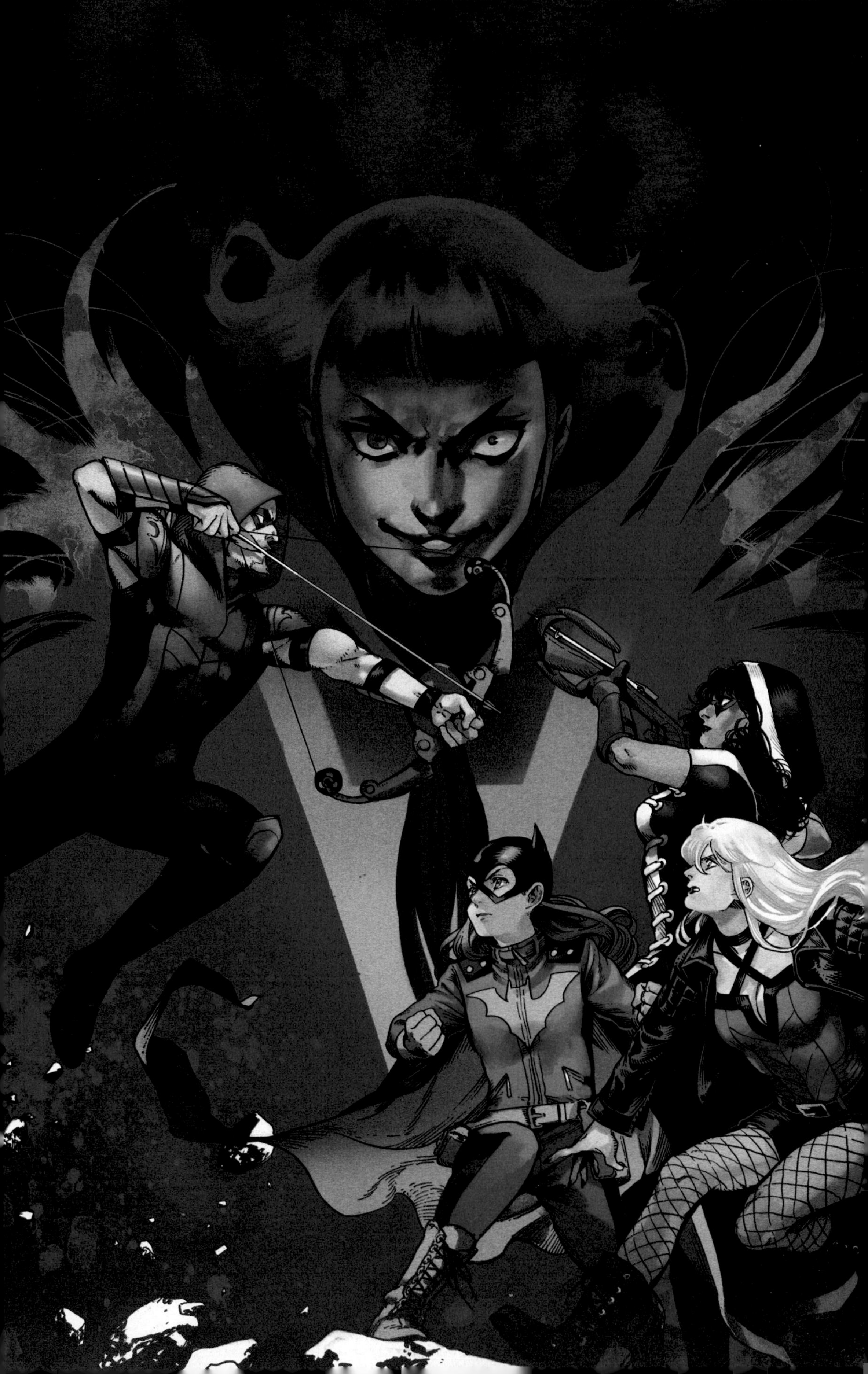

BATGIRL AND THE BIRDS OF PREY #11 variant cover by KAMOME SHIRAHAMA

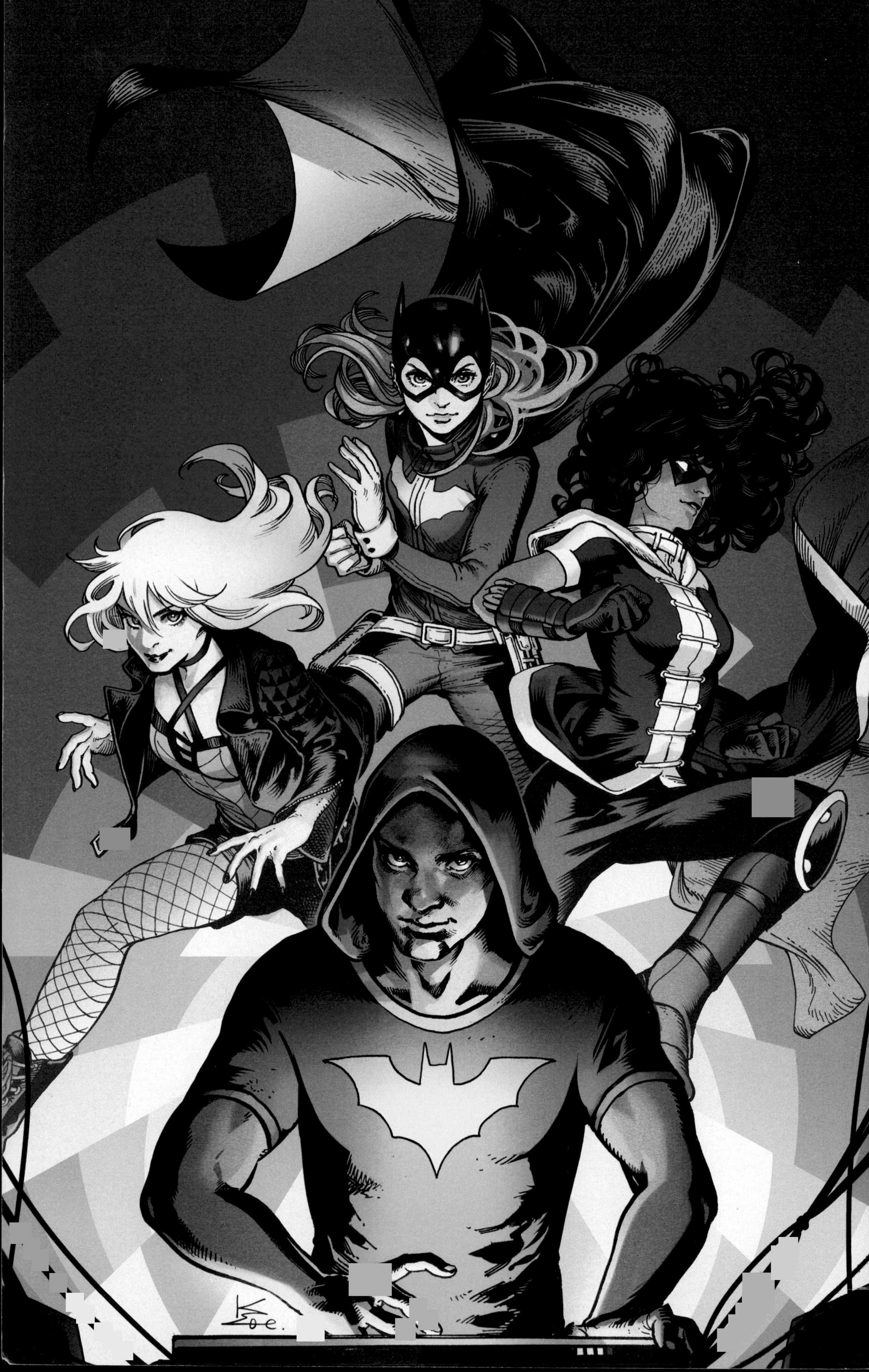

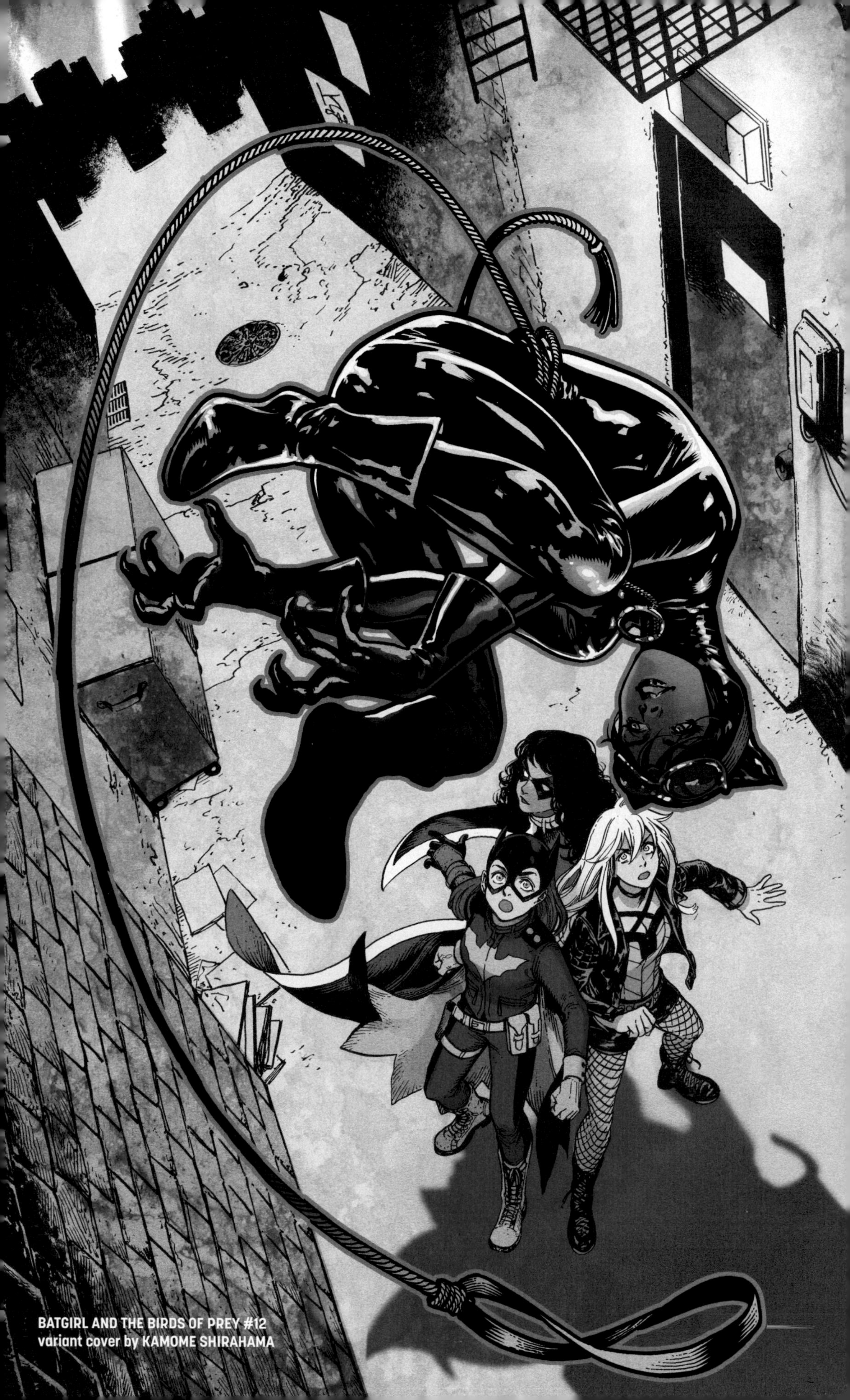

BATGIRL AND THE BIRDS OF PREY #12
variant cover by KAMOME SHIRAHAMA

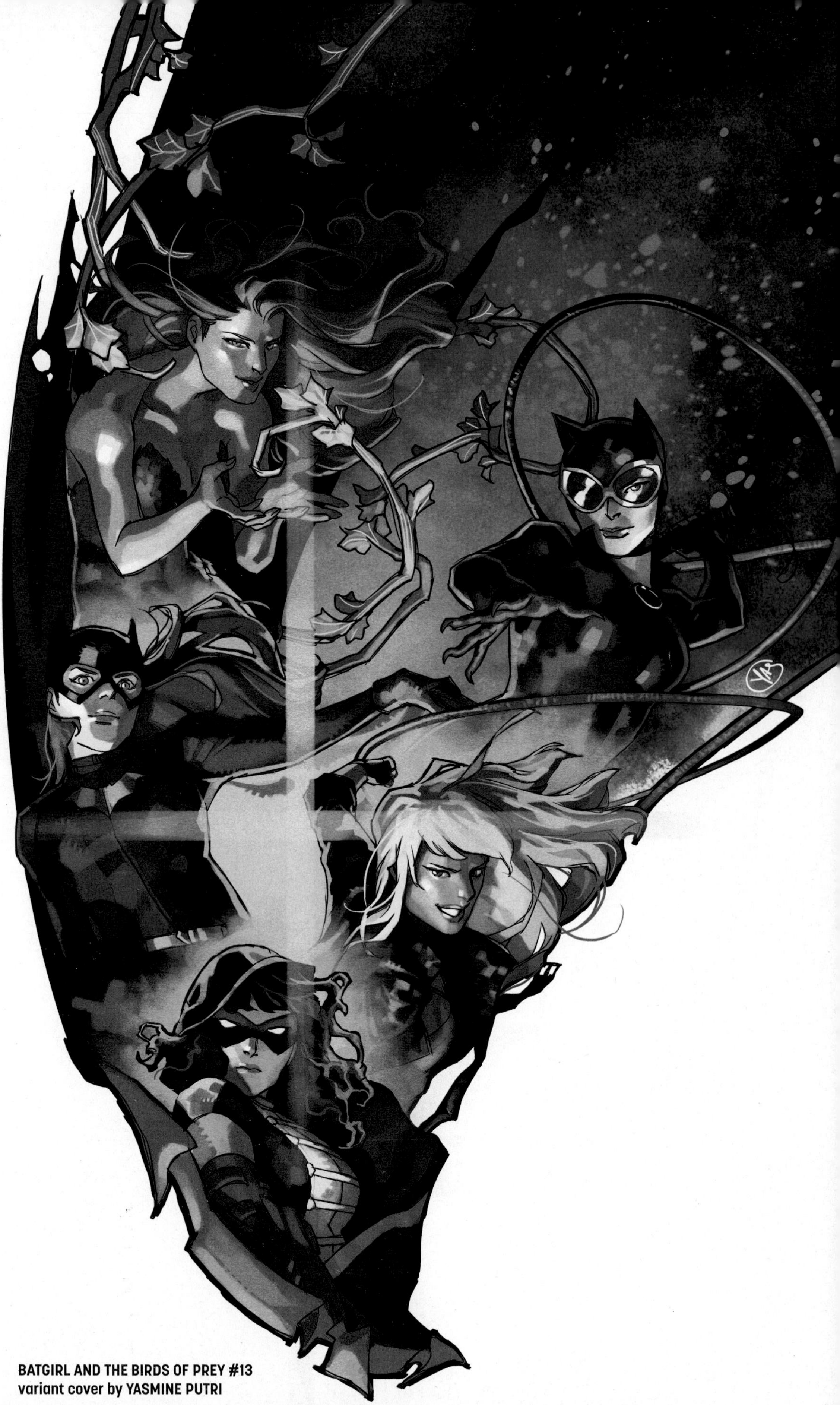

BATGIRL AND THE BIRDS OF PREY #13
variant cover by YASMINE PUTRI